MW00478226

Gossip and the Everyday Production of Politics

Published with the support of the
School of Pacific and Asian Studies,
University of Hawaiʻi

Gossip and the Everyday Production of Politics

Niko Besnier

University of Hawai'i Press
Honolulu

© 2009 University of Hawai'i Press
All rights reserved
Printed in the United States of America

14 13 12 11 10 09   6 5 4 3 2 1

Library of Congress Cataloging-in-Publication Data

Besnier, Niko.
 Gossip and the everyday production of politics / Niko Besnier.
  p. cm.
 Includes bibliographical references and index.
 ISBN 978-0-8248-3338-1 (hard cover : alk. paper)—
ISBN 978-0-8248-3357-2 (pbk. : alk. paper)
  1. Communication and culture—Tuvalu—Nukulaelae.
  2. Gossip—Tuvalu—Nukulaelae. 3. Political customs
  and rites—Tuvalu—Nukulaelae. 4. Nukulaelae (Tuvalu)—
  Politics and government. 5. Nukulaelae (Tuvalu)—Social
  life and customs. I. Title.
  GN671.T88B47 2009
  302.2'242099682—dc22
                                        2009000250

University of Hawai'i Press books are printed on acid-free
paper and meet the guidelines for permanence and
durability of the Council on Library Resources.

Designed by University of Hawai'i Press production staff
Printed by The Maple-Vail Book Manufacturing Group

For Mahmoud abd-el-Wahed

Contents

Acknowledgments | ix

Orthography and Transcription Conventions | xiii

1   Gossip, Hegemony, Agency | 1

2   The World from a Cooking Hut | 29

3   Hierarchy and Egalitarianism | 64

4   Morality and the Structure of Gossip | 94

5   The Twenty-Dollar Piglets | 120

6   The Two Widows | 143

7   Sorcery and Ambition | 166

8   Gossip and the Everyday Production of Politics | 189

Notes | 195

References | 213

Index | 241

Acknowledgments

In the early decades of the twentieth century, Marcel Mauss' exploration of what a gift entails appeared, at the time and still today, to go against the grain of Western middle-class commonsense. In many societies, he argued, being the recipient of a gift makes the recipient beholden in crucial and often onerous ways, placing him or her in the difficult position of indebtedness, which in subsequent anthropological works came to be known as "the tyranny of the gift." Working in a society where the gift figures so prominently in day-to-day experience gives an anthropologist more than a taste of this tyranny, of the feeling that whatever one does one will always disappoint. One can never adequately recognize the kindness and generosity, and match the effort and pain of food gathering, house building, speech making, traveling, becoming the target of anger and envy, all of which my relations on Nukulaelae Atoll experienced because of me. I cannot thank enough the late Faiva Tafia, Sina Tafia, Semolina Tafia, and Lamona Tafia for being my family on Nukulaelae, whom I have failed in so many ways. I cannot thank enough all the families, women, men, boys, and girls of the atoll and its growing expatriate communities on Funafuti, in Fiji, and in New Zealand, who shared their time, laughter, distresses, insights, meals, emotions, and material wealth with me. They all put up with my own quirks, opinions, and moods, meeting them with indulgence, edifying laughter, and the occasional justified impatience.

I am indebted to field research assistants with whom I have worked over the decades, among whom I wish to single out Mele Alefaio. Mele and I have worked together since 1980. Her insights into the life of Tuvaluan people perched on the unpredictable edge of change color this entire book. Her invincibly upbeat outlook on life in the face of so many setbacks is a lesson for everyone. I have seen her three children—Niko Jr, Nabil, and Maalosi—grow into beautiful transnational human beings in Tuvaluan Auckland, and I treasure their affection.

Money, without which this work would never have existed, was provided by several generous funding institutions over the decades. During my initial tentative fieldwork in the early 1980s I subsided on prize money from the Fondation de la Vocation (Paris), besides salaried work for the United States Peace Corps. In the mid-1980s and early 1990s, I received funding for fieldwork from the United States National Science Foundation (twice), the Harry F. Guggenheim Foundation, the Wenner-Gren Foundation for Anthropological Research, and the Yale University Center for International and Area Studies. I wrote parts of this book while benefiting from a Rockefeller Fellowship at the Center for Pacific Islands Studies of the University of Hawai'i at Mānoa in 1991–1992 and from a visiting professorship at the Kagoshima University Research Center for the Pacific Islands in 1999–2000.

An earlier version of the last section of chapter 1 was published as a chapter in *Ethnographic Artifacts: Challenges to a Reflexive Anthropology,* Sjoerd R. Jaarsma and Marta A. Rohatynskyj, eds. (University of Hawai'i Press, 2000). Chapter 3 is a considerably rewritten version of a chapter published in *Leadership and Change in the Western Pacific: Essays Presented to Sir Raymond Firth on the Occasion of His Ninetieth Birthday,* Richard Feinberg and Karen A. Watson-Gegeo, eds. (Athlone Press, 1996). In chapter 4, the section "Information Withholding" summarizes arguments I presented in "Information Withholding as a Manipulative and Collusive Strategy in Nukulaelae Gossip" (*Language in Society* 18 [1989]: 315–341), while the section "Animating Voices" is based on a discussion that appeared in much expanded form in a chapter in *Responsibility and Evidence in Oral Discourse,* Jane H. Hill and Judith Irvine, eds. (Cambridge University Press, 1993). Chapters 5 and 7 are extensively revised versions of, respectively, "The Truth and Other Irrelevant Aspects of Nukulaelae Gossip" (*Pacific Studies* 17(3) [1994]: 1–39) and "The Demise of the Man Who Would Be King: Sorcery and Ambition on Nukulaelae Atoll" (*Journal of Anthropological Research* 49 [1993]: 185–215). I thank Athlone Press, Cambridge University Press, the Pacific Institute at Brigham Young University Lā'ie, and the Department of Anthropology at the University of New Mexico for permission to develop arguments originally presented in these earlier publications.

Drafts of chapters or of the entire manuscript were read by friends and colleagues who provided invaluable comments, including Ping-Ann Addo, Philip Ells, Johannes Fabian, Peter Geschiere, Michael Goldsmith, Heather Lazrus, Dan Taulapapa McMullin, Peter McQuarrie, Susan Philips, and Gary Price. I have subjected students and colleagues at Yale University, Victoria University of Wellington, UCLA, and the University of Amsterdam to earlier versions of parts of this book, and their feedback was pivotal to the development of the final product. Philip Bock, Ivan Brady, Peter Geschiere, Linda Garro, Michael Goldsmith, Marjorie Goodwin, Alan Howard, Judith Irvine, Michael Jackson, Michael Lambek, Francesca Merlan, Isak Niehaus, Elinor Ochs, Susan Philips, Alan Rumsey, Deborah Tannen, Serge Tcherkézoff, and Geoff White were particularly encouraging and influential on my thinking at various stages in the development of the ideas I present in this book over almost three decades. Two reviewers for the press reviewed the manuscript anonymously; the generosity and insightful nature of their comments, however, betrayed their identity, and I wish to thank Don Brenneis and Joel Robbins for their hard work on the manuscript and their enduring collegiality and friendship. Masako Ikeda was an enthusiastic and thoughtful editor, and Joanne Sandstrom copyedited the manuscript with expert care. Juan-Carlos Goilo and Gabrielle Langdon came to my rescue with the illustrations. Marvin Harrison, Anne Kooy, and Ian Lincoln provided unmitigated encouragement in the writing process. Mahmoud abd-el-Wahed's large and wonderful family in Palestine embraced me, asking periodically over the phone how my writing was going, and not asking other questions whose answers would make no sense. Mahmoud put up with my frustrations as I sat in front of the computer for days on end with nothing to show for it, fed me, comforted me, and moved to places he had written off the map or that meant nothing to him. I am certain that I could not have been more patient than he has been with me.

Orthography and Transcription Conventions

Transcript excerpts in the Tuvaluan language that are quoted in this book follow a phonemic orthography, which differs from the various ways in which most Tuvaluans write their own language. In this orthography, double graphemes indicate geminated segments for both vowels and consonants except *h*, which in the Nukulaelae dialect of Tuvaluan has a restricted distribution. In Polynesia, geminated segments are an unusual feature that Tuvaluan shares with only a handful of minor Polynesian languages. In spoken form, geminated segments are held for a phonetic duration equivalent to slightly less than double their nongeminated equivalent. Geminated oral stops *(p t k)* are heavily aspirated. The letter g represents a velar nasal stop (phonetically, [ŋ]), *l* is a central flap, and all other letters have a phonetic value that approximates the value of the same symbol in the International Phonetic Alphabet.

The transcripts borrow conventions established for Conversation Analysis (see chapter 4), through the work of Gail Jefferson in particular (Atkinson and Heritage 1984). These conventions are designed to provide analytic information on the prosodic quality, rhythm, and nonlinguistic vocalizations audible in the recording. While these conventions have been subjected to criticism for their lack of precision and unsystematic application (e.g., J. Edwards 1993), they are nevertheless useful because of their readability and the fact that their widespread scholarly usage makes them easily recognizable. In this book, transcripts may differ in the level of specificity and detail, depending on the analytic context and purpose for providing the transcript (cf. Ochs 1979b).

Key to Transcription Conventions

(1.2)	length of significant pause in seconds, between or within utterances
(.)	untimed pauses (for pauses of less than 0.3 seconds)
word-	abrupt cut-off
WORD	forte volume

hhhh	exhalation (number of characters indicates approximate length)
.hhhh	inhalation
wo::rd	nonphonemic segment gemination
?	rising pitch (not necessarily in a question)
,	slightly rising pitch
.	falling pitch (not always at the end of a sentence)
!	animated tempo
word =	turn latching (no pause between turns)
= word	
word	overlap between turns (brackets mark the beginning and end of
[ ]	overlapping speech)
word	
((whisper))	information for which a symbol is not available
((high))	dominant pitch level of utterance string
((creaky))	voice quality
( )	inaudible material
(word)	conjectured material
[...]	untranscribed material
[1985:4:B:360–700]	transcript and page number or recording counter

1 Gossip, Hegemony, Agency

To the casual observer, gossip appears to be a quintes-sentially anthropological focus of inquiry. Not only is gossiping central to what ethnographers actually do during fieldwork, but it also encapsulates what anthropologists have come to think of as the essence of the discipline: an interest in the mundane, the overlooked, and the trivial, out of which the anthropologist distills not-so-mundane insights into how humans organize life in groups. Yet while gossip makes a cameo appearance in many ethnographic works, few anthropologists have engaged with an analysis of how it operates and articulates with other social forms. Of course, like all topics that anthropologists analyze, gossip can be seriously understood only if it is embedded in a larger context of social relations and symbolic dynamics, as it is only a vehicle through which agents get things done or undone. This book explores this embedding. In the process, it juxtaposes a number of themes that at first glance may appear unrelated. Its overarching theme is the emergence of political practice in the everyday and, in particular, the complexities of politics in small-scale societies where hierarchy and egalitarianism coexist in sometimes uneasy fashion and where the boundary between public and private is at best wafer thin. The analysis focuses in particular on power and agency, categories that are relevant not solely to public performances of political might, but also to everyday activities and unglamorous settings, where they sometimes fall into the hands of people whose hold on publicly sanctioned authority is tenuous at best. The book thus develops an analysis of the workings of power "from below," but departs from approaches to politics from below as resistance that preoccupied the social sciences in the 1990s: in the material that this work analyzes, who oppresses and who resists are very difficult categories to determine, either over time or at any given moment.

The analysis is also about emotions and morality, aspects of people's lives that anthropologists commonly subsume under the heading of "culture." Culture, however, has occupied an uneasy place in recent anthropological writings, from which it emerges as a heterogeneous entity, subject to contradiction and contestation, leading some to ask whether we should continue to talk about it at all. While

1

arguments about the heterogeneity of culture are easiest to make in the context of large-scale socially diverse postindustrial societies, small-scale societies also present complexities, even where members anxiously emphasize consensus and homogeneity, as is the case here. Emotion and morality, like other aspects of culture, are always unfinished projects that require constant reiteration, and it is this reiteration and its relationship to politics upon which my analysis focuses.

Emotions made a sudden appearance in the anthropological limelight in the early 1970s, and figured centrally in disciplinary debates for a couple of decades. This centrality has since somewhat waned, perhaps because of the association of emotions with the intimacy of private lives, from which anthropological attention has turned away as it shifted from local particularities to global flows, borders, history, and "multisited" ethnography. I will argue in these pages, however, that we should not dismiss the extent to which intimate events and experiences are intertwined with large-scale processes. I aim to explore the political nature of emotion (and the emotional nature of politics), and embed this "politics" in such large-scale processes as transnational labor markets, the turmoils of history, anxieties about self-representation to others, the potentialities of new (and not so new) communication technologies, and ecological changes seemingly related to global warming.[1]

Looming over the analysis is a concern with questions of how people construct and maintain a sense of localness in the course of history, particularly when outside forces, recent manifestations of which we have come to label "globalization," embed them in structures over which they may have little control. Some argue that the destabilization of local truths has given rise to new ways of understanding the self, ways that draw on multiple images no longer grounded in specific locales. I will maintain that such claims must be examined through an exploration of the everyday negotiations in which people engage over the meaning of the local and the global, the modern and the traditional, and the ephemeral and the enduring. I approach these questions stressing that large-scale global processes mean little if extracted from the quotidian experience of those who make them happen or endure them. For example, the experience of migrating, nurturing imaginings of a better life, or apprehending modern technology continues to be embedded in emotions, the senses, the body, kinship and friendship, desires and longings. It is on these intimate experiences that our search for an understanding of larger issues must focus, and I will illustrate how this approach can be fruitfully achieved by underscoring the multilayered complexities of language, interaction, and performance, taken in their broadest sense.

I bring together these various concerns by focusing on gossip, a form of interaction that in most societies variously provokes scorn, derision, and contempt, but also enormous interest. Precisely because it is the object of such contradictory sentiments, gossip embodies the complexities of social life. Confined to the intimacy of domestic contexts, gossip can nevertheless have a long reach, affect important events, and determine biographies. Through gossip, people make sense of what surrounds them, interpreting events, people, and the dynamics of history. On Nukulaelae Atoll in the Central Pacific, the ethnographic setting on which I base my analysis, the choice of gossip as a prime locus of social action was not a difficult one to make: Nukulaelae Islanders love gossip, a fact that their neighbors have enshrined in a stereotype of them, the validity of which they agree with (with some embarrassment). Nukulaelae Islanders devalue gossip as useless and dangerous because they view it as disrupting ideals of emotional equilibrium and stability, yet they all gossip with barely disguised enthusiasm. Thus, to understand what makes this society tick, one is almost compelled to focus on gossip while remaining cognizant that this focus may touch a raw nerve in Nukulaelae people's consciousness.

My discussion rests on two analytic traditions: the microscopic analysis of interactional data, traditionally grounded in linguistic anthropology, and the macroscopic analysis of large-scale social processes, an approach associated with the sociocultural subfield of anthropology. The kind of language-sensitive anthropology to which this book seeks to contribute is one that locates linguistic exchanges in a broad context of power relations, commodity circulations, and historical processes. Inspired by Bourdieu's (1977, 1991) programmatic call for a social science of practice, it is an approach that recognizes the language itself is a commodity, exchangeable for other commodities, but also deriving value and meaning from a preexisting market defined by local, translocal, and historical dynamics (Gal 1989; Hanks 2005; Irvine 1989). This engagement differs from works in linguistic anthropology that take language as the basis on which agents construct the social world. For example, a widely read ethnography of political meetings in a Samoa village assumes "a view of social structure as extremely dynamic or, more precisely, as a joint achievement produced by a number of individuals and institutions, tied by specific collective activities" (Duranti 1994, 7). The ethnography continues to provide an exemplary analysis of the way in which Samoan titled men utilize particular grammatical structures to assert, mitigate, and manipulate agency in meetings. However, while we are later told that political interaction also continuously reasserts differentiation, we learn virtually nothing about the material positions from which these men talk. In particular, we hear nothing of the fact that, by the late 1970s, there were already more Samoans living in industrial countries than in the islands themselves, that postcolonial Samoan village economies were crucially dependent on the diaspora, and that migrations had opened up furious debates about a host of issues, including land ownership, the conferring of chiefly titles, the behavior of return migrants, voting rights, and citizenship. Surely, these dynamics are determinative of linguistic strategies of agency in village meetings and probably are the focus of anxious debate in the meetings, rendering the analyst's engagement with the relationship between utterances and larger dynamics essential.[2]

In turn, sociocultural anthropological efforts to embed local processes in a historical and extralocal context are often based on interactional fieldwork material, but these materials rarely figure in the resulting analysis, or if they do it is in translated or paraphrased form, bearing the heavy weight of the analyst's interpretation. This book seeks to engage seriously "the (micro) study of face-to-face discourse strategies, and studies of macrohistorical processes; on the one hand the relatively well-understood role of, say, conversational inferences or participant structures in interpersonal power relations, and, on the other, the exercise of institutional power in which language is also a constitutive element" (Gal 1989, 349–350). Admittedly, "real-life" interactional materials are sometimes very difficult to obtain and analyze, and the specificity and quality of the data that I am able to present in this book vary in the different chapters. Using such materials also poses particular ethical and methodological problems. Yet, grounding myself in advances in linguistic anthropology since the 1970s, I will demonstrate the importance of analyzing what people say, rather than what they say they say or what I think they say (and of course, with Malinowski and every anthropologist since then, I will take as a problem the relationship between what people say they do and what they actually do). At the same time, I will demonstrate that an analysis of interactional data cannot be limited to a simple "reading" of the texts, but must invoke a more sophisticated theory of meaning and meaning-making.[3]

Nukulaelae Atoll, where I conducted the fieldwork on which this book is based, is a community of approximately 350 people, whose home is a graceful elliptical formation of islets surrounding a 3×8-kilometer deep-blue lagoon. The atoll is fringed by an outer garland of submerged reef intermittently broken by seawater channels rich in sea life but too shallow to allow crafts larger than canoes and dinghies to pass. As is the case of atolls worldwide, the 1.82 square kilometers of land barely rise above sea level, the soil is generally poor, and agricultural resources are limited and prone to environmental unpredictability. Along with eight other atolls and coral islands, Nukulaelae is part of Tuvalu, known in colonial times as the Ellice Islands and independent since 1978, and today one of the world's smallest microstates, peopled by 11,636 inhabitants (July 2005 government estimate). Nukulaelae's closest neighbor is Funafuti Atoll, the capital of the country, 121 kilometers away. To Western eyes, the atoll is a picture-postcard example of a South Sea Island, drenched by the almost-equatorial sun and covered, on clear nights, by a star-studded sky so bright that one can almost read by its light. However, Nukulaelae people are not prone to romanticizing the environment in which they live. This is an environment they know intimately, but which also embodies in very concrete terms the worries of everyday life: the search for fish on increasingly depleted fishing grounds, the growth of swamp taro now threatened by noticeable changes in the behavior of the sea and consequent seawater seepages, and the ever-growing need for cash, which remittances from overseas can never meet fully. Worrying about resources is hardly a new experience for them, as the atoll's history, or at least what we know of it, is replete with catastrophes and periods of hardship.

Since independence, and particularly since the beginning of the millennium, Tuvalu has become the object of frequent newspaper-column-filling journalistic attention in industrial countries, much of which emphasizes the remoteness and vulnerability of the country. These themes are attached in particular to the threat of complete disappearance that the country is under because of rising sea levels associated with global warming, which had not yet been constructed, when I conducted fieldwork, as an "issue," locally or globally. Vulnerability and remoteness do easily come to mind when one is on the atoll, and they have been recurrent themes in the history of Nukulaelae. At the same time, these themes are also constructs, and I will explore how and why these constructs arise, as Islanders negotiate and attempt to gain some control over the course of history and the course of their lives.

Politics, Agency, and Language

In her encyclopedic history of anthropology and politics, Joan Vincent (1990, 5–11) identifies in World War II a pivotal moment in the periodization of the anthropological analysis of political dynamics. It is at that moment, she argues, that the "anthropology of politics," hitherto a minor preoccupation in the context of other anthropological interests, transformed itself into "political anthropology," the product of concerted efforts to focus anthropological attention on political processes. Heralding this intellectual era were the "great monographs," such as Evans-Pritchard's (1940) *The Nuer,* Leach's (1954) *Political Systems of Highland Burma,* and Barth's (1959) *Political Leadership among Swat Pathans,* works that not only became foundational for the sub-subfield of political anthropology but also came to represent key moments in the development of structural functionalism, structuralism, and transactionalism respectively. My aim is not to analyze these well-known texts, but to focus instead on two directions taken by latter-day critiques of these works, mirroring the course of political anthropology itself in subsequent decades.

The first direction that critiques have taken is to fault these early analyses for being oblivious to larger political contexts of state formation, colonialism, and economic conflicts among world powers. Leach, for example, had analyzed political alternation between egalitarianism and hierarchy (as well as state structures) among Highland Burmese groups as evidence of the fact that the seed of instability was embedded within the very structure of these political systems. Nugent (1982) reanalyzes *Political Systems of Highland Burma* by demonstrating that what Leach had interpreted as pendulum-like oscillations between two political systems was in fact one single gradual change (Leach's [1983] virulent response notwithstanding). Precolonial chiefly systems were based on chiefly ownership of slaves, the controlled cultivation of opium and mining of precious stone, and the control of trade routes. Revolts in the lowlands in the nineteenth century led to the breakdown of the Burmese kingdom and the successful expansion of British colonial rule, which emancipated slaves and regulated trade, thus weakening chiefs and opening the door to revolt and the political rise of nonchiefs through the cultivation of opium. Embedded as it was in anthropology's then-ongoing return to Marx and concomitant engagement with history and globality (S. Mintz 1985; Wallerstein 1974–1988; Wolf 1982), Nugent's reanalysis locates society-internal political transformations at the convergence of forces larger than society itself, such as imperialism, colonialism, and world economic history.[4]

Other critics of early political anthropology have taken what appears to be at first glance a move in the opposite direction: politicizing the domestic. The insight that politics operates in "nonpolitical" domains, and operates there even more effectively, is of course not new. It underlies, for example, Gramsci's analysis of hegemony as located in civil society (trade unions, schools, churches), which is primarily nonpolitical, rather than in political society (Gramsci 1991–2007). The insight is also embedded in Althusser's (1971) distinction between repressive state apparatus (e.g., the military, the police, the law) and ideological state apparatus, namely institutions whose explicit purpose is to educate, inform, or entertain, but that also have the dissimulated function of indoctrinating people to think and act in a way that serves the purposes of the dominant system. But it is probably feminist anthropologists who, following in the footsteps of second-wave feminism ("the personal is political," remember?), questioned most effectively the confinement of the politico-jural to the public sphere, where men dominate, and the definition of what takes place in the domestic sphere, where women are confined, as irrelevant to politics (Rosaldo 1974, 1980b; Collier and Yanagisako 1987; Yanagisako and Delaney 1995). It is in this context that we can read McKinnon's (2000) deconstruction of another classic, Evans-Pritchard's (1940) *The Nuer*. By separating the political from the domestic, and concentrating exclusively on the former, Evans-Pritchard confidently characterized the Nuer as an egalitarian society organized in patrilineal lineages. Yet he also presented ample evidence of "matter that did not fit," particularly bilateral kinship, affinal relations, and status differences among children, all of which operate in the domestic sphere and are suffused with gender, but which he termed "transient." McKinnon's reanalysis, illustrating that "taking gender seriously not only adds to the analysis at hand but produces a different analysis" (Freeman 2001, 1008), makes the "matter that did not fit" fit, resulting in a picture of Nuer society as based on bilateral rather than patrilineal principles, alliance in addition to descent, and inequality despite a dominant egalitarian ideology (cf. also Hutchinson 1996).

The important lesson from both these critical trends is that an anthropology of politics must question the confinement of politics to what people themselves, as well as anthropological observers, overtly define as the political arena by taking account both of forces that transcend the boundaries of society and of dynamics that operate in the everyday, the domestic, and the mundane. While not alluding specifically to these critiques of earlier political anthropology, a congruent trend across the social sciences emerged in the late 1980s and throughout the 1990s, as anthropologists and other social scientists attended to the possibility that, because of their traditional preoccupation with structure and continuity, they had not been open enough to forms of action not defined as political but nevertheless politically consequential. Perhaps the most inspiring figure in this movement is James Scott. Based on ethnographic research among Malaysian peasantry and on a reading of historical and ethnographic works focused on a variety of contexts and times (e.g., Hochschild 1983; Thompson 1966; Willis 1977), Scott's successive monographs (1979, 1985, 1990, 1998) progressively refined a model that would recognize and showcase "everyday forms of resistance" among the subaltern. Even though they easily escape ethnographic scrutiny because of their seeming insignificance and disorganization, "weapons of the weak" have a cumulative effect on structures of power that is anything but insignificant. The foregrounding of resistance contrasts with the position, articulated in certain readings of Gramsci and in other versions of Marxism (e.g., Sennett and Cobb 1972), that hegemony has an all-pervasive effect, through which the powerless come to believe in the inevitability and just nature of unjust systems. Instead, Scott calls for an analytic recognition that, after all, the dominated are cleverer than those in power seem to think, and that life among the subaltern has a rich quality that agents of power fail to recognize, let alone control or defuse. This celebration of the revenge of the weak did not fail to generate enthusiasm in many social scientific circles, particularly an anthropology that had gradually come to define itself as the champion of the downtrodden in the course of its history.[5]

At first glance, the subaltern's quotidian resistance appears designed for purposes other than political action. Petty theft and minor acts of sabotage and obstruction, for example, seem driven by the desire to survive or take revenge, while the outcomes of disobedience, sarcasm, and foot shuffling are too insignificant to have an effect on structures of power. "Everyday forms of resistance," indeed, "make no headlines" (Scott 1986, 8). Yet the cumulative effect of individualized and often anonymous acts makes the exertion of power difficult, as long as they are consistent over time, coordinated (however loosely), and offstage. They also bear witness to the fact that, far from acquiescing to their own subordination and believing the system to be just (thus becoming active participants in their own oppression), the subaltern are perfectly capable of imagining alternative worlds while at the same time accepting more or less begrudgingly the terms of their oppression (what Scott [1990, 72] calls the "thin" theory of hegemony).

Going one step further, however, the subaltern's resignation is generally "read" in what Scott terms "public transcripts": social action that takes place in the open, particularly when interacting with the oppressor. But if we turn our attention to "hidden transcripts," forms of speech and behavior that occur when the subordinated congregate "offstage," particularly when the powerful are out of earshot, hegemony becomes thinner and thinner: through expressions of stories, songs, rituals, or gossip, the subordinate reflect on their subordination, defy its agents, and forge solidarity. Even seemingly compliant action in public can contain the seed of resistance, through subterfuge, indirection, and concealment: the Malay peasant's unctuous flattery of the stingy landlord's piety, for instance, can place the latter in the uncomfortable position of having to demonstrate generosity, one of the fundamental tenets of Muslim piety. The task of the social scientist is therefore to uncover the hidden transcripts of the subordinate, understand their dialectical and porous relationship with public transcripts, and more generally give voice to the voiceless.

Scott unravels in novel ways the complex relationship between material oppression and the symbolic realm, and this success has given rise to a veritable industry of ethnographic and other works that claimed to discover resistance where it was least suspected. The model, however, has also been subjected to serious critical scrutiny. The first concerns the implicit romanticism inherent to a search for resistance in every small act in which the oppressed engages. Let us not forget that for every small act of resistance there is a not-so-small act of increased oppression (Abu-Lughod 1990; also Comaroff and Comaroff 1992; Rebel 1989; Seymour 2006; Solway 1998; and many others). Abu-Lughod warns against the enthusiastic celebration of heroic resistance among the subaltern, evidence of the ultimately ineffectual nature of power and of the creativity and inventiveness of the human spirit. Heeding Foucault's (1980) warning that power has the propensity to lurk in covert ways, she reminds us that power and resistance are always intertwined in complicated and often unexpected ways. What may appear to be heroically resistant action to our well-intentioned ethnographic eyes or ears may in fact expose agents to broader, more diffuse, and thus more effective forms of oppression.

Furthermore, how we determine that particular forms of social action constitute resistance or not deserves serious scrutiny. Michael Brown (1996, 1997) demonstrates both the complexity and the importance of this question with ethnographic material from New Age spiritualism in contemporary America, which features the channeling of the spirits of the dead. Channeling, like the New Age movement in general, attracts middle-class, middle-aged Americans, arguably some of the most empowered people in the world, and is dominated by women. The highly gendered nature of channeling could lead one to propose that it represents resistance to male hegemony: after all, those who practice it occupy, as a group, a subordinate position in society, and the practice itself is nonnormative, somewhat secretive, and exclusive. However, everything that channelers say contradicts this interpretation: rather than performing a critique of gender hierarchy, Brown's women informants position themselves beyond gender, power, and resistance, working toward a deconstructions of gender binaries (an agenda largely made possible by material security). In fact, if hegemony is to be found anywhere in New Age spirituality, it is surely in middle-class mainstream New Agers' domination of the "indigenous" people from whom they borrow practices like Native American sweat-lodge rituals. Rather than being sites of resistance to structures of power of whatever kind, the burgeoning of the New Age industry is better understood as a response to the anxieties of the self associated with modernity. A form of action that has all the trappings of resistance (the right personnel, the right characteristics, the right relationship to the hegemonic order) ends up being about something entirely different. The moral of the story is that anthropologists should perhaps curb their enthusiastic search for resistance in every corner of the social map.

It is not only an obsession with power that plagues works on resistance, but also a blindness to forms of power that do not pitch, in a simplistic way, a dominant group against a subordinate group. Indeed, the subaltern is never single and unitary, since it is minimally transversed by dimensions of difference such as gender and age, structures of difference that are invariably transformed into structures of inequality, as feminist anthropologists taught us long ago. The subordinate thus always has its own internal politics beyond a reactivity to the domination it experiences as a group, and through this politics the very concept of subordination is negotiated, redefined, and contested (Ortner 1995, 175). In addition, in many societies, who is in positions of power and who is not may in fact be difficult to determine, as everyone can experience subordination or domination at different moments of their lives, given the inherently elusive and shifting nature of power (Gal 1995, 416). Such laminations can occur from moment to moment, and the exact configuration of power can even be indeterminate at any given social moment. It is precisely this indeterminacy that makes power potentially so effective, but can equally make it susceptible to resistant action.[6] Similarly, resistance never occurs in a "pure" form, that is, as action that is unquestionably designed to undermine domination and that is not motivated by any other design. In turn, the distinction between persuasion and coercion, the "obverse" of resistance, assumes a rational self-formed political subject whose goal in life is to free itself from structures of domination, a subject that is unlikely to exist outside of post-Enlightenment political theory (Mahmood 2005, 5–17; T. Mitchell 1990). Actions, be they authored by an oppressor, an oppressed, or anyone in between, are always the result of complex, multilayered, and ambivalent motivations, about which actors themselves are often unclear (e.g., Howe 1998; MacLeod 1992; Merry 1995; Reed-Danahay 1993):

"Real" actors, be they individual or collective, circulate among several "logics," choose among diverse norms, manage multiple constraints, are located at the convergence of several rationalities, and live in a mental and pragmatic universe transversed by ambiguities and ambivalences, located under the gaze of others, seeking their recognition or confronted with their hostility, and subjected to their multiple influences. (Olivier de Sardan 2001, 244–245; my translation)

Language and interaction figure centrally in works on resistance that Scott inspired. Indeed, much of the 1990 monograph is concerned with different kinds of linguistic activities that are foundational to resistant action. Hidden transcripts are forms of linguistic action that the powerless produce away from the punishing gaze of the powerful, and alternatively rely on formal features that presumably hide the "true meaning" of what is said, such as indirection, evasiveness, and anonymity, and thus shield the powerless from surveillance and retaliation. Gal (1995) articulates two important criticisms of these arguments. First, the assumption that public transcripts are somehow less "real" than hidden transcripts is problematic. All social acts are staged, if we take Goffman (1959) seriously, and interactions that take place in intimate contexts have as much dramaturgical quality as public interactions (Gal 1995, 411–414). Furthermore, hidden transcripts are not evidence of "truer" emotions and selves, since emotions and selves are always the product of culture, as decades' worth of work in psychological anthropology has demonstrated (Lutz and White 1986; Lutz and Abu-Lughod 1990). Of course, people can define certain manifestations of the self and certain emotions as more genuine than others, but such situations are always embedded in particular intentional dynamics that are matters of both culture and politics.

Gal's second criticism concerns the semiotic dynamics of linguistic disguise, interactional indirection, and opacity in talk, categories that are often the focus of ethnographies of resistance. In fact, in the work of Scott and of those who took up his lead (e.g., Levi 1999), hidden transcripts are almost invariably constituted of talk, even though the analysts assume that we can deduct unproblematically from the form of linguistic action its political meaning. However, "any linguistic form—such as euphemism, metaphor, indirection, trickster tale, or anonymous speaking—gains different meanings and has different social and political effects within specific institutional and ideological contexts" (Gal 1995, 419). For example, indirection, inarticulateness, and interactional reluctance are, in some celebrated cases, tools of the powerful rather than forms of resistance (e.g., Keenan [Ochs] 1974; Irvine 1990). Recognizing the contingency of the relationship between form and meaning has motivated linguistic anthropologists since the 1990s to turn their attention to the workings of linguistic ideology, that is, the ideological shaping of the link between social dynamics and forms of talk (Bauman and Briggs 2003; Kroskrity 2000; Makihara and Schieffelin 2007; Schieffelin, Woolard, and Kroskrity 1998; Woolard and Schieffelin 1994). These developments have demonstrated that, although ideas about and in language mediate the relationship between linguistic form and the sociopolitical context, this mediation takes on complex semiotic forms. Drawing on the classic semiotics of C. S. Peirce (1932), works in this vein have demonstrated that semiotic forms, including utterances, do not operate independent of a world of ideas, but do the work of meaning variously across different contexts (e.g., by invoking, through resemblance, or by means of social convention, or by suggesting and juxtaposing). It is in this more complex (and messier) model of meaning than conventional overcoherent Saussurean semiotics that we should embed our approach to performance, embodiment, and, in particular, language, and seek to understand the culturally and politically meaningful messages that people convey. These messages are not just embedded in the literal form of what they say or do, but in the way in which what they say or do evokes, insinuates, and alludes to dynamics that may be quite distant from the immediate context.

I locate my analysis of talk and political action on Nukulaelae at the juncture of Scott's theorization of hegemony and resistance and the critique of this theorization by cultural and linguistic anthropologists. I retain an important insight from resistance theory: politics "happens" where one may be led to least expect it—in the nooks and crannies of everyday life, outside of institutionalized contexts that one ordinarily associates with politics. This insight is not completely new, although works on resistance and contemporary critiques of earlier works have furthered it in two novel directions. One is that the politics penetrates much further into the "private" realm than the institutions of civil society and the locus of the ideological state apparatus, a point that Gramsci- or Althusser-inspired works, for example, have generally not explored (with some exceptions, e.g., Allison 1991). The second insight is that "politics," obviously, is much more than hegemony and coercion, a point that calls for renewed attention to the limits of hegemony and the potential effectiveness of alternative forms of action.

At the same time, I seek to shift the focus away from the unwieldy and theoretically problematic constraints inherent to the category "resistance," onto agency— "streams of actual or contemplated causal interventions of corporeal beings in the ongoing process of events-in-the-world" (Giddens 1979, 55). Two features are central to agency. First, at any moment in the stream of action, the agent "could have acted otherwise" (Giddens 1979, 56), either through an alternative intervention or through forbearance. Second, agency is not a universal capacity of precultural ahistorical individuals, but the product of particular cultural dynamics and historical antecedents. "The importance of subjects (whether individual actors or social entities)," Ortner reminds us, "lies not so much in who they are and how they are put together as in the projects that they construct and enact" (1995, 187). Agency can be resistant, but it can also be many other things, as humans negotiate their daily affairs with one another through social action.

Gossip is a classic form of agentive action. One of the most "hidden" of hidden transcripts, it is a quintessential tool for political action in private realms. A focus on gossip, as many have argued, enables us to understand politics "from below," particularly from the perspective of those whose voice is rarely heard in public or from perspectives that are deemed "not to matter." Such a focus diverges from approaches that seek to understand political action as primarily taking place in meetings, court proceedings, moots, parliamentary debates, bureaucratic encounters, and street demonstrations, and in the oratory and ritual that take place within them, about which we now have an extensive anthropological corpus. Anthropologists working in the Pacific region, for example, have long associated themselves with those in power, seduced, I suspect, by Islanders' flattering reassurance that anthropologists are themselves honorary chiefs or big men (the modern-day equivalent, perhaps, of early navigators thinking they were Polynesian gods; cf. Sahlins [1985] vs. Obeyesekere [1997]). Since Malinowski, who frames his classic *Argonauts of the Western Pacific* (1922) as a study of Trobriand men competing for prestige, anthropologists have predominantly been preoccupied with chieftainship, leadership, power, authority, and prestige. This is the case even in societies that anthropologists have considered relatively "egalitarian," such as big-men systems of Melanesia. In contrast to the multiple monographs on big or great men of the Papua New Guinea Highlands, for example, none exists on "rubbish men" (but see Wardlow [2006] on "wayward women"). Similarly, the lives of common people in Polynesia frequently often end up being couched in reference to chiefly persons, events, and categories. This book attempts to redress these biases.[7]

Gossip, of course, does not "do things" on its own; rather, like all other forms of discourse (Keane 2003, 140), gossip achieves whatever it achieves because it stands in relation to other forms of talk and social action. I seek an understanding of politics as the product of a relationship between various forms of action, from intimate contexts to events that involve the entire society. One insight I retain from works on resistance is that power and hegemony always constitute unfinished projects, structures that agents always potentially return to the drawing board through resistance or other forms of action. From critiques of resistance theory one can add the insight that resistance (and agency in general) is just as shifting, potentially contradictory, and incomplete. It is with these insights in mind that I now turn to gossip as linguistic activity, social action, and cultural form.

Theorizing Gossip

As many have pointed out (e.g., Besnier 1996a; Brenneis 1989; Haviland 1977, 28–47), gossip is notoriously difficult to circumscribe in the abstract, and this difficulty is a direct reflection of its inherent ambiguity: what a third party calls "gossip" is "information exchange" for those who engage in it. A general working definition identifies it as the negatively evaluative and morally laden verbal exchange concerning the conduct of absent third parties, involving a bounded group of persons in a private setting. As a social activity, gossip is often dismissed as lacking in importance and is equally often regarded as a reprehensible activity to be avoided or feared. Yet it is so pervasive that it is probably a universal phenomenon in one form or another.[8] It is closely related to scandal (Gluckman 1963), defined as gossip that becomes public knowledge, and rumor and hearsay (Rosnow and Fine 1976), defined as the unconstrained circulation of information about an event deemed important.

We find various versions of this definition in the now substantial literature on gossip in the social sciences and humanities.[9] Yet, not surprisingly, any version immediately raises a number of problems. First, what constitutes a private setting is a particularly thorny issue if we acknowledge that people frequently (perhaps always) gossip while being fully aware of the possibility that what they are saying will become public. What do we also make of "public" gossip such as celebrity tattler columns, tabloid journalism, and reality television, as sociologists of media remind us to ask (e.g., Gamson 1994), and of the increasing permeability of private boundaries that the Internet, for example, has made possible (Solove 2007)? What do we make of the recycling of public discourse, such as media talk, into private acts of collusion and complicity (e.g., Spitulnik 1996)? Even though the private and its contrasting category, the public, are highly elaborated categories in some societies, their definition is dynamic and never innocent of politics (Calhoun 1993; Gal and Woolard 2001; Habermas 1991; Warner 2005). Second, the seemingly innocuous issue of when a third party can be considered to be absent is in fact problematic. For example, interactors can make innuendos and veiled remarks about a person who is within hearing range for various purposes such as teasing, and these activities bear a close resemblance to gossip (Goodwin 1997). Similarly, conversationalists can make morally damaging statements about their own behavior, and whether this type of activity can be considered gossip is a pertinent question. Third, characterizing gossip as a form of criticism raises the question of whether any form of talk is ever devoid of moral evaluation, and this question leads us to ask from which forms of talk we should differentiate gossip. Furthermore, agents often skillfully disguise the evaluative character of gossip under the appearance of a straightforward narrative, in which case what constitutes gossip and what does not require careful analytic scrutiny.

These issues command that we focus our attention on the perspective of the actors themselves. Here again, however, analytic difficulties arise. Languages may lack a label for the range of activities roughly comparable to what English speakers term "gossip," or people may fail to recognize gossip as a significant interactional category. Such is the case of the Zinacantan of southern Mexico, who engage in verbal exchanges that anthropologist John Haviland clearly identified as gossip, even though Tzotzil, the language they speak, offers no specific descriptive term for such exchanges (Haviland 1977, 46). On Nukulaelae Atoll, people have strong ideas about gossip, and have a word for it: *fatufatu*, literally, "to make up [stories]" (reduplicated form of *fatu* "compose, begin to weave"). However, when pressed for a definition, a common answer is, "It's what people from family X do all the time!"[10] Alternatively, both women and men will often define gossip as "what women do," although women are also perfectly able to attribute the propensity to gossip onto men, pointing out that men's seemingly endless palavers in Council of Elders meetings are just as useless and morally suspect as gossip. Seemingly innocent conversation is *sauttala* "chat"; it is what men do, men say, aware of the fact that labeling their chatting as *fatufatu* would implicitly question their masculinity, even though their *sauttala* in many respects resembles what they say women do when they *fatufatu*. The characterization of women's communicative activities as reprehensible and unwholesome gossip and of men's as morally neutral talk is a phenomenon that finds echoes in many other societies: in the classic example of rural France, men's gossip "is *bavarder:* a friendly, sociable, light-hearted, good-natured, altruistic exchange of news, information and opinion. But if women are seen talking together, then something quite different is happening: very likely they are indulging in *mauvaise langue*—gossip, malice, 'character assassination'" (Bailey 1971a, 1). It enables men to denigrate women's social activities and justify gender hegemony, even when women's and men's talk may have similar structures and social organizations.[11]

In short, an airtight and cross-culturally valid definition of what constitutes gossip is probably not possible because the category itself is subject to context-dependent interpretations and possibly contestation by members of the same society. Indeed, an analysis of gossip must take into account the dynamic and shifting nature of the category, as well as its relationship to other forms of discursive and social action. To date, our theoretical and comparative understanding of gossip has been hampered by a dearth of detailed ethnographic investigations of gossip in specific societies. An artificial division of labor across disciplinary lines aggravates this ethnographic vacuum. On the one hand, anthropologists and sociologists have analyzed the sociopolitical "work" that people accomplish with gossip and rumor, while paying little attention to the form of talk. On the other hand, sociolinguistics has generated a sophisticated corpus of microanalyses of the structure of gossip talk, but these works adopt what most anthropologists would deem to be an impoverished theory of context.[12] This book seeks to establish a rapprochement between these analytic traditions and to demonstrate how an integrated approach can help us bridge microanalytic tools with macroanalytic concerns in a fruitful way.

Gossip is ethnographically difficult, for a number of reasons. One is that it typically takes place in small, intimate groups, which often exclude outsiders, including anthropologists. Particularly at the beginning of my fieldwork on Nukulaelae, I often experienced arriving at a house where people were engrossed in conversation to hear everyone shush each other because of my sudden presence. Even after I had managed to extricate myself from the isolating liminality of outsiderness, Nukulaelae people who did not know me well would express amazement (and sometimes amusement) when I dropped an ironic allusion, in good old Nukulaelae fashion, to a particularly juicy piece of gossip when the occasion called for it. It is not just that outsiders are excluded from gossip, but also that exclusion from gossip is one the primary means through which groups define outsider status.

However, some have advanced the exact opposite of this argument, claiming that the information ethnographers gather in the field consists mainly of gossip, or even gossip about gossip. Postcolonial critic Trinh Minh-ha (1989, 67–68) parades this view as an indictment of the ethnographic enterprise as a whole, arguing that anthropologists cultivate with informants a deceitful sense of solidarity that elides the erasure of coevalness that has plagued the discipline since its inception (Fabian 1983). I agree with the essence of Trinh's comparison, although I do not share her simplistic assumption that gossip is inherently idle, deceitful, and partial, and thus that the comparison is denigrating of anthropology. After all, anthropologists themselves have long been aware of the comparison ("scandalmonger par excellence," Gluckman [1963, 315] calls the anthropologist), and there is nothing inherently peculiar to the anthropologist's reliance on gossip as a source of insight, since all social knowledge consists of such "partial theories" through which actors make sense of the world (Van Vleet 2003).[13]

Another factor that has deterred anthropologists from studying gossip up close is that a careful investigation of gossip as a communicative and social practice necessitates a more than superficial command of language, norms, and presuppositions, as well as an intimate familiarity with the personal biographies of those who are gossiping and are being gossiped about. As I will show in chapter 4, Nukulaelae gossipers often do not even mention the name of the person about whom they are talking, to the extent that even autochthonous interlocutors sometimes have difficulties figuring out whom the gossip is about.[14] Understanding gossip thus presupposes a degree of intimacy with persons and events that anthropologists rarely attain. As Haviland (1977, 171–182) points out, it amounts to understanding a culture, with the caveat that "knowing culture" is always a partial, unfinished, and negotiated project (Van Vleet 2003).

Gossip as a legitimate object of anthropological inquiry first came into focus in a well-known paper by Max Gluckman (1963). True to his structural-functionalist intellectual roots but also inspired by his Marxist political leanings, Gluckman was concerned with both the inherently conflictual yet integrative function of gossip.

He argued that its principal role is to contribute to social cohesion and to distinguish the group from other groups: as "the hallmark of membership" (1963, 313), gossip provides a way of asserting the boundary between morally acceptable action and deviant behavior, and thus helps to solidify consensus and to control dissent without recourse to direct confrontation.[15]

Gluckman's analysis gave rise to a long series of exchanges pitting Gluckman against scholars (including some of his own students) inspired by versions of methodological individualism that were then emerging in anthropology and sociology, particularly transactionalism (Bailey 1960; Barth 1966; Boissevain 1968) and the symbolic interactionism of Erving Goffman (1959, 1963, 1967). Rather than being a harmony-maintaining mechanism, these analysts maintained, gossip is a tool that people use to foster their own agendas and undermine the interests of others (Faris 1966; Gilmore 1978; Handelman 1973; Hannerz 1967; Hotchkiss 1967; Paine 1967; Szwed 1966): "It is the individual and not the community that gossips" (Paine 1967, 280–281). Gossipers engage in "information management" that treats information as a precious commodity to be accumulated and jealously guarded, in capitalistic fashion, or doled out selectively in patterns of negative reciprocity, to use a concept from another anthropological subfield (Sahlins 1972). Human action is by nature unpredictable, and thus gossip does not have a "function," as it may create or exacerbate conflict as easily as it can contribute to group harmony.[16]

Sabini and Silver (1982, 93–94) capture the essence of the debate of the 1960s and 1970s about what gossip "does" by drawing a distinction between the end and the purpose of an activity: the end of a game of chess is checkmate, while the purpose may be to entertain, make money, impress, and so on. Viewed in this light, transactionalists focused on the purpose of gossip, while Gluckman focused on its ends, although the debate was also a debate about paradigms. Be that as it may, for many years this debate diverted analytic attention from what gossip "means" and what it looks like, themes whose importance later researchers would underline by turning to the aesthetic and micro-organizational aspects of gossip as verbal performance and communicative practice. Subsequent works (e.g., Abrahams 1970; Almirol 1981; Cox 1970) also argued that the positions Gluckman and his critics defended are not mutually exclusive: gossip can have both cohesion-building and self-serving purposes or consequences. Indeed, "taking the longer view, it seems almost obvious that many of the traditional devices which argue in terms of a public morality, (such as proverbs and myths), may also be applied to the prosecution of personal or factional ends" (Abrahams 1970, 290).

Furthermore, by focusing on the authors of gossip, scholars involved in the early controversy ignored an important aspect of the activity, namely the audience. In certain societies, such as Bhatgaon, a Fiji Indian village, author and audience are not even discrete categories, because gossiping is a joint effort involving many participants, and the authorship of particular gossip stories is fundamentally blurred (Brenneis 1984a, 1984b, 1987a, 1987b, 1990). Even in societies in which speakers rarely interrupt each other in the course of storytelling, gossip depends crucially for its effectiveness on the cooperation and participation of the audience. Perhaps more than any other form of interaction, gossip is a multiparty production, and attention to the microstructure of gossip interactions enable us to transcend largely speculative debates over whether conflict is personal or collective.

While many societies dismiss it as inconsequential, gossip can have dramatic consequences for its victims, a point that neither transactionalists nor structural-functionalists paid much attention to, and that leads us to return to problems of power, resistance, and agency. A focus on consequences differs from a focus on function, in that consequence is not an intrinsic characteristic of gossip. It is precisely the contrast between its social evaluation as trivial talk and the seriousness of its potential repercussions that endows gossip with potency as a political tool. According to Merry (1984), gossip can have economic consequences, in that it can restrict its target's access to resources, particularly those obtained through cooperative efforts. Gossip may have political consequences, in that it can mobilize support for particular agents, level structures of inequality, and delimit factionalism. Social consequences of gossip may include ridicule, ostracism, or even death. Finally, gossip sometimes has no consequences: people who are already socially marginalized (e.g., the rich, the poor, the abject) may be largely immune to it, and may even turn it to their advantage. An understanding of the consequences of gossip helps explain how gossip is embedded in a broader social and political context.

Closely related is the question of whom gossip benefits or harms, a question that brings us back to the problem, which underlies the debate about resistance of the 1990s, of whether and under what conditions resistance results in "real" social change. Because gossip is particularly difficult to repress or contain, it is a privileged instrument of protest and resistance in the hands of those with restricted access to public political action. It thus can provide a political voice to persons or groups that are excluded from more onstage political processes. Gossip, however, can just as easily be an instrument of oppression. Those in power can deploy it to control others or to control material and symbolic resources and thereby ensure the continuity of preexisting inequalities. Brison's (1992) exemplary ethnography of gossip and power demonstrates how Kwanga leaders, in the East Sepik province of Papua New Guinea, encourage rumors about their ability to perform maleficent sorcery to enhance their own prestige and intimidate potential rivals and dissidents. In short, the sociopolitical makeup of the group determines who benefits and who suffers from gossip, but the reverse is also true: gossip creates particular sociopolitical configurations. What may appear to be a tautology actually captures the constitutive relationship between gossip and politics, to which we should also add all other forms of talk and political action: agency, whether it manifests itself in talk or nonverbal action, creates structure just as structure gives rise to agency.

Anthropologists to date have mostly been concerned with the escalating consequences of gossip in fomenting conflict, oppressing the weak, or standing up to the strong, but gossip can also deflect conflict: people sometimes gossip in order to avoid aggressive confrontations. A celebrated example is Goodwin's (1990) analysis of African American children in a Philadelphia working-class neighborhood tattling on one another about each other's gossip, using narrative structures involving recursively embedded structures of reported speech (e.g., A says to B, "C said to me that you said to C something disparaging about me"). Because these narratives implicate several individuals, they obscure responsibility and thus avert more serious physical confrontation while allowing the protagonists to save face. Again, whether gossip aggravates conflictual situations or soothes strained relations hinges on the dynamics at play in the broader social setting.

What works such as Goodwin (1990) demonstrate is that the articulation of gossip with the broader sociocultural context in which it takes place is most fruitfully investigated through an approach that takes as its object of inquiry both the microscopic aspects of gossip and the sociocultural context in which the gossip is embedded. Research conducted in this vein recognizes that the meaning of gossip (and, for that matter, of talk in general) cannot be derived by simply analyzing words and limiting our analytic focus to the referential aspects of language. The structural and organizational aspects of the interaction, such as turn taking, reported speech constructions, and ways of interweaving evaluative elements with the narrative representation of events all carry great import. Attention to these interactional features demands a shift to the Peircean semiotics to which I alluded earlier, which locates meaning not solely in symbols and reference, but in a complex play of symbols, indexes, and icons, and the multiple ways in which they refer, resemble, allude, contextualize, confirm, and create what they mean (C. Briggs 1992, 2007; Keane 1997; Silverstein 2003; and many others). The richness of gossip as communicative and social action can be understood only through an investigation of minute aspects of actual samples of naturally occurring gossip in the original language (rather than in translated or paraphrased form), even though these details may appear at first glance familiar and unworthy of analytic scrutiny.

One particular aspect of the relationship between gossip and other sociocultural dynamics that has received relatively little attention is the articulation of gossip with emotions, particularly shame and pleasure. Shame will emerge in a number of ways in the analysis that follows: to the shame of the target of gossip, whose embarrassing deeds the gossipers divulge and ridicule, we can add the gossiper's potential shame for engaging in a socially disruptive form of action. But pleasure plays an equally important role in gossip. There is the pleasure that people experience in each other's company while denigrating absent parties, to which analysts of gossip as cohesive activity implicitly allude (Hornberger 1998; Strating 1998). There is also the pleasure of one-upmanship that skillful gossipers experience when they have a juicy story to tell to an attentive audience, particularly if they have few other occasions to have others listen to them (Bowman 1989; Gilsenan 1996). Gossipers also find pleasure in the aesthetic qualities of gossip and the creative enjoyment of deploying a skillful performance (Abrahams 1970; Brenneis 1984a, 1987a; Ghosh 1996; Guerin and Miyazaki 2003). Among rural Fiji Indians, for example, gossip has a sustained rhythmic structure and involves repetitions, strategically timed overlaps, and word play, features that all together provide a coordinated harmony to the interaction that is both aesthetically and socially pleasing to members of a society who value egalitarianism (Brenneis 1987a). Like other verbal arts that fall outside hegemonic aesthetic standards (e.g., Abrahams 1983; Labov 1972; Limón 1994), gossip can have a recognizable poetic structure, in the performance of which participants find pleasure. However, the reverse can also be true, as I will explore in chapter 5: gossipers can structure their stories as the antithesis of poetic language, turning them into a Rabelaisian performance that generates its own kind of enjoyment. But as we have come to realize in the last couple of decades (Butler 1990, 1997), "performance" and its companion "performativity" are also deeply political. Thus gossip emerges as the meeting ground for politics and aesthetics, and this dual nature enhances its efficacy as social and political action.

Ethical Entanglements

Nukulaelae people strive very hard to maintain, to themselves and to the outside world, an official version of their society as suffused with harmony and peace, an image that in the course of history has proved useful in coping with turbulent events (cf. Nader 1990). By documenting dynamics that precisely undermine the terms of this communal self-image, I am "exposing" aspects of life on the atoll that its dwellers consider unsanctioned, hidden, and unsavory, thereby undermining a mythology that has long served a relatively powerless community as a defense against the power of outside forces. As Luhrmann (1996, ix) did in her ethnography of Parsis in India, I run the risk of producing a document that Nukulaelae people, or rather the small but growing number of Nukulaelae people who will be able to read this book, will not like. This raises a set of ethical entanglements that have no simple solution, but that merit discussion.

The entanglements I face are not unique to this particular ethnographic project. Social scientists have long confronted the problems associated with presenting communities in a fashion that, as a corporate body, they do not find attractive, desirable, or politically useful. Communities' scandalized reactions to the ways in which researchers have depicted them have periodically rocked the boat of sociology (C. Allen 1997; Brettell 1993), a discipline that, in its ethnographic version, is perhaps more vulnerable to these occurrences than anthropology because the geographical, linguistic, and cultural distance between the describer and the described in sociology has traditionally been less dramatic. However, the anthropology of the Pacific has had its share of such controversies, particularly where anthropologists have scrutinized instances of the ill-named (and sloppily theorized) "invention of tradition" (Hobsbawm and Ranger 1983). Indigenous scholars and activists who have found useful political ammunition in stressing connections to a mythologized past have confronted anthropologists who have contended that the historical constructs in question may be fictional (although not necessarily illegitimate). This situation has arisen most notably when indigenous groups utilize these historical constructs in question to affirm empowered identities and claim for the return of resources, as is the case of Hawaiians and New Zealand Māori.[17]

For the moment at least, Nukulaelae Islanders live in a considerably less fraught and contentious world than the Fourth World populations that have been the context of these choleric exchanges (to my relief as well as theirs, I suspect). The stakes are arguably more modest, the colonial encroachment has been much less dramatic, and the history is relatively less tragic than in the Hawaiian and Māori situations, although Nukulaelae certainly has had its share of suffering at the hands of Westerners. Nevertheless, serious ethical questions remain concerning the depth and motives of ethnographic probing, the presentation of ethnographic materials and their potential consequences, and the nature of the relationship between the ethnographer and the ethnographed. While I am not going to tackle every single one of these topics in the same amount of detail, I describe in what follows several stances that have been taken in the recent literature on comparable situations and attempt to apply them to the Nukulaelae context.

The most radical stance is the assertion that no ethnographic research by outsiders should be allowed, on Nukulaelae or anywhere else, because anthropology is yet another instance of the colonization of the lives of Third and Fourth World peoples, particularly the sort of voyeuristic prying that my research could, at worst, be said to amount to. Trinh Minh-ha (1989, 47–76), again, condemns the hegemony that anthropological scientism exerts on its subjects, a hegemony that is so deeply embedded in the history and practice of the discipline that it is even perpetrated in the works of reflexive anthropologists, despite their claims to "expose the workings of ethnographic authority and ideology" (1989, 157). In less nuanced language, Trask (1991, 1993, 161–178) lashes out at anthropologists for robbing graves, treating other human beings as objects, and exploiting the intimate details of their lives to pursue highly lucrative careers in academic institutions of the industrial world.[18] In rather grandiloquent fashion, Bustos-Águilar (1995, 164) denounces the "apparatus of ethnographic surveillance" central to the "imperial anthropology machine."

There are several responses to the blanket identification of anthropological fieldwork with colonial exploitation. One is that this identification seriously lacks a sense of perspective. Harvey (1992) points out that there is a difference between the exploitativeness of cultural anthropologists and that of, say, multinational corporations intent on turning the forests of the world into logging quarries and its beaches into luxury resorts. Nukulaelae is too remote and lacking in resources to be a direct target of such exploitation, but it is vulnerable, along with the rest of Tuvalu, to less direct forms of neoimperialism. Among these figure most immediately the exploitation of Tuvaluan laborers by the Nauru Phosphate Company over past decades, as well as, since the early 1980s, their exploitation by German and Hong Kong shipping conglomerates who find in Tuvalu a source of non-union, eager seamen satisfied with deplorable wages. One also finds exploitation of a different kind in the gradual habituation of Tuvaluan children to imported junk food and trashy videos, particularly on Funafuti, and Tuvaluans' general vulnerability to the uncontrolled dumping of substandard consumer goods (Laban and Swain 1997; cf. also Gewertz and Errington 2007). Finally, yet importantly, rising sea levels, or at least the increase of violent storms and "king tides," seemingly tied to the greenhouse effect seriously threaten the very existence of exposed and low-lying island groups such as Tuvalu, to say nothing of radiation contamination from nuclear wastes dumped elsewhere in the Pacific.

To the extent that my prying into Nukulaelae lives can be labeled exploitative, this exploitation cannot compare, in intent, method, or consequences, with truly worrisome forms of economic and political colonialism that Nukulaelae and the rest of Tuvalu face. The intent of the ethnographic monograph, whatever it may be, is certainly not the enrichment of the author (*pace* Trask); it is even doubtful that it advances careers, in a climate of increasing distrust of intellectuals and in an academic market in which most scholars hang on precariously to part-time temporary employment in undesirable locations. An academic monograph may at best demonstrate to its limited readership that the image that a community finds useful to present of itself is a partial depiction (in both senses of the word "partial"). This threat is unlikely to leave the realm of ideas and representations, and is eminently resistible, in contrast to nuclear pollution, rising sea levels, and labor and consumer exploitation. As Ortner points out, "the notion that colonial and academic texts are able completely to distort or exclude the voices and perspectives of those being written about seems to me to endow these texts with far greater power than they have" (1995, 188).

Another response to the characterization of anthropology as neocolonial exploitation, voiced by Said (1991) among others, demands that close attention be paid to what critics of this exploitation propose to replace it with. Often, the most virulent critics of outsiders' entitlement to investigate the inner workings of Third and Fourth World societies are themselves in positions of intellectual and material hegemony over the "truly" disenfranchised members of these societies. Replacing the hegemony of outsiders with society-internal hegemony, which is potentially more veiled and thus more insidious, is hardly an improvement. Yet another, perhaps more dramatic, response would highlight the parallels between censorship and barring outsiders from knowing what goes on "inside." Preventing outside scrutiny is something that certain governments are very good at, because it allows them to kill, suppress, and sterilize in peace.

A final argument for barring outsiders' access to knowledge would invoke the fact that knowledge is irremediably tied to power, as Foucault (1980) has demonstrated and many others have reiterated, and thus that industrial-world knowledge of social processes in a developing world society further reinforces the power differential between industrial and developing worlds. This power differential, and the colonial oppression and other forms of hegemony that go with it, can be undermined only through a deconstruction of the mutually reinforcing linkage between knowledge and power. However, controlling access to knowledge is different from deconstructing this linkage; it is even antithetical to it.

A variation on the anticolonialist critique of anthropology would maintain that anthropologists should focus only on issues devoid of political sensitivity and that ethnographic attention to charged issues is unwelcome (as in the case that van Meijl [2000] analyzes). The anthropology of yesteryear, which focused its efforts on studying kinship, counting fish catches, or collecting plant names, tacitly followed this unstated precept, for one reason or another. Commonly, this focus results from the self-censorship that all ethnographers must apply to their field notes. Just as often, anthropologists have lacked the linguistic fluency, the time, and the personal connections in the field to become privy to the details of their hosts' lives. Some ethnographers have made explicit efforts to ensure that they not become affiliated with one faction or another in their host communities; while it may have personal or analytic advantages (which may well be illusory, as Barnes [1980, 115] suggests), this strategy has the unfortunate consequence of keeping the ethnographer well outside the workings of the community.

The confinement of anthropological inquiry to "neutral" pursuits may place anthropologists in a better position to deflect accusations of neocolonial exploitation, but it makes them subject to other criticisms. First, anthropology of this type erases lived experience from the picture, and with it agency, humanism, and the (inter)subjectivity that occupies a central place in the lives of members of all societies (as skillfully argued by authors such as Abu-Lughod 1991, 1993, and Jackson 1995, 1996, 1998). In addition, such research perpetuates understandings of non-Western societies as isolated, internally coherent, kinship-driven aggregates, whose members are concerned principally with cataloguing items in their environment and distributing the resources that their bountiful and benign environment provides them. The resulting picture is a familiar one in the history of anthropology, but also one from which anthropologists have tried hard to get away for decades in their deconstructions of "the romance of community" (Joseph 2002; see also Creed 2006; Ortner 1997, 63–64). Alternatively, my description could have focused on political strife, but only insofar as it pits Nukulaelae against outside forces, such as nineteenth-century slavers, traders, and missionaries, twentieth-century colonial rule, the late-millennium encroachment of capitalism, or even perhaps the contemporary dealings between Nukulaelae and the Tuvalu nation-state. Here again, problems emerge, of both an analytic and ethical nature. In particular, as Ortner aptly argues, "the impulse to sanitize the internal politics of the dominated must be understood as fundamentally romantic" (1995, 179).[19]

The more vociferous critics of anthropology maintain more or less explicitly that social research should be restricted to "insiders," namely individuals who belong to the same social group as the people being researched. My own employment peregrinations have taught me that these views do not have a uniform distribution the world: they are rarely expressed in Continental Europe, for example, while in postcolonial New Zealand they tend to dominate all discussion to the detriment of more significant dialogue, a fact that suggests that they may raise more questions than they answer. In the first place, there is ample evidence that "insiderness" has to date not turned out to be as privileging as it is cracked up to be, both in the First World and elsewhere. British anthropologists conducting fieldwork in Essex have as many barriers to overcome, albeit different ones, as English anthropologists conducting field research in Papua New Guinea (M. Strathern 1987). In Mithila (Bihar, northern India), Brahmin men are as predisposed to identify Tantric symbolism in rural Brahmin women's folk artistic production as are foreigner scholars, even though Tantric symbolism has little relevance to the paintings and their intended meaning (C. Brown 1996). "Insiders" in this case are thus not particularly privileged in their understanding of what is produced locally, sometimes in their very own houses.

More fundamentally, who counts as an insider or outsider is hardly a straightforward question. Insisting on an opposition between "inside" and "outside" generally assumes a tacit conceptualization of community, society, or culture as homogeneous, immanent, and well bounded, characteristics against which empirical evidence militates (Gupta and Ferguson 1997a, 24; T. Turner 1979). Furthermore, as Abu-Lughod argues, the very act of observing social behavior places the observer in a liminal position: "the [indigenous] anthropologist is still defined as a being who must stand apart from the Other, even when he or she seeks explicitly to bridge the gap" (1991, 141). This liminality is most dramatically illustrated by what Abu-Lughod (1991) terms the condition of the "halfie," the hybrid anthropologist with complex allegiances to multiple backgrounds and contexts (see also Narayan [1993] and, for a slightly different perspective, Cerroni-Long [1995]).[20]

These entanglements derive directly from the complexities of what constitutes identity in any context, not just that of the anthropologist conducting field research, complexities that postmodernist and poststructuralist scholars such as Butler (1990) and Spivak (1988) have brilliantly exposed. At the most basic level of analysis, one may share a racial, ethnic, or national identity with the villagers or islanders among whom one is conducting fieldwork, but remain fundamentally alienated from them by an elite or foreign education, privileged social class affiliation, and the dual citizenship or visas that afford the choice of residing in either the developed or developing world (Abu-Lughod 1991, 138–143). Any aspect of my identity can override whatever binds me to my kindred-hosts and establish a power differential between them and me. This power differential, incidentally, does not necessarily place the anthropologist in the superordinate position, as illustrated by the case of anthropologists (indigenous or not) who are, like me, of the "wrong" sexuality and find themselves in sometimes precarious positions vis-à-vis their hosts (Kulick 1995; Lewin and Leap 1996). In Bakalaki's apt words, "One becomes insider and outsider, representative of local or global discourses, in the context of social and especially power relations with others" (1997, 519).

To what extent am I deceiving my respondents by conducting research on something other than what they insist is, should be, and can only be the topic of my research? To what extent are my Nukulaelae informants really providing me their "informed consent," which some insist should be given as much importance in ethnography as in other human sciences (e.g., Fluehr-Lobban 1994)? As Barnes (1980, 89–133) discusses, the motives of social scientific research are never entirely clear to informants, even in contexts where no linguistic and cultural barrier separates researcher and researched, because informants generally lack familiarity with the intellectual and social context in which the research is embedded, that is, how questions arise, how they are addressed, how results are disseminated, and to what end. This is certainly the case of Nukulaelae society, whose members remain unacquainted with the basic precepts of academic research for the most part. For the moment at least, as far as I know, no one associated with Nukulaelae Atoll has raised any objection to any aspect of my representation of the society. Similarly, I know of no case in which my statements about Nukulaelae society have been used against the interests or endeavors of the atoll community, and thus the arguments I entertain in this section remain solidly grounded in the hypothetical, the eventual, and the contingent.[21]

This situation may change somewhat in the near future, as Nukulaelae's population becomes increasingly transnational and thus likely to be less impressed by academic credentials (as already evidenced by the pun that people have long made, converting the word *tiikulii* "[academic] degree" into *tae kulii* "dog shit"). Younger people are receiving university training in Fiji, New Zealand, Australia, and Hawai'i in growing numbers, and their reactions to my work are beginning to trickle back to me, thus far couched in polite terms. Nevertheless, the same people are unlikely to return to reside on the atoll (a situation that is itself potentially subject to critical scrutiny) and thus unlikely to have a direct impact on my own research practices and the responses of the atoll's residents to them. In the unlikely event that educated or otherwise privileged Nukulaelae Islanders would oppose my being privy to sensitive material, my documenting it in print, or even my conducting further research in the community, this opposition would undoubtedly be contested by other members of the community, even if it is as a matter of egalitarian principles.

These issues raise the question of who is entitled, on Nukulaelae or in any other society, to provide informed consent to the anthropologist. Indeed, Nukulaelae Islanders who are victimized by sorcery accusations, disparaging gossip, and other overt or covert forms of hegemonic action see in my fieldwork an opportunity to make their voices heard and the injustices that are perpetrated upon them documented. These people would urge me to write about what had happened to them, so that those who are the perpetrators of these injustices, many of which are never redressed, be exposed. These particular individuals subvert the prevalent image of outsiders being incapable of inside understanding. In many cases, they have come to know me well, which made them realize that an outsider may develop insights into the inner workings of Nukulaelae society after all. On the one hand, one can maintain that ethnographers are bound by the community's overarching desires to be presented under a certain light. On the other hand, this stance raises questions about who represents the "community" and the extent to which these desires are consensual. Standard professional codes of ethics are of little help on this issue because they conflate unproblematically the interests of individuals with those of the society to which they belong, in such statements as "anthropological researchers have primary ethical obligations to the people, species, and materials they study and to the people with whom they work" (American Anthropological Association 1998). In other words, codes of ethics continue to tacitly assume a definition of "community" as harmonious and cohesive, while anthropologists and sociologists moved away from such definitions decades ago.

Of course, people's attitudes and allegiances, like their identities, can be complex and change over time and across contexts. Could the same people who urged me to write about forces that have victimized them change their minds when they see the final product? Will they suddenly align themselves with the rest of Nukulaelae despite the pain it inflicted upon them, in contradistinction to a nosy anthropologist who had the nerve to paint a less-than-glamorous picture of their community? Here again, identities, affiliations, and sociopolitical stances are by nature shifting and negotiable, and at least at the local level, the anthropologist is as vulnerable to these shifts as his or her informants can claim some power through them. One possible escape route consists in simply deleting the identity of the field site by giving it a pseudonym and adopting a nom de plume, as van der

Geest (2003) did in Ghana in the 1970s, only to find out years later how displeased his informants had been about not having been identified. In this book, when writing about people in potentially compromising situations, I use pseudonyms and do not cross-reference details about them across chapters. While achieving complete anonymity in ethnographic writing about a very small group is impossible, the use of pseudonyms and other means of blurring recognition does provide a useful distance between anthropological descriptions and real-life actors and events.[22] However, I use real names when the context is positive and flattering, knowing that this is what people wish. One last factor on one's side is time: while I have published some of the materials I reanalyze here in scholarly journals, by definition relatively inaccessible, I waited to publish this book. Many people have died. For those that live on, the outrageous actions and scandalous events of two decades ago are now the object of mirth.

My field research benefited directly from the Nukulaelae enthusiasm for gossip, and many of its results focus on it in more or less direct fashion. In the first respect, my research may not differ greatly from most anthropological work. As if Trinh Minh-ha had written my fieldwork agenda, I obtained information over the years about social life on the atoll principally through gossip. But gossip has also figured prominently in my social and affective relations on Nukulaelae, in that my actions, intentions, and identity were common objects of speculation in the kitchen huts of the atoll. Gossip is Nukulaelae people's means of ethnographying the ethnographer, of turning the agent of description and analysis into an object of description and analysis.

Viewed from a local perspective, my retelling of the less-than-savory aspects of life on Nukulaelae could be seen as falling right in line with common social practices in the community: I, too, paint an unflattering picture ("disparaging" attributes the wrong connotation to my intentions) of close friends to my readership, that is, to complete strangers. However, the medium that I employ in my gossip is clearly different: no longer confined to the (albeit largely illusory) privacy of a cooking hut, my gossip is printed, and thus acquires an implicit claim to authority and truthfulness. However, the printed word only makes a *claim* to truth, and one that people can reject or resist, as Nukulaelae Islanders often do. As astutely literate people, they approach a written text with the expectation that it is authoritative, but they are also intensely aware of the fact that written texts are not end products, that their production and consumption are embedded in social contexts that determine the "truthfulness" of the text as much as its literal meaning (Besnier 1995, 165–166; cf. Lambek 1990). People can respond to texts, can evaluate, accept, or reject them. There are other differences between oral gossip in huts and ethnography-as-gossip. First, the latter makes serious attempts to maximize anonymity, while the former does everything to maximize recognition. Second, the gossiper's intent is very different from that of the ethnographer, whatever that may be. Third, and in a similar fashion, audience intentions differ in each case. Indeed, it is unlikely that many members of the anthropological community, to whom the work is principally addressed, will be interested in the specifics of the scandals on a tiny Pacific island. Readers with closer connections to the field site may have such interests, but it is difficult to imagine how they could use the specific knowledge they may acquire through the work for damaging purposes. In short, the parallel between gossip and ethnography breaks down under closer scrutiny.

Some may dismiss the conscience-probing exercise I have performed in this section as superfluous hand-wringing or as foolhardy self-exposure better suited to the confessional (or the wine-lubricated anthropologists' party) than to a "serious" published forum. Others may find that I have stopped short of deconstructing the sordid inner workings of the politics of an academic discipline. I conclude this modest effort by contending that anthropologists do not engage in such exercises often enough. For example, in an otherwise perceptive essay that I have already cited repeatedly, Sherry Ortner criticizes anthropologists' reluctance to study internal forms of hegemony in dominated groups as romantic (1995, 179). Yet she fails to give any consideration to the ethical implications that such research may have. All too often, anthropologists frame questions of representation only in terms of their intellectual content, while ethical considerations, or discussions of the political implications of anthropological field research, are relegated to newsletters and similar marginalia. The result is that ethical issues appear marginal to anthropological thinking, lending some validity to the strong reactions of the type voiced by the likes of Trinh Minh-ha and Trask.

However, what these reactions overlook is that the ethics of field research cannot be addressed by asking straightforward questions and expecting straightforward answers. Anthropological inquiry is embedded in social relations, just like relations with one's familiars, one's boss, and one's employees. And like all other social relations, relations in the field are potentially suffused with bonds of friendship and goodwill, as well as potentially fraught with difficulties (Luhrmann 1996, 233–236). Ethnographers are working with complex allegiances and obligations, and from complex identity formations. Field research is subject to local regimes of justice, cohesion, and social relations, as well as to more global regimes, and the interaction between these different regimes can be murky. Ethnographic works do not represent societies to their audiences, as M. Strathern (2005, 7) astutely remarks; rather, they establish a connection between societies and audiences, in some fashion or the other. What follows is my attempt at crafting this connection.

What Follows

The chapter that follows provides a description of life on Nukulaelae Atoll, focusing in particular on the intimacy of contexts in which gossip takes place. The chapter continues with a discussion of Islanders' self-representations to themselves and the outside world in the course of history and in modern times, self-representations that foreground problematically an ideology of harmony and consensus. In chapter 3, I further develop a discussion of this ideology, demonstrating that Nukulaelae people's anxious elaboration of it can be understood in terms of the coexistence of seemingly incommensurable discourses, one that calls for a hierarchical and authoritarian order, another for egalitarianism. This ideological landscape backgrounds the analysis of the microscopic structure of gossip interaction, to which I turn in chapter 4, in that this structure indexes the complexities of political ideology extant on the atoll. Chapter 5 puts the general discussion of the previous chapters "to the test" in an analysis of one particular event, a gossip session about a marginalized member of the society. I demonstrate how microscopic aspects of this gossip session relate to dynamics of marginalization and reputation, not only of the target of the gossip, but also of the gossiper and his or her audience. In turn, these dynamics are embedded in large-scale processes such as the politics of religious affiliation, encroaching capitalism, and novel discourses of human rights. Chapter 6 focuses on another set of events, the marginalization of two women through sorcery allegations, backgrounded again by changing economic and social conditions, in which I played a pivotal role as ethnographer. Here my focus shifts to the targets of gossip and seeks to make sense of their divergent responses to the gossip, responses that I contrast with those of another victim of gossip in chapter 7, also the target of sorcery allegations, who loses job and status as a result. I demonstrate that the latter's attempt to seek redress in a meeting with the entire island fails miserably because what can be whispered in gossip cannot be raised in public. The last two chapters demonstrate how different genres of interaction articulate with one another and highlight the extent to which gossip should be studied both in terms of what it is and in terms of what it is not. The concluding chapter brings together strands of my argument. Throughout the book, I seek theoretical inspiration from a variety of sources, which I introduce as needed: Peircean semiotics, which "complicates" the relationship between semiotic forms and what they represent; Bakhtinian understandings of the circulation across time, space, and contexts; the study of ideology in and through language; Foucault-inspired theories of power, coupled with poststructuralist insights into the work of performativity; and the feminist critique of received assumptions about the location of significant action in society and culture.

2 The World from a Cooking Hut

I WAS DROPPED OFF on Nukulaelae one stormy January evening in 1980 by a motor yacht on its way from Funafuti, the capital of Tuvalu, back to Fiji. The captain-owner, a former high-ranking government official of Fiji, member of an elite Fijian-European family not accustomed to being inconvenienced, had gruffly informed me that if Nukulaelae Islanders did not pay heed to the signals from his high-intensity lights, I would have to sail on to Fiji, take a flight back to Funafuti, and wait for the government ship, the venerable but tiny and by then miserably rusty *Nivanga* (figure 2.1), to take me to Nukulaelae on its monthly voyage. As it turned out, Nukulaelae people did notice the powerful beam of light he shone against the limestone church, the one edifice that towered above what was then a thatch-and-woven-frond village. Three young men came out in an outrigger canoe, which, to their bewilderment, I boarded precariously, with my shiny new blue suitcase. A cable was supposed to have been sent that morning from the prime minister's office on Funafuti to the Island Council president, but it got lost in the shuffle. I thus arrived unannounced, not a good start in a society that prizes predictability and order.

I begin this ethnographic chapter with a story of my fieldwork arrival, at the risk of subjecting myself to the severe criticism that in recent decades such introductions have received.[1] In her masterful deconstruction of the "classic Polynesian arrival scene," the utopian quality of which harks back to Enlightenment-era voyages, Pratt (1986, 35) demonstrates how such beginnings provide, in the classic texts of anthropology, the one glimpse that the ethnographer provides of himself (or, much more rarely, herself) to the reader before withdrawing behind the screen of impersonal and timeless authority that the arrival scene makes possible: "I was there, therefore I know." My arrival scene here has quite a different intent from those that Pratt deconstructs. This book in a sense is the story of my "discovery" of the workings of political life in a small atoll society on the edge of Polynesia. As the main narrator of this story, and in some cases one of the characters in it, I will remain embedded in it in more or less overt ways.

FIGURE 2.1:   The *Nivanga* docked at Funafuti, ca. 1982. When the ship calls at Nukulaelae, the shallow waters surrounding the atoll force it to anchor precariously at sea (photo courtesy Peter McQuarrie).

I use the word "story" because the narrative that follows is not a chronologically ordered chronicle of my hesitant progress in this process of discovery, a project in which I would be reluctant to engage. Nor is the discovery itself a simple progression from less to more knowledge, from lack of understanding to comprehension. Nor is it complete. Some of the roughest and most naïve impressions I formed shortly after my arrival on the atoll turned out to be as important to an understanding of political and social process on the atoll as the more nuanced insights I would eventually derive from the sheer experience of years of cumulative fieldwork. Often, my first-encounter impressions in fact matched closely the atoll dwellers' impression-management designs, the manner in which they want the rest of the world, including me, to perceive them, and in large part succeed in making the rest of the world believe is the one and only truth about themselves. The various versions of life on the atoll are thus equally valid, although each rubs shoulders with different positions and different projects.

Nukulaelae Atoll at first sight looks very tiny and vulnerable, and the possibility that a ship will miss it is not to be discounted, particularly if the captain is unfamiliar with the waters (it was a concern on that initial journey). Low-lying, it becomes visible only within a mile or so, although good navigators (as many Nukulaelae men still are despite the fact that interisland canoe trips had largely ceased by the end of the nineteenth century) can identify the presence of land from cloud formations, sea currents, and the presence of birds. Because of the small size of a population that hovers around 350, there is only sporadic transportation from the atoll to Funafuti, the nearest land, and from there to the world, via flights to Fiji. After an initial transportation boom following Tuvalu's 1978 accession to independence, which even included a weekly seaplane service to Nukulaelae funded by the New Zealand government for a little more than a year, conflict between parliamentarians and the country's economic difficulties have reduced links to the outside world to about ten visits a year by the sole government ship, the MV *Nivaga II*. Landing and boarding are precarious undertakings, as the ship's flat-bottom barges, the only craft that can approach the atoll, have to negotiate the pounding surf of the one shallow pass through the reef, and often overturn.[2]

It is with some apprehension about this perceived smallness and remoteness that I embarked on my first long-term stay at the beginning of the 1980s. Yet it took little time before I began to understand that size and isolation are deceiving, that life on the atoll could be as complex, fraught, diverse, and eventful as life in larger places, and that Nukulaelae was not a microuniverse turned upon itself. The last turn of the century has embroiled Tuvalu, including Nukulaelae, in some of the most dramatic and unanticipated global connections: from the international visibility it receives and seeks because of its vulnerability to global warming to the government's reliance on its "resources of jurisdiction" (e.g., leasing the ".tv" Internet suffix) to generate income. But even the least controllable of these forces, namely, rising sea levels related to climate change, generates an agentive response in the atolls, as Islanders argue among themselves what the best course of action may be and whether in fact the threat of the country's disappearance under the waves should be treated as the most important problem that Tuvalu currently faces. Large-scale processes and symbols not only shape atoll life, but often are shaped in turn by Islanders. My aim is to understand how the complexities, contradictions, and conflicts that characterize Nukulaelae's engagement with a larger context (e.g., visitors, the nation-state, labor migration, rising sea levels) are informed by historical and ongoing local dynamics.

The World from a Cooking Hut

Nukulaelae atoll has one village, huddled at the northern end of the tiny islet of Fagaua, on the western side of the atoll (map 2.1). When I last conducted fieldwork, in 1991, the village had become physically very different from when I first landed. In 1980, virtually all houses were rectangular structures neatly lined up on each side of two paths, resting on chalk-stone platforms raised about half a meter from the ground, with a gravel floor *(kilikili)* covered by layers of mats of increasing quality, topped by a roof of pandanus thatching, and walled in only in inclement weather with retractable woven coconut-frond blinds *(pola)*. A decade later, the only thatched structures that remained were cooking and storage huts. The main houses of the village now had corrugated-iron roofs, which, despite all their disadvantages (heat retention, high cost, danger in hurricane conditions), had finally alleviated the chronic water-supply problems of yesteryear: rainwater could now be collected in individual household cement water cisterns, an innovation funded by Save the Children. Most houses were now enclosed in cement-block walls, most of which remained permanently at waist level pending the arrival of elusive remittances from overseas. Houses still conformed to the careful, bylaw-mandated alignment patterns along the two main paths, forming two moiety-like structures *(ituuala)* that provide an organizational basis to many atoll activities (e.g., competitive gift giving, community labor, celebrations), but to me they looked considerably more temporary, uncomfortable, and unkempt than before. Yet to Nukulaelae people, cement floors, cement-block walls, corrugated-iron roofing, and water tanks made the village considerably more *gali* "beautiful" than before. Ah, modernity . . .

What remained constant in this whirlwind of change was the symbolic opposition between the village and the rest of the atoll. Many anthropologists working in Polynesia have analyzed life in Polynesian societies as being subsumed by what may appear to some a structuralist's paradise: sets of binary tensions, syntagmatically and paradigmatically ordered, between village and bush, land and sea, front and back, culture and wilderness, morality and lack thereof (e.g., Shore 1982 and Tcherkézoff 2003 on Samoa). Nukulaelae is no exception. Symbolically and materially, the village *(fakkai)* is opposed variously to the bush *(vao)*, the sea *(tai)*, and the household dependencies. The village is the site of culture, domesticated living, reason, and enlightened thought *(maalamalama),* in contrast to the bush and the sea, which are wild, undomesticated, emotional, and savage-like. Similar contrasts oppose the face *(mata)* or the front part *(mua)* of houses, the village, and persons, in contrast to the back part *(tua)* of these entities. Sociality and politics, the quintessence of culture, reason, and enlightenment in their more salubrious forms, are grounded in the village. In contrast, uncontrolled, unlawful, and asocial behavior take place in the bush, in the lagoon, or on the beach, where young men drink coconut toddy despite prohibition orders, where couples have sexual relations of a more or less licit nature, and where spirits roam, threatening to throttle *(kkumi)* mortals who trespass on their territory. However, as with all models—folk, analytic, or both—the relationship between these beautifully ordered binary tensions and lived experience is messy and full of contradictions. In particular, the boundaries between these seemingly contrastive categories always leak: the shadier forms of action that take place in the bush are never independent of the enlightenment

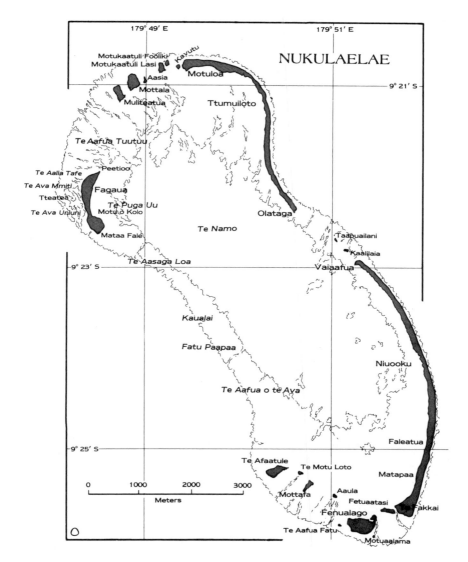

MAP 2.1:   Nukulaelae Atoll

that allegedly suffuses the village, and reasonableness and order cannot exist without unpredictability and wilderness.

As should be evident from my choice of examples, the sociocultural meanings of place and space are powerfully concrete instantiations of how life on the atoll is organized. One type of lived space that plays a central role in this book is the cooking hut, the site of a large portion of my data-gathering activities during fieldwork. Nukulaelae cooking huts are small and relatively frail constructions, many of which remained defiantly thatched with pandanus leaves while the rest of the village underwent momentous transformations, both cosmetic and of a deeper nature (figure 2.2). Skirting the boundaries of the village on its ocean, lagoon, and bush sides, this collar of small huts forms a liminal zone, whose overt purpose is to serve as a venue for cleaning fish, cooking, and storing such items as medicinal oils and pandanus leaves destined to be woven into mats. People refer to these cooking huts as *fale umu* "underground-oven huts" or simply *umu*, literally, "underground oven," a clear reference to the centrality of cooking activities among their overt functions. In general, the hut is informally divided into two areas. The smaller area is a section directly on the dirt floor and bounded at the far side by the open cooking fire, across which sturdy metal rods are steadied on rocks to hold in place pots filled with foods and liquids. The other, more substantial area consists of a raised platform, or *paapaa*, made of coconut-palm stems tightly held together with sennit or string or, more commonly today, wooden planks. Cooks rest on the edge of the *paapaa* to chop food and use it to set aside pots and bowls.

This is a gendered world: the *umu* is where Nukulaelae people try to demonstrate that Rosaldo (1974) was correct in equating domesticity with woman-

FIGURE 2.2:   Gossip by the cooking huts

hood. But space is always gendered in a messy fashion, as Shelly Rosaldo herself recognized later on (Rosaldo 1980b), and the *umu* is no exception. Thus it is also where men lounge around, their shorts or lavalavas wet or muddy upon returning from fishing or the swamp-taro pits, drinking cups of weak and very sweet tea to warm up. The *paapaa* is where entire families, women and men, young and old, take breakfast and lunch, shifting to the house in the village for the evening meal. And at night, the *paapaa* is cluttered with the sleeping bodies of family members and friends who have fled the stifling heat and bothersome mosquitoes of the village and sought in the cooking-hut areas, which are built strategically close to the beach and the bush, a soporific and soothing fresh breeze: *fakaagiagi i te matagi* "taking in the breeze" (literally, "making oneself be blown gently by the breeze").

For Nukulaelae Islanders, the cooking hut is a liminal and devalued context. Its physical location mediates between the village on the one hand and, on the other, the beach, the bush, and the taro swamps, which are undomesticated, dirty, and wild for different reasons. For example, the beach continues to serve as the community's toilet (despite Island Council efforts to encourage the use of the water-sealed toilets that were introduced in the early 1980s), and one always runs the risk of stepping on feces when walking on the coral sand. Fish caught in nets at night in the lagoon sometimes have the unmistakable scent of what they have just fed on, as I, through my enthusiasm to be useful, learned the hard way (one extricates fish from a net by biting its head and pulling its body through the mesh, a process through which one gets an intimate whiff of the creature's last meal). The bush is the location of pigsties and the graves of the dead, and where one risks being smothered by malevolent spirits. Young men go to the bush to drink fermented coconut toddy, in defiance of the prohibition that the Council of Elders tries to enforce, with little success. One goes to the bush to gather the dried spathes that have fallen off coconut trees for firewood, pandanus leaves for plaiting mats and thatching houses, and flower blossoms for garlands, fragrant body oils, and possibly magical ointments, tasks for which one wears one's work clothes. The same are also worn to go down to the taro swamps, enormous artificial pits dug by generation after generation of agriculturalists to the level of the brackish water that lies under the porous coral soil of atolls, up to thirty meters below the surface (the "Ghyben-Herzberg lens," freshwater that "floats" above underground seawater). There, gardeners sink to their knees in the brackish mud, hoping that a bare foot will not hit the sharp edge of a coral rock or the rusty blade of a lost knife buried under the mud. The huge leaves of the swamp taro *(pulaka; Cyrtosperma chamissonis)* can also serve as a welcome protection against prying eyes, and the taro swamp is where one can have sex, be it with one's spouse or an illicit partner. In short, the beach, the bush, and the taro swamp are potentially polluted and polluting, hidden and illicit, undomesticated and antisocial, and the cooking huts serve as buffers guarding the village from the potentially dangerous influence of these unsocialized areas.

Cooking huts are dirty, disorderly, and smoky. They smell of drying fish, fresh swamp-taro corms being peeled, and household scraps simmering for the pigs' meal. These smells connote abundance, but also invoke rawness and crudeness. Visitors and other outsiders are usually discouraged from visiting the cooking huts; receiving guests is what the village house is for. When they venture to the cooking hut areas, visitors are greeted with embarrassed apologies for the untidiness and dirtiness of the hut. A space will be hurriedly cleared for the visitor on the *paapaa*, as far away from the cooking fire as possible, and she or he will be warned about the smoke (*koe maa ausia!* "You are going to be overwhelmed by the smoke!").

For Nukulaelae people, society is elaborated in the village, in the context of each household, but most saliently in the *maneapa*, a large community house in the center of the village, designed to inspire awe and respect, although not always successfully. People refer to the *maneapa* metaphorically as *te fale o muna* "the house of words." Even though it probably is a postcontact or postmissionization borrowing from the Gilbert Islands that trickled down the islands of Tuvalu, first appearing in the northern islands and then the southern group (Goldsmith 1985), the building and its uses in contemporary Tuvalu embody tradition, continuity, and decorum. (The picture of a *maneapa* occupies a central position in Tuvalu's coat of arms, designed at independence.) However, it is in the cooking hut that reputations are made and undermined, actions are evaluated and condemned, motives are speculated upon and criticized, virtues are scrutinized and found wanting, and rumors are started and circulated. Everyone on Nukulaelae participates in and values the warm informal sociality of most social interactions in cooking huts. Islanders find intense enjoyment in each other's company in the midmorning, as early-morning fishing expeditions return displaying their catch and discussing it in detail with passersby; in the late afternoon, as men and women gather after work, and as women hurry to finish the preparations for the evening meal before dusk and the church bells announcing evening prayer; and in the late hours of the night, as groups of adults lounge around on the *paapaa*, fanning children to sleep and dozing off periodically themselves while the conversation continues around the fleeting light of a hurricane lamp and the large aluminum pot of weak and oversweetened tea, now cold, from which people halfheartedly pour themselves a cup. At other times, the cooking hut can be tense with scandal and abuzz with whispers. More rarely, it will be the setting for a screaming tantrum, the last resort for a young woman to express her exasperation at a mother's nagging or a brother's cruelty. In short, the cooking hut is the arena where all relationships are negotiated and where social life is constructed.

What Is He Doing Here?

During my initial stay on Nukulaelae in the early days of 1980, I was carefully kept at bay from the cooking huts for many weeks by the same empathetic concern (*alofa*) for my comfort that members of my host family, particularly the women, invoked when they jokingly threatened to commit suicide if I went net-fishing or to the gardens. White people, as is well known, are not only incapable of catching fish and climbing trees, but also squeamish about dirt and lack of comfort. As a twenty-year-old, I found these restrictions stifling, even though I was used to them from earlier fieldwork in Tonga. The justification for keeping me clean, comfortable, and securely entrenched in stereotypes about white people (formed and confirmed by a century of sporadic encounters with colonial Europeans) was only one of a complex of motivations, many of which were either unconscious or unspoken. There was, for example, a dose of self-concern about the possibility that my presence in the cooking hut could have brought upon the family the disparagement of neighbors for not treating their foreign guest properly. "People will talk!" I was told more than once after I had negotiated my way around other excuses.

Gradually, my forays to the cooking hut (and on the reef and fishing canoes) became more frequent, and eventually the cooking hut and its own dependencies became my world. My forced entry into the private world of my adoptive family generated fewer and fewer protests. It was backed up by unimpeachable local logic: I, too, wanted to *fakaagiagi i te matagi* "take in the breeze." The process was also expedited by the fact that my activities became increasingly centered on the cooking hut. My friend Selau, three years younger than I, started taking me net-fishing, angling, and fly-fishing early on, and was instrumental in demonstrating to others that I was more or less capable of looking as if I could become a productive member of society, one who could bring fish back to its logical landing place, the cooking hut. The first few net-fishing forays, where my more or less pathetic efforts were visible to all from the huts of the lagoon side, were not easy for me: I seethed at the laughter I could clearly hear, and even at the ostensibly approving calls of "*poto!*" (clever, capable), full of matchless Nukulaelae sarcasm, that young women would yell out when I did manage to extricate a furiously flapping surgeonfish (*manini*, a common Indo-Pacific small reef fish) from the meshing of the net. Selau and I also regularly got tipsy on coconut-sap sour toddy in his or my family's cooking hut, at a time when prohibition was not as contentious an issue as it would later become, requiring that drinking be done in high secrecy, further into the bush. Later, no one would pay much attention to my net-fishing, nor eventually my deep-sea fishing for bonito, unless the catch was particularly large.

Slowly, I changed status, from a guest of the family to a family member, albeit a liminal one. As the cooking hut gradually became my usual haunt, I began to understand that initial concerns about the cleanliness of my clothes were also concerns about my stepping into private lives too quickly. Eventually, though, such concerns were no longer of much import, at least for my closest kindred. The human aspects of quotidian interaction began overshadowing, in many contexts, differences in background, skin color, access to the outside world and its bountifulness (as well as misery), life designs, sexuality, and many other things. My adoptive father barked at me when I overreacted, drowsy from lack of sleep, when a deep-sea fish bit my trawling bait at 5 a.m. (a *valu*, given the nature of the jolt), and I lost it; my adoptive mother had and still has many reasons to be annoyed at me; and my little sisters found me too protective of my books and papers and a slow eater as they waited for their turn. Yet concessions for my privileged status continued to be made, as the cooking hut where I began sleeping and working and living was renovated from one fieldwork period to the other from a basic storage hut to a magnificent little thatched structure with an enclosed sleeping area and a table and chairs in the work area.

For many, though, what I was doing on Nukulaelae remained a mystery, and there was plenty of gossip about it. In the initial few months, when rationalizations were lacking, I was widely suspected of being a "spy," as are so many other anthropologists all over the world. Fortunately, in the Pacific Islands (in contrast to areas of the world such as South America), what a spy looks like and does is quite vague, and the consequences of these suspicions would eventually amount to little more than the good laughs that everyone would have when they were later mentioned, even as I later engaged in activities, such as tape-recording and videotaping, that could have reinforced the image of a spy. During my original stay on the atoll, I was in the employ of the U.S. Peace Corps, which had found in me a cheap way of having language and culture materials developed for the training of the first substantial contingent of volunteers that were about to be posted to the various islands and atolls of Tuvalu. (The agency was then a growth industry in the Pacific, as newly independent states such as Tuvalu were flirting with the Soviet Union as a way to encourage foreign aid from the United States and its allies.) Therefore, for Nukulaelae Islanders with familiarity with the world of governments and bureaucracies, my original stay on Nukulaelae was easy to account for: I was "sent" there by the branch of a large and powerful state. This association was not without its advantages for me, since Nukulaelae Islanders hold Americans in higher regard than other Westerners (ignoring, with everyone on Nukulaelae, the fact that I, not an American citizen at the time, was working for the Peace Corps as a "third-country national," a category whose precariousness and suspect nature the organization and its representatives never missed the chance to point out).

During my subsequent stays on Nukulaelae, my motivations for residing on the atoll became the subject of more specific rationalization, but these were also more diverse. People who had relatively little intimate contact with me understood that I had by then formed serious personal bonds with one family on the atoll and that my visits were "holidays" *(malooloo)* comparable to the sometimes lengthy leaves periodically taken on the atoll by Nukulaelae Islanders in the employ of the Tuvaluan government on Funafuti or other bodies further afield. In this context, I was also taking advantage of the special bond to my adoptive family to find a place to live, have fun, and partake of a simpler lifestyle. This slightly reified "simpler lifestyle" was manifest in the sorts of activities in which I engaged, like off-island Nukulaelae people during *malooloo* visits. I would go fishing in the early morning hours, feed ducks and pigs, work on a vegetable garden (in vain, as "other people's chickens" always got to the seeds before they had a chance), and participate, with relatively few obligations, in the activities of the atoll community *(mea fai a te fenua)*. People generally described what I did on a day-to-day basis as devoid of effort: speaking to old men, tape-recording meetings, typing mysterious things into a laptop computer I had hooked up to a solar panel (in 1990–1991), all of which amounted to *sagasaga fua* "just sitting around" (cf. Bashkow 2006). Only when I went fishing or when I brought swamp taro back from the gardens *(umaga)* were my activities recognized as work. Occasionally, a young man I knew well would come and watch me work at the solar-panel-powered laptop computer I brought in the 1990s and admit to me that it did not look that simple after all. These experiences are of course not unique, as many anthropologists will report similar receptions.

Many people were aware that I had a research interest in aspects of Nukulaelae society and culture. Opinions nevertheless diverged about what the focus of the research was and should be. Individuals with whom I developed intimate rapport over the years generally developed an understanding of the nature and scope of my fieldwork that was close to my own. Other people thought I was interested in studying "sanctioned" representations of life on the atoll, such as what is displayed, on special occasions, in the middle of the village. Feasts in the *maneapa*, for example, with conspicuous displays of culinary wealth, songs and dances, and speeches about togetherness, peace, and cooperation, are excellent manifestations of what Nukulaelae people, particularly older men, think of as *tuu mo aganuu* "customs and traditions" and wish outsiders like me to think of as such (cf. Keesing 1985, 28–29). Some people did their best to draw my attention toward manifestations of this communally institutionalized representation and away from competing ones. For example, the first time I videotaped a Women's Council meeting, hoping to capture glimpses of how Nukulaelae women handled disagreements, the president of the council explicitly forewarned, to my dismay, some of the feistier elderly women to watch what they said because, in her words, what I wanted to record on video footage was the island community in all it peacefulness, harmony, and beauty.

After a few months, I began interviewing people individually, as well as tape-recording casual conversations by placing a tape recorder in the corner of the family kitchen hut, warning everyone that it was on, and remaining next to it to observe. The practice quickly became accepted as yet another of my strange activities and interests, but some people at the same time enjoyed the complicity of stimulating juicy talk among the conversationalists present. The kitchen hut was an ideal site for my endeavors, because its strategic location by the lagoon-side path on the edge of the bush made it a favorite venue for socializing. The collection method, which in later years my assistant replicated with her host family, worked so well that it enabled me to obtain highly naturalistic sample of the most informal of Nukulaelae interactions, and this is how I came to obtain audio recordings of gossip.

Like Harvey (1992, 82), whose Quechua informants suspected that she had chosen the wrong fieldwork site, I was sometimes told that Nukulaelae was not the best place to see "Tuvaluan culture" in action. Rather, islands and atolls in the north of the group, such as Niutao and Nanumaga, are widely thought to be more conservative and "traditional" (although circumstantial evidence indicates that Niutao and Nanumaga Islanders are as adept at constructing tradition as Nukulaelae Islanders). At the same time that Nukulaelae Islanders admire northern Tuvaluans for "hanging on" to their traditions, they also see them as quaintly backward because of it. Thus, for example, when a government dignitary originally from a northern island paid an official visit to Nukulaelae, the fact that he made speeches in his native dialect, rather than the de-facto national standard dialect of Funafuti, was the subject of some behind-the-scenes ridicule (*Koo oko loa te maatagaa!* "How unseemly!").

For most Nukulaelae people, the focus and limits of my understanding were determined by the strongly held belief that outsiders are by definition incapable of acquiring anything but the most superficial understanding of their society. Despite my competence in the language, fictive kinship affiliations, long association with the community, and adeptness at gossiping, I was no exception, except for those who knew me well. Islanders also frequently warned me not to believe particular people and expressed worries that I would swallow everything I was told wholesale, a naïveté that goes hand-in-hand with the impossibility of an outsider's knowing anything. When I cracked an inside joke, dropped an innuendo, or teased someone with kinship details, interlocutors and overhearers would often express amazement and often hilarity: *Palele ne iloa nee ia!* "He knows it all!" But these flashes of evidence failed to shake most people's disbelief that I too could understand what was going on, in part because people found them more entertaining than worrisome, I suspect.[3]

However, the strength of these beliefs about epistemological limits did not preclude some people from expressing worries about my nosiness. Well into my second long-term visit in 1985, for example, one relative of the family into which I had been incorporated attempted to dismiss me from a family event that was turning into a session designed to iron out interpersonal problems (*faipati fakallei*, literally, "speak properly"); the head of the household contradicted him and told me to stay. The same person continued to communicate in no uncertain terms his unease about my position in the family and community. When my host family threw a feast for the entire island to celebrate my return in 1990 and the fact that I had obtained a Ph.D. since my earlier fieldwork, this person formally declared in speech during the feast that I would bear from then on the name of my now-deceased adoptive father. ("Sending me to the community" on the occasion of my return had been my adoptive father's intention before his untimely death, and therefore the feast was also a posthumous commemoration of him.) He was later criticized, however, for exerting authority over a name that belonged to the patri-line, while he was matrilineally related to the deceased name bearer. It is possible that his action were a carefully calculated plan to grant me a powerful symbol of localness while knowing full well that it was invalid and would therefore have the opposite effect. Whatever may have been his intentions, the act stands out as a particularly complex enactment of the continued misgivings that some on Nuku-laelae had about my presence on the atoll, my status in the community, and my research and other activities in the course of my long-term involvement.

There were other, less dramatic, more mundane, but equally multilayered responses to my continued and mysterious involvement with persons, families, and the community. For example, my linguistic competence was sometimes a topic of revealing commentary. When I arrived on Nukulaelae, I was quite pro-ficient in Tongan, and was able to use this proficiency (coupled with focused lin-guistic efforts) to learn Nukulaelae Tuvaluan quickly. On an everyday basis, my ability to partake fully in conversation, make speeches, and overhear gossip was taken for granted. But in 1990, when my then-graduate-student Miki Makihara spent three months on the atoll, members of the community told her that I spoke their own language better than the Islanders themselves, because I knew *pati lloto* "deep words" and *pati taumua* "ancient words."[4] Such indirect flattery is subtly effective: placing me on a pedestal for my linguistic competence is one way of encouraging me not to meddle with the less exalted and more reprehensible ways of using the language, in contexts like arguments, disagreements, and gossip. I am certainly not claiming that Nukulaelae Islanders consciously devised this sce-nario to ensure the continuity of my marginal status. However, these actions, and many others like them, had the tacit effect of drawing an epistemological cordon, either around me or around the social areas into which I should not peek. Yet not everyone had the same idea about where the cordon should be placed, and the same person could be motivated by different agendas in different contexts. Thus the people who appeared most keen to insulate me from the affairs of the family and the community were the very same individuals who, in other contexts, would complain bitterly to me about the atoll's authority structure and lampoon those in charge for my benefit. These inconsistencies and contradictions ensured the ineffectiveness of the epistemological insulation. As with all human relationships, the relationships between a fieldworker and "the field" are complex, contradictory, ambiguous, and motivated by a host of possible agendas, many of which lie well below the surface of the various agents' consciousness.

History and the Outside World

The thrust behind developing a detailed discussion of the complexities and contradictions of my position in the Nukulaelae community is not to provide a narrative of self-absorbed reflexivity. Rather, I am attempting to provide an instance of Nukulaelae Islanders' dealings with tokens of the outside world, a particularly vivid one I hope since I am retelling some of it in the first person, in an attempt to tap the most useful form of reflexivity, "the kind that places the cultural assumptions of the ethnographer in question—that clarifies the ethnographic encounter and its limitations as predicated upon the imperfect meshing of two different codes, with its multiplicity of divergent identities and presuppositions" (Herzfeld 2001, 45–46). The relationships I formed over the years on the atoll are of course embedded in a long history of contacts between Nukulaelae people and outside agents, a history that I will outline in the next chapter and that will prove essential to an understanding of the materials I present in this book.

An important theme underlying the account I provide of my position in the Nukulaelae community is the tension between harmony and conflict, oneness and divisiveness, peace and discord. (I use the vague term "tension" to avoid the greater specificity of terms like "contradiction," "conflict," or "incommensurability.") This theme will figure prominently in the discussion in subsequent chapters, but it is also a salient theme in Nukulaelae's history of contact with the outside world. In other words, the issue is both a topic of great concern in local processes and discourses of self-understanding and a subject of heightened awareness in Nukulaelae's relationships with the external world.

How people first came to settle on Nukulaelae is not known, as archeological work remains to be conducted on the atoll. One can surmise, however, that settlement was not a single event, but instead consisted of arrivals from different parts of Western Polynesia, periods of relative stability, and momentous natural events like hurricanes and droughts that would leave the atoll uninhabited until the arrival of a new wave of settlers. Prehistorians have documented such patterns on other small islands of the Central Pacific where field research has been conducted (Kirch 2002, 171–182). Virtually nothing is known either about the Nukulaelae social order prior to the end of the nineteenth century. What can be pieced together of the precontact past suggests a loosely hierarchical social structure headed by a chief, selected from among the members of one particular clan or kin group, who ruled with the help of a council. Chieftainship may have been based on a mixture of ascription and achievement, and chiefly as well as nonchiefly descent was reckoned bilaterally with a patrilineal bias. In short, Nukulaelae society was structured like that on other atolls of Western Polynesia, exhibiting the least amount of hierarchical elaboration in the spectrum of Polynesia's systems of social organization (Sahlins 1958, 92–106).

There has been no dearth of outsiders on Nukulaelae since contacts with the greater world began in earnest in the latter part of the nineteenth century. From Samoan pastors and visiting English missionaries to assorted whalers, traders, planters, and beachcombers of varied origins, a host of personalities from the outside peppers historical records, memories, and genealogies of the late nineteenth and early twentieth centuries. Some stayed one day, others twenty years, while the physical presence of yet others remained a fleeting illusion. During the colonial period, colonial officers visited only occasionally, although their specters loomed large in everyone's quotidian consciousness, through codes of colonial laws, for instance, that regulated minute aspects of personal lives. When the Pacific War broke out, as elsewhere in the Pacific, it shrouded with complexity hitherto seemingly straightforward relationships between colonial agents and the colonized. Later, relatives from other islands, government workers, American Cold War servicemen, a historian, a few lost tourists and yachters in search of "true Polynesia," and two successive Peace Corps volunteer couples would sojourn on the atoll for varied lengths of time and with varied consequences. Yet another type of outsider remained over as many generations as it takes to become "local." For example, in the second half of the nineteenth century, following the slaving raid that took a large percentage of the local population and the plantation venture that brought to the atoll the human capital that would quickly replace those who were taken into slavery (to which I turn presently), "outsiders" greatly outnumbered "locals," and in turn became the new locals. In this society, despite the hugely determinative role that people bestow on "origin" (particularly on the contrast between local and extralocal blood), localness in practice is as shifting as it is in all other societies.[5]

By far the most important outsider residents since the mid-1860s have been the pastors. The agent of missionization in Tuvalu was the Samoa-based London Missionary Society (LMS).[6] However, society authorities deemed the atoll environment too harsh for any Westerner to adapt to it, and sent Polynesians, not Westerners, to convert and minister to Ellice Islanders. While it is amply clear that Samoans accustomed to rich high-island environments found living in tiny, poor, and nonhierarchical atoll communities beneath their station, 1865 marks the beginning of a long succession of Samoan missionaries. The first on Nukulaelae, Ioane, disembarked with his wife Saili from the ship *Augustita* only after a great deal of "persuasion" from the British missionary John Murray (Elekana 1872, 196), but stayed more than two decades, while the last departed in 1958, the year in which the localization of the church in Tuvalu was complete. While the pastors that the LMS distributed across the atolls differed in their personalities and approaches (Munro 1978), they all shared a background in a deeply hierarchical society in which pastors figured prominently, and they did not hesitate to either demand or accept high status. Oral history maintains that the traditional tokens of chieftainship, such as the wearing of precious pearl-shell fish-lure necklaces *(paa kasoa)* and the right to the head of any turtle caught, were immediately bestowed onto Nukulaelae's first Samoan pastor, Ioane, upon his arrival.

However, the relationship between the LMS's Samoan envoys to Tuvalu and their hosts was complex and multilayered. On the surface, the religious teachers appeared to have wielded tremendous authority and to have thought of themselves as infinitely superior to the recently converted atoll dwellers. However, their authority was circumscribed. First, they were themselves under the much more formidable authority of the British missionaries who would visit each atoll for a few hours once a year. During this visit, the missionary would assess the Samoan teachers' progress and perform all the important ritual work, such as testing potential new converts and baptizing them. If the congregation had not made appreciable progress in such areas as literacy and Bible knowledge, the Samoan teacher was made to bear responsibility, and some were actually sent back home. Once a year, therefore, Nukulaelae Islanders were offered a dramatic demonstration of the limits of the authority to which they were subjected the remainder of the time. Generally speaking, the British churchmen kept a tight rein on the missionization process and entrusted the Samoan teacher with very little (Goldsmith and Munro 1992). It is telling, for example, that the LMS did not see it fit to ordain their "native teachers" as pastors until they finally yielded to the latter's demands in 1875.

All church pastors who have served on Tuvalu's islands and atolls have been Tuvaluans since 1958 (significantly, the last Samoan posting in Tuvalu was on Nukulaelae), yet many aspects of their relationship with the congregation are reminiscent of the olden days. The now localized Christian Church of Tuvalu (Eekaaleesia Kelisiano o Tuuvalu, or EKT) follows a policy of appointing to each congregation a pastor from another island, ostensibly to prevent the pastor from demonstrating favoritism toward any particular family. A pastor is always a guest of his congregation, and his spiritual power and personal importance are constantly acknowledged, both symbolically and materially: not only is he generally the first person that orators refer to in the standard panegyric preface of all formal speeches *(fakalagilagi),* but the island community meets all of his and his family's material needs, taking particular pride in ensuring he be supplied vast quantities of food, money, mats, and other gifts, competing in generosity with other islands of Tuvalu, in ways that resemble competitive gift giving to pastors and chiefs in other parts of Polynesia. At the same time, the community controls, circumspectly under most circumstances, the extent of his influence on the political life of the atoll and does not hesitate to resort to drastic measures if a particular pastor betrays an inappropriate interest in secular affairs, usually by asking the church to remove him (Besnier 1995, 39–43, 154–160; Goldsmith and Munro 1992). Gossip figures prominently in such cases. Rumor circulated in the mid-1980s that the pastor, who was meddling in politics, was having an affair with a young woman; whether the accusation was founded or not, he lost his posting as well as his job. (I refer to the pastor with a masculine pronoun because to date the Church of Tuvalu has never ordained a woman, not for lack of qualified candidates I must add.) The congregation's relationship with its guest pastor is thus one in which it exerts a lot of control, not unlike the control Islanders seek to maintain in their dealing with the outside world.

What dominates many of the accounts that we have of Nukulaelae's historical contacts with the rest of the world is a complex of values and representations that echo discourses of self-representation on the atoll today. This complex centralizes the peacefulness *(fiileemuu)* of the atoll community, the mutual empathy *(feaalofani)* that reigns among its members, and oneness of spirit and action *(fai mea fakatasi* "do things together," *loto tasi* "oneness of heart").[7] These are the values that Nukulaelae people tirelessly celebrate today in songs and speeches, kitchen-hut conversations, and interviews with ethnographers. They are the values that, in my initial months of fieldwork, struck me as the most impressive characteristics of the society. They loom large in local depictions of the "enlightenment" *(maalamalama)* that characterizes the Christian, progress-oriented, and reason-driven present times, in contrast to the "dark ages" *(aso o te pouliuli)* before Christianization, from which contemporary Tuvaluans distance themselves and during which they allege that coercion, unpredictability, and violence reigned. The idealized depiction of the society as peace-loving, cohesive, and consensus-driven is central to the "officializing strategies" (Bourdieu 1977, 38–39), communally ratified self-representations that Nukulaelae Islanders provide to others and, in many contexts, to themselves.

Beauty, mutual empathy, and serenity are states of maximal emotional balance, and Nukulaelae people are anxious to project to outsiders an image of communal harmony driven by these emotional experiences. For example, visitors to the atoll are treated to marvelously well-coordinated dance performances called *faatele,* in which the tension and tempo of the choreography and the volume and tempo of the singing and percussion accompaniment gradually increase in tightly controlled unison, and finally come to an abrupt end. It is particularly important for the success of the performance that everyone (dancers, singers, percussionists) end it at exactly the same moment. During performances, individuals may engage in isolated trancelike displays of intense excitement called *matagi* (literally, "wind[y]"), which can "hit" *(poko)* dancers, singers, or spectators. When this happens to dancers, they "break frame" from the otherwise highly controlled choreography and execute a brief twirl on their feet with arms extended while whooping and smiling rapturously; when members of the chorus have a *matagi* episode, they get up from their seated position and gesticulate wildly in time with the singing or join in the dancing. However, the actions in which individuals under the spell of a *matagi* episode engage are carefully coordinated with the ongoing action and only serve to underscore the unified quality of the communal effort. It is through such highly charged symbolic action, and through talk about it, that the Nukulaelae community displays its emotionally harmonious oneness of spirit.

There are striking similarities between the vocabulary of self-representation that Nukulaelae Islanders elaborate today and outsiders' representations on the atoll, be it in ship logs, colonial reports, travelers' narratives, or reports by foreign experts in modern days. The pattern began with the first Western commentator, George Barrett, captain of the first Western ship to sight Nukulaelae, in 1821, which he named "Mitchell's Island," a name by which it was known on navigational charts for the rest of the century. In his logbook (now lost, but an extract of which was published in a New England newspaper), Barrett auspiciously reported that the two crew members he sent ashore "were treated very kindly by the natives who made them presents" (Ward 1967, 257). The same images are encountered with consistent regularity in missionary journals, whose authors were generally not predisposed to commending the habits and characters of pre-Christian or recently converted "natives." "As a race," wrote visiting missionary S. J. Whitmee in 1871 about Tuvaluans, "the Ellice Islanders are very quiet and peaceable. Quarrels are rare, and ordinary disputes are settled by the authority of the king or chiefs" (1871, 27).[8] As is the case of other groups elsewhere in the world, such as the Zapotec villagers of Oaxaca, Mexico, among whom Nader (1990) conducted decades of fieldwork, "harmony ideology" on Nukulaelae is a coconstruction, the product of both autochthonous efforts and outsiders' perceptions and actions.

For four decades after the initial 1821 encounter, whaling ships roamed the oceans surrounding Nukulaelae and the rest of the Ellice Islands, but very few bothered to call, for many different reasons, not the least of which was that the atolls' poverty and isolation offered little of interest to the whalers. In a similar vein, colonial powers and other agents paid no attention to the group, preferring to concentrate their commercial and politics efforts on larger, more fertile, and more populated island groups like Samoa, Hawai'i, and the Society Islands. Nukulaelae and its neighbors were thus spared the encroachment of Euro-American colonialists experienced in what the latter perceived as the more desirable areas of the Pacific. But at the same time, they were never subjected to the influx of literate eyewitnesses from whom we have inherited voluminous accounts of life in other parts of Polynesia around the time of contact. Consequently, information on the atoll's social organization at the time of contact is extremely scant, although events are inscribed in visitors' records and local memory practices.

Of these events, the most pivotal for Islanders' identity formation is conversion to Christianity (cf. G. White 1991, 7, on Santa Isabel in the Solomon Islands). Before the 1860s, the inhabitants of the atoll had already become acquainted with the new religion, purchasing at least one Bible from a passing ship and conducting, with the help of a beachcomber named Tom Rose, rudimentary services (Elekana 1872, 148). But for contemporary Nukulaelae Islanders the climatic and epoch-making event was the chance arrival, in 1861, of Elekana, a Manihiki Islander (Northern Cook Islands; see map 2.2) who, along with several others, had drifted fifteen hundred miles over several weeks in a canoe after being blown off course by a storm during a routine interisland trip (Goldsmith and Munro 2002). The Cook Islands having long been Christianized, Elekana was a lay deacon and, during his stay on Nukulaelae with his fellow survivors, began converting people to Christianity, a process that, according to contemporary narratives, met no resistance. A while later, Elekana secured passage on a ship bound for Samoa, promising to alert the Samoa chapter of the LMS of the need to attend to the pastoral desires that Islanders harbored. In Britain at the time, Elekana's involuntary voy-

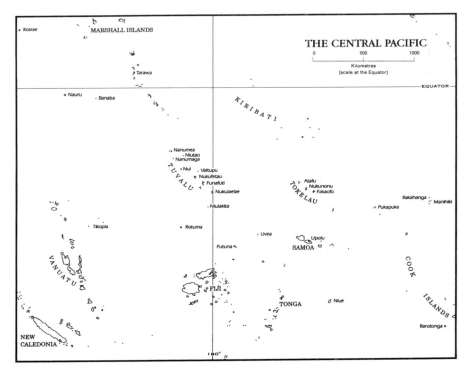

MAP 2.2: The Central Pacific

age, his "miraculous" beaching on the eastern side of the atoll, and his conversion of Nukulaelae Islanders became enshrined in missionary propaganda as a well-known parable (Elekana 1872; Murray 1865; G. Turner 1865). On Nukulaelae today, the events are anchored in the collective consciousness as the foundational events of the atoll's history, marking it as the anointed source of Christianity for all of Tuvalu. Important celebrations commemorated the centenary of Elekana's arrival in 1961 and its 125th anniversary in 1986, the preparations for which consumed minds and bodies for an entire year.[9]

Elekana's episode marks the beginning of a period that is remembered today as a dense concentration of events, "landmarks in time that are placed close together—and usually in a very irregular manner, since for certain periods they are almost entirely lacking—whereas around such salient events sometimes many other equally salient events seem to gather" (Halbwachs 1992, 175). In 1863, three Peruvian slaving ships or blackbirders dropped anchor off the atoll, enticed a large percentage of the population to come on board, and made off with them. Approximately 250 Islanders, out of a total estimated at 300, were transported to the island mines of Sala y Gomez, off the coast of Peru, from which none ever returned (Maude 1981, 74–82; Munro 1990). Other islands of the region lost many inhabitants to the Peruvian slavers who plied their trade in the Pacific from 1862 until they yielded to the mounting international protest in 1864; among these in particular figure Tongareva in the Gambier Islands, Rapa in the Austral Islands, and Easter Island. But probably none were as devastated as Nukulaelae (Maude 1981, 194). According to an English missionary who visited Nukulaelae in 1870, most able-bodied adults had been taken away, leaving only older people and children: "[T]he strong men and women were advised to leave their small children in charge of the aged. In some cases they did not; in others the men went, and left their wives and children behind" (Whitmee 1871, 11). Three years later, when missionary John Murray called at the atoll to drop off the first Samoan teacher, Ioane, there were only sixty-five pitiful people on the atoll, which puts into perspective Ioane's initial reluctance to stay as their guest pastor.

Further hardship followed the slavers' raid. In 1865, whoever was left on Nukulaelae entered in an unfortunate contractual arrangement, the terms of which were undoubtedly incomprehensible to them, with the Samoa office of the Hamburg-based corporation Godeffroy und Sohn (sometimes referred to as the world's first transnational business conglomerate), which would soon reconstitute itself as the Deutsche Handels- und Plantagen-Gesellschaft der Südsee-Inseln (DHPG) and dominate trade in the region, altering irreversibly the economic landscape of the Pacific Islands. On Nukulaelae, the firm leased the largest islet, today called Niuooku (New York; see map 2.1), and turned it into a coconut plantation. To the Islanders' surprise, the islet became off-limits to them; since it represents a fourth of the atoll's total dry-land area, the local population was deprived of substantial food-gathering grounds and went hungry. In 1883 and 1886, major hurricanes devastated the atoll repeatedly, interspersed by droughts (McLean and Munro 1991). Disagreements also arose between the successive managers of the DHPG plantation and the Islanders about the length of the lease. The former insisted that they had the islet for twenty-five years, while the latter thought that they had agreed on twenty-five lunar months. (Contemporary accounts on the atoll also assert that the latter received total compensation of 10 shillings for the duration of the lease.) This classic case of cross-cultural misunderstanding, undoubtedly aggravated by the German planters' opportunistic duplicity, accentuated the food crisis and plunged the atoll population into a turmoil of conflict and desperation until 1890, when DHPG finally pulled out (Munro, Iosefa, and Besnier 1990).

The plantation did leave one indelible positive mark on the atoll. Instead of hiring labor locally, the planters imported contract workers from other Pacific islands, including the Gilbert Islands, Kosrae, Niue, Rotuma, Fiji, Samoa, and the Marshall Islands (see map 2.2). The practice was customary on nineteenth-century plantations around the colonial world (Wolf 1982, 368–371) and was in part designed to circumvent the possibility that autochthonous workers could have a local power base. In this case, Nukulaelae did not even have a labor pool to offer, at least at the beginning of the lease. Many workers whom DHPG brought in did not return to their home islands at the end of their contracts but instead stayed on and married Nukulaelae Islanders. Their warm bodies and working hands were undoubtedly eagerly sought by the widows of the raid, and Nukulaelae continues to be one of the most exogamously oriented islands of the Tuvalu group to this day.[10] Thus the plantation conveniently provided what Nukulaelae was in dire need of, new blood. Consequently, many contemporary inhabitants of the atoll have substantial kinship networks on several Pacific islands, many of which they still sustain.

The various events of the last four decades of the nineteenth century had a considerable impact on the atoll. The personnel associated with high-ranking positions was seriously reduced by the slavers' raid. While there is a place in contemporary Nukulaelae historical memory for Tafalagilua, the chief during whose tenure these events took place, and while Tafalagilua himself was probably not kidnapped, the chiefly descent group to which he belonged was undoubtedly as drastically reduced by the kidnapping and other disasters of the period as any other descent groups.[11] Today, no one on Nukulaelae claims direct descent from Tafalagilua, a fact that strongly suggests, given the specificity of Nukulaelae genealogical memory, that he died leaving no living survivor. His successor was his classificatory sister's son (*tuaatina*) Laapana, whose tenure marks the end of hereditary title holding, even though Nukulaelae people still speak, in very vague terms, of a chiefly lineage, the identity of which differs from one person to the next, although no one generally expresses concern about these discrepancies.

Nukulaelae's population was so reduced that the land tenure system needed to be completely revised. Significantly, two strangers accomplished this task. According to a written record of genealogies *(tusi gafa)* I consulted on Nukulaelae, Vave and Taupo of Funafuti arrived on Nukulaelae in the years following the Peruvian raid and were entrusted with dividing up the land among twenty-eight men, whose identities and origins are not known. Following is the relevant passage from this document, in the original orthography, which appears to have been compiled around 1945 from earlier documents:

Vave se tagata Funafuti laua mo Taupo. Taupo ne fakafolau kako Vave ne tautali mai ia Taupo. Mai ki Nukulaelae fai te mavaega a Valoa i te mea ka galo, muna Valoa kia Tepuku, ka vau Vave ke tuku te filifili kia Vave. Ko Vave mo Taupo ne tofi ne laua te fenua nei. E 28 tagata ne vaevae ei te laukele[.–torn]

Vave [was] a Funafuti man, together with Taupo. Taupo was set adrift [as punishment], and Vave followed Taupo here. They came to Nukulaelae[.] Vaaloa was making his will because he was about to die, and [he] told Tepuku to let Vave partition [the land]. Vave and Taupo partitioned this atoll. The land was partitioned among 28 men.

What this document suggests is that the blackbirding raid and other late-nineteenth-century disasters left the atoll's authority structure so weakened that land redistribution had to be performed by outsiders. These outsiders, however, do not appear to have dominated the rest of the population, despite the fact that the scenario lent itself to the creation of a stranger-king complex.

The discontinuities of the late nineteenth century not only explain why contemporary Nukulaelae historical memory (e.g., genealogies) begins abruptly with the early 1860s, but also have implications for a reconstruction of the historical trajectory of the atoll's political history to this day. They also created a peculiar situation on the atoll at the end of the nineteenth century, in that virtually every inhabitant of the atoll could claim recent ancestry elsewhere, and, conversely, no one could claim "pure" Nukulaelae or even "pure" Tuvaluan ancestry. The Islanders therefore faced the task of constructing a common culture despite highly diverse identities. We know nothing of the process through which they approached this task. All we can say today is that it was achieved with a great deal of efficiency, as contemporary Nukulaelae society and culture retain no trace of their eclectic origins. In fact, Nukulaelae seems to have experienced surprising continuity in many aspects of social life and culture in the midst of these troubles. One of these is language: the situation of the atoll in the second half of the 1800s could have been a propitious context for language death, and yet the Nukulaelae dialect of Tuvaluan appears to have survived.

The discontinuities and selectivity that characterize Nukulaelae histori-cal memory today are of course not unusual and surprising, in that all acts of remembering and forgetting are social, as many scholars have demonstrated (e.g., Carsten 1995; Halbwachs 1992; Lambek 1996; Rappaport 1990). Are the blanks in Nukulaelae historical memory evidence of trauma-induced repression, as a classic Freudian account would maintain? Hardly, since what is remembered are precisely the most traumatic events, in minute and often harrowing details: the slave raid, the hardship following the lease of Niuooku, the famines. I do not discount the fact that some of this memory may have found some boosting through access to writ-ten accounts authored by outsiders, such as Maude's (1981) chapter about Nuku-laelae in his history of Peruvian slave raiding in the Pacific, copies of which I took to Nukulaelae and which atoll elders read with enormous interest and pride.

Characteristic of present-day Nukulaelae Islanders' talk about their ancestors' misfortunes is an ambivalent mixture of empathy and distance. The descriptor that dominates these characterizations is *fakaalofa* "pitiable, arousing empathy" (the causal version of the emotion term *alofa* "empathy, pity, provoking one to wish to feed or care for"): nineteenth-century Nukulaelae Islanders were pitiable because they were uncivilized, ignorant, and poor and were not yet acquainted with Christianity. Sometimes, the characterization verges on condescension, of the kind that Islanders express when they hear stories about unclothed savages inhab-iting the outer edge of Christianity or stories about the terrible deeds that people in industrial countries are capable of.[12] The other side of this moral coin is that the atoll and its population were and continue to be vulnerable, easily victimized by the depredatory actions of outsiders, a morality of victimization that continues to suffuse Nukulaelae Islanders' and Tuvaluans' self-representations in the context, for example, of the threat that global warming poses for the continued existence of the atoll and country. More on this topic anon.

In 1892, chief Laapana signed with his mark a treaty of cession to Britain, and after his death in 1897 the colonial authorities appointed a man called Malaki as "native magistrate." To the now well-entrenched LMS was added yet another force from abroad, the colonial administration. Great Britain reluctantly declared a protectorate over the Ellice Islands to fulfill its treaty obligations with Germany, though the islands were of little interest to the Colonial Office because they lacked resources it could exploit, in contrast to phosphate-rich Ocean Island to the north. Britain eventually amalgamated the Ellice Islands, somewhat arbitrarily, into a large area of scattered islands for administrative expediency. The resulting Gilbert and Ellice Islands Protectorate (Colony after 1916) included, besides the Ellice Islands, the Gilbert Islands, a much larger and more populated island group to the north of the Ellice Islands, peopled by Micronesians, and Ocean Island (as well as, between 1916 and 1926, Tokelau, then referred to as the Union Islands).

The colonial authorities administered Nukulaelae and the rest of the colony from far-away Ocean Island or Banaba (1916–1942) and subsequently Tarawa (1945–1975) with a painfully meager understanding of their sociopolitical circumstances (Brady 1975). Colonial authorities at first insisted on seeing a highly hierarchical structure where it might not have existed, at least as long as it suited their purposes (Macdonald 1982, 69–78), but happily left the task of regulating atoll life to the Samoan pastors. While they issued successive editions of *Native Laws* in the Samoan language from 1894 (Ellice Islands Protectorate 1894), which spelled out rules of daily existence in increasingly minute detail (a fine for breaking prayer-time curfews, imprisonment for drinking coconut-palm toddy), these pamphlets were merely reiterations of policies already put in place by the pastors.[13]

A tantalizing if fleeting text of Nukulaelae Islanders' engagement with missionizing and colonizing modernity can be read in an 1897 photograph, possibly the first ever taken on the atoll (figure 2.3). The photograph appears as one of the plates in Cara David's (1899) "unscientific account" of the Royal Society's six-month scientific expedition to Funafuti to investigate coral-reef evolution, which her geologist husband led and which called at Nukulaelae, sixty-five nautical miles south of Funafuti, for a day on its return trip to Australia.[14] Western shirts, trousers, lavalavas, hats, and even two coats (presumably brought out for the occasion) are in evidence, although just as evidently not affordable to all Islanders, as about half the adults, including the "chief justice," wear pandanus-leaf skirts and no shirt. The European trader, clearly unable to cross his spindly legs tailor fashion, sits on one buttock in the front row, a position he presumably claims as the go-between

Chief Justice of Nukulaelae
in Native Costume

The Trader.   The Jamaica Man.

NUKULAELAE NATIVES.

FIGURE 2.3:   "Nukulaelae Natives," in David (1899)

between Islanders and visitors, but one that also places him at the undignified end of the row of children rather than standing with the rest of the men. Also pushing himself forward and ending up surrounded by kids is "the Jamaica man," another beachcomber probably identifiable as Charles Barnard.[15] The "chief justice" is the native magistrate appointed by the colony, probably Malaki. Conspicuously absent is the Samoan pastor, who may have found the occasion beneath his dignity. The overall picture is one of conflicting definitions of the modern, probable power struggles among agents of modernity and Islanders' cautiousness vis-à-vis them all.

Modernity and the Outside World

When the war in the Pacific broke out, things would never be the same again on Nukulaelae as in the rest of the Pacific. The United States posted substantial contingents of troops on Funafuti, which became an important air base on the edge of the southbound Japanese advance. Military authorities hired Islanders from all parts of the Ellice Islands, including Nukulaelae (McQuarrie 1994). Those momentous times gave Ellice Islanders their first glimpse of working-class male *Ppaalagi* "Westerner" and specifically American culture, categories that became tightly bound to one another. Like inhabitants of other Pacific Islands (White and Lindstrom 1990), Ellice Islanders were impressed by the cargo-cult-generating abundance of resources, potlatch-like wastefulness, apparent easygoing nature, and generosity that they came to associate with Americans. For Nukulaelae Islanders, that Americans were particularly "good" Whites was further reinforced in the 1960s when a contingent of Cold War aviators and servicemen were stationed on the atoll for several weeks or months, leaving once again a long-lasting favorable impression that was still very vivid in the early 1980s.[16] Americans had by then also become a standard against which Ellice Islanders could compare British colonial authorities, which until then Ellice Islanders had thought of as representing Whiteness. The British, and to a certain extent colonialism, emerged from this comparison cast in distinctly unfavorable light.

Nukulaelae Islanders learned early in their history of dealings with the outside world that presenting oneself through an "ethno-orientalist" (Carrier 1992, 198) lens that highlights peacefulness and harmony had serious advantages. Indeed, "harmony ideology can be powerful even when it contradicts the common realities of disputing" (Nader 1990, 2). This was particularly the case during the colonial period; in the triangular relationship among Ellice Islanders, Gilbert Islanders, and the British colonial authorities based in the Gilbert Islands, Ellice Islanders were the most vulnerable numerically, and their home atolls constituted a mere remote outpost of an already distant and insignificant colony. However, Ellice Islanders, including Nukulaelae people, knew how to play their cards, and maneuvered themselves into positions of favoritism vis-à-vis the colonial authorities, benefiting from the colonial regime, of which most were passive supporters. (Chambers and Chambers [1975] provide a brief account of the puzzlement that this attitude generated amongst a team of UN decolonization officers in the mid-1970s.) They presented themselves as having qualities to which the British would respond favorably, including peacefulness, internal cohesion, industriousness, and "civilization." While "civilization" and "enlightenment" would take a few more years to anchor into this complex of symbolic associations, peace and harmony were already strongly associated with the Tuvaluan ethos in the early years of contact and missionization. This portrayal was not free of caveats, but it prevailed in the discourse of the day, as the following illustrates:

> The Gilbert Islander is not a model domestic servant; his talents are adapted to sterner conditions. Though he is faithful and shows much desire to please, his forgetfulness and lack of method seldom prove amenable to teaching. As a policeman, under conditions of strict discipline, he shines: without unremitting "nursing" he is a failure. The Ellice boy, who is much inferior to the Gilbertese in all things that really matter, makes a better house servant. He springs, not, as the Gilbertese, from a warlike stock, but from a peace-loving race. He is quicker to learn than a Gilbert Islander, and also makes an excellent policeman, but his chief talents are domestic. As a personal servant he is ready, hard-working and retentive, but too often dishonest. Cases of dishonesty among Gilbert houseboys are exceedingly rare. (Gilbert and Ellice Islands Protectorate 1916, 15–16)

Despite its mitigated enthusiasm for the "Ellice boy's" character, this passage establishes a clear pecking order between Ellice and Gilbert Islanders, in which the one can be given authority over the other, although it also reflects the ambiguous and shifting nature of the relationship among the colonizing and the two colonized groups.[17] To this day, the colonial era, which ended in 1978, is not remembered as a particularly trying period, although no one misses the toughness, distance, and difficult personality stereotypical of British colonial authorities.

Colonial officials, missionaries, and other Western observers needed little encouragement to buy into the image of Ellice Islanders as more peaceful and "civilized." Rather, they took an active role in constructing it. First, the purported contrast between the lighter-complexioned Polynesian Ellice Islanders and the darker, more "savage" Micronesian Gilbertese fell right into the groove of European racialist expectations that the former would necessarily be further along the path of human evolution than the latter. While these expectations may not have been always explicitly articulated in this particular context, they are strongly rooted in Western constructions of Polynesia since the Enlightenment's initial encounter with the islands at the end of the eighteenth century (as Smith [1985] and Thomas [1989] have discussed, among many others). They also fall right in line with colonialists' predilection for understanding the colonized in terms of overdetermined notions of "peacefulness" versus "violence."

Second, the depiction fits the "facts" of early contact history. While relations between nineteenth-century Euro-American voyagers (e.g., explorers, whalers, traders) were often tense in the Gilbert Islands, interactions with Ellice Islanders, although much less common, were rarely violent. The prominent role that firearms played in early trade with the Gilbert Islands contrasted with the lack of such a trade in the Ellice Islands (Macdonald 1982, 29). So did Ellice Islanders' alleged enthusiasm for Christianity with Gilbert Islanders' lack thereof in the nineteenth century (Goldsmith and Munro 1992; Macdonald 1982, 31–53). Some islands of Kiribati experienced periods of extreme violence in the nineteenth century. A ruthless tyrant who reigned over the island of Abemama in 1878–1891, Tem Binoka, is reputed to have forced his subjects to crow like roosters around his house in the morning and to have used his slaves as targets in rifle practice (Maude 1970). His cruelty and despotism have been folklorized both in Western literature (e.g., Stevenson 1924) and in the oral lore of modern-day Tuvaluans, who relish telling Tem Binoka stories as evidence of the violence and cruelty they see as inherent to the Gilbertese character.[18]

The persistence of these expectations, or more accurately of Tuvaluans' use of them, is particularly evident in the debate over the separation of the Gilbert and Ellice Islands, which occupied the first half of the 1970s. Beginning in the 1960s, Britain busied itself with unloading its colonies, and began talking of independence for the Gilbert and Ellice Islands Colony. Ellice Islanders argued for the separation of their group from the rest of the colony, invoking, among other things, "the Gilbertese predilection for fighting [in contrast to] the low incidence of violence in the Ellice" (Macdonald 1982, 254). Despite the fact that the British authorities who heard these particular arguments were not entirely convinced that they constituted compelling grounds for the establishment of a separate state, Tuvalu did separate from the rest of the colony in 1975, and gained independence on its own three years later.[19]

The discourse of community cohesion, peacefulness, and harmony is not merely a historical phenomenon. Rather, it continues to emerge at strategic moments in interactions between Nukulaelae Islanders or Tuvaluans and the outside world. Nukulaelae Islanders use it in their dealings with the national government of Tuvalu. In turn, the national government invokes it as a useful way of presenting itself in interactions with representatives of Western nations and similar bodies, particularly when foreign aid is at stake. Tuvaluan immigrants in New Zealand, whose numbers are increasing, invoke it in their sometimes strained relations with the New Zealand government (immigration authorities in particular), in order to distance themselves from groups from other Pacific Island groups, particularly Tongans and Samoans, which are substantially more powerful and numerous but are plagued with negative stereotypes of violence. In short, the image of their societies as free of conflict has worked in Nukulaelae and Tuvaluan people's favor and has enabled them to turn to their advantage historical situations in which they could have fared very poorly as marginal and numerically insignificant players in a remote colonial outpost. As it has for Zapotec villagers (Nader 1990), history has proven to Nukulaelae Islanders and to Tuvaluans in general that emphasizing peacefulness, communalism, and concomitant values can be a powerful political tool for their island communities in the face of potential threat from the outside.

A useful comparison can be drawn with the well-documented case of the !Kung-San of the Kalahari Desert in southern Africa. This group has for centuries figured prominently in the exoticizing fantasies of travelers, missionaries, colonial agents, freak-show organizers, and travel writers like Laurens van der Post. From early on, anthropologists were enthusiastic participants in this tradition. Touting the !Kung-San as heir to an ageless continuity of life-ways, anthropologists (e.g., Shostak 1981) have presented them to generations of first-year undergraduate students as the prototype of successful hunter-gatherer adaptation to a hostile ecological environment. According to these accounts, the timeless and harmonious integration of !Kung-San daily lives, egalitarian social structures, and cultural formations with their natural surroundings is only "now" being disrupted by outside forces, which demand that they lead a settled lifestyle, don Mother Hubbards and khaki shorts, and seek jobs in town, like everybody else. However, as Pratt (1986) and others have argued, these representations studiously ignore the centuries of not just "contact," but more or less systematic genocide, marginalization, resettlement, and redefinition that the people now known as "the !Kung-San" have experienced at the hands of Western conquerors of southern Africa and of their own African neighbors, often in collusion with Europeans. Wilmsen's powerful *Land Filled with Flies* (1989) demonstrates that the !Kung's cultural conservatism is the consequence of their integration into capitalist contexts, rather than a reenactment of a timeless past. The admirably successful adaptation to a harsh but ultimately livable ecology is best understood as "a delicate and complex adaptation to three centuries of violence and intimidation" (Pratt 1986, 49; see Barnard [2006] for a summary of the !Kung debate). Clearly, the boundary between representation and represented is a highly porous one, and "life-ways" should be located at the convergence of historical dynamics including colonialism, conflict, displacement, as well as representation by others and by self.

It is not only outside forces coming to Nukulaelae that have represented potential danger and uncertainty, but also what Islanders encounter when they leave the atoll. From early contact days to this day, Nukulaelae men have offered their labor as seamen and traveled the world, sometimes ending their days in other parts of the insular Pacific (e.g., Samoa, Tonga, Rotuma, Kosrae, Marshall Islands). In the late nineteenth century, Tuvaluans worked on sugarcane plantations of Melanesia and Queensland. A few Nukulaelae Islanders worked as missionaries in Melanesia. During my fieldwork, one old lady with Alzheimer's would regularly launch into oratorical performances in Toaripi, a coastal language of southern Papua New Guinea that she had learned as a child on a mission, which everyone found utterly hilarious. The war brought young men's migration to Funafuti. During the colonial period, employees of the colony (policemen, secretaries, laborers) and their dependents lived on Tarawa. Today, a significant number of Nukulaelae Islanders live on Funafuti, Tuvalu's capital, and there is brisk passenger and goods traffic on the monthly ship between the two atolls. Suva, Fiji's capital, the Pacific region's metropolis, the seat of the main campus of the regional University of the South Pacific, and the destination of most flights out of Funafuti, attracts Nukulaelae Islanders both temporarily and permanently.

But what looms large in contemporary memories and imaginations is labor migration to the phosphate mines of Banaba (Ocean Island) and Nauru, fifteen hundred miles to the north. The British Phosphate Company (BPC) and, after the Republic of Nauru's independence from Australia in 1968, the Nauru Phosphate Company (NPC) recruited their labor force almost entirely from overseas, originally mostly from China. After World War II, however, Chinese laborers were gradually replaced with recruits from the Gilbert and Ellice Islands Colony and later Tuvalu and Kiribati, which soon became the mainstay of the phosphate workforce, with some reinforcement from other Pacific Island nations and Pacific Rim countries like the Philippines (Macdonald 1982; Williams and Macdonald 1985). The 1979 census of Tuvalu enumerates thirty-five Nukulaelae Islanders on Nauru, out of a total of four hundred Tuvaluans, twice the ratio of Nukulaelae Islanders to the country's total population. These numbers remained essentially the same throughout the 1980s and the 1990s, and included principally able-bodied young men, but also a number of married couples and their children, since the NPC allowed workers of a certain seniority to bring along their spouses and up to two children. Workers signed up for contracts of two to five years, which they sometimes renewed repeatedly, which meant that some Tuvaluans have spent most of their early years on Nauru. Men were employed as laborers, petty clerks, service-industry workers, and sometimes foremen, and workers of both genders could also find jobs in the service industry for the NPC or the Nauru government. Wages were generally very low, although they seemed luxurious to many Islanders with little experience of labor markets. Rights and benefits were few, and workers could be sent back to Nukulaelae at a moment's notice for disciplinary reasons. They faced the same fate if they were found to be in poor health or if they ran into any difficulty with Nauruan citizens, no matter where the responsibility lay. However, mining exhausted Banaba's phosphate in 1980 and most of Nauru's in the early 2000s, leaving both islands in desperate ecological condition and, in the latter case, stranding hundreds of Gilbertese and Tuvaluan workers for years with no employment or means of repatriation as Nauru's economy faced collapse (Radio New Zealand International 2006).

For Nukulaelae Islanders, modernity saturates all these locales and historical moments, in a variety of forms. They encountered electrical lights, gas stoves, movies, motorbikes, and outboard motors on Ocean Island, Tarawa, and later Funafuti. They brought back from Nauru vivid tales of Nauruans' arrogance and of their deadly infatuation with fast cars, fast food, and strong liquor. They still reminisce about the cantilevers, deep-sea wharves, and expatriate compounds of the Banaba and Nauru mining industries. From the multiethnic intermingling of the mine-islands, they returned with stories, stereotypes, and snippets of Cantonese, Tagalog, and Nauruan, as well as, more concretely, large wooden crates (*kaakoo* "cargo") full of pots and pans, table servings, clothing, textiles, ropes, fishing gear, cooking oil, tools, and outboard motors, some of which they put to use upon return, while the rest stays stored inside crates stacked up in homes. But Nukulaelae Islanders also treasure memories of modernity and development in these distant locales almost as much as their crates of consumer goods.

The younger generations' encounter with far-flung modernity takes the form of employment in the German, Hong Kong, and Taiwanese merchant marine. As independence approached, the Tuvalu government strove to find a substitute for the imminent end of contract labor on Banaba and Nauru, and in 1978 established the Amatuku Tuvalu Maritime Training School on Funafuti, with the intent of training young men for employment as seamen employable by shipping conglomerates. The school's admission criteria were originally high, but its standards relaxed as the demand for seamen increased.

For the shipping corporations, Tuvaluan seamen represent a nonunion and therefore cheap workforce, but also one that, once again, has a reputation for compliance, obedience, and relative peacefulness, echoes of the same stereotypes that have suffused history. For the seamen, seamanship represents not just historically and ideologically sanctioned adventure, but also a unique opportunity to fulfill the duty that Tuvaluans expect of young men, namely to meet their families' and island communities' needs, increasingly counted in dollars. By the 1990s, a significant proportion of able-bodied men from Nukulaelae and other islands of the group was either working overseas on a ship or on leave between assignments, leaves that are generally too short to allow the seamen to make it to their home island. In December 1994, I enumerated fifty-four Nukulaelae young men who were either at sea or on short furlough, which is most of the younger male population. In 2005, seamen's remittances for all of Tuvalu were estimated to be between A$4M and A$7M (cf. Borovnik 2006 on Kiribati).

While here again the image of quietness and obedience serves Tuvaluans well, this particular form of encounter with modernity is considerably more gendered, individualistic, and problematic than past forms. In contrast to phosphate-industry contract laborers, who could move with families and would live in island-based communal compounds, seafarers are lone male workers relatively isolated from one another, a situation that encourages new forms of individualistic and entrepreneurial thinking and, more generally, new views on the relationship between person and society. Their prolonged absence from their home communities also results in significant demographic imbalance, and they bring back to Tuvalu not just money, but also serious binge drinking or alcoholic tendencies and sexually transmitted diseases. Nukulaelae has long suffered from a gender imbalance in its demographic makeup, in that young women are disproportionately numerous, a situation that is now further exacerbated. The recruitment of seamen has given rise to a wave of shotgun marriages between very young adults, who end up spending very little time living together before the young man's departure. The divorce rate has also increased dramatically as a result. Impressionistic observations indicate that fertility is also affected in ways that demand analytic attention, particularly because of the STDs to which seamen are exposed during their long overseas assignments. The threat of AIDS is not an insignificant factor, and Tuvalu and other sources of seaman labor are widely reputed to be sitting on a time bomb.

Seafarers' income, which pales in comparison to the income of their workmates from industrialized nations, nevertheless greatly exceeds the sums that Nukulaelae Islanders were used to earning. At the local level, young seamen have consequently become the key to a type of wealth (e.g., money, imported goods) that is becoming both more important and more conspicuous than "traditional" tokens of wealth (e.g., land, exchange networks). They favor the creation of capitalistic inequality and private enterprise, and are often strongly disaffected with the gerontocratic organization of sociopolitical life, themes that I explore in greater depth in the next chapter.

Global Warming and Clashing Discourses

Perhaps the most dramatic contemporary "encounter" between Tuvalu and the rest of the world is global warming and the predicament it poses for a nation whose topography barely rises above the level of the sea. At the time of my fieldwork, "global warming" had yet to become anchored in the international consciousness. Politicians, better-educated Tuvaluans, and Tuvaluans living overseas are quite cognizant of the potential danger of global warming for the country. Tuvaluans on the outer islands are also conscious of changes in the behavior of the sea, even though they are as unclear about their global causes as are most scientists, although many journalistic reports in the West attribute to Tuvaluans a confident belief that God will come to save them from the Flood as He did with Noah.[20]

The fact that changes in the environment had not gelled into an "it-entity" at the time does not mean that Nukulaelae Islanders, like people on other islands of Tuvalu, had not noticed that something was amiss. It is true that coral atolls are ever-changing environments, with or without rising sea levels. In 1985, for example, a large sandbank appeared in one curve of Nukulaelae's lagoon, and disappeared a couple of years later. But already in the early 1980s, the one form of employment on Nukulaelae that did not involve exile was working on the seawall, something that all young, able-bodied men did for the better part of their waking hours, receiving a daily wage of 25 cents, paid out of the development grant that the central government allotted to the Island Council. Painstakingly built with coral slabs, the seawall was designed to protect areas of the beach on Fagaua Islet, where the village and the largest swamp-taro pit are located. Seawater seemed to be attacking the shore particularly ferociously, causing seepage into the swamp-taro pits and attacking the otherwise highly resilient swamp-taro plants. The seawall figured prominently in everyone's consciousness. Working on it was backbreaking work, and many young men complained of eye and skin irritations brought on by the salinity of the sea. When a journalist from Radio Tuvalu visited Nukulaelae on one trip of the MV *Nivanga* in 1980, she interviewed children for a radio program, asking them what they would like to do when they grew up, to which one five-year-old boy replied in a shy whisper, "seawall." (The whisper was broadcast nationally, to everyone's hilarity.) Older people worried about the crops, since swamp taro on Nukulaelae continued to be the staple of both everyday and feast meals, not yet supplanted by imported food like white rice, as it already was for most people on Funafuti, and they took painstaking care of the plants, sometimes spending hours working in the pits, up to their knees in brackish mud.

The seemingly changing conditions with which Nukulaelae Islanders and other Tuvaluans were attempting to cope in the years following independence only got more worrisome with time, with the noticeable erosion of beaches and soils, the increasingly frequent storms, during which the sea lashes at the shore, and "king tides" that inexplicably flood low-lying areas of the islands. The most dramatic occurred in January and February 2006, when the meteorological office on Funafuti measured high tides 1.5 meters in excess of its average level. The scientific jury is still out on the significance of global warming, its mechanism and rate, and, of course, what or who bears responsibility: the figures and calculations continue to be manipulated, yielding contradictory results, providing conflicting angles on an issue around which the stakes are high. Right-wing proindustry politicians continue to ignore the Kyoto Protocol and to muzzle in their own countries' refractory scientists who sound the alarm too loudly by cutting off their research funding or laying them off for "irresponsibility."

Like all disasters or impending disasters, the effects of ecological changes on Tuvalu are as much a matter of material events as they are a battle of representations, and it is on the latter that cultural anthropology can shed the kind of light that few others can. I will not attempt to do so here, since my own fieldwork preceded the emergence of climate change as a global concern in general and in particular as a concern for Tuvalu. However, I will explore a number of historical and ideological continues that link the dynamics I analyzed earlier in this chapter with some of the representations operative in relation to global warming and Tuvalu.

Since the late 1990s, Tuvalu has emerged as the poster child of global warming. While in fact much larger countries and much more populated areas of the world are as vulnerable as Tuvalu is to rising sea levels (e.g., Bangladesh, the Netherlands, London, Tokyo, and New York), a combination of agents with few connections to science have promoted little Tuvalu to front stage of the global warming scare. Journalists and other producers of representations for popular consumption in industrial societies play a major role in this politics of representation. In a textual analysis of representations of Tuvalu's relationship to climate change in Australia's leading daily newspaper, the *Sydney Morning Herald*, Farbotko (2005) identifies a number of recurrent themes. One is a discourse of vulnerability and tragedy, pitching the continental security of the Australian environment against the fragility of tiny atolls. This discourse of physical fragility easily skids into a discourse of social and cultural fragility, through depictions of timeless atoll cultures in danger of disappearance as Islanders face the future as environmental refugees, themes that are solidly anchored in the popular Western imagination about the Other (cf. Kirsch 2001). These representations are not innocent of politics: not only are they grounded in a formidable genealogy of uncritical and patronizing associations between non-Western societies and timelessness, sedentarism, and lack of agency (Lutz and Collins 1993), but they also rob Tuvaluans of resourcefulness and resilience. The analogy with the flood of the Bible that journalists love to attribute to Tuvaluans' understanding of global warming brings to the fore another underlying message: Islanders are puerile and superstitiously religious. At the same time, journalistic coverage is analytically selective, displaying a conservatism that "limits critique to the realms of government policy without questioning the social practices of mass consumption that also contribute to the climate change problem" (Farbotko 2005, 287).[21]

Nowhere are these themes more transparent than in the veritable industry of documentary film production that Tuvalu has been subjected to in recent years. Bearing predictably dramatic and exoticizing titles like *Before the Flood* (Lindsay 2005), *Tuvalu: That Sinking Feeling* (Pollock 2005), and *Paradise Drowned* (Tourell, O'Connor, and Jones-Middleton 2001; also Bayer and Salzman 2005; Horner and Le Gallic 2004; and numerous others in multiple languages), these documentaries elaborate uncritically familiar themes of victimhood, "paradise lost," and "disappearing cultures," which endure in the Western imagination as they produce an orientalized context for thinking about the dynamics at play (Chambers and Chambers 2007).

A couple of anecdotes of my own (very marginal) involvement with the production and consumption of these images are revealing. In June 2002, filmmakers

Julie Bayer and Josh Salzman (*Time and Tide,* 2005) grilled me on camera for a couple of hours on the UCLA campus, where I was teaching at the time. Despite being trained in anthropology, Julie Bayer was very insistent that I substantiate the "disappearing culture" scenario, and clearly found my noncompliance frustrating. (Not surprisingly, no footage of the interview made it into the final product.) In 2005, another filmmaker, Christopher Horner, came to the same film-happy university for a screening of *The Disappearing of Tuvalu: Trouble in Paradise* (Horner and Le Gallic 2004), along with Nukufetau Islander Enele Sopoaga, a gifted Tuvaluan civil servant who was then ending his term as Tuvalu's ambassador to the United Nations.[22] At "Q&A" time, I got up and asked why the film had focused only on Funafuti, which after all was least immediately at risk from the effects of climate change, since most Funafuti residents had for a long time been getting their food from the cooperative store, not the swamp-taro pit, a situation that results in part from the fact that many residents of the capital-atoll have access to no garden land because they lack local kinship ties. In contrast, residents of the outer islands, smart enough and not wealthy enough to rely on often-interrupted food imports like white rice, do depend on swamp taro, which will be the first victim of rising sea levels. I realized that the filmmakers probably had not been enthusiastic about the long uncomfortable trips to the outer islands on the *Nivaga II* and about being stuck on an outer island without basic comforts for an indeterminate number of weeks. Furthermore, most residents of the outer islands probably would not have made good interviewees, compared to the Funafuti elites who invariably appear in the films: not only would they have not spoken good English, but they also would have been unlikely to talk the talk of global warming. I was not prepared, however, for the fact that the filmmakers had not even thought about the issue. The problem of garden-based food supply simply had not entered the consciousness of these agents of representation (however well-meaning), for whom food can only logically come from the supermarket and for whom global warming engenders problems that have nothing to do with the food supply and everything to do with the Rousseauesque mourning over the impending loss of pristinely primitive atoll cultures.[23]

At the same time, some Tuvaluan politicians have contributed spectacularly to the global image of Tuvalu's vulnerability to global warming. One prominent agent was Nukulaelae Islander Bikenibeu Paeniu, who served as an astute prime minister of Tuvalu for two nonconsecutive terms (1989–1993 and 1997–1999) and as cabinet minister at other times, and was someone whom I saw grow over the years from an insecure young man recently returned from obtaining his undergraduate degree at the University of the South Pacific to an important international politician. Bikeni made memorable speeches at the United Nations Conference on Environment and Development in Rio de Janeiro (the "Earth Summit") in 1992 (Leggett 2001, 97–98) and at the annual meeting of the parties of the United

Nations Framework Convention on Climate Change in Kyoto in 1997. In 2002, he dramatically threatened to enlist Caribbean and Indian Ocean nations to launch joint legal action against the United States for not signing the Kyoto Protocol. Both actions received wide coverage in world news, as their "David and Goliath" undertones captured, for better or for worse, the imagination of many in the industrial world, and made for very good journalistic copy.

Clearly, consequential Tuvaluan agents are principally those who benefit from knowledge of the larger perspective on high tides and pounding surf, namely the politicians. These same agents are also able to turn Western romanticizations of timeless cultures in danger to good use. In the same way that Kayapó activists in Brazil find in their carefully selected body adornments important ways of combating state-sponsored encroachments by loggers into their forest habitats that resonate with Western romantic understandings of primitive innocence (Conklin 1997), Tuvaluan politicians build a sense of presence and urgency through the interest of Western journalists and filmmakers, which is continuous with responses and representations of past ills like slaving raids, plantations that won't go away, and debts to traders: discourses of communalism but victimhood, encapsulated in the notion of *fakaalofa* "pitiable, arousing empathy," a characterization that Nukulaelae Islanders commonly apply to their ancestors fighting formidable forces coming from the outside. However, it is not clear that an alliance with Western journalists and filmmakers is a dependable strategy, as journalistic interests can be terribly fickle, even when they are grounded in resilient Western romanticism about disappearing cultures or ecological natives (cf. Conklin and Graham 1995; Doane 2007). Furthermore, not all Tuvaluan politicians are united in this discourse, as some argue that Tuvalu has more pressing concerns, including sanitation, nutrition, and access to labor markets in the industrial world. It is in these historical and discursive contexts that we need to embed further work on climatic and cultural change in Tuvalu.

The very nature of climate change, rising sea levels, and holes in the ozone layer, the threat that they represent to Tuvalu's existence, and the local grounding of peoples and cultures are all "situated knowledges" (Haraway 1988), tied to particular positions and embedded in particular politics of representation. What is revealing and inaccessible to most outside observers is the extent to which the Tuvaluan response, or at least one of the responses, is colored by the same ideological stance that has colored Nukulaelae's engagement with the outside world in the course of its history.

3 Hierarchy and Egalitarianism

IN LIGHT OF THE TURMOIL of the last century and a half of Nukulaelae's history, it should come as no surprise that political life on the atoll is rife with tensions. Beneath the overelaborated veneer of harmony and peace that people try so hard to maintain are long-standing conflicts, contradictions, and complexities about how the island should be organized. In this chapter I turn to a basic ideological tension between what I call a "discourse of nostalgia" and a "discourse of egalitarianism." Both are part and parcel of what Nukulaelae people articulate quite readily to one another and to the prying anthropologist, although the discourse of nostalgia is more closely associated, in the local logic, with the image of the atoll community as harmonious and peaceful than the discourse of egalitarianism is. In turn, the discourse of egalitarianism is invoked to undermine the hierarchical order put forth in the discourse of nostalgia, and this undermining frequently takes place in gossip. I am not, however, seeking to locate Nukulaelae's "genuine culture" in either a harmonious order or a conflictual disorder, or in either hierarchy or egalitarianism. Rather, the atoll's culture and politics are located in the tensions between these different qualities, at the convergence of these various seemingly incommensurable discourses.

Reinventing Chieftainship and Controlling Resources

Just as the nineteenth century was for Nukulaelae Islanders a time of probably unprecedented upheaval, the seven decades of colonial rule were characterized by far-ranging change. The colonial administration first decreed that each island of Tuvalu be headed by an *aliisili* "paramount chief" (rough translation of the Samoan term used in those documents), who in the first *Laws of the Ellice Islands* (Ellice Islands Protectorate 1894) is seconded by a magistrate *(faamasino)*, secretary *(failautusi)*, and police officer *(leoleo)*, a structure that reflects colonial endeavors to implement both indirect rule and a check on it (figure 3.1). In later versions of these laws, the chiefly structure gets replaced by a six-person body called the *kau pule*, literally "group of rulers," a phrase that in colonial papers appears as *kaubure* or *kaupuli*—the former being the Gilbertese borrowing of the word, the latter a misspelling by administrators unfamiliar with (and uninterested in) the Tuvaluan language. This body consisted of four appointed elders *(toeaina)* and the colony-appointed magistrate, and was headed by the elected "chief." That the names of these various roles are all borrowings from Samoan is indicative of the influence that the Samoan pastors exerted by the turn of the century. Later, wavering between "traditional" and "progressive" colonially inspired systems of leadership and political organization, the atoll reinstituted and did away with chieftainship on several occasions, alternating it with an acephalous organization, although the extent to which the colony controlled these changes is unclear. Following is a description of these alternations by one of my more cynical Nukulaelae interviewees:

> *Koo fanaka fua peelaa, olo aka, "Ulu aliki!" Fano, fano, toe masolo foki, seeai foki ne ulu aliki. Faatoaa fakatuu atu fua fakamuli fua nei, [. . .] toe fakattuu aka mea konei, te ulu fenua mo ttaupulega, [. . .] a koo leva tausaga ne ssolo peelaa, seeai, koo nnofo loo ko toeaina o te fenua. [. . .] Peelaa foki loa mo te vaa mai mua atu foki loo i seeaiiga o se aliki taumua atu foki loo, i te vaa teelaa, nnofo loo ko toeaina. Kee oko mai ki ttaimi teenei i ttaua lasi eeloo. Mai tua o ttaua lasi foki eeloo, vau eiloo i ttaimi teenaa, ne toeaina eiloo. Naa fua kaati ko ttausaga teenaa, faa iva ki te lima sefulu, teenaa ne toe fai i ei te ulu aliki. Toe masolo atu i ei, e fia tausaga ne olo aka i ei, e fia a- a pule fenua ne olo, aku muna me toko- e- e lua taimi, toe masolo atu i ei, nofo mai loa i ei, teenei fua [. . .] toe f- fakatuu aka. Teenei loa koo nnofo nei, see iloa foki laa me ssolo maafea! [V 1991:1:B:285–309]*

[It then] came up again, [they] announced, "A chief!" Time went on, and it was abolished again, again there were no more chiefs. It just got reinstituted recently, [. . .] these things were reinstituted, the chief and the Council of Elders, [. . .] but there were many years during which they were abolished, they did not exist, there were just the atoll community's elders. [. . .] Just like the previous period when there were no more traditional chiefs either. Until World War II. After the war, for a time, there were just elders. Then perhaps around the year forty-nine or fifty, the chief was reinstituted. It was then abolished again after a few years, after a few chiefs' tenures. I believe it was abolished again twice later on, till now [. . .] when it is reinstituted. And here it is, we don't know when it's going to be abolished again!

The rapidity and ease with which these seemingly fundamental changes took place pose particularly thorny questions, which the dearth of data on the socioeconomic background of these changes makes it impossible to answer. How did they take place? What triggered them and who enacted them?

MATAUPU I.

Alii Sili.

I nuu taitasi o le Alii sili e pule i le faáleleiga o nuú.

MATAUPU II.

Le alii nofonuu Peretania.

O le Alii sili, poo le Faipule, o soó se nuu faitalia ia se itula e fia fesili ai, i se tonu, poo le fesoasoani o le Alii nofonuu Peretania.

MATAUPU III.

O Faamasino.

1. Ia iai i nuu sili taitasí, se toatasi poo se toalua o Faamasino, o lolatou tofiga ona faáiú i le faigá o le Tulafono o mataupu uma e aumai i olatou luma.

2. A tatau i le Faamasino, nate valaauina Faipule e le sili le toaono, e fesoasoani ia te ia i le suesueina o lea mataupu.

3. I le faamasinoga o le fasioti tagata ua faáleiloa lelei e fesoasoani le sefulu ma le lua o Faipule, e faalogologo.

4. O faamasinoga uma, e faaoó sala le Faamasino auá o ia e pule.

MATAUPU IV.

O Failautusi.

1. Ia iai i Nuu sili taitasi, se Failautusi nate tusia uma faamasinoga sa fai e le Faamasino, i le Tusi Tulafono, ma o ia e súe atu iai uma tupé, o sala ua aó.

2. O le failautusi na te tusia uma tusi a le Alii siḷi, poo Faipule.

3. O le failautusi na te faamauina uma tupe o Lafogá mai le Alii sili.

FIGURE 3.1: *Tulafono o le Atu Elisa* [Laws of the Ellice Islands] (Ellice Islands Protectorate 1894:1)

Translation from the Samoan:

"ARTICLE I, *the Paramount Chief:* On each island it is the Paramount Chief who overseas the welfare of the community.

ARTICLE II, *the British Resident:* The Paramount Chief, or the Council of Elders, shall decide all matters brought before him, or else seek help from the British Resident Governor.

ARTICLE III, *Magistrates:* 1. On each island are one or two Magistrates, whose duty is the administration of the Laws in all matters brought before them. 2. In the case of supposed murder the Magistrate shall be assisted in the hearing by twelve elders. . . .

ARTICLE IV, *Scribes:* 1. On each island a Scribe shall write down all judgments rendered by the Magistrate in the Book of Laws, and he will keep records of all money, and be responsible for it. . . .

In 1965, the colony established a new body, the Island Council (Fono Pule), on every island of the Ellice group. This Island Council was headed by an elected island president *(pelesitene)* assisted by an island executive officer *(aaioo)*, a civil servant who after independence was appointed by the Ministry of Local Governments. The principal responsibility of the council was to mediate between the island community and the central government, but at the time of my initial fieldwork in 1980–1982, it was the most visible decision-making body on the atoll, with control over the budget for "development," including water catchment, path maintenance, government buildings, the telegraph, the school, and health programs. A Council of Elders was in existence, but its jurisdiction at the time was confined to such ceremonial tasks as organizing feasts for important occasions. Initially, I did not even realize that the Council of Elders existed, while I became immediately aware of the Island Council. But in 1983, the pendulum swung again, with important implications for the present-day political life. A "traditional" chiefly system was reinstituted, and power shifted from the *Fakkai o te Maaloo*, literally, "Government Settlement," at one end of the village, where the Island Council holds its meetings, to the *maneapa* in the center of the village, where the Council of Elders meets once a month, presided by an *ulu fenua*, literally, "head of the community." Because the boundary between "development" and "ceremonialism" is porous, it was not difficult for the Council of Elders to claim control over a large portion of the budget previously assigned to the Island Council. The investiture of Faiva Tafia as the first *ulu fenua* of that epoch was by many accounts a major catalyst for the change: a charismatic person of superb gravitas, with worldly experience working as the driver of the governor of the Gilbert and Ellice Islands Colony (until he crashed the car) and later as foreman on Nauru, a biography punctuated by youthful drink-inspired and fist-wielding bravado that gave him both the required warrior background and fuel for impassionate exhortations to today's youth to quit drinking and fighting and follow the Christian path, Faiva had all the personal attributes traditionally associated with the position (figure 3.2).[1]

The relationship between the chieftainship and the authority structure of former days is difficult to assess. Tellingly, the Tuvaluan terms used to refer to the various relevant entities are either borrowed from another language or a bit unstable. The term *maneapa* is of Gilbertese origin, as is the institution to which it refers even though it has come to represent "tradition" locally (Goldsmith 1985), while *taupulega* "Council of Elders" is borrowed from Samoan. What I translate here as "chief" is in fact any of several terms, some of which are used as synonyms while others characterize particular historical periods. The term *aliki*, cognate of terms usually translated as "chief" in other Polynesian languages, appears to have been the original designator for the chiefly role; but a borrowing from Samoan, *tupu*, commonly rendered in English as "king," is also used retroactively to refer to the chief of pre-Christian days. Nineteenth-century Western visitors commonly used the term "king" in their accounts of Nukulaelae social structure, which allowed

FIGURE 3.2: Faiva Tafia (1932–1986), *ulu fenua* at the reestablishment of the chiefly system, photographed at a relaxed moment by the cooking hut

them to deride the incongruity of a "king" ruling over a few dozen subjects (e.g., David 1899, 280–291). Today, the terms *ulu fenua* and, less frequently, *ulu aliki* "head chief" are in common usage. But the important point is that Nukulaelae Islanders consciously historicize today's roles and structures in a distant past that may be beyond the reach of memories but not beyond the reach of imaginations and desires. Their syncretic quality, merging Tuvaluan, Samoan, Gilbertese, and probably colonial images, is precisely what gives them their contemporary vitality and authority.

For Nukulaelae Islanders, the chieftainship derives legitimacy from the continuity with the former times that it allegedly represents. It is in this vein that Bikenibeu Paeniu, a Nukulaelae Islander who served two terms as Tuvalu's prime minister, writes, "[T]raditional governing systems of the island or village communities, whether changed or not, are still existing and will never disappear" (1995,

7). Today, Nukulaelae political discourse is suffused with talk about the Council of Elders, the *maneapa* (a metonym for chiefly authority), and *tuu mo aganuu* "customs and traditions." The latter are invoked today in ways that are familiar from other contexts in the Pacific (e.g., *fa'a-Sāmoa* "the Samoan way," *i-tovo vaka-Viti* "Fijian customs," and *kastom* throughout Melanesia).[2] Although before 1983 they were either absent from or incidental to comparable discourse, they now have important implications. For example, after several years of the universal suffrage system invariably producing major factional conflicts, elections of the Nukulaelae representative to the Tuvalu national parliament have in recent years been elected *faka-maneapa* "in the way of the *maneapa*," that is, by the Council of Elders. The Island Council was further subordinated to the Council of Elders in 1986 when the *maneapa* began choosing the Island Council president, who was formerly elected by universal suffrage. The authority vested in the newly reconstituted tradition is far-reaching, and receives some legitimacy from Tuvalu's central government, whose policy since independence has tended to increase decentralization, localize decision making, and uphold *tuu mo aganuu* (Paeniu 1995).

At first glance, the political oscillations that Nukulaelae continues to experience appear to be both internally motivated and purely political in nature, and indeed they are talked about as such on the atoll. However, they cannot be understood without reference to the broader context of Nukulaelae's changing economic dependence on the external world, the position of the atoll in the nation-state, and the economic and political relationship between the state and agents of the West that provide the aid necessary to its survival. A separate monograph would be necessary to do justice to each of these topics, and an understanding of these areas would have required field research of a different sort (and in different sites) from the fieldwork that I have conducted on Nukulaelae. However, a few words about these issues are necessary as background to the analysis of local politics with which I am preoccupied here.

Nukulaelae and Tuvalu in general have virtually no commercially exploitable resources. The production of copra (dried and treated coconut meat), the great Pacific Island industry since the earliest days of contact, was virtually eliminated in the 1970s because of decreasing world demand and competition from much larger centers of production like the Philippines. Attempts over the years to introduce such cash-generating industries as mother-of-pearl cultivation, bêche-de-mer processing, and fish drying have consistently failed. To be exploitable, the country's only substantial wealth, marine resources, would require an infrastructure on an unaffordable scale (e.g., for harvesting, transportation, processing, and distribution). While many local needs continue to be met through reef and deep-sea fishing and subsistence agriculture, principally of swamp taro, the atoll has depended on imports for many decades, and money has a well-established history in this society. Items like soap, cloth, nylon fishing line, metal fishhooks, pots and pans, knives, tobacco, matches, cloth, and writing implements have long figured on the list of items sold at the trade store and later the cooperative store, and most of these items are now considered necessities, along with more modern items like fuel, batteries, and junk food. Islanders can easily live without store-bought food, but many find it difficult to weather periods when tea, sugar, and rice run out between ship visits, and they would now find it impossible to fish and garden without manufactured tools. Regular customary gifts to the pastor have long included cash, and the sums involved in fund-raising competitions and other forms of gift giving have increased dramatically in recent years, as I will document in a later chapter. The rebuilding of houses in the early 1980s with imported material, which I described in chapter 2, created an unprecedented demand for money, aggravated by the simultaneous appearance of fuel-guzzling outboard motors.

At the national level, Tuvalu's economy has emerged in the course of its nearly three decades of existence as one of the most postmodern economies on the planet (Finin 2002), a point that has often provided fodder to the Western journalistic hunger for quirky exoticism. In the rocky postindependence years, when national reserves amounted to less than US$1M, the state became embroiled in several ventures that turned disastrous, including the purchase of useless Texas desert under the advice of an American adventurer named Sidney Gross. (Other Pacific Island states, including Tonga and Vanuatu, have also periodically lost precious funds in similar schemes and to similar con artists.) Then Tuvalu turned to "resources of jurisdiction," that is, resources that only exist because of its status as a state. It began with the issuing of increasing quantities of postage stamps, which depicted images of locomotives, pure-bred dogs, and, of course, Princess Di and Elvis Presley. When that market became flooded and the British company contracted to produce the stamps was found to be defrauding the government, the second minister of finance, Nukulaelae Islander Henry Faati Naisali (1930–2004), persuaded Western donor nations to contribute to a trust fund instead of providing direct economic aid. From the mid-1980s, the state was kept afloat thanks to interest earned. Besides collecting license fees from foreign ships fishing within its 200-mile exclusive economic zone (totaling 600,000 square miles), the country also leased out its telephone country code (688) to international corporate interests, although the Church of Tuvalu pressured the government to end the lease when it found out that the code was used mainly for phone-sex services. Most spectacular is the lease to a Canadian dot-com corporation of the Internet suffix, which fortuitously happens to be ".tv" (thus homophonous with "television") and is now ubiquitous on the Internet. However, the extent to which these state-level dynamics have a significant impact, materially or ideationally, on the life of the average Tuvaluan citizen, particularly on the outer islands, remains unclear.

In the mid-1980s, geographers and development-studies scholars focusing on the Pacific Islands began referring to the national economies of microstates like

Tuvalu with an acronym, MIRAB, which seeks to capture their four cornerstones: migrations, remittances, (foreign) aid, and bureaucracy (Bertram and Watters 1985; Bertram 2006; Poirine 1998). MIRAB economies are said to be characteristic of Pacific microstates with little exploitable potential and to be remarkable for their resilience and stability despite the appearance to the contrary. Of the various defining characteristics of MIRAB economies, foreign aid and bureaucracy are relevant to Funafuti in particular, although they indirectly affect Nukulaelae and Tuvalu's other outer islands: foreign aid trickles down in small doses to the local level, and many Nukulaelae Islanders migrate to the capital, whether temporarily or permanently, because of employment opportunities in the government bureaucracy. These migrations in fact concern many more people than the employable sector, as illustrated for example by older mothers spending extended periods of time on Funafuti on the occasion of their employed daughters or daughters-in-law giving birth. The most relevant economic factor to Nukulaelae are remittances from migrant workers.[3]

Since the 1990s, the young men employed on ships around the world have become the major source of remittances, as I discussed in the previous chapter. In addition, Tuvaluans have been migrating to New Zealand in recent years, doubling their number with every five-year census in New Zealand between 1991 and 2006. While the New Zealand government is unenthusiastic about the idea of relocating Tuvalu's population should rising sea levels threaten the atolls' existence (and Australia has been categorically opposed to it), it established in 1999 a work scheme bringing in up to eighty Tuvaluans (and citizens of a few other Pacific Island countries) at a time for a maximum of three years to work as farmhands and factory workers. During my fieldwork, however, the second most important destination of migratory movements from Nukulaelae after Funafuti was the phosphate-rich Nauru, as spelled out in chapter 2. (The last workers from Ocean Island returned to Nukulaelae during my first stay there.) There, workers from each island of Tuvalu including Nukulaelae formed a miniature community, housed in the workers' compound, structured as a replica of the *fenua* "atoll community" back home: its members held frequent feasts and dance performances, sponsored a soccer team, and formed a natural unit for socializing activities (this structure is also found among outer islanders living on Funafuti). At the head of the Nukulaelae community on Nauru was a *toeaina* "elder," whom the Nukulaelae Council of Elders chose from among the workers employed by the Nauru Phosphate Company (NPC). The *toeaina*'s responsibilities included overseeing fund-raising, controlling law and order among Nukulaelae people on Nauru, and liaising between this community, other Tuvaluan communities in Nauru, the government of Nauru, and the NPC. The position was an enviable one, since it required no physical labor, while being considerably more remunerative than other forms of employment on Nauru. When they returned to Nukulaelae at the end of their contract, former *toeaina* could commonly claim a loud voice in the political life of the atoll because of their comparatively substantial financial wealth. In short, the Nukulaelae community on Nauru served as a training ground for Nukulaelae leadership.

Most importantly, the Nukulaelae community on Nauru staged fund drives, during which they gathered significant sums of money to fund development endeavors and other communal activities on Nukulaelae. Indeed, the very reason for Nukulaelae people to be on Nauru was to procure cash for the *fenua,* for their kin groups, and for themselves. Nukulaelae people on Nauru were crucially important to the economic viability of the atoll, and they faced enormous pressure to hand over the fruit of their labor to relatives and to the atoll community. The financing of community projects, such as the construction of a new meetinghouse and of seawalls to fight what would become known later as the effects of global warming, was carried almost entirely by Nukulaelae workers on Nauru, who were talked about as the "hope" *(fakamoemoega)* of the atoll community:

> . . . *tamaliki Nukulaelae i Naaluu, e* fakamoemoegina *kkii nee te fenua mo ttau-pulega i mea fai a te fenua i feituu tau sene, e* fakamoemoegia *kkii a tamaliki i Naaluu e lasi telotou fesoasoani ki te fenua ki mea tau sene.* [F 1991:1:A:178–182]

> . . . Nukulaelae's sons on Nauru are the atoll community's and the Council of Elders' very *hopes* for the community's plans that involve money, the sons on Nauru are the very *hopes* because of their important assistance to the community with respect to money.

In turn, members of the Nukulaelae contingent on Nauru often expressed their discontent about the demands that they were placed under and the dearth of gratitude they received in return. This is evident in the often pleading and sometimes bitter tone of letters home: [4]

> My contribution to the atoll community is done, [and] now what's left is the gift [to the pastor], and I have not made my contribution to the church yet. I'll do that at the end of May. . . . I can't even keep up with money matters any more. My mind is hurting just to think about it all. The contribution we [each] have to make is greater than my own salary. So I wish I could just run away from here and return home. But despite that, here I am, applying myself to my work. If I don't send you soon the dinghy propeller and the fishing lures [that you've requested], it's probably because I don't have enough money in my hands to buy them. [Letters 1985:558]

> So some members of our atoll community go on living in peace, while here is the rest of us [on Nauru] killing ourselves providing for the atoll community's

projects. We should not be called [Nukulaelae's] sons on Nauru. . . . And then when we reach land on our atoll for holidays, no one wants to pay any attention to us. They pay attention only to their own children. [Letters 1985:537]

People from Nukulaelae and the rest of Tuvalu would make periodic communal trips to Nauru on the MV *Nivanga* (see figure 2.1), following a tradition, borrowed from Samoa, of group visits from one community to the other called *malaga*, the occasion for the renewal of kinship ties, the exchange of gifts, the sealing of new marriage alliances, and the conception of many an out-of-wedlock offspring. Among Nauru-based Tuvaluans, the *Nivanga* was nicknamed *te vaka aakai* "the begging ship."

The discontent worsened with the gradual shift in employment from phosphate labor to seafaring, as seafarers' income is higher than contract laborers' and their work is now individualized. Upon their return to the atoll, seamen are increasingly reluctant to participate in a political structure that has traditionally placed them at the bottom of the hierarchy, under older people's authority. They raise far-reaching questions about the status quo, demanding a political voice that they have not had, thereby creating much tension in meetings of the Council of Elders. Holders of positions of power and authority view these young men as potentially disruptive of the social order, and have plenty of reasons to hold this view, as I will illustrate presently. And indeed, the reestablishment of a more blatantly hierarchical political system has close links to the emergent possibility of a power struggle associated with changing economic conditions. What better way to detract attention from threatening socioeconomic change than to reinvent tradition? But these changes are also steeped in long-standing discursive tensions.

The Discourse of Nostalgia

Nukulaelae people of all ages and both genders frequently voice the belief that their community prospered when it was ruled with an iron fist. (I will justify presently my use of the past tense in this characterization.) The term "prosper" captures the essence of several notions that go hand in hand in Nukulaelae discourse: the community prospers when food and labor are plentiful, when the sea is fecund, and when *fiileemuu* "peace" and *feaalofani* "mutual empathy, harmony" reign, which is *ttonu* "right, straight" and generally *gali* "beautiful." These vignettes, which are familiar from other societies in the Pacific Islands and beyond, such as in Ancient Greece, where "beauty" and democratic order went hand in hand (W. Murphy 1998, 566), compose an idealized picture of life in the best of times. In the past, prosperity legitimized authority, while legitimate authority engendered prosperity.

The constitutive link between authority and fecundity is evident in discourse about the past. With surprising unanimity, Nukulaelae people reminisce longingly about the days when everyone would cheerfully comply with any command that the chief or council would issue. In those days, they maintain, the grumbling and negotiations one hears today would never have arisen. The following, extracted from an interview with an elderly man, is a typical example of this discourse:

> *Aso mua i loto i te maneapa, kaafai ko koe te pule o- o faiva o te fenua, seeai se muna peelaa, peenei mo aso nei e fai peelaa, kee lluki aka tamataene kee faippati taatou ki te faiva. Seeai! Kaafai e- e onoono au ko- ko au ttagata teelaa e pule i faiva, "Aa! koo llei te koga teelaa maa fai te faiva o te-," e tasi fua, vvalo i loto i te fenua, "Te faiva kaa fano!" te fenua, seeai ne tino e mmai o tau pule mai ki-. I aso mua, nee?* [K 1990:1:A:550–556]

In the olden days, in the *maneapa*, if you were in charge of communal fishing for the atoll community, [you] didn't say things like, like what one hears today, the young men should gather so that we can all talk about going on a fishing expedition. None of that! If I, the man in charge of communal fishing, see, "Oh! there is a good spot for a fish drive-," I would proclaim in the middle of the village, "There's going to be a fish drive!" [and from] the community, no one else comes to try to contradict me-. Those were the olden days, you see?

The same metaphors and rhetorical structures emerge over and over again in discourse about the authoritarian past. The rhetorical parallelism of the last three words in the following excerpt (*"Fai!" fai eiloo!* "'Do [this]!' and [it] was done!"), in which a command is reported in direct speech and echoed by a description of the action that followed from the command, is particularly conspicuous in such discourse (it is also frequent in certain other contexts, as when adults *polopolooki* "admonish" younger people):

> *Peelaa foki laa i aso kolaa, peelaa me e muna tasi fua, nee? Kaafai e muna pee- laa, "Taatou koo- koo ssai te koga teelaa, see- see faaika ki ei," peelaa me seeai ne manatu foki e fai ki ei, nee? "Fai!" fai eiloo!* [T 1991:1:B:214–217]

Like, in those days, only one command, you see? If it was said, "We will reserve that area [of the lagoon], no fishing is to be done there," no one ever voiced an opinion about it, see? *Do [this]!* [and it] was done!

In the past, legitimate authority brought *manuia* "prosperity, fortune" to the atoll. Under the authority of the right individual, the sea yielded its bounties, so that dolphins and whales, neither of which is consumed as food, were the only things that stayed at the bottom of the sea:

A te salala koo asu fua ki pakau. Au see loi! A maatou nei tamaliki koo ttele mo pakau, kaallaga mai, "Ee, mmai mo pakau!" A salala e asu aka eeloo paa ki pakau, lligi ki uta, oko eeloo ki tua i koga kolaa i te faifeau, a te ika mo te mea ki te ika sake! [. . .] Kae nei, se aa laa i te salala koo fakapugapuga mai loo i koga ppoko. Aunoa loo ne ika sake nei e ssake aka ki uta i te fenua, io me ne fonu e ssolo. Ko aso mua, ttaapaa!, a te akau e ssoko eeloo te sisi, olo atu, katoa, katoa. [. . .] Aso kolaa, e tufa eeloo, ttamaliki nei, tena atu, ttamaliki nei, tufa eeloo. Kaafai e toko uke te kaaiga, e fia te atu. A te akau e ssoko eeloo te sisi. Avaka ki uta, ave aka ki uta, katoa fakafia vaka. Kae nei, se tasi, se lua, fanaka te pooti, fia te kaalone penitiini ne ave ki ttai, aunoa eeloo se manuia o te fenua. [L&S 1991:1:A:560–597]

[In those days, we] would gather mullets by the basketful. I am not exaggerating! We children would run with coconut-frond baskets, [they]'d call out, "Hey! Bring [your] rough mats!" [We] would gather mullets, like, by the mat-ful, empty them on the beach, all the way down to where the pastor lives, there was so much fish, it would beach itself! [. . .] While today, mullets just sound down into the deep sea. No school of fish ever beaches itself onto the land, no turtle crawls on shore. In the olden days, heavens!, schools of bonitos were harvested by fly-fishing, [canoes] went out, a catch of one hundred, a catch of one hundred. [. . .] In those days, [bonitos] were just distributed; there was a bonito for each child, just distributed. Kin groups with many members got heaven knows how many bonitos. Schools of bonitos were constantly harvested by fly-fishing. [Canoes] brought [their catches] back to land, many hundreds. But today, one [bonito], two [bonitos], a dinghy comes back to land [having used up] heaven knows how many gallons of fuel, the atoll community has no prosperity.

The land was equally bountiful, coconuts fell like rain, and rats did not reproduce:

A te fuaa niu nei, peenei, manafa peenei e nnofo ei taatou, te fuaa niu koo ttoo eeloo me se vaiua ki lalo. Kae nei laa, kilo mai ki te oge! Laavaki te fenua. Ausage ne fuaa niu. E peelaa foki mo taagata i luga i te laukele, koo lausevasseva faaka. [L&S 1991:1:A:600–603]

And coconuts, like, [on] the land that we own [as a family], coconuts fall to the ground like rain. But today, just look at the dearth of coconuts! The land is barren. Not a single coconut. It's just like men on land, they are incapable of producing anything.

These depictions represent the atoll's *discourse of nostalgia*. Whether the time that the discourse of nostalgia depicts ever existed is of little relevance. The important point is that Nukulaelae people engage in these reminiscences and attribute positive value to them. The discourse of nostalgia contrasts with characterizations of the present time. Today, men in position of authority "allow" younger men to voice dissenting opinions, to challenge their authority, and to negotiate orders. The elders' words are no longer deeds.

The discourse of nostalgia is characteristic of opinions articulated by the least powerful as well as by those with the most secure claims to power, in both public and private contexts. Everyone upholds the discourse of nostalgia on the atoll, including those who are most likely to be barred from political power in a geronto-cratic and gendered authoritarian system, namely women and younger men. Wit-ness how a twenty-five-year-old interviewee, with a solidly established reputation as a troublemaker, narrates some of his recent counterhegemonic exploits, ending with the familiar rhetorical parallelism described earlier:

> *Peelaa kaafai foki e fai peelaa se mea peelaa, "Taatou e taki taattasi kaauli!" peelaa me se tii s-, te mea teenaa- te mataaupu teenaa e faigataa o fai peelaa, "Ikaai, kee fai se manatu ki ei." Kaa fai peelaa, "Taatou e taki taattasi kaauli moo fai te mea teelaa!" "Teenaa!" teenaa eeloo!* [T 1991:1:B:196–200]

> Like, when [someone] says, "We'll [contribute] a swamp-taro corm each!" there isn't any-, this- [in] this type of event, it was impossible to answer, "No, let's discuss it [first]." When [someone] says, "We'll [contribute] a swamp-taro corm each!" *"This is [what's going to happen]!" this is [what happened]!*

Importantly, in the views of the powerless, what the discourse of nostalgia depicts is a desirable state, even though it defines their powerlessness, and not simply the price one has to pay to maintain prosperity and social order.

The positive image of the olden days as a time when authority was strong and life was good is held by every member of the community, including those who would have most to lose in a hypothetical return to authoritarianism. The major difference between invocations of the discourse of nostalgia by the less powerful and by the more powerful is connotational: for the powerless, the deterioration of the authority structure is blamed on the chief and the elders. Thus those in positions of authority do not have much authority nowadays because they are not capable of exerting control. In this discourse, there is little room for attenuating circumstances deriving from changing social and economic conditions. However, this difference is peripheral to the fundamental similarities in the discourse of nostalgia as it is maintained across segments of the society.

The Discourse of Egalitarianism

In the very same breath as they articulate the discourse of nostalgia, Nuku-laelae Islanders are also virulently critical of anyone with pretensions of rising above others. Those whose actions or words suggest even remotely that they see themselves as wealthier, more powerful, better informed, or otherwise superior to others are greeted with scorn, mockery, and suspicion. Such people are considered dangerous, and, in the words of one of my respondents (himself extremely ambitious in the political arena), are *alamati* "watched in ambush" by everyone else on the atoll:

Te fenua teenei ne faaite ki luga i kau papa o mea konei, faaite ki luga i kau papa o mea konaa, paa, e ita ssuaa tino i ssuaa tino maa fano ki luga, e nofo faeloa i te lamatiiga, nee? A ttino teelaa, kaa tasi, sae aka loo se tino, "Aa!, ko- kooi teelaa?." "Ee! Fai (kee) maasei!." Te- te uiga o te fenua teenei, te mea koo iloa nee au. [. . .] Te mea teenaa ne faanau mai loo mo te fenua teenei. Se uiga tuutuumau eeloo o te fenua teenei. See manako se tino Nukulaelae kee maaluga aka ssuaa tino Nukulaelae iaa ia. [N 1991:1:A:591–595, B:001–005]

This atoll is made of coral reefs fashioned out of such material, like, people do not want other people to rise above [others], *they keep watching in ambush,* right? That person, one person, who rises to the top, [everyone says], "Oh!, who's he [to do such a thing]?" "Hey! Try to tarnish [him]!" That's the- the way of this atoll, the way I know it. [. . .] That trait was born with this atoll. It's a trait that's deeply ingrained in this atoll community. Nukulaelae people do not want another person to be higher up than themselves.

These statements are evidence of another set of discursive practices, which I refer to as the *discourse of egalitarianism.*[5]

The discourse of egalitarianism proclaims that everyone is on the same footing and that no one is entitled to have access to more resources than others or exert any type of authority over others, thus leaving little room for hierarchy and leadership. This discourse can take a variety of forms. For instance, people articulate it in statements about the importance of equality between members of the community, as the last quote illustrates. In more recent years, it has manifested itself in arguments that rest on the constitutional protection of human rights. Most saliently, the discourse of egalitarianism surfaces as gossip, grumbling, and ridicule. Whenever the chief attempts to exert control over the atoll community, for example, he is reproached and ridiculed for being too bossy, and the same goes for the Council of Elders. Any public action by the chief that might betray a claim to power and authority is torn to pieces in gossip. In the following example, a woman ridicules the chief's speech-making habits, while imitating his quirk of pulling down on his shirt while speaking in public:

A ko tena pati muamua eeloo e tau ave teelaa eeloo, "Nofoaki te mmalu o Avafoa i ona feituu e faa!." See mafai loo te pati teenaa o sui aka! Faipati katoa loo a Tito, teenaa eeloo tena pati! [L&S 1991:2:B:422–424]

And the very first thing he keeps saying [when making a speech], it's always the same thing, "[I pay] respect to the four sides of Avafoa [name of Nukulaelae's *maneapa*]!" He doesn't seem to be able to change [his routine]! Whenever he speaks up, that's what Tito says!

At times, criticisms of those in positions of authority are clearly motivated by the simple fact that being in that position raises one's station above that of others. Witness the following tirade, in which the speaker rails against the atoll's current authority structure:

> *Nei laa i aso nei, koo tino lima matai o Nukulaelae, kae isi e tino lima matai foolliki, kae toko tasi te matai putaputa, ka ko ia eeloo e lasi kae puta, teelaa e aumai ki te pou i te kogaa loto, fakasagasaga i ei, te mea kee kai saale, kee lasi tena laulau, kee fai ana laauga kee ggali.* [N 1991:1:A:239–245]

These days, there are [about] fifty heads of household on Nukulaelae, there are fifty small heads of household, and one plump one, the latter is big and fat, he's brought to the post in the middle [of the *maneapa*], he's made to sit there, so that he can keep eating, so that he gets a big leaf tray [during feasts], so that he can make nice speeches.

In short, in the discourse of egalitarianism, leaders are reproached for being leaders because leadership gives them a claim to a higher position than the rest of the community.

In contrast to the discourse of nostalgia, the discourse of egalitarianism associates with (although does not equate) morally reprehensible emotions. When people express it, they open themselves to the possibility that others will describe them as *kaimanako* "envious, covetous" or *kaisano* "jealous, resentful" (the term usually occurs in its reduplicate form *kaisanosano*), two emotions that go hand in hand in terms of their occurrence and their moral weight. Witness how one elder, who for years was the person appointed by the Council of Elders to redistribute food at communal feasts (events that can occur on Christmas Day, on the occasion of a family's important occasion, or the occasion of a particularly abundant fish catch), describes people's reactions in a spontaneous conversation with his cousin:

> *A te vaegaa faiga teelaa,* ai! *au e iloa tii maasani. (0.2) Tufa mua te pou loto. (0.2) Te faifeau, (.) Pou loto. Tufa aka, kaa muuttana ika, onoono aka ki tino matuattua kolaa e nnofo ki tua. A kolaa laa mata o ttokoukega! (.) Ppula katoa eiloo. Kaa tai uke aka muu mea a ssuaa tino- ((very fast)) "Aa- aa- ss- ss-! Kiloko laa ki te faapito, koo asu aka kee uke aka mea a ttinoohh!"* hhhh hhhh! H::eeeehehehe! (1.0) .hhhee. [V 1985:4:A, 38:43–39:12, CONV 113:13]

That kind of thing, oh! I know it well. I distribute first to the inside part of the *maneapa*. The pastor, the inside part. I distribute, and when the fish is not plentiful, I look around to the older people sitting in the outside part. And then you've got the majority's eyes [on you]! All looking. When someone's share is a bit bigger- "Ah- ah- sh- sh-! Look at the way he favors, he is scooping a lot for so-and-so!" ((laughter))

Envy, jealousy, resentment. Murmurs, gossip, grumblings. Antihierarchy, counterhegemonic, and cohesion-disruptive emotions. These are just as real as the mutual empathy, peacefulness, and communalism that the discourse of nostalgia promotes.

Two seemingly incommensurate discourses thus coexist on the atoll, but the characterization of Nukulaelae's discourses of authority and egalitarianism as "incommensurable" needs some qualification. Throughout this chapter, I hedge this qualifier with modifiers like "seemingly" and "apparently" because it raises an important problem of representation: to what extent are these discourses incommensurable for Nukulaelae Islanders themselves? There is strong evidence that the coexistence of these discourses is as problematic from a local perspective as it seems from the outside. Indeed, Nukulaelae Islanders themselves talk about this coexistence as a *fakalavelave* "problem, cause for preoccupation." Furthermore, the coexistence of two discourses presents serious problems for the practice of leadership and authority, as I shall illustrate in the next section. Contradiction, tension, and ambivalence are best viewed as constitutive of Nukulaelae political ideology and practice. Viewing the coexisting discourses as contradictory does not preclude management in praxis, even though the resolution of contradictions might never be achieved.[6]

Understanding incommensurability in terms of tensions between different contexts does not provide an adequate resolution to the problem. First, Nukulaelae Islanders can switch very quickly, in the same interaction, from one discourse to the other, without any observable change in other aspects of context. Indeed, the discourse of egalitarianism and the discourse of nostalgia sometimes reinforce one another, even though the enactment of one makes the enactment of the other impossible. Second, discourse and context are in a constitutive relationship; accounting for tensions between conflicting discourses in terms of tensions between contexts resolves very little, because the coexistence of conflicting contexts still remains to be accounted for. Indeed, context may be defined solely in terms of the discourse that characterizes it. Thus, for both ethnographic and theoretical reasons, the ideological problem presented here remains a problem of discourse.

The coexistence of discourses of nostalgia and egalitarianism is of course not particular to Nukulaelae and Polynesian atoll societies. Even in Samoa, traditionally viewed as one of the most stratified Polynesian societies, tensions exist between dignified and elaborated manifestations of the political process on the one hand and a distinctive taste for offstage satire of the dignity and elaboration of political life on the other. What takes place offstage in Samoa is not just a marginal aspect of political life; it is constitutive of political life, on par with onstage political action (Shore 1996).

What Nukulaelae lacks in comparison to the Samoan village is a built-in system of inequality in the inheritance of chiefly prerogatives and the complex system of entitlement found in Samoa. While kept more or less honest by the offstage presence of potentially subversive satirical discourses, the Samoan political system still guarantees the presence and survival of hierarchy and the ensuing system of inequality. In Nukulaelae's case, the legitimization of power and authority is considerably more problematic. Authoritarian action and the exercise of power lack a solid foundation, which, even if it existed prior to contact, has been thoroughly undermined by a tormented history. As a result, the discourse of egalitarianism has the potential of gnawing at the very base of the authoritarian edifice that the discourse of nostalgia calls for, as I shall show in the rest of this chapter. Conversely, the discourse of nostalgia calls explicitly for the undermining of equality. In no way can we posit either discourse as encompassing, in Dumontian fashion, the other (Robbins 1994).

Managing Incommensurability

The coexistence of two seemingly incommensurable discourses has obvious but complex implications for the practice of power, authority, and leadership on Nukulaelae. How can power be exerted, and what shape does it have against a background of discursive contradictions? One of the most common ways in which Nukulaelae Islanders in positions of leadership negotiate their difficult station is by avoiding at all costs presenting themselves as speaking or acting on their own behalf. Instead, they invariably present themselves as *sui* "representative" of a group. The term *sui,* a borrowing from Samoan, has many referents: it is applied to any element of a set that stands in a metonymic or metaphorical relationship to the set with which it is associated; possible translations are "representative, delegate," "illustration, example," or "replacement." Acting as the *sui* of a group has positive connotations: it implies that one is willing to place the concerns of the polity before one's own selfish priorities or the localized interests of one's kin group. Comparable strategies are found in other communities that emphasize egalitarian ideologies, such as various groups in the Papua New Guinea Highlands (Goldman 1983, 134; Rumsey 1986, 290).

The group that individuals can claim to represent can vary from context to context: a person can claim to represent part of the atoll community (but, interestingly, generally not the entire community), small subdivisions of particular groups, or anything in between. The position of *sui* is stressed whenever a leader uses his or her position to take the floor. For example, the chief during my 1991 fieldwork invariably prefaced his speeches in the *maneapa* with some variation of the following utterance: *e tuu atu moo fai te sui o maaua nei* "I am getting up [to make a speech] as the representative of the two of us here," in which the first-person dual exclusive pronoun *maaua* refers honorifically to the elders seated in his vicinity. This strategy became so much his stock phrase that he was constantly ridiculed about it behind his back. His constant references to the fact that he was speaking as a representative came to be seen as yet another index of the poverty of his speech-making skills and of the inappropriateness of his being in a position of leadership.

Similar patterns are found in expressions referring to *groups* in positions of authority. All members of the community commonly refer to the Council of Elders as *te fenua* "the atoll community."[7] Similarly, the Council of Women is not referred to as a council, but as *faafine o te fenua* "the atoll community's women." Yet the membership of the Council of Elders excludes most adult women, every-one classifiable as a "young man" *(tamataene)* or "young woman" *(tamaafine)*, and all children. In the same vein, the Council of Women comprises mostly the wives of members of the Council of Elders; younger married women do attend meetings of the council, but are under much pressure to be seen and not heard, to acknowl-edge and respect the older women's authority with their silent presence. Referring to these bodies with metonymic labels has a legitimizing function: it provides the illusion of adhering to egalitarian ideals while covertly facilitating the authority of a small subgroup over the rest of the group's membership.

Labeling is a powerful manipulative tool in that, like other features of language, descriptors are in a constitutive relationship to the social categories and institu-tions they refer to: not only do they reflect these categories, but they also create them, reinforce them, and present them in a specific light. But descriptive labels are not enough. To be maximally effective, the institutions thus labeled must be associated with discourses that confirm, reinforce, and reify these labels and their connotations. And indeed, decision making on Nukulaelae is invariably framed to create the illusion that decisions are reached by corporate entities, even when a small group or single individual is ultimately in charge.

The example I use to illustrate this point is extracted from a meeting of the Council of Women, a group that was constituted after the 1983 reestablishment of the "traditional" political structure, in overt emulation of the Council of Elders. Once a month, this council meets and negotiates such issues as how the next round of feasts should be run or the number of mats women will have to weave for an upcoming gift to the pastor. The unifying characteristic of all topics broached dur-ing these meetings is that they concern *mea a faafine* "women's affairs," the exact definition of which is a complex question beyond the scope of this chapter. The extract I present here is of a meeting during which the president of the council announces the "program" *(polokalame)* of the Women's Day celebrations, to be held the following August. Such programs include rigorous dress codes and regulations regarding the type of food that should be brought to and consumed during the feasts:

> *(Ei!), i te taeao, lanu tasi katoa eiloo. [. . .] Ttaeao, (taki ttunu mai eiloa te) vai vvela, (kae aumai kkonei kee palu i ei). [. . .] Ia, gatu lanu tasi! Heei loo he gatu lanu tasi kee- kee matea atu, peelaa, e isi he mea maasei i ei. A-. Mata eeloo! A ttino teelaa e matea atu he tamaa ila me he taelagoa i tena lanu tasi, sala. Tasi ttaalaa. Taatou lanu tasi, ggali katoa katoa katoa eiloo. Lanu tasi konei e pei nei, hee toe matea kee pei mai i te- te Aukuso teelaa, nee?, i te Aukuso. Fai eiloo fakallei ttou gatu kee ggali taatou.* [Fono o Faafine 1991:1:B:588–600]

(Hmm,) in the morning, everyone will wear solid colors. [. . .] In the morning, everyone will boil her own hot water, (and brings it here [to the *maneapa*] for it to be steeped and sweetened). [. . .] So, clothes of solid colors! No clothes should be seen with, like, a spot of dirt on it. Hmm. I'm not kidding! Whoever is seen with a spot of dirt or a stain on her solid color, [she']ll be fined. One dollar. We all wear solid colors, everything everything will be beautiful. These solid-colored clothes, they should be different from the ones that were worn last August, right?, last August. Let's get our clothes ready so we can all be beautiful.

Several characteristic patterns emerge from the above extract. First, as in many other Nukulaelae contexts, authority is presented as having one purpose: that of enforcing conformity, equality, and uniformity, the achievement of which is equated with beauty *(gali)*. Second, authority is frequently agentless: authoritative commands sometimes have the structure of statements (e.g., "clothes of solid colors!") or bear no overt subject (e.g., "[She]'ll be fined"), in which case I have used in the above translation a passive construction, the closest English equivalent to the original construction. So the voice of authority, which is typically impersonal, owes its existence to the furthering of egalitarianism, the very value that disenfranchises authority. What we are witnessing here is an astute management of the potential conflict between egalitarian and authoritarian ideologies, in which the latter neutralizes the former by appropriating it. This discursive practice then becomes a political practice that benefits those who achieve it.

When the voice of authority is named, it is attributed to the group, not to an individual: decisions are not made by any single person, but by the entire group. As is the case of political talk in Western societies (Seidel 1975; Urban 1986; J. Wilson 1990, 45–76), pronoun choice is a particularly rich area in which those in control of the floor can manipulate authority and agency in general because the indexical nature of pronouns makes them potentially less open to accountability and scrutiny than more straightforwardly referential areas of language structure (Besnier 1990b; Silverstein 1981). In the following aside, which the Council of Women's president utters between the two halves of the last quote, the speaker draws an explicit contrast between *taatou* "we [inclusive]" and *maatou* "we [exclusive]," the former being a reference to all women present, the latter to the council's governing committee:

> *I mea oki loo a taatou, heeai ia maatou, e ia taatou fakatasi, kolaa ne iku foki i te fono.* [Fono o Faafine 1991:1:B:595–597]

> These are things we [inclusive] all decided, it wasn't us [exclusive], but all of us [inclusive] together, what was decided in the [previous] meeting.

Further on, as she "displays" *(folafola)* the details of the program, the president states that all women must wear new undergarments, which will be "examined" *(aasi)* on Women's Day to ascertain that they are indeed new:

> *A mea konaa e aasi. E olo atu eiloo a faafine, a- a mea konei o- o fakamasuesue peelaa ttou gatu, maalie ua peelaa, kee lavea ttou sooti, nee?* [Fono o Faafine 1991:1:B:601–603]

> These things will be examined. Women will go around and- and lift up our skirts, just a bit like that, so that our shorts can be seen, right?

Newness and cleanliness, concerns for which echo directly nineteenth-century missionary discourse, together with uniformity and equality, are the ingredients of that sought-after condition, "beauty."

Again, the authoritarian control of intimate details of people's lives is legitimized by the fact that it was *taatou* that made these rules; as in talk among "occasionally" egalitarian Fiji Indians that Brenneis analyzes, the overt message is that "no single voice has control, and no individual is responsible" (1987b, 506):

> *Pati a taatou ne hai, fai eiloo.* [Fono o Faafine 1991:1:B:603–604]

> What we [inclusive] said [should be done], that's what will be done.

What is at stake here is not simply the extent to which agents of authority control symbolic tokens. A more important aspect of the authority being exerted in the "program" I have just discussed is economic and practical. Indeed, as I was told by several women after the meeting, the "program" for Women's Day celebrations places participants in a position where they have to obtain new garments in order to perform their duty of willingly contributing to the spirit of togetherness. Because new garments are usually not available for purchase on the atoll, many women have to rely on whatever reciprocity network they have previously established with the outside world to procure these goods. Many personal letters written around the time of such events include panicky requests for money, clothing, and whatever else has been made de rigueur for these events (Besnier 1995, 93–101). Women also have to deal with timing problems: the ten ship visits a year do not lend themselves to the rapid turnover of goods. Thus the economic and logistic hardships created by such "programs" are potentially very burdensome. But the alternative to not finding a way of procuring new outfits is to face both shaming and further economic hardships in the shape of fines.

I have illustrated here how the authority structure seeks legitimacy by invoking and appropriating for itself a discourse of egalitarianism under many different guises. These invocations not only provide the desired legitimacy, but also ensure that overt opposition in the name of the egalitarian ideology will not be possible. These strategies work in many cases, particularly when the motivation for authoritarianism is of relatively little consequence, of relatively little material or symbolic significance. Against this backdrop of ideological indeterminacy, it should come as no surprise that Nukulaelae Islanders regard leadership roles with ambivalence. On the one hand, individuals sometimes accept positions where they stand a chance to have their voice heard, if not respected, and their symbolic capital increased in terms of the prestige that they might accrue. On the other hand, Nukulaelae Islanders know the precariousness of positions of leadership, the stratagems leaders have to devise to make their authority appear to be something else (Bailey 1988), and the difficulties involved in maintaining a presentable image in the eyes of others. As a result, positions of leadership are frequently difficult to fill. For example, at the beginning of 1990, the chieftainship of the atoll was left vacant by a resignation; as the following account illustrates, the Council of Elders had difficulties finding a new chief:

> *Kae ona ko te mea e toko uke tino ne fai atu, see talia nee ttinoo. Fili atu ttinoo, see talia. Teenaa, e toko fia tino kolaa ne tuku atu ki ei, see talia, tuku atu ki ei, talia nee ia. Teenaa te- te- te mea ne iloa nee au, te filiga teenaa. Seeai ake foki se tino ne talia nee ia kee fano ia o ulu fenua, a koo tuku atu ki ei, mea loa koo talia nee ia.* [V 1991:1:B:102–108]

Because many people were asked [if they could fill the position], but they all turned it down. Every time someone else was chosen, he refused. Who knows how many people were asked who refused. [Then] it was given to him [the current chief], and he accepted. As far as I understand of that investiture. No one else would accept the position, but when it was given to him, he accepted.

Firth (1960) describes comparable ambivalence at times of chiefly succession on Tikopia, but Nukulaelae differs from Tikopia both in the cause and procedure of ambivalence: while there is no instance of any Tikopia refusing a chiefly position, such instances abound on Nukulaelae. One feature of Nukulaelae chiefly succession (and of ascendance to any position of leadership) bears strong resemblances to the Tikopia material: enthusiastically welcoming the offer of a position of leadership is seen as evidence of a lack of humility and met with great scorn.

And indeed, in the above quote, the speaker thinly disguises his contempt for the man who accepted the chiefly position after so many had turned it down. The odds were against this particular Nukulaelae leader right from the beginning, and things quickly went downhill. Many in the atoll community shared his contempt for this man; all the quotations in this chapter in which the chief is ridiculed in fact focus on this individual. Lacking the gravitas that Nukulaelae people expect of holders of positions of consequence, unkempt in his appearance (he is overweight, his shirts are always torn, etc.), erratic in his decisions and actions, this man harangues everyone with his repetitive, unimaginative, and tactless public speeches, which he delivers at great length while constantly pulling down on his rent shirts in an attempt to cover his protruding belly. But at the same time, the limelight in which his prominent position places him is wonderfully functional for the island community: his actions and words are mercilessly ridiculed in backstage clowning and gossip, even by his own close kin. When his verbal blunders and nonverbal improprieties are particularly blatant, ridiculing even takes place, more or less discretely, right under his nose. In short, this leader's desperate attempts to claim the attributes that the discourse of nostalgia associates with his social position constitute superb material for the discourse of egalitarianism.

Those Pesky Young Men

In the context of the ideological ambivalences I have analyzed, the atoll's authority structure is terribly fragile, and when the Council of Elders tried to enforce in the course of the mid-1980s a ban on the production and consumption of alcohol, it got a dramatic reminder of this fragility. Prohibition has historical antecedents on the atoll, as both Samoan missionaries and colonial authorities had enforced it from the late nineteenth century until the end of the colonial period. While most other islands of Tuvalu did away with prohibition in the 1960s, Nukulaelae remained dry until the late 1970s, by which time no one deemed it an important issue any more, although the moralistic discourse on drinking did not change. In 1988, however, the reconstituted Council of Elders began worrying about what it judged to be an increase in drinking-related violence, and it voted to outlaw liquor. By then, prohibition had become a symbolic terrain on which the struggle between the tradition-oriented older men and increasingly powerful younger men was played out.

The ruling targeted the production and consumption of "sour toddy," or naturally fermented coconut sap. Young men harvest fresh coconut sap twice a day by climbing to the top of the tall trees (an athletic feat in itself), binding the green spathes before they effloresce into coconut bunches, and, after several weeks, delicately shaving the tip of the bound spathe with a very sharp knife (known as *naifi Paanapa* "knife from Ocean Island," where people used to purchase it), allowing the sap to drip into an emptied-out coconut shell or empty glass bottle. The process involves considerable skill and experience, which are markers of youthful manhood. In its unfermented state, the sap *(kaleve)* is a major ingredient in everyday atoll diet, but left to ferment naturally for more than twenty-four hours, it becomes a powerful wine comparable to West African palm wine. The toddy comes in two forms: the sweeter *kao,* fermented on the tree while fresh toddy continues to drip into the container, and the bitter *kamagii,* taken down from the tree before the onset of fermentation. Drinking is almost exclusively a young men's pastime. But it is after drinking that young men fight and engage in displays of bravado (e.g., shouting, throwing stones, expressing defiance) that, in the opinion of older people, threaten communal *fiileemuu* "peace" (cf. Marshall 1979). The reinstituted prohibition is thus deeply embroiled in a politics of power and control, as it is in many other comparable situations (e.g., Haugerud 1995, 86–91; Marshall 1975).

In the course of the mid-1980s, drinking became one of the central concerns of the Council of Elders. Few meetings were held during which the issue was not discussed. For one of my female interviewees, the centrality of this concern fits perfectly with the discourse of nostalgia:

A taimi kolaa, te fakaala koo ssoko eeloo, mo te fiafiaaga, te faatele, koo-! Seei koo- seei loo ne mea peenei! Kae nei, koo fakamuamua mai faeloa te inu. [. . .] Teenei faeloa te mea koo tuu muamua i ttaimi nei. Se aa laa?, e (isi) sou manuia e maua mai? Faitalia ttino teelaa kaa maua nee te agasala, avegina koe o fakasala nee ttulaafono, me e isi ne tino tausi o te fenua- ttulaafono, maafai koe koo soli nee koe. Teenei eeloo te mataaupu koo mili! O le aa fono nei? "Aumai tamaliki kolaa, e iinu, e peipei fale!" [L&S 1991:1:B:006–023]

In those days, it was one feast after the other, rejoicing, *faatele* dancing! Now, none- there isn't anything like this any more. Instead, now the foremost thing [in

Council deliberations] is drinking. [. . .] That's what's foremost these days. What's in it, what good [*manuia*] does one get from it? Just leave the sinner alone, let [him] be judged by the law, since there are people who are in charge of the atoll-of the law, if you break it. [But] that's what keeps being mulled around! [*switching to Samoan for dramatic effect*] What are these meetings about? [*switching back to Tuvaluan*] "Bring those children, they've been drinking, they've been throwing stones at houses!"

Nukulaelae people refer to the rod that the Council of Elders initially tried to use in enforcing prohibition as *faleesea*, a word borrowed from Samoan and rarely or never heard on other islands of Tuvalu. Following is a succinct account by a young man of the range of restrictions included under the heading *faleesea*, which I translate loosely as "ostracized":

Mea laa e faleesea maatou, tapu maatou i faigaa mea a te fenua, tapu i loto i te maneapa, tapu i ttaafaoga, i taafaoga kolaa e maaopoopo ei tamataene mo tamaa-fine. Tapu i- fakatapu foki maatou i gaaluega, nee?, kolaa, peelaa mo te siiuolo, [. . .] Mo te- a ko gaaluega kolaa fakagaamua a te fenua, kolaa fua, fai, see ttogi, ee, maatou e gaalue ki ei. [T 1991:1:A:036–046]

So we were ostracized, we were forbidden from the community's feasts and events, forbidden to [enter] the *maneapa*, forbidden to [take part in] games, including games where young men and young women get together, forbidden to- we were forbidden to work [for money], to work, like, on the seawall, [. . .] And the- but unpaid communal work, work that doesn't get you any money, we [had to] work at those.

By all accounts, *faleesea* is very serious in a society where happiness can only be derived from participating in communal activities. The economic implications of being *faleesea* are equally severe: while the Council of Elders can no longer block the hiring of seamen, it can close the doors to the meager local employment opportunities (e.g., working on seawall construction for minimal wages).[8]

The problem is that without young, able-bodied men, the community cannot operate, a fact that the young men themselves were quick to note. Not only does everyone need their age- and gender-specified labor (beginning with the production of fresh coconut toddy), but also, at the time, young men were leaving the atoll in increasing numbers to work on ships and well on their way to become the economic lifeline of the atoll. Almost as soon as prohibition went into effect, young men violated it. One by one, no matter how careful they were, they were discovered, as the potent smell of fermented toddy easily betrays it. One by one, they came to make a formal apology *(fakatooese)* to the Council of Elders. One was fined A$500, an enormous sum of money. Tuvalu's senior magistrate on Funafuti got wind of it and sent word to the Nukulaelae Council of Elders that the fine was illegal, and the money was returned. Others were required to *faagai te fenua* "feed the atoll," that is, throw a feast for the 350 inhabitants of the atoll, while others were severely admonished *(polopolooki)*. Some elders called for a return to one old form of punishment, consisting in the culprit's being hoisted to the rafters of the *maneapa* and dropped to the hard floor. The Council of Elders' debates turned to whether or not ostracized young men should be reintegrated at all, and at what cost. They engendered factionalism, pitching "traditionalists" against younger, better educated, and worldlier members. The clashes became extremely heated.

Prohibition also raised the problem of whether the Council of Elders had the authority to enforce prohibition at all. As everyone on Nukulaelae knows well, Tuvalu's constitution calls for the protection of human rights *(saolotoga o ttino)*, which can be argued to include the right to drink liquor but, of course, not to disrupt community peace, a crucial factor if one defines drinking and disorder as constitutively related.[9] Opponents of prohibition (i.e., all younger men, some elders, and many women of all ages) argued that controlling antisocial behavior was the task of the policeman and the government-appointed magistrate, not the Council of Elders. As the council became increasingly entrenched in its opposition to abolishing prohibition, the situation became a perilous test of the legitimacy of its authority.

And perilous it was. In 1989, a group of about twenty ostracized young men (a significant percentage of the total number) asked for a hearing, in which they would have essentially questioned the authority of the Council of Elders to impose prohibition. The result was predictable:

Teenaa ne maannako maatou o faippati, nee?, paa, o fesilisili ki luga i te-. [. . .]
E fia iloa nee maatou i maatou laa, paa, e iloa nee maatou, maatou e ppei motou
[. . .] laafoga foitino, a kaiaa kaa fakatapu ei maatou i luga i gaaluega kolaa a
te maaloo, mea kolaa se mea loo faka-te-fenua. See talia nee laatou, kae olotou
pati, "Teenaa te ttonu." "Teenaa," teenaa eeloo, kee olo maatou ki tua. [T 1991:1: A:046–055]

So we wanted to talk, right?, like, to ask about the-. [. . .] We wanted to know, like, as far as we know, we pay our head taxes, but then why were we forbidden to take up government-funded work, in that this [i.e., our being ostracized] was an atoll-community affair. They [i.e., the Council of Elders] refused [to speak to us]. They said, "That's our order." "This is [how it will be done]," [and] this is [the way it's to be done], we should go away.

After this initial shunning, the young men in question decided that they would "do something bad" to the community *(fakamaasei te fenua)*. They felt angry *(kaitaua)* and hurt *(mmae te loto,* literally, "the heart aches"). After several meetings held in the bush around sour-toddy containers, they decided that they would set fire to the store's supply of engine fuel and to strategic houses, then commit suicide together by setting themselves adrift *(fakataapea)* in the communal catamaran.

Predictably, given how difficult it is to keep secrets secret on the atoll, word of these plans reached those in power. Even though the young men's plans had by that time died a natural death, the alert was sounded:

> *Naa naa, paa mo koo llogo te fenua. A te fenua ne llogo, aati koo tasi te maasina tupu, i te faiga o temotou aofaga teelaa, nee? A ko ttaimi foki teenaa, maatou paa mo koo see maaopoopo tasi saale. Paa mo koo maofaofa, nee?, koo see loto tasi. [. . .] Teenaa, taumafai ei te fenua o aa?, o tiute te fale penitiini. Ttaimi teenaa, ee, katoa ttagata, aati peelaa mai te tolu sefulu tausaga, ki luga i te lima sefulu, paa, silia atu foki mo te lima sefulu, ttagata taa koi tai maalosi taa sili atu, palele katoa, olo o onoono i- o tausi te fale penitiini.* [T 1991:1:A:177–192]

So, the community heard [about our plans]. The community heard [about them], it must have been about a month after we had made those plans, see? But by that time, we had sort of stopped getting together. We had sort of broken up, see?, we had stopped being of one mind. [. . .] So the community began trying to guard the fuel shed. At the time, every single man, from perhaps the age of thirty up to the age of fifty, and probably even older, every man that was still able-bodied, every single one of them would go and guard the fuel shed.

For several weeks, no able-bodied man managed a full night's sleep, and daily routines were completely disrupted. The community organized vigils, during which some people guarded the fuel shed while others patrolled the paths, spying on those suspected of being ringleaders, who were enjoying every minute of the panic they had caused. Finally, the pastor was asked to step in, a typical response to very serious disruptions of social order. This move contributed to the sense of emergency, since the pastor, as an outsider to the atoll and as its spiritual protector, should ideally be kept out of the atoll's secular problems. The pastor "invited" *(aami)* the young men and "helped" *(fesoasoani)* them by advising them to *faipati fakallei* "speak properly" with the chief:

> *Naa laa i ei, aami maatou nee Palu. Faippati maatou, aa, silisili katoa ki maatou tamaliki kolaa faleesea, fai maatou, "Ao, e isi nemotou maafaufauga ne fai peenaa. Kae nei laa nei, koo seeai, nee?" Naa, fesoasoani mai Palu, peelaa loo mo tena*

tuulaga, iaa ia se faifeau, nee? Fesoasoani mai tou tagata, kee olo maatou kiaa- te
ulu fenua, [. . .] kee faippati fakallei, faippati maatou ki te mea teenaa. [T 1991:1:
A:202–210]

So at that time, [the pastor] Palu invited us, and we had a chat. So he interrogated
all of us who had been ostracized, and we said. "Yes, we had voiced these thoughts
[of burning down houses]. But no longer, right?" So Palu helped us, since that's
his job as a pastor, see? He helped us and told us to go to the chief, [. . .] to speak
properly, to speak about what happened.

The situation cooled down and the young men were eventually reintegrated into
the community after making a token apology. The main leader of the movement,
Taukiei, whose voice suffuses the above narrative, left the atoll for a year, and
returned to nothing more than memories of the events in which he had played a
central role. Such is the course of the numerous conflicts that characterize daily
life on Nukulaelae: extraordinarily disruptive events are left to fade away. However,
the debate over prohibition was far from resolved, and would remain on everyone's
minds until more pressing matters dislodged it in the course of time.

What can be gleaned from the events I have described is that a traditionally powerless group on the atoll can mobilize enough agency to immobilize the
Council of Elders. With a very few but carefully chosen tools, among which rumor
figures prominently, the ostracized young men managed to disrupt the life of the
entire community. While exhibiting all the expected deference in their dealings
with the Council of Elders, the ostracized group created a situation that put into
question the very legitimacy of the Council of Elders' authority. The struggle for
egalitarianism is of course framed differently in this situation. Since egalitarianism
does not apply equally across age categories in the "traditional" system, the young
men invoked instead a discourse of human rights as protected by the country's
constitution. In short, the coexistence of various discourses on Nukulaelae makes
the exertion of authority a very hazardous enterprise. The power that even the
most marginal individuals have in undermining the authority of leaders is simply
too great.

Ideological Dilemmas

This chapter has sought to unravel the ideological complexities of power in
Nukulaelae society and to analyze the relationship between these complexities and
political praxis. One question that I have yet to tackle is to what the discursive tensions I analyzed here can be attributed. The most obvious place to look for their
roots is in history. I have hinted at the potential role that Nukulaelae's tormented
postcontact history may have had in the emergence of multiple discourses. It is

tempting to attribute an extraterritorial origin to one or the other discourse that I have identified as constitutive of political ideology, or to search for a link between one of these discourses and either Nukulaelae's precontact aboriginal culture or postmissionization religious ideology. But there is no evidence to support this analysis. While colonial authorities squeezed out of Nukulaelae and the rest of Tuvalu every shred of hierarchy that the precolonial system might have been able to offer, there is no evidence that authoritarianism was a postcontact introduction (even though it is commonplace for the incorporation of egalitarian societies into a larger state system to engender inequality and hierarchy; cf. Etienne and Leacock [1980]; Flanagan and Rayner [1988]; Leacock and Lee [1982]). For that matter, early colonial authorities were hardly dealing with a precontact social order, since missionization had already altered it fundamentally in the three decades that preceded the establishment of the protectorate.

The reverse hypothesis, in which contemporary discourses of nostalgia represent the precolonial situation, is equally difficult to support, in that we do not know whether chiefly authority was indeed more firmly established in precontact days or whether the discourse of nostalgia is simply an instance of invented tradition whose grounding in the past is the product of present-day reification. Similarly, Christianity has penetrated Nukulaelae life so thoroughly since the late nineteenth century that it makes little sense to try to distinguish Christian from other types of ideology on Nukulaelae. Rationalizations based on Christian principles are offered for both authoritarianism and egalitarianism. Clearly, historical trajectories are never straightforward, and the ideological makeup of culture always derives from the past though multiple interlocking dynamics. Here and elsewhere (e.g., G. White 1991, 52), chiefs are neither the remnants of precolonial society nor the creation of colonial times, and the same applies to the idealization of equality.

While history does not provide clear answers, contemporary dynamics do help shed some light on the ideological dilemmas that characterize Nukulaelae thoughts about power and governance. Like the inhabitants of so many other villages and islands in the Pacific Island region, Nukulaelae Islanders often feel as if they were suspended in a worrisome web of indeterminacy. They find themselves on the edge between subsistence and a monetized economy in which the stakes are becoming dangerously high, while sources of income are fragile, elusively far away, and shifting in unpredictable ways. The high expectations that followed independence in 1978 were in many ways never met, or they were met in oblique ways, fueling suspicion and resentment, justifiably or not, that a few were benefiting from newly discovered resources while the rest were left in limbo (cf. Gewertz and Errington 1999). Aggravating the sense of uncertainty are the new forms that labor migration is taking, from temporary (if potentially long-term) relocation by nuclear families to Banaba and Nauru until the turn of the millennium to potentially permanent relocation to New Zealand or long-term labor on foreign ships traveling from one industrial city to the next. The potential disappearance of the country under rising sea levels, and the bombardment of publicity about it, have undoubtedly done little to alleviate these anxieties. It is little wonder that a less tormented past is the focus of nostalgia, appeasing at least in symbolic terms the anxieties about the bases of social control and other forms of control. At the same time, the discourse of egalitarianism responds to anxieties about new forms of unfairness and their seemingly haphazard configuration. Seemingly incommensurable discourses thus provide answers, or at least ways of questioning, a troublesome present and an anxiety-filled future.

My analysis of leadership and authority refers specifically to Nukulaelae atoll. There is evidence that tensions between an egalitarian ethos and a stratified authority structure do exist on other islands of the group. For example, on Nukufetau, one of the southern atolls, in 1991, young men contested the hourly wages they were earning for work on development projects around the atoll, principally at the time seawall construction. Funds for these projects came from the Tuvaluan government, which provided grants that the Island Council administered. When the Island Council refused to give them a pay raise, the young men refused to participate in any further work. Able-bodied women have had to take over seawall construction, probably a well-calculated move on the part of the Island Council to shame the young men. In retribution, the young men boycotted community gatherings, including feasts and dances that depended on their participation for their success.

Parliamentary elections have given rise to serious rifts on several islands of Tuvalu. Both Nui, in central Tuvalu, and Nukulaelae were torn in the 1980s by disputes over election results. Nanumaga, in the northern part of the group, is "traditionally" divided into four clanlike entities, called *fale* (literally, "house"), membership of which is determined in part by residence. In 1983, an American town planner funded by the Save the Children Fund redesigned the village, and disagreements arose among the members of one of the clans over details of the design of its part of the village. The clan failed to resolve the disagreement, and one faction went on to create a fifth clan. The remaining three clans excluded both clans from community activities until they resolved the rift. In 1989, both the original fourth clan and the new clan were reintegrated into the community.

Thus the tension between egalitarianism and authoritarianism is not an exclusive feature of Nukulaelae Atoll, although they do appear to be more serious on Nukulaelae than elsewhere. Why this should be so is a complex question. The social and cultural discontinuities that Nukulaelae experienced in the late nineteenth century are likely to have had a major role in the creation of multiple discourses. The tiny population of the atoll is another explanation that inhabitants of other islands of the group commonly invoke to account for the frequency of social disruptions that, in their eyes, characterize Nukulaelae life, referring in the same breath to Nukulaelae Islanders' love of gossip, scandal, and intrigue. When pressed, they explain that events and actions that would remain inconsequential in larger communities come to have disproportionate visibility and consequences among so few people. It is indeed the case that social relations have a concentrated quality on Nukulaelae, not just in terms of space but also in terms of emotions, drama, and a multiplicity of meanings. This quality is what I seek to capture in this book.

4 Morality and the Structure of Gossip

NUKULAELAE ISLANDERS PRODUCE prestige, reputation, morality, and political action across multiple contexts, not the least of which is gossip. As I mentioned at the beginning of this book, Nukulaelae has a reputation throughout Tuvalu as the "island of gossip." The vanguard that nurtures this reputation is the handful of civil servants and other workers from other islands of Tuvalu posted on the atoll, who often complain bitterly about Nukulaelae people's love of confabulation, exaggeration, and drama. This is particularly the case of workers who oversee potentially charged matters, like money, goods, and news: the island executive officer, who doubles as bank teller; the wireless operator *(tama uaeelesi)*; the manager of the Tuvalu Cooperative Society store; and the primary-school teachers. *Ttamaa fenua fua, a ko te uke o tala!* "Such a small island, but so many stories!" they often exclaim. Even pastors, who are always strangers to the atoll, as I discussed in chapter 2, have been known to comment on the matter and, when they have suffered directly from gossip, to do much more than just comment on it.

Nukulaelae people are embarrassed by this reputation, although they concede that it holds more than a grain of truth. When in a good mood, they dismiss gossip amusedly as *pati agina i te matagi* "words blown about by the wind." Publicly, they condemn it as antisocial behavior. In speeches delivered in the *maneapa*, in church sermons, and in interviews with the anthropologist, they deplore gossip as an insidious, immoral, and dangerous activity. "What do you think of gossip?" I asked one of my informants, an elderly man who had then just retired as the long-standing island magistrate:

> *Ttoe mea maasei eiloo teenaa. Ttoe mea maasei eiloo teenaa. Kaafai au e isi se mea e- e ita au kiaa koe, kaa fano au, koo sauttala maatou mo- mo te kau i te umu, "Taapaa ee!, a Faiva peelaa, peelaa, e fai peelaa," nee? Teelaa laa, olo atu te kauu, koo olo foki o- o toe- o toe ave, ko- konaa feituu e ttupu ei fakalavelave i luga i- i te fenua, nee? Konaa aku fakalavelave, kaafai e sauttala taaua nei, kae faippati mai*

*nee koe, kae fakattau- fakattau au se mea e see ttau o-, koe laa e faipati ki luga iaa
Sina, nee? Kae fakattau au me see ttau au o faipati kiaa Sina, e nofo eiloo mo au te
mea teenaa, kae teelaa laa kaa fano au o faipati kiaa Sina, kaa-, peelaa, fai fua nee
au a- a te fiileemuu o te kaaiga kee maasei, nee? Kaa kosu nee au te fiileemuu mo
te ola fiafia o te kaaiga i luga i vaegaa tuu konaa. A konaa foki eiloo fakalavelave e
ttupu i loto i te maaloo. Konaa ko vaegaa fakalavelave peenaa, te fatufatu, fano au
o fatufatu a ttinoo ki ttinoo, ia, logo koe, aa!, ave au ki te- tagi a koe ki te fono, ia!,
maua tou- toku kaitoa.* [Kelese 1990, vol. 1]

It's the worst of all things. It's the worst of all things. If I am angry at you about
something, and I go and chat with the guys in the cooking hut, "Hey!, Faiva [i.e.,
Niko Besnier] is doing this and this and this," right? So then the guys go and- and
again- again- they repeat it, these- these are the ways in which problems arise on
this atoll, right? These are the problems, if you and I chat, and you tell me something, and I figure- I figure that it's something not right, and you talk to Sina,
right? And I reckon that I should not talk to Sina, I stay with that information,
but then I go to Sina and talk to her, so I mess up the peace *(fiileemuu)* of the
family, right? I disturb the peace and the happy living *(ola fiafia)* of the family
with that kind of behavior. This is also the kind of problem that arises in the
government. This kind of problem, gossip, I go and gossip from this to that person, and you hear of it, ah!, you take me to- you file a complaint with the court,
and there you go!, I get what I deserve.

Public discourse of this kind articulates a morality bound to Islanders' anxious
self-presentation as a harmonious and peaceful community.

Pleasure and Danger

For people on the atoll, gossip is a trait that runs in certain families. Members of those families have *gutu faipati* "talking mouths" and engage in *poolitiki*
"politics," a category that always connotes deceit and trickery (cf. W. Murphy 1998,
510). They "make up" stories, as attested by the fact that the term that is closest in meaning to "gossip," *fatufatu,* literally means "to make up [stories]." These
people are often jokingly called *looia* "lawyer" (a role with which Islanders have
little direct experience but of whose possibility they are intensely aware), a term
that bears an amusing resemblance to *loi* "lie, tell lies," to which many think it is
related. These attributions are examples of what is referred to as a *pona* "stigma"
(literally, "bump"). People inherit their *pona* from their parents and grandpar-
ents, be it through filiation or adoption, so that one's biography begins before
one is even born. Some *pona* are explicitly grounded in the extralocal origins of
particular families (e.g., a quick temper in a family's Gilbertese ascendance).[1] The
descendants of the Jamaican beachcomber Charles Barnard, whom I mentioned

in chapter 2 and who appears in figure 2.3, are saddled with the *pona* of gossip, the exact reasons for which have been lost in time, but that people today associate with the dark complexion that runs in the family, a sign of the lack of beauty, dignity, and peace associated with gossip (as well as with unflattering memories of Charles Barnard, who is reputed to have been caught red-handed in the pastor's pig pen with his pants around his ankles).[2] Whenever an individual's *pona* is mentioned, people immediately relate it to the familial *pona,* and the local discourse of personhood consists principally in searching for explanations of people's conduct in terms of the *pona* associated with their family. While one can also inherit positively valued attributes, these are considerably less interesting than negative traits. This model of personhood does not preclude the possibility that an individual will break the familial pattern; however, to do so, the individual must work awfully hard to "prove" to the community that *pona* does not always run in families because, at the slightest slip, everyone nods knowingly.

Furthermore, within the families stigmatized by gossip, women bear the heaviest burden, a classic pattern that is reminiscent of the crosscultural gendering of gossip and the reinforcement of gender hierarchy through ideologies of verbal behavior. The resulting pattern is one of "fractal recursivity," which occurs when "the dichotomizing and partitioning process that [is] involved in some understood opposition . . . recurs at other levels, creating either subcategories on each side of a contrast or supercategories that include both sides but oppose them to something else" (Irvine and Gal 2000, 38; cf. Besnier 2004b, 316–320). Here, Tuvaluans stigmatize Nukulaelae people for their propensity to gossip, Nukulaelae people attach the stigma to particular families, and family members (as well as Nukulaelae people in general) attach this stigma to the women of these families. The pattern is not peculiar to this ethnographic context: in Greece, Cretans consider apprentice artisans rude and uncultured, Greeks consider Cretans rude and uncultured, and Europeans consider Greeks rude and uncultured, in what Herzfeld (2003) calls a "global hierarchy of values." (Few people outside of Tuvalu are concerned about what Tuvaluans do or don't do, so in this situation, in contrast to the Greek case, the recursivity stops at the national level.) Such is the reifying power of stereotypes in creating and nurturing inequalities.[3]

Like the cooking huts in which it takes place (chapter 2), and like the discourse of egalitarianism of which it is constitutive, gossip lacks "beauty": it is disorderly, rude, and undomesticated. It stands in sharp contrast to forms of interaction like *maneapa* oratory, church sermons, courtroom interaction, and meetings, where people are supposed to be calm and words are expected to be deep and thoughtful, their delivery elegant. Gossip is the opposite of "speaking properly," the ideal way with which conflicts should be managed, during which older people, usually men, calmly admonish and instruct the conflicting parties, who are too "weak" *(vaaivai)* to control their impulsivity and remember their place in the hierarchical order, and ask them to exchange apologies at the end, asserting that no hard feelings (*loto maasei*, literally, "bad heart") remain (Besnier 1990a). *Faipati fakallei* does not aim to establish an objective truth, but to establish a workable form of sociality, connoting civilization, modernity, and Christianity. It associates with both the discourse of nostalgia, for being orderly, *gali* "beautiful," and *fiileemuu* "peaceful," and the discourse of egalitarianism, because it places everyone on an equal footing through mutual apologies (see Watson-Gegeo and White [1990] for comparable ethnographic cases).

Unlike *faipati fakallei*, gossip is above all dangerous, as the above quote spells out. It can lead to shame, escalated conflicts, and lawsuits for defamation. I learned it the hard way, as I began to take gusto in gossiping during fieldwork (to my own surprise at times, and certainly to my retrospective embarrassment). In one incident, a distant relative of the family came to our cooking hut to ask for some salted fish, of which we had an abundance at the time, and shortly after she had left I remarked disparagingly that she seemed to be treating our cooking hut like her own larder (a complaint that Nukulaelae Islanders would easily voice). It was not until Sina pointed it out to me that I realized that the old lady was hiding behind the water tank to listen to what we would say about her. I was embarrassed and everyone was amused.

However, morality is also contextual, and the public denigration of gossip does not prevent the very same people who condemn it from finding great pleasure and few qualms in participating in gossip as either narrator or listener. Gossip is pleasurable, for various reasons: the pleasure of the forbidden fruit, the pleasure of collusive intimacy with one's interlocutors, the carnivalesque pleasure of Bakhtinian inversion. The pleasure of companionship and intimacy is evident, for example, in the long pauses between gossip narratives, during which participants fan sleeping children, roll cigarettes, and drink oversweetened weak tea. While gossiping, Nukulaelae people negotiate pleasure and danger in a variety of ways. Witness one interlocutor's conspiratorial reaction when she thinks that a young woman, E, is about to initiate a juicy gossip session during a casual after-dinner conversation among women:

E *F ne faipati mo-* =
   "F talked to-"

S = *ia!*, ((rising pitch, whisper)) *muu mea laa* hhh! (3.0) ((high pitch, whisper)) *Muu mea mai laa o faipati mai!* ( )
   "Hey! Come closer! Come closer and talk to us! ( )"

E ((high pitch)) *kae aa?, e llei hua.*
   "Why?, it's ok."

S *Taatou koo t:oo meaga,* ((fast)) *i tino e tii olo i auala,* =
   "We might be too loud, because people keep walking along the path,"

?   ((laughter))

S   = *kae muna aka, "ne aa::?" Mo te fale oki teelaa e pili mai, moo mea mai o*
      takato fakafaauli kia au. (2.6) *Fakapaa peelaa ki lalo.*
      "and they'll start to ask, 'uh, what is it?' Also the house here that's close by,
      [so] come closer and lie down facing this way. Take a load off your feet."
      [1985:4:B:360–700, Transcript 111]

This conversation encapsulates the mixed emotions that gossip engenders: the danger of being overheard by inquisitive ears in crowded and wall-less huts, the pleasure of conspiratorially whispered information exchanges (here at a time when the atoll was torn apart by conflict over parliamentary elections), and the pleasure of relaxed intimacy.[4]

The immorality and pleasurability of gossip has different implications for different people, and different consequences for the form that gossip takes. Those who fear being branded as inveterate gossipers are people who claim to be morally upstanding Christian community members, whose words and deeds are without ulterior motives and are only designed to strengthen peace and beauty, and who show the same face in public as in private. Others have little to lose, because such claims are not available to them or because they are members of families whose *pona* is gossip. In this category fall younger people, whom the gerontocratic order excludes from power, as well many adult women and older men who, for one reason or another, are relegated to marginal social roles. All, however, have to negotiate the conflicting values of which gossip is the object, evaluating, as narrators or listeners, the relative weight of these values and the extent to which they stand to gain and lose from particular moves.

In this chapter, I turn to a microscopic level of analysis of gossip interactions to explore how the way in which people actually gossip articulates morality. I analyze fragments of gossip that I recorded and transcribed during fieldwork and borrow analytic tools from a sociological tradition commonly referred to as "conversation analysis" (overviewed in Drew and Heritage [2006]; Hutchby [1998]; and Schegloff [2007], among others). Conversation analysis is an offshoot of ethnomethodology, the sociological tradition concerned with how social order is produced and enacted, founded by Harold Garfinkel and grounded in Husserlian phenomenology. Conversation analysis is primarily concerned with discovering, in detailed transcripts of naturalistic conversation, the procedures that social agents employ to produce conduct and understanding. Conversation analysts, however, operate with a peculiar understanding of "context," which they view as produced in interaction and consider as analytically irrelevant any material extraneous to the transcripts, such as class, gender, or situation (Schegloff 1987, 1992; and see Billig 1999; Blommaert 2003; and Wetherell 1998 for critical deconstructions). In contrast, this chapter in particular and this book in general focus specifically on the relationship between interactional dynamics and the extrainteractional context, such as ideology, history, the structuring of power, and the production of locality and globality.

Ideology in the Interactional Structure of Gossip

We can read the moral and political complexities of Nukulaelae gossip not just in the literal text of what people say in and about gossip, but more importantly in what they do while gossiping, whether strategically or unconsciously. For theoretical inspiration I turn here to a dynamic body of work that linguistic anthropologists have been developing since the 1990s, commonly referred to as the analysis of "language ideology," which Judith Irvine defines as "the cultural (or subcultural) system of ideas about social and linguistic relationships, together with their loading of moral and political interests," adding that "the cultural system (including the linguistic ideology) is a mediating factor, not necessarily a causative one" (1989, 255). As a substantial corpus of analyses of linguistic ideology demonstrates, ideology is embedded in language structure at different levels (phonological, grammatical, interactional), and this embedding often takes on the semiotics of indexicality and iconicity, rather than symbolism.[5] Irvine's insistence on the mediating power of the cultural system captures the fact that we cannot attribute a universal context-independent sociocultural meaning to linguistic form (e.g., grammatical constructions, silence, prosodic features) since such meaning is only retrievable in reference to local ideological constructs. Thus, for example, speaking loud and fast may be an assertion of power in one society, but the exact opposite in a different society, depending on the ideological constructs at play in each context. However, since ideology is always an unfinished project, characterized by contradictions and a vulnerability to contestation, the relationship between ideology and linguistic practice is unstable and dynamic, and linguistic practice can in turn contribute to the construction of ideology. Thus linguistic production does not just reflect ideology, but also produces and reproduces it. Indeed, linguistic ideology and linguistic form are constitutive of one another: one maintains the other, in mutually reinforcing fashion.

Accordingly, many aspects of the interactional organization of gossip on Nukulaelae reflect and in turn produce the ideological tensions of which gossip is the object. Gossip interactions are organized differently in different contexts, depending on the gender, age, number, and interests of the participants, as well as the conversationalists' relationship to the information that they circulate. At one extreme, gossipers who happen to know a juicy story that their interlocutors have not yet heard can be in full control of their audience, which they can monitor and enlist through strategies that I will analyze presently, and command their rapt attention, punctuated by expressions of amazement, disbelief, and exasperation. In such cases, we can talk about a principal gossiper, in charge of the deployment of the gossip narrative for the benefit of his or her audience, frequently several people and overhearers (given the crowded conditions in which most gossip takes place). But these situations are potentially dangerous, as the party who controls everyone's attention later risks being laughed at, disbelieved, or accused of being a *looia* "lawyer, liar." So gossipers with reasons to be concerned about their reputation take on this role with some trepidation, and when they do, they strategize so as to dilute the responsibility for the gossip, as I will explain presently.

In other circumstances, gossip can be deployed in interactive fashion involving many people whose turns overlap, latch together, and parallel one another. The following humorous fragment is a good illustration of the resulting effect. Here, two elderly male relatives allude jointly to a humorous incident involving a husband and wife. One speaker (F) provides the beginning of the narrative of a well-known anecdote about this married couple, part of the corpus of lore about particular people and families, and the other speaker (S) provides the punch line:

> F   ((high pitch)) *Kae aa::? (Koo fai) p(ee)laa mo te fueega: a: Tito* ((mid-high pitch)) *nee Tausi,* ((normal pitch)) *fue atu loo i te afiafi, (f)ano, koo vvini te moa,* ((laughter)) =
> "Yeah, it'd be like when Tausi started fanning Tito, (she) started fanning (him) in the evening, went on and on, (until) the rooster crowed [i.e., until morning]."
>
> S   = ((laughing)) *Kae poko makalili a- hah Thhithhho. .hh*
> "And then Tito caught a cold [as a result]."
> [CONV 102:11]

Part of the humor of this anecdote is that it exposes an intimacy between married couples that on Nukulaelae is deemed inappropriate for public eyes. In contrast, humor is not what is at stake in the following example, in which two men (T and F) and two women (S and Si) co-construct, at the close of a particularly virulent gossip session, the indignant narrative, which exhibits many of the characteristics of a "degradation ceremony" (Garfinkel 1956), of an elder's behavior during a recent Council of Elders' meeting. The tempo is fast, the pauses are short, and most turns are latched:

> S   *me ko mea katoa, mea katoa a:iloo::, koo:: ita ailoo maa hai mea:::,* =
> "because everything, absolutely everything, he is displeased by everything that,"
>
> T   = *Soko ki tena tamana,* =
> "He takes after his father,"
>
> Si   ((in background))   = mm, =
> "hmm,"

S   = ((falsetto, fast)) *Aku muna, "E tonu kkii*
eeloo!" ((creaky, high pitch)) *kae::-*
"I say, 'You're absolutely right!' but-"
(0.5)

F   *Kae, ko t- ko te:: aakoga o ia i te faiaakoga teelaa.*
"Also, it's what he learns from that teacher of his."
(2.0)

S   ((soft)) *Mm.* (1.0) *Tonu koe,*
"Hmm. You're right,"

F   *Teelaa i uta-* =
"Over there in the bush-"

S   = *Olotou fai aakoga konaa.*
"That's their teacher."
(1.0)

T   *Teketeke nee laatou a mea a te fenua.*
"They opposed everything that the island community wants to do."

S   ((mid-high pitch)) *Ailoga eeloo:: e:: isi ne mea e llei e:: toe: maua i:::*
"I doubt anything good will ever come out"
(1.5)

F   *manafai*   *e toko uke te lauvaaega*   *teelaa.*
    "if"   there are many from   that species."
               [   ]

S   *mana toko*   *uke te vaegaa (tino) ko=*   =*laa?*
    "if"   there are many of that   kind of people?"

[1985:1:A:129–143]

While we can identify in this fragment a leading gossiper, S, who describes the target of the gossip as someone who is constantly displeased with every decision made by the Council of Elders, other interlocutors explain this trait by claiming that it runs in the family (true to the workings of *pona*) and that the gossip target is imitating the community's black sheep, the one who lives "over there in the bush" (a location with fortuitous connotations of disorder and danger).

This kind of interaction is reminiscent of what Reisman (1974), in an early but enduring contribution to the Ethnography of Communication tradition, termed "contrapuntal conversation," referring to interactions that are co-constructed by several participants at once (also Brenneis 1987b; Watson-Gegeo and Boggs 1977).[6] Counterpoint typically operates in egalitarian contexts, and foregrounds both the sociability of the setting and the aesthetics of the discourse. On Nuku-laelae, contrapuntal exchanges take place when allusions are made to common-knowledge information rather than "new" gossip that one person divulges to uninformed others. By collaborating as coauthors in the production of the gossip, participants underscore the fact that they are of one mind and that they have the same affective responses to the content of the narrative. Convergence of opinion is so essential that adult audiences rarely disengage from gossip interactions by expressing disagreement or doubt about what the principal speaker is saying. Counterpoint in gossip has the effect of turning the activity into a joint effort, which fits well with central values of Nukulaelae society, in which individualistic endeavors and achievements meet little appreciation. The sheer pleasure that Nukulaelae Islanders find in being together and focusing on the same task is evident in gossip, where the joint construction of a good degradation ceremony and of the concomitant emotional tenor clearly fuels the conviviality and sociability shared by the participants. They highlight a warmth and interpersonal harmony that are not just desirable in gossip, but also essential to its success. Indeed, in order to gossip successfully, conversationalists must enlist their audience's cooperation in the development of the moral world that the gossip constructs (Brenneis 1984a). The creation of collusion between the author of the gossip and the audience is the driving motivation of contrapuntal organization.

The simultaneously pleasurable and dangerous quality of gossip means that initiating gossip has to be done delicately, and the boundary between "conversation" and "gossip" as events is just as blurred as the boundary between them as genres. It is indeed potentially hard work to turn a casual conversation, about the weather, the tides, the catch of the day, and the growth of swamp taro, into disparaging talk about the deeds of others (cf. Bergmann 1993, 86–91). Whenever the conversation focuses on other people, and even when it focuses on nonhuman subjects, it can suddenly turn to gossip, and conversationalists often appear to be on the lookout for the opportunity to turn casual conversation into derogatory talk. At any given moment, what is actually going on is largely subject to different interpretations about the speaker's intentions, and speakers themselves play on this ambiguity to negotiate the delicate balance between immorality and pleasure. The success of this play depends on whether gossipers can infuse the conversation with a particular affective quality: lowered voices, whispers, falsettos, bodies leaning in, and condescending laughter.[7]

The mastery of these skills is the subject of a short passage in one of the few colonial-era candid documents about Tuvalu, the autobiography of Lucille Iremonger, wife of the administrative officer for the Ellice Islands before the outbreak of World War II:

> The main trouble again, as with Falavi and Melitiana, was the native love of gossip, especially about other Europeans who had visited the island in the past. However plainly we had stated our dislike of it, they would work their way round by devious routes, and you suddenly found that you were nodding interestedly to a hair-raising piece of scandal. (Iremonger 1948, 132)[8]

The fact that "other Europeans" were the focus that Islanders chose for gossip with the colonial couple raises unanswerable questions about motives and dynamics, in light of the fact that the latter's worldview left little room for doubt about the righteousness of colonial hierarchies (both husband and wife would eventually become Tory MPs in Britain, the former an active advocate of capital punishment).

Not all attempts at gossip succeed, even when no outsiders are involved. The following example of a failed transformation of small talk into gossip illustrates the difficulties involved in creating and maintaining the quality required. The excerpt is part of a conversation between several adult men socializing around a cooking hut; when one of the men, T, hears a cracking noise down in the *pulaka* pit, he attempts in a tense tone to rally the other's interest in what may be suspicious activity:

T   ((fast)) *Ttino teelaa e pakeekee mai, e a ai te vai teelaa i feituu ki tua o saa*
    Ioopu?
    "[There is] someone making cracking noises, whose grove is it behind
    Ioopu's?"
    (2.0)
F   ((laconic)) *(o) Laapana,* =
    "(it's) Laapana's,"
T   = *Laapana? Me e isi ttino e pakeekee mai,* =
                                     "Laapana's? Because there is someone making
                                     cracking noises,"
K   ((mid-falsetto)) = *M- me ne vau hoki laa ki te umaga!*
    "an- and he's already been to the taro swamp!"
[1985:1:B:046–048]

In the first turn, T frames a question about the identity of the individual making noise in terms of the ownership of the banana grove from which the noise emanates, rather than simply asking who the person might be, suggesting that the person might not be where he should be, a suggestion that his fast tempo and level intonation contour accentuate. F does not take up the lead, since he knows that the person in the grove is its rightful owner. K, however, tries to rekindle the gossip on a different note, and does so in a mid-falsetto pitch that also suggests urgency: Laapana has already been to the taro swamp, and now he is again down in the banana grove, a zeal that is testing the bounds of common sense. (People who work too assiduously at a single task are labeled *fakavalevale* "asocial, crazy.") Both T and K tried to transform an innocuous exchange into gossip, but their efforts failed. The last turn was followed by a lengthy pause. The missing ingredient in both cases was the cooperation of the interlocutor, which neither T nor K was able to mobilize. Indeed, gossip and the emotional intensity necessary for its success is contingent upon interlocutors cooperating, and getting them to cooperate can be hard interactional work. Since gossip is at best morally tainted, people (men in particular) will generally need to be pretty certain that it is worth their while before they accept someone's invitation to gossip.

Information Withholding

There are several ways of encouraging one's audience to agree to switch from small talk to gossip. One is to simply flout social mores and initiate gossip, as F and K try to do in the previous extract. Through the urgency that their voice, tempo, and intonation convey, they attempt to get their interlocutor to respond with the same. This strategy is not the subtlest, in that it presupposes more interlocutor collusion than may be forthcoming, and it is potentially dangerous for those who are concerned about their public reputation. A subtler move consists of creating suspense in the narrative and drawing in the interlocutors through it. A common strategy for doing so is that I called in an early article "information withholding" (Besnier 1989), whereby a gossiper withholds an essential piece of information or proffers an ambiguous or problematic reference at strategic locations in the gossip interaction, commonly at the beginning, thereby "forcing" the interlocutor to ask for the missing piece of information. Most commonly, withheld information is the name of the person whom the gossip is going to be about, as in the following superb example of the discourse of egalitarianism I described in chapter 3, in which K begins to ridicule another man for showing off his *tautai* "fishing knowledge":

K   *A koo vau o fakatootoo mo tena tautai i aso nei.* =
    "And [he] comes along and [starts to] pontificate about how much fishing knowledge [he has]."

F   = *A ai?* =
                                                     "Who?"

K   = Manono.
[CONV 102:06]

This sequence of turns takes place after a long pause, and is thus the beginning of a new conversation. In the first turn of the sequence, K, a middle-aged man, initiates the gossip by introducing a new topic, referring to an individual by using a zero-pronoun (third-person pronouns are very commonly expressed by the absence of a referring expression) in the main clause and a possessive pronoun (tena *tautai* "*his* fishing-knowledge") in the subordinate clause. Lacking the background information to enable him to identify the referent of these pronouns, the interlocutor F asks whom K is referring to, and K provides the identification in the third turn.

The first turn of information-withholding sequences can be thought of as an invitation to the interlocutor to initiate what conversation analysts call a "repair."

These particular repairs are unusual in that they violate the cross-linguistic "preference" that repairs be resolved quickly, unobtrusively, and by the same person who uttered the problematic utterance in the first place, be it a hesitation, a slip of the tongue, or an outright error (Schegloff, Jefferson, and Sacks 1977). Clearly, in Nukulaelae gossip, something else is at stake: the frequency of information withholding in gossip, the predictability of where it occurs (usually at the point where small talk switches to gossip), and the predictability of the kind of missing information that triggers the withholding all conjure a more or less calculated conversational move on the part of the gossiper to recruit the active participation of his or her audience.[9]

Several other aspects of information withholding deserve mention. First, when the gossiper is confident that he or she has a good story that will capture interlocutors' attention, he or she can deploy quite a bit of gossip before giving interlocutors a chance to ask for the identity of the target. A particularly vivid example is the following narrative of an old lady's unfamiliarity with the trappings of modern life, in this case a flush toilet, while traveling away from the atoll. The gossiper refers to the old lady in the first turn with the expression *ttou fafinee*, literally "our woman," a common expression that conveys a mixture of empathy and condescension, and it is not until after she has told a fair bit of the narrative that participant V can ask, "Who?":

S   ((very high pitch)) *Kae aa laa aka ttou fafinee,* ((mid-high pitch)) *ulu ki loto i te: meaa,* (1.5) ((fast)) *tiko.*
"What about our woman, (she) walks into the thing [i.e., the toilet], she shits."
(2.0)
"*E aa koee na?*" ((normal tempo, normal pitch)) *Au e kilo atu nei, koo ggalo* hh *ana vae* hhhh *i loto i te poo::?* Hhh
"[I say to her,] 'What are you doing?' I look at her, she's got both her feet deep inside the toilet bowl."

All   ((laughter)) =
V   = *A ai?*
"Who?"

S   ((high pitch)) *A Saavave!* hh hh hh hh hhh
"Saavave!"
((very high pitch)) "*Saavave ee! E aa?*" hh *ttaa!*
"'Saavave! What's going on?' Hey,"
Iaa ia hee iloa o ppaki te mea! ((mid-high pitch)) *kae* ((normal pitch)) *teenei laa tena vae i loto* hh *o te* hhhh *poo* ( ). hh ((laughter))
"She doesn't know how to flush, so there she is with her foot inside the toilet bowl."

V   ((breathy)) *E akaaka ana tae* hh *kee ggalo ki lalo.*
     "She's kicking down her shit to make it go down."
     (2.0)

S   ((very high pitch)) *Kee-* hh *kee ggalo ki lalo::!*
     "To make it go down."
     Ttaapaa ee! ((normal pitch)) *Mata eeloo, ttamaa ee!*
     "I swear, that woman!"

[CONV 108:08]

The high pitch that S uses to finally reveal the identity of the target also illustrates the dramatic suspense that information withholding generates, further heightened in this case by the humor of the narrative, to which everyone responds with derisive laughter.

A second notable feature of these gossip strategies is that gossipers can keep their audience guessing about the identity of the target of the gossip by failing to identify it fully even after being prompted to do so. In the following excerpt from a gossip interaction about an older male relative of the conversationalists who is being stingy with his radio, the gossiper's interlocutor asks who the gossip is about, but the gossiper only identifies him with an insult, *a puunana hoki teelaa!* "that asshole again," forcing another interlocutor to offer a guess about who the person might be in the last turn:

S   *Ko au i ei, fakalogo mai i te leet:ioo e tagi atu,* (3.0) *me ulu mai maaua ki loto i te fale kae taamate aka tena leetioo!*
     "Me, I heard that the radio was playing, so I came into the house [to listen to it], but then he just turned it off!"

T   *A ai?*
     "Who?"

S   *A puunana hoki teelaa!*
     "That asshole again!"

V   *Neli?*
     "(You mean) Neli?"

[CONV 111:07]

This kind of delayed identification accomplishes two tasks at once: it increases the suspense and it allows the gossiper to provide a derogatory description of the gossip target, which she or he must nevertheless do with some caution because bad-mouthing others too overtly is disruptive of the social and moral order.

A third noteworthy characteristic of information withholding demonstrates its usefulness as an attention-getting device and a tension-building mechanism. After the gossiper discloses the identity of the target, it is very common for the interlocutor(s) to react with a dramatic expression of disapproving amazement. The all-purpose expression of surprise and exasperation *ttaapaa ee!* often occurs there, or a comment that the interlocutor provides with a dramatic voice quality. In the following excerpt, the interlocutor responds to the disclosure with an incredulous *e aa?*, literally "what?":

K   ((whisper)) *Ae (muimui) hoki naa a te- te::-*
"And then there was a complaint from the- the::-"
            ((chuckle))
            [   ]
F   ((whisper, smiling)) *A ai?*
                  "Who?"
K   ((high pitch)) *Aalisi mo Faalogo!* =
     "Aalisi and Faalogo!"
K   ((mid-high pitch, whisper))   = *E aa:?*
     "Don't tell me!"
[CONV 112:06]

Information withholding is so prevalent in Nukulaelae gossip that, besides the interactional "work" that it accomplishes, it serves as an index through which gossipers announce to their audience, "This is gossip" or "I am now initiating gossip," reminiscence of the Goffmanian notion of "frame" (1974). Such is the work of indexes in language: multifunctional and multilayered, they signal stance, affect, and genre all at once (Silverstein 2003).

Information withholding emerges in at least one other interactional genre, teasing, which occurs frequently in Nukulaelae social life, in tune with the general love of talk as a regulator of social relations. In teasing, the teaser often withholds the punch line from the generally unsuspecting "victim," thus encouraging the latter to elicit the playful insult. One particular type of teasing that is particularly well suited for this routine is called *fakkata ffula* (*fakkata* "to make [others] laugh," *ffula* "bloated"); it consists in implying that the "victim" is socializing in an inappropriate way with his or her classificatory cross-sibling (particularly patrilineal or matrilineal cousins of the opposite sex), a relationship that normatively calls for a classic kind of respectful avoidance *(fakammalu)*. This kind of teasing is "close to the bone" and can easily lead to offense, and it should not take place if the cross-sibling is within earshot.[10] The following anecdote is a particularly striking example of the importance of information withholding in teasing. I was at festivities in the *maneapa*, which included a Western-style dance party (*tuisi*, from "twist") that was about to begin, when I saw a woman in her seventies leaving. As politeness calls for, I asked her where she was going, but then added a *fakkata ffula* line (the following is from my field notes):

N	*L, e aa? Kaa fano koe o moe?*
	"So, L, you're off to sleep?"
L	*Oo, au e fano o fakamoe oku mokopuna.*
	"Yes, I'm off to put my grandchildren to bed."
N	*See nofo koe kee tuisi koulua mo K?*
	"You're not staying to dance with K [her equally elderly cross-sibling]?"

One bystander found my repartee utterly hilarious, for several reasons: the age of the woman and her cross-sibling made the image of dancing together particularly funny, in addition to their being in an avoidance relationship, and the age of my "victim" made the teasing particularly risqué, in part because of the incongruity of the white man having enough kinship knowledge to construct the teasing. When he re-created the interaction in my presence for the enjoyment of others, he inserted an information-withholding sequence into the dialogue as follows (also from field notes):

N	*See nofo koe kee tuisi koulua?*
	"You're not staying so that the two of you can dance?"
L	*Maaua mo oi?*
	"Me and who?"
N	*Koulua mo K?*
	"You and K?"

Had I been a more competent teaser, I probably would have constructed the dialogue as he re-created it, inviting the "victim" to elicit the punch line.

Placing information withholding within the ideological context in which gossipers deploy their narratives on Nukulaelae, we note several dynamics. First, information withholding provides a dramatic framework to the gossip, making it worthwhile for interlocutors to engage in what morality tells them is not a proper thing to do. The fact that interlocutors have to fish for information that the gossiper has not divulged but that is essential to the intelligibility of the narrative makes them complicit in the deployment of the narratives and allows the gossiper to manipulate the interlocutors into taking an active role in the co-production of the gossip, thereby dissipating the responsibility for engaging in an activity that all know is immoral. Assigning a manipulative function to withholding sequences does not necessarily imply that they are intentional activities although, as noted earlier, there is evidence that they are at least in some circumstances.

While engaging in gossip, conversationalists have two options at their disposal: they may either involve everyone in the production of the gossip, or they may redefine the activity as something other than gossip. Withholding sequences (and probably other micro-organizational strategies) offer both options at once. On the one hand, their collusive effect ensures that both the gossiper and his or her interlocutors are involved in the production of gossip. On the other, withholding sequences dilute the gossiper's responsibility in the production of the gossip. Until the interlocutor requests a specific identification of the central element, the speaker may pose as simply divulging common knowledge, which he or she does with as much indexicality as can be afforded.

Animating Voices

A striking aspect of gossip narratives on Nukulaelae is the extent to which they consist of reported dialogues, in which narrated voices carry not only the narrative of events, but also the moral and emotional quality of events, people, and deeds. These characteristics demand analytic attention.

Reported speech in written and spoken language has been the object of much attention in literary criticism and sociolinguistics.[11] Linguistic anthropologists who have studied reported speech have sought inspiration from the work (long neglected until its revival in the 1980s) of Russian formalist literary theorist Mikhail Bakhtin, who in the 1930s already insisted that there is no such thing as neutral discourse (Bakhtin 1981; also Medvedev 1985; Voloshinov 1978). All utterances are embedded in a particular context and derive their meaning from this context. In particular, utterances have the potential of articulating the multiple voices that are part of the context of utterance, each of which can potentially be charged with ideological meaning, a process that Bakhtin termed "heteroglossia." Sometimes these voices can be disambiguated by the fact that they are associated with different languages or dialects (as in Tolstoy's *War and Peace,* which Bakhtin famously analyzed) or with different characters in a reported dialogue, but in other instances the distinction between voices is opaque and ambiguous, yet heteroglossia suffuses the text (C. Briggs 1992; Hill 1995; Irvine 1996). All discourse, for Bakhtin, is heteroglossic, in the sense that it articulates past and future relevant discourse, although different genres and instances of discourse differ in terms of the extent to which this heteroglossia is transparent. The resulting overall epistemological effect is what Bakhtin termed "dialogism." These characteristics of speech reporting have led Deborah Tannen to prefer the term "constructed dialogue" to the term "reported speech" (1989, 1), capturing (in a way that I suspect Bakhtin would have applauded) the extent to which voices interpenetrate one another in reported dialogues.

Nukulaelae gossipers typically structure their gossip narratives as sequences of reported turns, even when verbal actions are less important to the events than nonverbal actions, so that reported speech can be viewed as the primary action-reporting device. The following excerpt is taken from the narrative of a confrontation between the gossiper and a young female relative who had recently "married well" and as a result was beginning to put on airs. Backgrounding the narrative was a wrongful allegation that the young woman had made to the effect that the gossiper had chopped down banana trees he was not entitled to chop down, and a third party, whom I call Samasone, relates this allegation to the gossiper, who begins his narrative with this encounter. The narrative is carried forward almost entirely by reported speech:

> K   *Koo fakafetaui ifo Samasone au. "ššš! Au e ssili atu hua kia koe i te:: fekau*
> *nei a: Luisa ne hai mai kee taaofi koe i te:: te faamanatuga."*
> "Samasone came down to meet me. (He said) 'Hey! I just want to ask you about Luisa's request that you should be prevented from (taking) communion.'"
> *"Io? I te aa?"*
> "[I said] 'Oh? And why?'"
> *Me i te tala teelaa ne hai i: i: i futi kolaa o: laatou ne taa nee au.*
> "[He said that] it was about the story to the effect that that I chopped down some banana trees of theirs."
> *Aku muna "ttaa, a ko au nei e- e(i) he tino fakavalevale?"*
> "I said, 'Come on, am I crazy or what?'"
> [1982:1:13–14]

Direct quotation—the representation of quoted discourse as an unmodified representation of its original occurrence—is much more frequent than indirect quotation, which occurs mainly when a narrator provides a quotation within another, as in the third line in the above excerpt. Thus Nukulaelae speakers prefer what Voloshinov (1978) called a "linear style," in which the grammar helps maintain a clear distinction between authorial and reported voices, reflecting a concern that reported dialogue represent original utterances authentically.

The same concern is also reflected in the role of speech-act expressions as framing devices for reported speech. The most common speech-act expression is a noun phrase that consists of the noun *muna* "word" in the plural, modified by a possessive phrase denoting the identity of the person whose utterance is reported (e.g., *ana muna*, literally, "his words [were]"). The speech-act expression and the quoted string form an equational structure (equivalent to the copula uses of "be" in English):

> K   *Muna a Tito "Ia, naa ttoki laa ttuaakoi!"*
> "Tito said, 'OK, get that boundary-marker planted, then!'"

However, dialogues in gossip can simply consist of sequences of directly reported turns at talking, without speech-act expressions. The gossiper distinguishes the different reported turns by ventriloquizing the speakers' voice qualities and intonations. The following excerpt from a gossip narrative of events that took place on Funafuti (hence the reference to the airstrip) is a typical example:

V   ((whisper)) *(aku muna,) "Sss! taaua kaa alo!"*
       "(I say,) 'Hey! let's go!'"
       Muna a Moose, "Ki fea?"
       "Moose says, 'Where to?'"
       "Taa alo ki te malae. ((normal voice, addressing someone else)) Pasoni!
       Maaua nei (kaati) kaa ttipa aka peelaa."
       "'Let's go to the airstrip. Pasoni! We are off that way to the airport.'"
       ((animated)) *"E aa?!"*
       "'What [did you say]!?'"
       ((normal tempo)) *"Maaua nei kaa tipattipa aka peelaa ki te airport i koo."*
       "'We're off that way to the airport.'"
       ((high pitch)) *"Io!"*
       "'OK!'"
       ((normal pitch, quiet)) *Saasaale laa maalie.*
       "We walk slowly."
       "Taatou kaa nnofo loo i se koga, kaa mmai loa a tino nei mo olotou pati,
       taatou see::i eiloa se fia fakalogollogo e tasi ki olotou-."
       "'Let's sit down somewhere, and if other people always come and want to
       talk at us, we'll act as if we have absolutely no interest in listening to what
       they want to-.'"
       E muna aka, ((mid-high pitch)) "Taatou see fia fakalogollogo ki lotou mea."
       "He says, 'We'll won't want to listen to what they want to say.'"
       [1985:4:B:078–083]

The gossiper here pays minute attention to the details of the reported dialogue. His dramatic animation includes vocalizations with no referential meaning (e.g., *sss!* "hey!"), requests for clarification that his interlocutor presumably made in the original dialogue (e.g., *ki fea?* "where to?" *e aa?!* "what [did you say]?"), vocatives (e.g., *Pasoni!*), and confirmatory back-channel cues (e.g., *io!* "OK!"). The painstaking care with which he performs the dialogue bears witness to an extreme concern for presenting a seemingly unedited verbal transcript, a concern that is deeply grounded in local communicative ideology.

The preponderance of reported dialogues in gossip serves as a dual index. First, like information withholding, it "entextualizes" (Bauman and Briggs 1990) the ongoing performance in past interactions that exhibit similar characteristics, that is, to other gossip sessions. Second, it grounds the narrative in interactions purported to have taken place in real-life settings. As many researchers have demonstrated (e.g., Hill and Irvine 1993; Tannen 1989), reported speech can provide a compelling sense of dramaturgic reality. In the case of Nukulaelae gossip, which occupies a fragile position in the local moral economy, this feature is crucial: attention to the interactional details of reported dialogues subtly provides the legitimacy and credibility of a real-life happening, thus deflecting the morally tainted character of gossip activities (cf. Bauman [1986] on "tall tales" in small-town Texas). In other words, reported dialogues help frame the gossip as something other than gossip while at the same time indexing it in the particular genre of gossip, and thus provide a solution to the gossiper's moral dilemma.

While purporting to provide a "true" representation of dialogues that took place in the past, gossipers also use the indexical means available to them to color their gossip with affect, and embed this affect in morality. One obvious such index is intonation, which is by nature "fundamentally emotive" (Bolinger 1982, 530). On Nukulaelae, as in many other societies, high pitch, flaring timbre, and a fast rate of speech are all associated with subjectively active feelings, while low affect is associated with low pitch, soft voice, and a slow rate of speech. These associations are also morally charged: people associate the former with unpredictability, anger, and lack of control, while the latter are constitutive of the overelaborated *fiileemuu* "peace," *feaalofani* "mutual empathy, harmony," and *gali* "beauty." Well-adjusted adults do not let their emotions and internal states interfere with their social relations: they remain calm and predictable. The poorly socialized are absorbed in their personal emotions and let them govern their actions.

These linkages suffuse gossip. Gossipers generally cast others in a negative light, not by making negative comments about them (although it does happen), but by reporting their utterances with "nonsegmental" characteristics (i.e., characteristics that are not part of the grammatical or lexical structure of the language) that portray them as emotionally erratic, angry, and out of control. Observe the high pitch, animated tempo, and whispered voice quality of the reported speech in the following narrative of the old lady unable to cope with the flush toilet:

S ((normal pitch, normal tempo)) *Muna mai* ((high pitch, animated tempo))
"PPAKI-! PPAKI-!"
"[She] tells [her]: 'Flush! flush!'"
((whisper)) *"Taapaa ee!* ((very high pitch)) *A te mea laa maa ppuna mai kia AKU!"*
"'Hey! But the (water) is going to jump at me!'"
[1985: CONV 108, p. 5]

Prosodic structure is thus one of the primary means through which Nukulaelae gossipers communicate affect in reported discourse, as well as the moral value of this affect. Crucially, it is also one of the levels of linguistic structure that most effectively eludes "metapragmatic awareness" (Silverstein 1981) and, in consequence, one for which speaker responsibility is least imputable. Prosodics is a level of linguistic structure at which the voice of the reporter is allowed to infiltrate the reported discourse. Gossip narratives organize events and people on a moral map, and do so with indexical tools that are maximally difficult to pin down.

In a similar vein, the pragmatic organization of quotes (length, degree of planning, rhetorical style) is a level of structure at which gossipers encode morally laden affect. In the following, which continues the banana-tree-chopping allegation, the gossiper narrates the final discussion he has with his accuser. The quoted conversation consists of two turns, his own and his accuser's, which have radically different qualities:

K *Aku muna "Luisa, lle:i, (0.3) i au ne m- manako kee: fetaui taaua i Fagaua kae:- mea aka laa koe koo tele mai ki Oolataga.*
"I said, 'Luisa, good [that we are running into each other], because I wanted to meet you on Fagaua [the main village] but- the thing is that you had escaped over here to Olataga."
(1.2) Ko au fua e: faipati atu kiaa koe ki luga i te: (0.3) peelaa mo tau: fekau ne avatu nee Samasone.'
"I just wanted to talk to you about, like, your complaint to Samasone.'"
(2.2)
((high pitch)) *Muna mai "io-, ((fast)) io- io-!"*
"She says, 'Yes, oh, yes- yes-!'"
((laughter))
(Muna) hh a t̪ou fafi(ne)!
"The woman said!"
[1982:1:36–37]

The speaker's self-reported turn at speaking has many features characteristic of "planned" discourse (Ochs 1979a): the turn is long, the sentences are complex, the tone is poised, and repetitions of words and repairs are kept to a minimum. The turn also has the prolix quality characteristic of rhetorical performances (which I will discuss in the next chapter). The turn that the gossiper attributes to his accuser has the opposite characteristics: it is short, full of repetitions, and erratic in tempo as it speeds up halfway through. As the narrative progresses, the representation of the gossiper's opponent digs her moral grave deeper and deeper. After tripping, fumbling, and backtracking, she finally declares harboring no hard feelings, while in fact it is the gossiper who is entitled to harbor such feelings, and the gossiper suggests that they apologize to one another (*fakatau fakamaagalo*, literally, "exchange apologies"), even though the gossiper has nothing about which to apologize:

K   *Muna mai. 'Koo hee:ai- HEE:ai he: mea e:* (0.7) *onosai e:i-'*
      "[She] says to me, 'There is nothing- no harbored bad feelings any more.'"
      (M)una: au, (0.7) *fakatau fakamaagalo nei taaua.* ((laughter))
      "I say, 'Let us forgive each other now.'"
      [1982:1:46–49]

By attributing to different people rhetorical styles associated with specific moralities, the gossiper assigns moral attributes to them. The rhetorical style of quotes
allows the gossiper's voice to "leak" onto the quote in heteroglossic fashion, but to
do so in imperceptible fashion, while the gossiper presents himself as deploying
"just the facts."

Laughter

Laughter does not just simply communicate inner joy; "in fact, often it does
not even do this" (Billig 2005, 189). Substantial work on laughter in sociology and
cultural anthropology has stressed that there is nothing simple about laughter,
but one thing it is not is a "spontaneous" or precultural action. Instead, laughter
is deeply embedded in culture, particularly morality, and is suffused with intersubjectivity (Apte 1985; Billig 2005; Norrick 1995). Yet laughter *appears* to be a
spontaneous event, and it is precisely this cultural-yet-natural quality that turns
it into a particularly attractive index of morality in Nukulaelae gossip, where it
appears frequently. While it is difficult, if not counterproductive, to try to attribute
a specific meaning to laughter where it occurs (such is the nature of indexes), its
presence alone may be interpreted as a significant factor.

Nukulaelae Islanders talk a lot about laughing and smiling (*kata*, a term that
encompasses both), elaborating them as markers of desirable sociability and predictability, of one's willingness to contribute to the peacefulness and beauty of society. People are praised for being *mata katakata*, literally "having a laughing appearance," which usually forms a pair with another term, *mata fiafia* "appear happy,"
both antonyms of *mata itaita* "dour-faced, prone to contrariety." Even though the
default morality of laughter is positive, there are many types of laughter, some more
"sociable" in intent than others. At one extreme is the very loud whooping laughter
in the *maneapa* in response to an old woman's lewd antics during a dance performance or an old man's joke (*tala fakkata* "funny story") in a middle of a speech,
laughter that begins and ends in perfect unison, three hundred voices perfectly
coordinated. Similar unison, superb icon of togetherness, is performed in many
different contexts, such as the *faatele* song-and-dance performances I described in
chapter 2, or the loud monophonic but multivocal and perfectly timed voicing of
annoyance and disgust referred to as *aali ("TTAAAA!!")* at a child's unruly behavior or at the morally reprehensible sight of a teenager's spirit possession.

Laughter emerges in a variety of contexts, particularly in response to jokes, predictably. But jokes on Nukulaelae are almost always about real events involving known people, sometimes even the teller him- or herself in the case of a self-deprecating story, but more commonly others.[12] A large repertoire of funny stories concern embarrassing mishaps that particular people met with in the sometimes distant past, such as losing one's lavalava in public, getting a fishhook stuck in one's penis, or not knowing how to switch lights on and off when visiting modern locations. These funny stories form a canon of formidable longevity and become part of one's personal *pona* as well as the *pona* of one's descendants, who can be teased mercilessly long after the death of the unfortunate protagonist. Known to everyone, these stories are nevertheless reiterated periodically, sometimes only with a one- or two-word allusion, enough to provoke great hilarity. Fresh funny stories are sometimes broadcast nationally on one of the most popular programs on Radio Tuvalu, *Tala Fakkata* "Funny Stories." Throughout my years of fieldwork, an elderly Nukulaelae Islander named Peifaga, resident of Funafuti who informally claimed the role of national trickster, would host the program, inviting a guest or two to the studio to narrate mishaps that they had heard through the grapevine, or that people had telegraphed from the outer islands to Peifaga. People finding themselves in an embarrassing situation sometimes expressed apprehension that someone would report their story to Peifaga for national broadcasting, although often in good humor. I appeared in several of these stories, usually as an agent of modernity. In one, Nukulaelae young men visiting Funafuti had watched the video of a B-rated action film called *Above the Law,* in which Steven Seagal plays a character named Nico. When they returned to Nukulaelae, they told my adoptive mother, Sina, that they had seen me in a film, partaking in deadly car races and shooting people indiscriminately (in contrast to my "peaceful" behavior on the atoll), a story that Sina swallowed wholesale. Sina's gullibility articulated the belief (common among less-worldly Tuvaluans) that there can only be few people out there with the same name and that movies represent real-life events that happen to occur while the camera is running, all of which made superb fodder for Peifaga's program.[13]

Some stories and some retellings are more edgy than others, and laughter varies from the good-hearted to the cutting. It is to the latter kind that I now turn. Laughter is common in gossip designed to ridicule others, and it occurs in a variety of ways. First, people sometimes refer to laughter, commonly their own, since laughing is positive and moral. In the following excerpt, the gossiper relates an interaction that had taken place during a Council of Elders' debate about how to organize a feast in honor of dignitaries who were coming on the next ship to visit. One elder, whom I call Manono and who did not belong to either village moiety, argued in the meeting that communal labor should be organized by moiety, which the gossiper states made him laugh, since the argument would have had the effect of relieving Manono of having to provide food for the communal feast:

F   *Ee- ee Saapolu, a (k)o au e: kata,* (3.5) *ttaaofi o Manono t(eel)aa: (e) tau*
      fakatuu mai, kee faa ituuala,
      "Hey, Sapolu! And it makes me laugh, the suggestion that Manono keeps
      making that [the work] be distributed by moieties,"
      kae heea(i) laa he ituuala e fh:ano i h ei hhhh!
      "and he doesn't even belong to a moiety!" ((laughter))
      [CONV 102:03, 1:A:157]

Second, and more frequently, gossipers enact laughter in and around the narrative, in a variety of forms (e.g., chuckling, chortling, sniggering). Such laughter can
overlay reported turns of the narrative, providing an unspoken, indexically super-
posed editorial voice, to which the gossip interlocutor sometimes responds with
an explicitly articulated moral commentary about the target of the gossip:

K   *Hanatu nei Lootau ssili atu teehee Sulu,* (0.6)
      "Lotau comes around and asks where Sulu is,"
      ((high pitch)) *muna mai* ((mid-high pitch)) *e galo i te umu.*
      "he says she's not in the cooking hut."
      (0.6) *Aku muna koo atuli eiloa a ia n(ee) thena* ha.hha.hha.h
      "I said, 'She was chased away by her ((laughter))'"
                              (*au* hahaha e hehehe)   .hhh
                        [   ]
F   ((mid-high pitch))   *Ko te fia pule: laa::-*
                              "She just tries to be so bossy-"
      [CONV 113:07, 0:B:629]

As conversation analysts have demonstrated (Jefferson 1979, 1984; Sacks 1978),
there is a clear systematicity to locating laughter, a systematicity that is particularly effective here given on the one hand the positive value attributed to it and on
the other its spontaneous and unplanned appearance. Laughter is rhetoric (Billig
2005, 189–192), and, like all rhetoric, it is designed to persuade while appearing to
be doing something else.

    The third noteworthy aspect of the organization of laughter in gossip on the
atoll is its frequent occurrence as the gossiper "trails off" in his or her narrative,
gradually replacing segmental material (i.e., words organized in sentences) with
laughter, thus failing to provide a conclusion to the narrative. Such is the case in
the previous example, in which the gossiper appears to be about to provide an
evaluative judgment of his opponent, an explicit guidance to his interlocutor of
how the latter should evaluate the situation and the person being denigrated, but
stops short of doing so, his voice gradually giving way to laughter, leaving it up to
his interlocutor to provide the final incrimination and confirming the success of

the gossip insofar as it has rallied the interlocutor's alignment with the gossiper against the target of the gossip. Laughter thus replaces what would otherwise be the most explicitly damning, and thus most sensitive, segment of the narrative, distancing the gossiper from a socially disapproved act of denigrating others and undermining communal togetherness (cf. Jefferson's [1979] analysis of laughter overlaying and distorting obscenities).

Lastly, it is not only gossip narrators who laugh, but also interlocutors. The gossiper may "invite" other people to laugh by laughing, or interlocutors may begin laughing, ambiguously indexing appreciation for a good gossip story, amusement about other people's self-inflicted embarrassment, moral condemnation of the target of the gossip, alignment with the narrator, or the pleasure of sociability. In the following, narrator L complains about a young married couple's antisocial behavior, selfishly wanting to spend time together rather than with the rest of the family as is normally expected. The complaint ends with an allegation that all they want to do is to have sex and bear children (why else would a couple want to be alone?), an allegation that generates a general guffaw:

L   ((mid-high pitch, fast)) *Telaa mea mo Iee::liko i (te) f:ai mea maassei i (   )*
      fakaffua laa tama:, =
      "Those two and their habit of doing bad things [i.e., having sex] in (   )
      they go and make children ="
      [

S   *hm hm hmhmhmhmhmh*
      "((laughter))"

M (falsetto)) = *ihm   ihhhhhhhhhhm   hmhmhmhmhmh*
S   [   ]
L   *hm hm hm hm   hm*
S   = *teenaa!*
                           "That's it!"

      (0.5)
      .HHHHH =
      "((laughter))"
M = *.hhh iiiiii*
      "((laughter))"
[CONV 118:26:46, 5:B:187]

Laughter thus provides important nonsegmental tools that enable gossipers and interlocutors to walk the fine line between the conflicting moral groundings of gossip. Available to all present, laughter is carefully organized over and around verbal material, contributing to the heteroglossic quality of the gossip in powerful yet efficient and disembodied fashion.

Knowing How to Gossip

All utterances, Bakhtin argued in the early decades of the twentieth century, are potentially suffused with a multitude of prior utterances, each associated with different voices, persons, moral stances, and historical precedents. However, the resulting heteroglossia can be subtle and complex, as voices loom circumspectly over utterances, hidden in difficult-to-pin-down indexicality, operating in the intersubjectivity of the discourse. Nukulaelae gossip is no exception. Embedded in different ways of gossiping on the atoll is the imprint of the moral instability of gossip: pleasurable and dangerous, gossip is moral talk about moral deeds, but at what point does the immorality of engaging in it becomes more serious than the immorality of the deeds it chronicles? The answer to this question is shifting and contingent, which makes gossip both exciting and scary. Gossipers can easy misjudge situations and interlocutors. But the consequences of misjudging are different for different people. If you are a morally upstanding and politically ambitious member of community and congregation, the consequences can be serious. But if you have little social standing because of your youth, gender, biography, or ancestry, then gossip can become your one fragile claim on other people's attention. This is what I turn to in the next chapter.

"Skilled gossiping is done in such a way that the speaker either conceals the fact that he is gossiping or else behaves in such a way that no-one can possibly say that he is gossiping. The unskilled gossip leaves himself open to accusations of malice and consequently his words are ineffective" (Bailey 1971b, 300–301). What I have done in this chapter is to demonstrate how, in the context of Nukulaelae at least, these concerns for concealment and subterfuge are implemented in the microscopic form of gossip. Using tools from conversation analysis, but departing from that analytic tradition by focusing on how the organization of conversation embodies the ideological world in which it is embedded, I have demonstrated that information management, reported speech, intonation, voice quality, and laughter all provide multiple layers of meaning, which are always open to ambiguous and multiple interpretation, true to the heteroglossic and uneasy nature of gossip. These interactional tools locate meaning-making in an intersubjective space, not only the intersubjective space that gossipers create in the act of gossiping, but also the intersubjective space that agents re-create and animate in narrative dialogues.

Intersubjectivity figures prominently not just in gossip but also in many other aspects of social life that have preoccupied anthropologists since the late nineteenth century, even though the term "intersubjective" may not appear in their analytic repertoire. Take, for example, exchange, which has been treated across divergent analytic perspectives since Marcel Mauss' 1925 paradigmatic essay (Mauss 1967) as a fundamentally fraught social fact, loaded with both pleasure and danger, potentially generative of both solidarity and humiliation. Decades ago, Bailey (1971a, 1971b) captured the relevance of this ambiguity by showing that gossip is in fact a form of exchange, thus inheriting the anxieties that envelop exchange in general. Is one's audience going to receive gossip as gift or poison? What I have added to the insights that gossip inherits both the pleasure and danger of exchange is a demonstration of how, in one society, agents deploy particular microscopic aspects of interaction to cope with the ambiguity and incertitude of the intersubjective in gossip as exchange.

This microanalysis provides a useful perspective on the old debate that pitched structural-functionalists against transactionalists I summarized at the beginning of this book, the former claiming that gossip integrates people with one another, the latter maintaining that gossip is all about one-upmanship, interpersonal competition, and negative reciprocity with informational commodities. Social psychologists Sabini and Silver (1982) attempted to solve the disagreement by arguing that collusion is what gossip creates as a *process*, while one-upmanship is its *product*. My microanalysis confirms their insight that the two approaches are not mutually exclusive, but it also shows that drawing a distinction between process and product does not solve the disagreement. In the process of gossiping, Nukulaelae people create both collusion and one-upmanship: they manipulate their audience into collaborating in the production of the gossip, but they also claim control of a juicy story. But like all social designs, collusion and one-upmanship as products are fragile, temporary, and unfinished. What will prevent someone who has colluded with you in a gossip moment from laughing at you after you go home? What ensures the longevity of the personal triumph you obtain from impressing others with how well informed you are and making them laugh at other people's expense?

5 The Twenty-Dollar Piglets

THROUGHOUT THE ANALYSIS of the structure of gossip that I developed in the previous chapter, I insistently returned to the contingent nature of gossip: whether it takes place or not, how abrasive or indirect it is, and the particular tools that gossipers employ all depend on a variety of contextual concerns. One of these contextual concerns is who is in charge of it: some people are good at it while others are less enthusiastic or skilled, some have a great deal to lose if caught spreading false rumors while others don't, and some suffer from familial *pona* that imprison them in the image of an incorrigible gossiper, no matter what they do.

There is a clear inverse relationship between, on the one hand, a person's aspiration and opportunity to be viewed as an upstanding member of the community and, on the other, a person's enthusiasm for gossip, particularly in producing it. Like all bad deeds, gossip can land one in trouble, be it through embarrassment, a lawsuit, exclusion from church communion, or the loss of church or political office. Reputation is thus doubly implicated in gossip: most straightforwardly, gossip puts the reputation of its target on the line; more subtly, the gossiper's own reputation as a troublemaker and a teller of tall tales is also on the line, where it competes with the possibility that he or she will also be viewed as a trickster whose humorous company others find desirable.

I turn here to the analysis of an incident that revolved around a very brief gossip session that took place during my 1985 fieldwork. My analysis of the incident enables an exploration of how texts articulate with reputation, morality, the truth, personhood, and large-scale forces. In this process, I mobilize the microscopic tools for the analysis of gossip talk that I developed in chapter 4 to demonstrate how they can help us understand these various articulations. Indeed, analyzing the formal structure of gossip talk is not an end, but a means of apprehending issues of more general import. But first I must make a brief excursus to explore what gossip maximally contrasts with, formally, ideologically, and contextually: oratory.

What Gossip Is Not: Poetics and Antipoetics

Discourse genres are permeable categories, in that they never operate in isolation from one another (Keane 2003, 240). For instance, intimate talk has the potential of leaking into various forms of public talk (as when gossip "gets out," as I discuss later in this chapter) and vice versa; within the same event, people can "genre-switch" or laminate different genres, as when casual conversation subtly turns into gossip; and people are always potentially aware, when they use a particular genre, that they are not using other genres. It is to this last form of simultaneous permeability and incommensurability that I turn, by asking, From what kind of talk does gossip differ?

The most radically divergent ideology of interaction from the one that operates in gossip is found in public talk on Nukulaelae. Speeches in the *maneapa*, family homes, Council of Elders meetings, Island Council meetings, village-moiety meetings, meetings of church deacons, meetings of the multitude of interest groups that continually emerge and disappear, family meetings, church sermons, and radio-telephone conversations all fall into a broad category of "public speaking," characterized by a number of recurrent interactional and organizational features: calm, orderliness, an emphasis on clear turn-taking (only one person speaks at a time; interruptions are rare), a high degree of fluency, a rich vocabulary replete with borrowings from Samoan, and long, complex, and complete sentences. Oratorical performances in the *maneapa* are perhaps the best illustration of public talk, the *maneapa* being also called *te fale o muna* "the house of words." Utilizing a genre called *laauga* (a term that also applies to church sermons; see Besnier 1995, 125–128), these performances are primarily the domain of elderly men, and occasionally adult women. Younger people who would attempt to make a speech in the *maneapa* under other than the most exceptional circumstances would be quickly shut up with scandalized exclamations of "*te tautalaitiiti!*" ("the impertinence, the insolence," a word borrowed from Samoan). *Laauga* punctuate the very frequent feasts, dance performances, and other communal events referred to as *mea a te fenua*, literally, "things that the community does," which always mobilize the enthusiastic participation of most of the atoll's population. After communal meals in the *maneapa* or *fakaala*, orators from alternative village moieties deliver a series of *laauga*; between dance numbers (during which almost everyone either sings or dances), they get up to "rest" (*fakamaanava*) the dancers and singers. Getting to their feet from their seated position on the floor against posts supporting the high-status inner square of the *maneapa* (*pou loto*) or more rarely around its lower-status portico (*poletito*), orators commonly begin by calling out the name of a senior member of the opposite moiety and then launch into a formal opening, which in its most refined form is referred to as a *fakalagilagi*. The following was one of many speeches delivered by the *ulu fenua* Faiva in 1985, on that occasion to bid farewell to the island's member of Parliament leaving for Funafuti after a particularly tense reelection:

Nafatali! Ia, e fakamaaloo fakafetai moo te poo o taatou, koo nofoaki te mmalu o te fale.

"Nafatali! Indeed, thanks and congratulations for this evening of ours, the respectfulness of the house is acknowledged."

Ia, fakafetai moo te fuafuaga teenaa koo oti ne maallie fakatasi a taatou ki ei, kaati koo lava kae ttoe a te fakaasiiga o te loto fiafia o taatou, fakamaavaeega i te toe poo teenei.

"Indeed, thank you for the thoughts [in previous speeches] that we have enjoyed together, perhaps we have amply demonstrated the happiness of our hearts, [in] this farewell on the occasion of the last evening."

Peelaa laa mo aofaga me ko fakanofoga o te fenua o taatou.

"According to the desires and decisions of this community of ours."

Ia, kae e fakamaaloo foki ki toeaina mai te taeao eiloa, laauga kolaa koo oti ne paak-kuu i loto i te fale, kee fakattau katoa moo te- te sui o taatou i te vaai taimi teenei, io mo ko te maaloo foou teelaa kaa maua, i te toe tuuakaaga nei.

"Indeed, thanks in addition to the old men from the very morning, speeches that have been pronounced within the house, that were commensurate with the- the parliamentary representative of ours at this time, as well as the new government that is going to be constituted, in this last reunion." [Maneapa Speeches Faiva 1985:219]

Rhetorically beautifully formed, elegantly delivered with virtually no hesitations or stumbles, replete with parallelisms, "exuberant" (Becker 1988) and "articulate" (McDermott 1988), oratorical texts constitute the epitome of positively valued language: clarity, beauty, and power, indexes of the beauty, communal together-ness, strength through hierarchy, and Christian enlightenment *(maalamalama).*

These themes are indeed some of the most frequent topics of *laauga,* which are a treasure trove of explicit pronouncements on morality. For example, in the following passage from the same performance as the above, the orator exhorts the youth of the community (*te maalosi o te fenua,* literally, "the vitality of the island") to seek inspiration from the beauty of the *faatele* performance (itself derived from its unison) and work together, a theme that was particularly pertinent at the time, as fission was tearing the atoll apart in the aftermath of the elections:

Ia, kae i te poo foki teenei au e tuu atu o mmoli atu te fakamaaloo mo te fakafetai lasi ki luga i te maalosi o te fenua, moo te faatele gali teelaa koo oti ne fakaasi nee koulua.

"Indeed, this evening I am also standing up to offer big thanks and congratulations onto the youth of the community, for the beautiful *faatele* that you have displayed."

Ia, kaafai teenaa ko te fiafia, io ka ne aa foki niisi mea teelaa e mafai o ulu mai?

"Indeed, if this is happiness, so what else can also penetrate it [and disturb it]?"

Teelaa laa, au e fakamolemole atu ki te mmalu o te maalosi o te fenua, seeai se mea e mafai manafai ne tino a taatou e ttele valevale,

"Therefore I am beseeching the youth of the community, we can accomplish nothing if some of our people run around all over the place,"

mmai kee nnofo tasi taatou i te koga e tasi, ko te maalosi teenaa.

"come so that we can stay together in one place, this is strength." [Maneapa Speeches Faiva 1985:219]

In short, oratory *is* the discourse of nostalgia.

Without oratorical skills, one makes one's voice heard in public: to open one's mouth in political meetings, at feasts and dances, in church, or at family feasts, one must control the genre, lest one be laughed off the stage. People who cannot make speeches are simply left out of the limelight and hence out of the race for key political positions. At the same time, one cannot aspire to positions of power and prestige without at least paying lip service to the spirit of egalitarianism that pervades the community's political ideology, one of the major tenets of which is the establishment of consensus. Thus, an ambitious individual will strive to become the voice of consensus as often as possible and to emerge as the person best able to become the spokesman for the truth that most will agree with, while skillfully inserting, of course, a perspective that will benefit him- or herself (cf. Lindstrom 1992, 112). Without oratorical skills, one cannot assume this responsibility. At the same time, oratory alone cannot insure political success. Certain individuals may be good orators, but other social traits (e.g., raw ambition, or the fact that they are women or too young) thwart political ambition. The relationship between oratory and politics is therefore not straightforward.

An important characteristic of Nukulaelae oratory is its intimate connection to the truth. Nukulaelae Islanders spend much time talking about the truth, and they talk about it in ways that centralize informational repleteness and exuberance of form. In oratorical contexts and other forms of formal language, the word *tonu* "truth, true" (etymologically related to *ttonu* "straight") frequently co-occurs with the word *kaatoatoa* "complete, whole," with which it forms a doublet, *tonu kae kaatoatoa*, "true and complete." The frequent association of these two terms is not simply a rhetorical device but is symptomatic of a conceptual linkage central to Nukulaelae communicative ideology: what is true is also complete and whole (for further discussion of this point, see Besnier 1994). In addition, truth and completeness entail issues of authority and entitlement, particularly when they concern history, a recurrent feature of oratorical performances. Like names, history is generally "owned" by particular families through genealogical links, and only senior members of these families are in theory entitled to retell historical narratives. Nukulaelae Islanders are reluctant to publicly narrate history that does not "belong" to their kin group, for they risk sharp criticism. Owners of narratives control what completeness consists of in particular narratives.

Oratory is everything that gossip is not and vice versa. Formally, gossip is blurred, incomplete, and unframed, while oratory is clear, complete, and framed. Oratory's form is predictable, its delivery poised, its voices seemingly monologic, while the gossip text is messy, full of pitch variations, and heteroglossic. Laughter can respond to oratory, but it is good clean communal laughter triggered by an orator's joke, while laughter in gossip is more often than not ill-intentioned and insidious. Gossip's relationship to the truth is, at best, in serious competition with other concerns, like denting other people's reputations, having the proverbial good story to tell, and being appreciated as a good storyteller. Gossip's pleasure resides in its subversiveness, while oratory's derives from its beauty, fluency, and depth. Gossip is dangerous, immoral, and intentionally opaque; oratory is tame, Christian, and transparent. And, of course, gossip takes place in dirty, smelly, and messy cooking huts, the antithesis of the *maneapa*'s order and cleanliness.

Nukulaelae Islanders do not have an explicit theory of poetics, nor do they elaborate genres of oral or sung performances associated with formalized rhetorical forms, as are found in more hierarchical societies of Polynesia.[1] To be sure, certain formal features recur in valued texts and performances, but these features are not articulated as a self-conscious aesthetics. Despite the absence of a theory of verbal aesthetics, one can still speak of a sense of poetics. Nukulaelae audiences discriminate between good orators and poor rhetoricians, and can be moved by the form and substance of particular oratorical performances or the lyrics of certain songs, even though they do not generally reflect explicitly on the basis of their appreciation, in contrast to an informed audience of a Tongan song-dance performance, for example, who are able to deconstruct in detail the aesthetic qualities of what they are witnessing. A tripartite constitutive link thus emerges between the truth, completeness, and verbal aesthetics. Because of its formal repleteness and exuberance, formal oratory is maximally truthful. In oratorical and related performances, the truth is maximally thematized, and it is thus not surprising that older men, who have the authority to assert what is true and what is not, have almost exclusive control of these contexts.

Antithetical to poetically valued speech is talk whose formal features and context place it in the most devalued regions of Nukulaelae social aesthetics, and I apply the term "antipoetic" to this kind of talk. Although this term does not correspond to any particular descriptor in Tuvaluan, the category it denotes captures a logic that underlies local practice.[2] The truth is minimally relevant to antipoetic performances. Because such performances leave much unsaid, understated, or waiting to be filled in by the audience, they lay few or no claim to truthfulness. There, the truth is diffuse in terms of what actually gets said, which the performance style sometimes makes difficult to decipher, and in terms of who assumes responsibility for what gets said, as the audience is a coconspiratorial entity.[3]

Religious Conversion and Anxiety

During the nine months I spent on Nukulaelae in 1985, there was a lot of anxiety in the air, and this anxiety was palpable in all social interaction, from *maneapa* oratory to whispered conversations in cooking huts. Nukulaelae was feverishly preparing for the following year's *kuata senitenali* "125th anniversary" of Elekana's chance landing in 1861 and the mythologized arrival of Christianity on Nukulaelae and all of Tuvalu, an event whose magnitude required absolute unity of effort. Unfortunately, parliamentary elections were held in mid-1985, during which a young civil servant decided to contest the parliamentary seat of a seasoned politician and close relative, the late Henry F. Naisali. The very tense "campaign" (in essence, a count of how relatives would split their vote) led to an agonizingly close victory by the latter and to the immediate fission of the community, as the defeated candidate and his supporters moved to the other side of the lagoon and refused to partake in *mea a te fenua* "communal events," including feasts, dances, communal work, and, of course, preparations for the *kuata senitenali*. This act of self-ostracism, a textbook enactment of the discourse of egalitarianism, was not motivated by any disagreement over the vote count or the electoral process, only by anger over defeat and what the rest of the village characterized as the dreaded emotions that undermine hierarchy and cohesion: *kaimanako* "envy" and *kaisanosano* "resentment." Young women from the fissional faction added fuel to the fire by sending telegrams to the Radio Tuvalu studio on Funafuti, requesting songs (*manako*, literally, "desire") to be dedicated to "the 'B' of Nukulaelae" (i.e., Nukulaelae-B vs. Nukulaelae-A), thereby exposing the rift to the scrutiny of the entire nation, undermining Nukulaelae's anxious self-presentation as harmonious. But there was another, more enduring source of anxiety: one family had left the church congregation, setting a worrisome example that others might follow. Very tense *poolitiki* was in the air, and the tension could be cut with a knife.

Since mid-nineteenth-century missionization, the congregationalist church that would eventually become the Christian Church of Tuvalu was the only denomination allowed and logically possible. The Samoan pastors and, after 1958, their Tuvaluan successors, "stranger-kings" whose hallowed presence ensures that God bless the congregation, are bound to their congregation in a *feagaiga* "covenant," according to which the pastor prays for community welfare while the congregation feeds, clothes, and takes care of him and his family (and does so lavishly). Congregation and community are coterminous because everyone benefits from the propitiousness that the pastor ensures, and taking care of the pastor can only be a communal project, so that for a long time leaving the congregation was logically impossible (other than by leaving the atoll altogether). It would have affirmed that individual "choice," a category of little relevance to the traditional order, could be as important as community cohesion and service. While easily appearing to err on the side of unbalanced reciprocity, for mainstream Tuvaluans, the material capital (food, fine mats, money, consumer goods) that flows from congregation to pastor is largely reciprocated by the "spiritual" capital that flows in the other direction. But certain dynamics can interfere with this reciprocity, such as pastors being too obvious in their worldliness, individuals accumulating an excess of material goods, and people becoming exposed to *talitonuga ffoou* "new beliefs" while traveling, through relatives, or by reading.

There was one brief incursion of a *talitonuga foou* onto the Nukulaelae scene in the 1950s when a Catholic convert decided to set up household on the atoll, but his house unexpectedly catching fire in the middle of the night quickly persuaded him to leave. In the 1980s, however, *talitonuga ffoou* (plural form) became more difficult to control, as people traveled more and more frequently away from the regulating communal gaze, encountering Jehovah's Witness missionaries or Baha'i teachers.[4] These conversions generated a great deal of anxiety across the island nation, particularly on Nukulaelae (the mythological foundation of Christianity in Tuvalu, remember), where fragmentation and dissolution are viewed with horror because of the very small size of the population, its history, and its present troubles. So when a man I will call Vave, a very likeable upwardly mobile father of two in his late forties at the time, decided to become a Baha'i along with his spouse, all hell broke loose.

Why Vave left the EKT congregation is complex. In interviews with me, he proposed that he had always been a nonconformist and that he found the ecumenical outlook, humanistic focus, and generally progressive politics of the Baha'i Faith particularly attractive. The Baha'i Faith in Tuvalu tends to be the thinking person's religion, or at least the religion of choice for Tuvaluans who think in modernist fashion, as witnessed for example by the overrepresentation of its adherents in prominent government positions. But the main reason he articulated for leaving the church was his displeasure with what he saw as the highly materialistic basis of Nukulaelae Christianity. The atoll's pastor, in Vave's opinion, receives far too great a share of the atoll's resources, at a time when capitalism is gaining prominence in the life of an island with no direct access to a steady source of cash. While grumbling about this issue is not uncommon, few dare to be as vocal in their criticisms as Vave. At the same time, Vave and other Baha'is in Tuvalu see in the Baha'i Faith a way to pursue values that are identical to the values of the EKT majority: peacefulness (fiileemuu), mutual empathy (feaalofani), enlightenment (maalamalama), being loto fenua "community-hearted," and so on. The added twist perhaps is a sense of frugality and a sense of scale commensurate with need, reminiscent of a Weberian take on the Calvinist and capitalist geist and in opposition to the spectacular displays of abundance associated with mainstream practices.

Because religious affiliation and economics are so intricately entangled, switching religion and leaving the EKT congregation seriously compromises one's role in the atoll's economic and social life. After conversion, Vave and his wife were quickly marginalized from exchange networks and became the targets of palpable harassment: angry words, threatening gestures, vandalism, and of course gossip. Cut off from exchange networks that underlie social relations, the person on Nukulaelae, as in many other societies, is something less than a person, but Vave's case was somewhat complicated by the fact that he was wealthy. Economic autonomy and the new off-island networks that his and his wife's religion made possible helped them cope comfortably with marginalization, but it also threw oil on the fire of others' resentment. In addition to the abundant land he had inherited from his ascendants, Vave had more pigs, chicken, and ducks than anyone on the atoll, in part because he did not have to kill any to fatten the pastor and his wife, and everyone was reminded of this fact several times a day, as he walked back and forth between the village, the gardens, and the pigpens in the bush, laden with feed, vegetables, and tools, past cooking huts, from which people quietly scoffed.

Crying and Trembling

The other person whose reputation comes on the line in this anecdote is an elderly man I will call Maika. Poor and long widowered, Maika lacked the gravitas in public settings that most of his age-mates cultivated, and as a result he never acquired the political importance or social status commensurate with his age. The synecdoche for this lack of a public presence is Maika's very poor or nonexistent skills at public speaking. Judged to be incapable of speaking up in public, though his status theoretically entitled him to a voice in contexts such as feasts and political meetings, he differed from most elderly men, who were generally eager to display their oratorical skills. He inherited this lack of rhetorical confidence from his forefathers, and his children continue the tradition. It is the family's *pona:*

M *Teenaa, teenaa te kaaiga teenaa kaafai e faippati i taimi peenei mo taatou, e mafai o faippati, nee?*
"Like that, that's a family which, if they are just talking to us at a time like now, they can talk, right?"
A kaafai koo faippati i loto i se fakapotopotoga, peelaa, e tagi, e polepole kae see iloa o fakavasega pati, nee?
"But if they talk in a group of people, they start crying, they tremble and they no longer know how to articulate the words, right?"
Aati laa se- se vaegaa kaaiga peelaa e- e ppoi, nee?
"Perhaps it's a kind of family like that, they get scared, right?"
[...]
Kae vaaivai o te- o te loto, nee?
"It's- it's the weakness of the heart, right?"
[Mataua 1990:3:A, p. 3]

And, another interviewee adds, the *pona* has run in the family for generations: *Mai mua i- i lotou tupuga e peenaa eiloo, e see mafai nee laatou o faippati i koga e toko uke ei a tino, e faigataa i laatou* "From long ago, their ancestry has been like that, they can't speak when there are many people around, they find it very difficult" (Kelese 1990:1:A, p. 3).

For an elderly man, the consequences of public voicelessness are grave. Prestige and, to a large extent, social standing depend crucially on one's ability to deliver, as the occasion arises, the kind of complex and elegant rhetorical performance I described earlier. Oratory is one of the few means through which one can acquire prestige and lay claim to power. Even this process is never straightforward, as the competition is fierce. Talking a lot in public places an individual in the running; talking well in public opens the door for accruing prestige. This prestige is in turn closely linked to power and leadership. Thus the most important role of the island's *ulu fenua* "chief," an elected position that theoretically any adult can fill and arguably the most powerful role on the atoll, is to *fakafeagai* "face" the island community, visiting dignitaries, and representatives of island-external powers like the national government. Crucial to the ability to *fakafeagai* is the ability to manipulate high rhetoric. For example, when asked why women are almost never chosen to be chiefs, Nukulaelae men invariably explain this exclusion in terms of women's assumed inability to speak well. Echoing arguments made in many other societies to justify the exclusion of particular groups from positions of power (e.g., Irvine 1990; Keenan 1974; Lutz 1990; and for general discussion

Besnier 1990b, 434–437), they maintain that women, in contrast to men, are great gossipers, have little sense of *mmalu* "dignity," and lack self-control in their interactional habits. Women sometimes contradict these judgments, but sometimes acquiesce with them, particularly in interactions with men in public settings. On the rare occasions when they are called upon to speak in public, for example, they frequently ask for forgiveness for their alleged inability to speak: *e valea te gutu* "my [literally, the] mouth is unsocialized, ignorant," they say, sometimes while in the middle of a beautiful speech. Voicelessness in public contexts, be it constructed or not, guarantees that one will never have much of a claim to any form of prestige or power. There is thus little room in the competition for prestige and power for voiceless men such as Maika, who, unlike women, cannot rationalize voicelessness in terms of gender.[5]

However, Maika compensates for his exclusion from orthodox forms of public politics with an expertise that we can term "heterodox" (Bourdieu 1977, 164–171), for it goes against the grain of the taken-for-granted assumptions underlying ordinary behavior. In old age, he has become a confirmed trickster, adopting a role to which his seniority entitles him in principle, though it is more commonly associated with older women than older men (cf. Hereniko 1995; W. Mitchell 1992). Throwing all claims to *mmalu* to the wind, he would engage in antics that blatantly violated propriety. For example, pushing the notion of burlesque inversion to its literal extreme, he would periodically squeeze his genitals between his thighs and display the result from behind by lifting his lavalava. This sophomoric behavior provoked ambivalent responses. Women were torn between being horrified and choking with laughter, while men were furious: *'Kaiaa e kkata ei koulua i aamioga vaallea a ttoeaina teelaa?'* "'Why are you two laughing at that old man's stupid behavior?'" one senior man impatiently reprimanded the women of his household. It is in this context that we should understand how Maika emerged as a valued conversationalist in kitchen huts. Everyone gave him as much conversational floor as he wanted and took delight in listening to his subversive narratives, even when everyone thought that he was going too far. Maika thus had a strong and loud voice in private contexts, even if his more morally upstanding interlocutors considered his verbal antics as outrageous as his nonverbal ones. Instead of capitalizing on the poetic manipulation of language in public contexts, Maika capitalized on what I characterized earlier as an "antipoetic" performative style, thereby laying some claim to prestige, albeit prestige of a different kind from that which his age-mates fought over in the *maneapa*.[6]

The Twenty-Dollar Piglets

At the time, the elderly Maika's chores had been reduced to feeding the pigs that his family kept but did not bother to take care of. On his way to and from the pigpens, he had made our family's cooking hut his regular haunt and the setting for many of his outrageous acts and hilarious stories. I had been recording casual conversations through the usual method, placing a tape recorder in the corner of the hut, warning everyone that it was on, and remaining next to it to observe. As I discussed in chapter 2, it was well known on the atoll (if not terribly well understood) that I used taped interactions for ethnographic analysis. I would first listen to the tapes to make sure that they did not contain any material that could potentially backfire against those involved. Dealing with recordings of gossip requires care in a tightly knit society whose attitude toward gossip is full of ambivalence and complexity, and where privacy is limited to what one does not say. I would then hand over my tapes to my research assistant, a Funafuti Islander who helped me transcribe and frequently obtain these recordings. My assistant was a well-known, very gregarious person, well liked, despite the fact that she was also a Baha'i. For the duration of my fieldwork, she was staying with Vave, with whom she not only shared a religious affiliation but also ties of kinship. On one memorable occasion, however, my screening was not as thorough as it should have been, my judgment slipped, and the recording turned from being a representation of gossip to being its conduit, with embarrassing consequences.

That late afternoon, I recorded a gossip fragment that, at first assessment, appeared banal. In my view at the time, nothing particularly scandalous was uncovered, and the tape had recorded more silence than talk as the participants lounged around, enjoying the late afternoon coolness that, despite the lack of a breeze, provided a break from the oppressive heat of the day. Present were the "regulars" of that period, consisting of the head of the household, F, who was Maika's *tuaatina* "classificatory sister's son," a relationship marked by affection and care; the head of the household's adult younger brother; and me (figure 5.1). We sat around in the platform area of the kitchen hut, while the women of the household were making dinner at the other end of the hut. Smoke from the cooking fire filled the air.

A brief excerpt of what I recorded turned out not to be as banal as I had originally thought, and my misjudgment triggered an incident that highlights the fragility and permeability of gossip. Maika had been jokingly discussing with the women his (fictitious) plans to purchase ducks and then, with an analogical change of topic, began to gossip about a recent event in which Vave, my research assistant's host and kinsman, had allegedly offered to sell a pair of piglets to someone I will call Teao, an old friend of the latter, for which he eventually asked ten dollars each. Even as they were becoming more frequent, monetary transactions other than gifts still played an uneasy role on the atoll and provoked shame *(maa).* As in other Pacific Island societies (e.g., Addo and Besnier 2008; Besnier 2004a), selling is shameful because it implies that one is poor in social relations, forcing one to commoditize exchanges with others that should really be gift giving. Selling became necessary when people began fishing in motor dinghies rather than sailing canoes, but the sale of tuna that follows a deep-sea fishing trip is always permeated

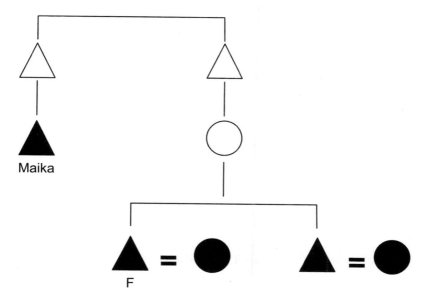

FIGURE 5.1: Participants (shaded symbols) in the gossip about the twenty-dollar piglets

with an atmosphere of embarrassed evasiveness, which is sometimes alleviated through joking. These emotional dynamics explain why Nukulaelae people avoid directly asking the price of items they are buying from others, opting for indirect means such as sending a child to ask how much money is due, for example, as is the case in this story. Sometimes what begins as a monetary transaction becomes a gift, particularly when recipients find themselves unable to meet their debts; the reverse is very unusual and morally tainted. One thing was clear in the context of Vave's piglets: no one asked twenty dollars for a pair of animals that might not even survive piglethood.

In the gossip excerpt, typical of private discourse targeting Vave at the time, fueled by a mixture of condescension and envy, Maika and his interlocutors squeeze out of the incident confirmation of Vave's avarice and social isolation, which go hand in hand with his accumulation of wealth and his exclusion from exchange networks resulting from his religious conversion. According to Maika, upon learning the price of the piglets from a child he had sent to inquire, Teao had paid up, being too embarrassed to return the overpriced piglets, and had fallen victim to his own stupidity for conducting business with an untrustworthy character. To add insult to injury, one of the piglets promptly died, while the other was barely hanging on for dear life.

Following is the narrative I recorded. It is quite difficult to follow, even for native speakers, for reasons that I will elaborate presently:

1 Maika ((snorts))   *I au e ttogi peelaa m- m- mo Vave te punuaa pu- (ee)*
puaka a: Theao.   hhehe ehe ehe
"I'm gonna pay [for my ducks] just like Vave- the piglets- the piglets
that Teao bought [from Vave]."

                        [   ] =
2 F   ((breathy))   *Lua sefulu taalaa!*
                       "Twenty dollars!"
3 Maika = .hhh (   ) *Puaka a Teao koo mate ssuaa puaka.*
"One of Teao's pigs is dead."
4 F   *Tteehhh!*
"You're kidding!"
5 Maika *Te puaka. A ssuaa puaka LAA: (t)EELAA e: tuu, e: tuu (k-) eeloo pee-*
laa::, (a p- p-) pe te ola po ko te mate. =
"One of the pigs. And the other pig, it just keeps standing there, you
don't know whether it's dead or alive."
6 F   ((semifalsetto))   = *Kae fia ttogi?*
                                     "And how much did they cost?"
7 Maika *Sefulu taalaa.*
"Ten dollars."
(1.5)
8 F   ((very soft)) *thhhaaphhhaa eehhh!*
"You don't say!"
9 Maika *Te avaa puaka e:::- teelaa laa, e lua sefulu taalaa te avaa puaka.*
"The pair of pigs, like that, twenty dollars for the pair of pigs."
(5.0)
10 F   ((falsetto, soft)) *Se aa te ttogi naa? A Teao naa e fakavalevale?*
                       "What kind of price is that? Is Teao out of his
                       mind?"
(3.0)
11 Maika *A Tinei e too sala te pati a Teao ki ei,* ((clears throat)) ( ) *e fakatonu*
tena pati kia Elekana, a ia hoki laa koo maa maa fakafoki te-:::- peelaa
iaa ia e:- muna ake loo hoki, e nofo fua peelaa, ko te lima taalaa. Iaa ia
e hai ki ai i puaka a::, (.) a Isa ne ttogi i ei,
"What Teao said to Tinei did not go down well, ( ) he says to
Elekana that he was too ashamed to take back the- like because he
had thought [originally] that they'd be like five dollars. Because he
remembers the pigs that Isa had bought from him,"
(2.5)
12 F   *Mm:* =
"Hm."

13 Maika   = *taki lima taalaa.* (4.0) *Naa a ko ia hoki laa hEE:: ssili atu hoki*
laa me::, me e fia te ttogi o puaka. (4.0) *(oti n)aa, a(e) (h)ano ia,*
(.) puke mai tena avaa puaka, ((semifalsetto)) *kae llei eilaa*
e- e lua ana puaka. A ko ia teenei e: tolu ana punuaa puaka.
(4.0) ((low voice)) ( )   ( )
"Five dollars each. But then he didn't even ask how much the pigs
were going for. This done, he goes off, and grabs himself a pair of
pigs. While that guy's got three pigs [left]."

                            [   ]
14 S   ((to N))   *Niko koe naa maa ausia.*
"Niko you're gonna choke on the smoke."
15 Niko   *llei.* =
"'t's all right."
16 S   *Mm.*
"Hm."
= [   ]
17 Maika   *Naa laa, puke aka ana: avaa puaka,* (.) *vau ei ia, feeppaki mai mo:::*
ttamaliki teelaa a Vave, fai (atu) ei kia:- .hhhh (.) *Faauga kee (hano o*
aasi) kee vau ia::- (.) *Vave me fia ttogi o:-* (.) *punuaa puaka.* (4.0) ( )
a puaka kia:- ki fale, a ko au e toe fanatu koo muna mai me e lua- e::
sefulu taalaa, taki sefulu taalaa i te puaka. ((high falsetto, very fast))
Taapaa ee! (.) *koo hei laa (o) fakafoki eiloo puaka i puaka koo oti*
ne aumai nee:- (6.0) *Aku muna, "koe e ssee. Moi puke pee(laa) koe i*
puaka teelaa:-, puaka kolaa koo llasi,"
"Then he grabs himself a couple of pigs, comes back, [and] runs into
Vave's boy, he tells that boy Faauga to go and (have a look) if Vave's
come back [to ask him] how much the piglets cost. ( ) the piglets to-
to the village, and then I come along again and he tells me that they
cost twen- ten dollars, ten dollars for each pig. What?? [I] tell [him]
to return the pigs but he's already brought the pigs- I say to him,
'You made a mistake. You should've taken those pigs, those larger
pigs,'"
(3.0)
18 F   *Koo fua ei.*
"And they [should] be weighed."
[   ]
20 Maika   *Peelaa a puaka kolaa::*
"Pigs like that"
21 F   *Mm.*
"Hm."

22 Maika   *kolaa eeloo: koo ssao:-*
            "the ones that have already made it-"
23 F   *A koo fua ei.* =
            "And they [should] be weighed then."
24 Maika   = *Koo fua ei, kae hano (mo) au puaka kolaa::*
            "And they [should] be weighed, and you [only] take those pigs tha::t"
            (4.0)
25 F   *Teenaa te faiga, maasei maa puke i punua me:: see iloa me e oola me*
                                                                e mmate.
            "That's the way to do it, it's no good taking piglets cuz you don't
            know if they're gonna live or die."

                                                    [   ]
26   Maika   *oo:::*
                                                    "Right."

     [1985:1:B:258ff.]

When my research assistant heard the recording, she became indignant. She
already had been irritated by another of Maika's pranks, during which he had
jokingly suspected that she regularly spent the night in my hut "fanning" me, a
remark with sexual undertones inappropriate to the close personal and professional bonds between us. She dropped her work (I was out fishing at the time) and
went straight to Vave to report what she had heard, urging him to go and confront
Maika. Vave's and my assistant's version of the affair was that Vave had offered the
piglets as a gift to his old friend Teao, who instead had insisted on paying for them,
at an inflated price. Teao's unusual insistence to turn gift giving into a sale may
have had different motivations, including a desire to put social distance between
himself and Vave.

What happened next is opaque. At the time, my assistant told me that Vave
had gone to Maika and had *faipati fakallei* "spoken properly" with him. Five years
later, Vave told me that he had talked to Teao semiformally to avoid involving me
directly. The long and short of it is that everyone was embarrassed. Maika abruptly
stopped his late-afternoon visits to the kitchen hut and did not resume them for
several weeks. Not knowing how to handle the situation, I did my best to avoid
him. But the person who ended up with most egg on her face was my assistant,
whose precarious position as a stranger and a Baha'i made her an easy scapegoat.
According to subsequent gossip (some of which I simply overheard), she had mis-
interpreted Maika and overreacted. No one seemed to blame Maika for having lied
or told an uncorroborated version of the story. He had told the story, gossipers
pointed out, to *fai fakkata* "to make jest." Why had my assistant failed to recognize
a funny story when it had been meant to be nothing more than that? A well-
adapted adult on Nukulaelae must always take life in stride and maintain a benign

attitude toward the rest of the world. There is no greater compliment than being characterized as *mata katakata* "having a laughing appearance" and *mata fiafia* "appearing happy." A moral person is one who is *fiileemuu* "peaceful," one who knows how to control his or her anger at all times (cf. G. White 1991, 125–130). By having reacted the way she did, my assistant was not abiding by these ideals.

Form and Ideology

I now turn to an analysis of some of the transcript's formal features, using tools I developed in the previous chapter and evaluating what these features tell us about the place of the fragment in Nukulaelae "social aesthetics" (Brenneis 1987a). The most striking characteristic of the fragment is its opacity, which is in fact not untypical of Nukulaelae gossip in general where, as among Fiji Indian villagers, "it is often difficult to reconstruct underlying events on the basis of [gossip] texts themselves" (Brenneis 1987a, 244). Nevertheless, several interesting features emerge. First, the story emerges in the conversation in a highly incidental fashion. Maika raises the topic of the piglets as a casual and rather unlikely analogy to his nonexistent ducks, with the comparative conjunct *peelaa m- m- mo* "like, as if."[7] The analogy is followed by several seconds of talk (turns 2–4), during which Maika informs his interlocutor that one of the piglets is dead and the other is not doing well. In these turns, Maika moves away from the main story line and would perhaps have continued doing so (or at least he gives his interlocutor that impression) had F not rekindled the gossip in turn 6, with *Kae fia ttogi?* "And how much did they cost?" He already knows the answer to this question since he himself already provided it in turn 2, so his question is not a request for information, but clearly an encouragement for Maika to return to the juicy gossip. By turn 4, Maika has done little more than drop a hint, make an allusion, and laugh about it. As in Bhatgaon, "one is rarely told why a story is being told, and the links between the account and preceding discourse are not made clear" (Brenneis 1987a, 244).

The performance is highly dysfluent, even by the standards of everyday informal conversation. (It is certainly recognized as such by native speakers.) The narrator hesitates a great deal (e.g., turns 1, 5, 9, 11, 13, 17), repairs himself many times, and pauses at syntactic junctures where pauses are not expected—for example, in turn 17, between three prepositions and their objects (the preposition *kia* "to" and the name Faauga, the preposition *ia* "to" and the name Vave, and the preposition *ki* "to" and the noun *fale* "village"). He fails to carry several of his utterances through to completion, which is one factor that contributes to the lack of clarity, and leaves unsaid what appears to be the most significant element of several utterances. When he snorts and clears his throat (turns 1 and 11), he does not pause, and the words that follow are colored by the snorting and throat clearing. At the level of phonology and prosodics, Maika's delivery is breathy and creaky, and he switches to falsetto or semifalsetto voice in several instances, a common characteristic of informal talk that certainly would never occur in oratorical genres. Throughout the extract, he voices oral stops in words. Tuvaluan, like most Polynesian languages, does not have a phonemic voiced-voiceless contrast in oral stops (e.g., /b/ vs. /p/, /g/ vs. /k/), and the contrast can be exploited for purely affective purposes. Thus, in turn 1, he pronounces the phrase *punuaa puaka* "piglet" as, phonetically, [bunua: buaga], and later on (e.g., line 42) even utters the /k/ sound in *puaka* "pig" as a voiced velar fricative [ɣ] (i.e., phonetically, [buaɣa]). The voicing of stops is characteristic of very casual talk, and conveys the impression that the speaker is too uninvolved to pay much attention to the contrast between the voicing of vowels (which always follow consonants in this language) and the voicelessness of oral stops. Finally, he uses Nukulaelae dialect forms in /h/ throughout, which are devalued, even locally, compared to the corresponding standard Tuvaluan forms in /f/ or /s/. In one instance (turn 13), in the word *(h)ano* "go," the /h/ sound is almost imperceptible.

The text is rhetorically poorly formed. It is common for Nukulaelae narrators to "ground" narratives in a great deal of background detail—thus the invocation in turn 11 of many names of individuals playing only marginal roles in narrated events is not unusual—but the narrative in this turn and in turn 17 is highly unfocused. Maika clearly is not concerned with producing an elegant rhetorical performance in the degradation ceremony he is orchestrating. Lastly, the responsibility for providing moral evaluations of the story falls on the all-too-willing interlocutor, not on Maika. For example, it is the interlocutor, F, who utters the interjection of scandalized outrage *taapaa ee!* in turn 8 and the interjection *ttee!*, which has a similar force, in turn 4. The audience is highly involved as coauthor of the discourse and is primarily responsible for producing the affect, Greek chorus–like. The result is a shared complicity in the production of the degradation ceremony, which both diffuses responsibility and binds the interactors together. In short, the gossip victim's public biography, woven out of many strands, has more than one weaver. The evaluative statements that the narrative contains (e.g., *koe e ssee* "You made a mistake" in turn 17) are carefully framed as directly reported speech; the utterance is thus deeply embedded in the story world, which makes it particularly resilient to scrutiny (cf. Besnier 1992; C. Briggs 1992; Hill 1995). Note that the coda of the fragment is about how to choose pigs, not about Vave. Vave's reputation is confirmed as dead, and what is left to do for the gossip accomplices is to learn how to keep clear of the likes of him.

Maika's performance thus epitomizes Nukulaelae gossiping styles but pushes their characteristics to an extreme. It contrasts sharply with what the local linguistic ideology considers beautiful and important, as canonically embodied in oratorical performances in the *maneapa*, which are fluent and well formed, rich in parallelisms and other poetic devices, and framed by elaborate opening and closing devices. Maika's gossip is the opposite: dysfluent, fragmented, and disorganized, poorly linked to the previous conversation, its phonological and rhetorical structures sloppy. It falls squarely in the ideological construction of gossip as the antithesis of beauty because of its physical location, purpose, and form.

Heterodoxy and Orthodoxy

Biographies are paradoxically both complete and unfinished. They are complete in the sense that everyone knows what everyone else is doing, what motivates them, and the decisions they take, and people's "personalities" begin even before they are born, as I demonstrated in the previous chapter. But biographies are also unfinished projects, placed on the chopping board over and over again to be scrutinized and evaluated, and that is one of the main motivations for gossiping. In the story of the twenty-dollar piglets, two biographies come to the fore, Vave's and Maika's. Both politically marginalized for different reasons, they do not have much agency in public contexts: they have no say in communal decision making and occupy no position of importance (although Vave would later find important alternative avenues of power). But they both are the focus of attention on the atoll: Vave is wealthy, independent, envied, and reviled; Maika is outrageous but generally liked, and he sides with majority opinions. Thus neither is in any clear sense a "subaltern," in that the inequality from which Vave and Maika suffer does not derive from a differential access to material resources that delimits clear society-internal boundaries between groups and persons. In terms of material accumulation, Vave is better off than most, although he is also excluded from most exchange networks. Maika is poor, but his exclusion from politics has a symbolic foundation, not a material one.

It is Maika's biography that preoccupies me here. Maika may be a failure when it comes to orthodox forms of speaking and what one can claim through them, but he is a success in a number of other, heterodoxic ways, which question the status quo and potentially undermine it. Like the trickster of many societies, he commands his audience's attention and makes people laugh and desire his company. He capitalizes on gossip's polymorphous pleasure. In particular, the efficacy of his performance as a form of political action depends crucially on its relation to the truth, and Maika emerges as a master in placing his performances outside the regimes of truth articulated in the atoll's formal institutions. The formal features of this performance converge on this purpose. The breathy and creaky voice quality, the unfinished utterances, the switches in the narrative, and the snorting, throat clearing, and laughter all make the narrative difficult to follow, and hence at the moment of its delivery there is little specific information (in the form of segmentable linguistic units) that the audience could have focused on and ask Maika to justify or corroborate, yet the narrator succeeds in establishing a negative atmosphere around Vave in the narrative. The interlocutor, acting as a cooperative gossip recipient, in fact has other purposes in mind than scrutinizing the truth of the story, since he contributes, invited and uninvited, to the narrative's affective atmosphere: by rekindling the gossip when it seems to be on the verge of dying out (turn 6) and providing interjections and comments laden with negative affect (turns 4, 8, 10, 25). Maika's skill as a gossiper thus resides in his ability to make the truth irrelevant to the narrative, extracting the text from potential scrutiny for truth. By doing so he escapes, at the performative moment at least, potential accusations that he is lying. The more adept at making the truth become irrelevant to a performance, the more appreciated the gossip performer, and the greater the alternative prestige he or she accrues.

Maika's gossip highlights the limitations of theories of resistance that I discussed in chapter 1 that read "weapons of the weak" and "hidden transcripts" in the private words of the disenfranchised. On the surface, Maika's gossip could be construed as resistant action: it is hidden, it subverts dominant symbolic forms in which the truth is formed and reproduced, and it is directed against the actions of a materially powerful person. In these respects, it resembles canonical examples of resistant linguistic practices: the heroic narratives that poor young rural Lebanese men with little social status tell one another of their alleged exploits against the agents of their oppression (Gilsenan 1996); the lyric poetry that Bedouin women and youths of the western Egyptian desert sing surreptitiously about forbidden sentiments of loss, abandonment, and unrequited desire (Abu-Lughod 1986); the episodes of spirit possession that young Malaysian women have in the oppressive environment of the factories that employ them (Ong 1987); or the ritualized wailing that Warao women intone on the death of relatives in eastern Venezuela, through which they voice accusations and criticisms to which they are otherwise not entitled in public (C. Briggs 1992).

With these examples Maika's gossip shares a context-boundedness, a veil of secrecy and stealth, and stylistic characteristics that set it apart from other forms of talk. But there are many differences. Unlike the young Lebanese villagers, wailing Warao women, and many other comparable categories, Maika targets his gossip at someone who is not part of an oppressing class and who does not oppress him directly. In many ways, Vave is more oppressed than anyone else on the island. What provides Maika's talk its subversive quality is the absence of verbal skills; its evasive, marginal incoherence; and its dysfluency. Indeed, the relationship between particular linguistic forms and their aesthetic or political value is always mediated by linguistic ideology, and thus completely divergent patterns of valuation can operate in different societal contexts. In short, a "hidden transcript" approach to Nukulaelae gossip can only lead one to undermining the usefulness of resistance as an analytic category.

Nevertheless, we must contend with the possibility that producing devalued antipoetic discourse as one's trademark is a legitimate trajectory for at least one person on Nukulaelae lacking more solid symbolic or material resources, a legitimacy that others confirm by laughing at his jokes and pranks, egging him on in his gossip, and acknowledging his claim to an alternative form of prestige. The persona that Maika adopts enables him to confront the very processes that place him at a disadvantage and turn these inside out in sabotage-like fashion. At the same time, he chooses his victims well: by focusing on the actions of an already marginalized individual to nurture his own alternative prestige, he contributes to the reproduction of structures that marginalize this other person, thus lending further legitimacy to his own project. Working within the bounds of orthodoxy, since he is gossiping about an individual already bracketed for criticism, enables him to engage in his self-serving heterodoxic enterprise. The success of this balancing act depends on a complex linkage among performative style, regimes of truth, and the construction of biographies (both the gossiper's and the victim's) in the context of large-scale processes such as emergent capitalism, the maintenance of traditional forms of exchange, the politics of religious affiliation.

However, the alternative prestige gained through antipoetic performance is even more fragile than the type of prestige one can claim through valued rhetorical performances, for two major reasons. First, alternative prestige on Nukulaelae depends crucially on social boundaries being kept intact. Had the tape recorder not been there, Maika would probably have enjoyed on that day the success that he enjoys on a daily basis: his audience would have been amused by his performance, dismissed it as unimportant talk, but also retained one of its basic messages—Vave is not to be trusted. However, when one's antipoetic performance is tape-recorded by an annoying anthropologist and heard by others, the performance can be challenged, its text scrutinized and placed again in a universe of discourse in which truth and lying are again relevant. The basis of one's claim to alternative prestige collapses, and loss of face ensues. As in other cases of sociopolitical action initially intended to challenge structures of social inequality, but that ultimately promote these structures (cf. Merton 1957, 421–436), the gossiper is reminded that communally sanctioned structures are powerful and not easily challenged.

Maika's political project represents one extreme of a continuum, or perhaps of a series of continua, of strategies that community members may opt for at different times and in different contexts to maximize their chances of having a voice, and thus their social resources and their share of power, prestige, and status, while remaining within the bounds of "acceptable" behavior, or perhaps while negotiating what these bounds are. It is suggestive to compare this approach to communication and micropolitics on Nukulaelae with the way in which adaptive mechanisms to the impoverished atoll environments of Tuvalu operate. The limited resources of atoll environments engender many "crunches," for land, food, and, increasingly nowadays, money. A fruitful way of coping with these crunches is to maintain flexibility in the kinship structure, land-tenure system, and residence patterns (Brady 1974, 1976, 1978). A flexible kinship structure, for example, allows adoptive relationships of various types to play an important role in descent and inheritance, thus enabling members of the group to maximize their access to economic resources, since adoption adds to rather than replaces kin ties. Land is owned in corporate fashion, and the right to the fruit borne by particular parcels of land is not a matter of absolute legal entitlement but of degree, and this right is in turn tied to emotions like *alofa* "empathy" but is also vulnerable to feuds and fissions. In recent history, the inventive way in which the Tuvaluan state has banked its "resources of jurisdiction" (see chapter 2) mirrors on a global scale the socioeconomic bricolage that makes life possible in atoll environments. Though the dynamics I have described in this chapter are of a different nature from these adaptive socioeconomic patterns, they nevertheless suggest interesting parallels. Gossip, like other maneuvers to seek access to symbolic or economic resources, is a prime locus of the interplay between structure and agency, created by agents' attempts to handle structural constraints and find ways of circumventing aspects of the structure that place them at a disadvantage.

Most agents in this community will bank on a variety of resources, adjusting them to the context, foregrounding some while backgrounding others as the situation arises. Few will, like Maika, bank so radically on one type of resource, such as gossip. What is interesting about Maika's case is precisely its atypicality. His marginal status in Nukulaelae society helps us locate the outer edge of agents' struggle to deal with preexisting structures. The tools used in that struggle exploit aspects of a system that otherwise places the agent on the boundary of society. Yet as I have shown here, much can go wrong in the process, and the results often represent a rather meager reaping, in that Maika's project depends for its success on its being bound to a specific situational scale. The instant this scale is enlarged by the presence of an ethnographer and his tape recorder, things go awry.

From Micro to Macro

In this chapter, I have demonstrated how the microanalysis of particularly strips of gossip interaction can be tied to a variety of concerns of broader import: how biographies emerge, how divisiveness and marginalization are reproduced, how anxiety arises in the context of changing forms of exchange and changing definitions of belonging. In this process, I had to invoke the instability of the truth, the way in which interaction and truth are tied to the community's social aesthetics, and how agents seek to follow particular projects, some more orthodox than others, but always negotiating the boundary between orthodoxy and heterodoxy. An approach that links an analysis of minute aspects of interaction to an analysis of larger sociocultural, economic, and historical dynamics can provide a goldmine of insights into how moments of agents' everyday lives embody the larger context in which they operate.

The strip of gossip I have analyzed in this chapter demonstrates an important point that underlies works on gossip but is not often stated explicitly: that particular instances of gossip are not "about" the events that the narratives recounts, nor simply "about" morality and reputations, but perhaps more importantly "about" issues and events of much more enduring longevity, schisms and fissions, and biographies that begin even before individuals are born. "Aboutness" is of course a notion of malleable and telescopic scale, and addressing this complexity enables us to transcend earlier debates concerning the nature of gossip for agents and for communities. Attention to these complexities motivated my switch in this chapter to a mode of analysis that focuses on a concrete situation as a means to capture general principles of social life, from the perspective of both structures and agents, akin to the classic "extended-case method" (van Velsen 1967). Here I add to the classic form a micro–macro linkage that ties the features of interaction to processes of a general and enduring nature.

In chapter 1, I spent quite a bit of time exploring the ethical implications of conducting ethnographic research on a topic that members of the society spend considerable energy sweeping under the rug. I return here to the ethical consideration brought to the fore by my misjudgment in the situation I analyze here, a misjudgment, I should add, of a kind that is rife in every anthropologist's fieldwork, despite its almost complete silencing in the production of ethnographic writing. The situation (and others like it) has destroyed any illusion I might have started with regarding the possibility of "distance" between the community that "generates" the "data" I write about and myself as observer and recorder. My tape recorder, innocuous at first glance, ended up acting as an instrument of social disruption, of which I became the agent. Despite its conspicuousness in the kitchen hut and the fact that I drew everyone's attention to it before recording, the reality of "data gathering" receded from interactors' consciousness as the gossip progressed. In a sense, the tape recording became surreptitious, and all the ethical discomfort associated with such recordings quietly emerged (cf. Larmouth, Murray, and Murray 1992). Where do we locate the boundary between clandestine and consensual audio recording? Alternatively, are the ends of any ethnographic work ever explicit from the perspective of those being observed (Barnes 1980)?

In two provocative essays, Harvey (1991, 1992) analyzes how, while conducting fieldwork in a Peruvian Andes village bilingual in Quechua and Spanish, she clandestinely tape-recorded people talking while drunk. The villagers, who appeared docile and compliant when sober, became loquacious and defiant when inebriated. In drunken talk, villagers voiced complex emotions about their oppressed status as poor peasants, which never surfaced otherwise. Had she failed to take into account drunken talk, Harvey would have presented villagers as passive victims devoid of agency, thus providing a distorted depiction of their ideological stance. In the same fashion, failing to take into account the microscopic forms of prestige seeking that Maika engages in while gossiping would not do justice to the complexities of his position in Nukulaelae society, and to political and social processes in Nukulaelae society. Although recognizing the contentious nature of her methods, Harvey questions the extent to which her taping practices were more problematic than any other anthropological method: "it is the relationship between researcher as member of a particular and powerful social group and that of the researched as members of less powerful groups that constitutes *all* data collection, covert and overt, as problematic" (1992, 81, emphasis in the original; see also Dwyer 1982, 255–286).

I would take Harvey's point further, suggesting that anthropological methods that base ethnographic analyses on impressionistic re-creations of what is said during a drunken episode or a gossipy moment are more abusive of scientific authority than methods based on the microscopic analysis of a transcript of what is said, without ignoring, of course, the ethnographic authority embedded in the transcribing process. Meaning (in the most general sense) resides not just in the strings of words that make up an utterance, but also in the form of words, in the organization of interactions, and in the positioning of interlocutors vis-à-vis the text and context of the interaction. To derive an analysis of social relations solely on the basis of a re-created and translated representation of what the ethnographer (who is often unskilled at listening to the interactors' language) thought was said fails to do justice to the social dynamics at play even in the most inconspicuous interactions. Clearly, the ethics of fieldwork are considerably more complex than they may appear at first.

6 The Two Widows

DESPITE ITS SHORTCOMINGS, Gluckman's (1963) early analysis of gossip as a cohesion-enhancing mechanism, which I discussed at length in the introductory chapter, did rest on the basically correct insight that gossip is always embedded in a larger social context and that people can use gossip to "do things" to that context. In the previous chapters, I focused primarily on the way in which this larger context (political, ideological, symbolic) was related to particular aspects of the structure of Nukulaelae gossip texts. In this chapter and the next, my attention shifts to the potentialities of gossip in reproducing or changing social relations and the course of events. Gossip can work on old resentments and ongoing dislikes, as much as it can alter the life of other people and the shape of relationships. Equally, the targets of gossip are not necessarily passive victims: their response to gossip about them articulates with many other dynamics, including their own life projects, the source of their sense of selfhood, and their economic positioning.

In this chapter, I explore two questions, which I will further develop in the next chapter. The first is the extent to which gossip is both a local process and a process that transcends the local. In an atoll world in which print literacy is limited and Internet communication has yet to make its presence known, gossip requires the face-to-face copresence of participants at some point, but it can also take place over vast distances, through letters, phone calls, and telegrams. It can involve participants emanating from nonearthly dimensions of reality, in this case the world of spirits. Both familiar and distant, spirits and their actions play an important role in the logic of earthly social relations, and gossip furnishes an ambiguous context that is particularly well suited to spirits' interference in worldly affairs. The extralocal and extraworldly potentialities of gossip provide its users a useful mechanism to make sense of the relationship between the local and the nonlocal, as well as sociocultural transformations, the encroachment of capitalism, and the desires and expectations that come with it.

The second aim of this discussion is to shift the focus from the production of gossip to the interplay among its producers and its targets. In particular, I embed gossip in the context of a broad range of forms of knowledge production, which involves not just many different parties but also different channels with different levels of specificity and vagueness, all contributing either to giving gossip the power that its users intend it to have or to thwart this power. But it is not only epistemological entanglements between producers and targets that are at play, not just a politics of knowledge and evidence, but also the materiality of social relations, a politics of who is entitled to own and control what resources (even if these resources remain hypothetical, as will become clear presently).

The narrative to which I turn brings to the fore several additional themes to which I alluded, but did not develop, in earlier chapters. Gender becomes important, as the situation that I analyze involves only women. Gossip, knowledge, and morality become embroiled with the complexities of beliefs in sorcery, spirits, and spirit mediumship, themes that often go hand in hand cross-culturally with gossip and rumor but that require careful contextualization in local dynamics. This contextualization in turn raises questions about the nature of localness because, on Nukulaelae, neither gossip nor the supernatural is local in any straightforward way. The situation I analyze also involves me directly (in rather frustrating ways), and its analysis demands an even more reflexive stance than my previous discussion, whether I like it or not. This situation is, however, not unique, in that ethnographies of sorcery and witchcraft demand that ethnographers understand their role in the development of the ethnography, beyond a faddish interest in ethnographic reflexivity. When spirit discourse turns into sorcery or witchcraft, which is epistemologically sanctioned by some institutions but not others, no one is innocent. This point is one of the more memorable lessons from Favret-Saada's (1977) celebrated ethnography of sorcery in the Normandy bocage (also Favret-Saada and Contreras 1981). In Normandy, the peasantry is more open about sorcery and witchcraft with the Catholic Church hierarchy than with the city slickers, including the anthropologist. In Tuvalu, where the church acts at least in principle as the epistemological watchdog, the opposite is the case, or perhaps the choice of whom one confides in is more modulated. Whatever may be the case, the anthropologist's inability to take on a neutral position is aggravated in cases where she or he is implicated in what spirits declare and in the transformation of spirits' declarations into sorcery accusations. In this chapter, I am fully implicated in all of the above.

I am departing here from the kind of fine-grained textual analysis that I developed in chapter 4 and used as an analytic platform in chapter 5, since the ethnographic data that I have about the particular situations on which I base my arguments do not include specific gossip texts. It would have been quite an extraordinary stroke of ethnographic luck to obtain both naturalistic microscopic and macroscopic data on the same set of events, given the elusive nature of both. In particular, as I will explain presently, much of the gossip implicated in the events I will analyze took place either on Funafuti, where I have not spent much time, or on Nauru, a place that I have never visited. I do have rich textual material, however, that consists in *maneapa* speeches, church sermons, and of course interviews with a broad range of Nukulaelae people, samples of which I analyze. Yet despite its textual absence in what follows, gossip is at the core of the events that I analyze here, and its formal characteristics are very similar to the gossip I examined in detail in the previous two chapters.

The Omniscience of Spirits

The events I analyze began in September 1990, when several Nukulaelae people boarded the new national ship, the MV *Nivaga II*, for the overnight trip to the capital, where they were to attend to a variety of communal and private matters. At that time, rumor had reached Nukulaelae that a spirit medium on Funafuti, whom I shall call Suunema, had been holding mediumship séances (*fakalleo*, literally, "to make [spirits] have a voice"), eagerly if somewhat surreptitiously attended by people from all over Tuvalu who had questions they wanted answered. These queries ranged from the whereabouts of lost keys to considerably more dramatic matters such as what had happened to the Funafuti child who, found lying unconscious by the road with a large dark stain over one side of his body, was taken to the hospital, where he promptly died (the spirit declared that she had eaten him). The spirit whom Suunema was hosting knew everyone's name, and she knew who had committed incest, where stolen money was concealed, and who had ensorcelled whom. For many, despite the church's strong disapproval of it all, this omniscience was undeniable proof that the spirit was among them and that the medium was not "lying" (*ppelo*), both topics of some preoccupation. Witness a Nukulaelae woman's amazement that the spirit knew about a letter she had written before a séance:

Ko au laa e ofo i au e nofo mo taku tusi, ne tusi nee au i te Ossaa peenei i te ao.

"I am amazed, because I held on to my letter, I wrote it on Sunday, during the day, at about the same time as now."

Au heki teka eiloo mo taku tusi, ffao nee au ki ttaga, moe loa mo au i te moega.

"I never parted with my letter, I hid it in my pocket, I slept with it on the bed."

Hano au ki te lotu, vau au i ei, te poo kaatoa naa, au e moe eiloa mo te tusi.

"I went to church, came back, the entire night, I slept with my letter."

[. . .]

A koo hai mai, "Oo! Koo tusi aka tau tusi?"

"And then [the spirit] tells me, 'So, you've written the letter?'"

Mea loo koo ttala mai nee ia taku tusi, aku pati kolaa ne tusi ki taku tama, mo oku maafaufauga kolaa heki tusi ki lalo, palele katoa ne fai mai nee ia!

"Then she goes on to tell me what's in my letter, the words I had written to my child, and the thoughts I never wrote down, she tells me what they are!" [Saumaiafi 1990:1:A:037–045]

The spirit, which continues to haunt to this day, goes by different names, the most common at that time being Saumaiafi or Saumaiafe, but also Te Lasi, literally, "the big one," a slightly old-fashioned version. For Nukulaelae Islanders, spirits *(agaaga)* are outsiders in multiple ways. Saumaiafi only manifested herself on Funafuti, where the larger land area, the migrant residents emanating from all the islands of the group, and the trappings of modernity render the church's panoptical surveillance more difficult to implement than on Nukulaelae. On Funafuti, there is no curfew at evening prayer, the Sabbath is broken at will, denominational fragmentation is rampant, and no one quite knows what happens inside the tightly packed cardboard houses, sorry-looking leftovers of the 1972 posthurricane housing relief—to say nothing of the two bars (one making valiant attempts at maintaining dignity, at least until sunset), the video parlors operated by seamen's relatives in private homes, the disco hangar, and the seamen on furlough who never sober up. According to the medium, whom I interviewed four years later, and people who attended the séances, Saumaiafi had been all over the world and in particular to all atolls of Tuvalu, except Nukulaelae, which she found to be "as hot as a fire," in which I read an obvious reference to Nukulaelae's status as the "chosen atoll" of Christianity. Indeed, when a young woman is possessed on Nukulaelae, she is immediately dragged away from public view, accompanied by a unison of *aali,* a loud expression of annoyance and disgust *("AAAAAAA!!").* On Funafuti, there may be no one around to nip these events in the bud, and few feel entitled to deter outer islanders, through disapproval or other ways, from flocking to the medium's house to query the spirit.

Another index of outsiderness is that Saumaiafi is Samoan. The various versions of her name, as Sauma'iafi and Sauma'iafe, are well known in Samoan lore, as names of both spirits and people.[1] On Funafuti, Saumaiafi speaks through the spirit medium in Samoan, a fact in which some read further convincing proof of the "truth" of the mediumship although, at skeptical moments (which can rapidly alternate with moments of conviction), my respondents were quick to point out that all Tuvaluan adults speak at least rudimentary Samoan, a relic of the days of Samoan pastors and of reading, until the 1980s, the Samoan translation of the Bible. When Saumaiafi dances, it is a perfect Samoan village ceremonial virgin's *taualuga*. A Funafuti elder anxious to ensure that the Funafuti soccer team win the yearly national tournament apparently recruited her from Samoa initially, and she stayed on. Again, for Nukulaelae Islanders, spirits and their activities always originate elsewhere and act in nonlocal ways. It is when they can come close to the local that they become dangerous, as if they had read Mary Douglas' (1966) *Purity and Danger*.[2]

Saumaiafi had been visiting the medium Suunema for a long time, but the latter had been living on Nauru, and her séances received relatively little attention in Tuvalu until her return in 1990, after which her husband promptly abandoned her. Her séances then increased in frequency and so did people's interest in them, including Nukulaelae visitors to the capital. At more skeptical moments, friends invoked a classic instrumental analysis of Suunema's possessions as "indirect claim for redress" (Boddy 1994, 415): she was distraught about her divorce, and the mediumship was a way of calling attention to her distress. At other moments, the evidence for the "truth" of her possession was overwhelming. But as Irvine (1982) argues, the "truthfulness" and authority of spirit possession is always a joint effort involving many parties (medium, spirit, audience, bystanders, overhearers, ancestors), and is not simply determined by the way in which the possessed person speaks and acts (cf. Lambek 1993).

The renewed interest in the mediumship was rooted in a palpable general malaise and jumpiness that reigned over Nukulaelae at the time and spilled over to Funafuti, or at least to Nukulaelae people's cultural map of the capital. For example, one morning on Nukulaelae, several people (including me) around the cooking huts heard what sounded like a *vvalo* "town crier's call." One woman conjectured that it had come from the northernmost point of the islet, while other people thought that it had come from the ocean side of the islet *(ttua fenua)*. People close to me reasoned, with some trepidation, that it was "some sort of warning to the community." The anxiety that this event generated did not readily abate, even after we eventually figured out that a man in a net-fishing party had shouted at younger men not to let a school of fish escape. It is in this anxious context that Nukulaelae people traveled to Funafuti to consult the spirit, and returned with much to talk about.

Spirits, Sorcery, and Christianity

Spirits, mediumship, and sorcery figure prominently in the analysis I present in this and the next chapter, and it may come as a surprise to readers familiar with the anthropology of the Pacific Islands that I would invoke these themes, particularly sorcery, in the context of a Polynesian society. While sorcery has a very robust genealogy in the anthropology of Melanesia, to the point of having almost gained the status of "regional typification" (Fardon 1990, 27) alongside exchange and millenarian movements, it is almost entirely absent from anthropological writings on contemporary Polynesia. Among contemporary Polynesians, it appears, sorcery is rarely mobilized outside of the construction of the "darkness" of the heathen past (in Tuvaluan, *pouliuli*), where it coexists with violence, discord, and self-centeredness, ideological foils of the "enlightenment" *(maalamalama)* of the Christian present (see chapter 3). Two factors may explain the prominence of sorcery in one region and its apparent absence in the other. One, harking back to Sahlins (1963), is the classic greater preponderance of chiefs with a more stable power base in Polynesia than in Melanesia, who historically ensured the more absolute hegemony of Christianity and who do not have to rely on (the fear of) sorcery to maintain their power, as Melanesian big men and chiefs do. The notable anxiety about sorcery on Nukulaelae supports this hypothesis despite Nukulaelae's self-avowed Polynesian identity, given the instability of chiefly power on the atoll in contrast to the rest of Polynesia. The other is the longevity of Christianity in Polynesia and its concomitant repression of pre-Christian belief systems in contrast to its relatively shallower history in Melanesia. But as Lamont Lindstrom reminded me (personal communication), there is plenty of hegemonic Christianity in contemporary Melanesia, as well as Christian big men who make a career out of sorcery by selling antisorcery Christian revival campaigns.[3]

The regional contrast may be not as clear-cut as it appears at first glance, and is perhaps as much an artifice of the areal structuring of anthropological knowledge as it is a reflection of what concerns people in the respective regions (cf. Thomas 1989; more generally Gupta and Ferguson 1997b, 8–11). Indeed, like Freudian polymorphous desires, sorcery in Polynesia always threatens to reemerge alongside other manifestations of "darkness." Its containment is a difficult and unfinished project, and hence the object of anxieties similar to Melanesian ones (e.g., G. White 1991, 135–139). Whatever may be the case, an explanatory excursus into the ideological context of Nukulaelae sorcery is necessary before I turn to the events that concern this chapter.

Nukulaelae cosmological understandings of sorcery and spirits are inseparable. Without spirits there is no sorcery, and the primary task of spirits is to enable sorcery. Nukulaelae Islanders define sorcery as the harnessing of the power of spirits. While the nature of spirits and of their actions is a controversial topic, people generally agree in private that their principal function is to enable the work of sorcerers, and when spirits visit mediums, it is often to make accusations about who meddles with sorcery. There is a continuum between local medical practices and sorcery performed for malevolent ends, the distinguishing factor being the practitioner's intentions rather than the means employed. As is common cross-culturally, the same term refers to both curing and sorcery: *vai laakau*, literally, "liquid [or water or juice] of vegetable [substance]." In its least morally marked sense, *vai laakau* refers to Western medicines, like aspirin and antibiotics, or to local pharmacopoeia and medical practices, such as oils for rubbing and infusions for ingestion. In its morally most marked sense, *vai laakau* refers to substances and practices using substances that have the power to change the normal course of events so as to benefit the practitioner at the expense of others, an act that is euphemistically referred to as *taafao ki mea maassei*, literally, "to play with bad things." As in many other societies (e.g., Whitehead and Wright 2004, 3), medical practitioners are capable of engaging in both curing and sorcery, although moral rectitude and adherence to a church-sanctioned sense of selfhood restrain most from engaging in the latter.[4]

Spirits always demand a *taui* "reciprocity, compensation" (a term borrowed from Samoan) for their assistance with sorcery, typically a misfortune that affects either the person or his or her kin: childlessness, a debilitating disease, or a disabled offspring. Certain misfortunes are associated with particular types of *vai laakau*; for example, one of the dangers of using *vai laakau* for erotic purposes is that it can unwittingly affect a close relative, leading one to commit incest, the most horrifying of all transgressions in atoll societies. Such compensations are most immediate when a person dabbles in *vai laakau* that does not "belong" to his or her family (like most knowledge, *vai laakau* is the property of a particular descent group), and the visible evidence of these compensations is often the basis of suspicion that one is up to no good. But so is being particularly successful at fishing, gardening, sex, or politics (as well as soccer).

The target of *vai laakau* is usually a person or group unrelated to the sorcerer, unlike sorcery in many African societies, where relatives, affines, and neighbors are the prime target of sorcery suspicions, although, of course, relative relatedness can be the product of sorcery rather than its preexisting context.[5] The tools of both sorcery and curing are concoctions of vegetable ingredients, usually infusions of herbs, barks, and coconut oil, all referred to as *fagu* "bottle," short for *fagu vai laakau* "bottle of liquid of vegetable substance." *Vai laakau* can be used for a whole panoply of purposes: killing opponents and enemies, increasing one's success in fishing, increasing one's erotic success with persons of the opposite gender, prescience and divination, and making soccer teams from one's home island win in Tuvalu's national tournaments. There is constant gossip about who possesses a *fagu*, although no one admits to having one, and bottles are covertly transmitted from one generation to the next. I never saw one, although I had occasional moments of doubt when confronted with odd-looking containers.

Beyond these basic observations, Nukulaelae Islanders' relationship with sorcery and sorcery-enabling spirits becomes complex and, at the same time, gendered. First, Nukulaelae discourse about the existence, importance, and relevance of sorcery and spirits is shifting and full of contradictions. The church treats them with disgust, as remnants of the darkness of yesteryear. Elderly men, whose claims to political power depend crucially on their hanging onto church appointments as deacons and lay preachers, stay close to the church-sanctioned discourse whenever the topic arises in public. They publicly refer to sorcery and spirits with the distancing expression *mea kolaa* "those things [over there]," implying that using a more precise term for sorcery is beneath their dignity. Women, who can only aspire to become lay preachers, have less to lose, and thus have an easier time claiming control over spirit and sorcery discourses.

However, overtly incommensurable epistemologies easily rub shoulders with commensurability. When I presented an oral version of this chapter at the University of Auckland in 1995, I bravely invited to the lecture a number of recent Nukulaelae migrants, the forerunners of a now extensive expatriate community. The lecture became an uneasy event, at the end of which the patriarch of the small group declared to me, "There is no *vai laakau* on Nukulaelae," despite the fact this man (now deceased) was widely known to have sought the services of sorcerers to treat his debilitating ailments. Even on a historical-cosmological level, spirits are in fact uncomfortably close to Christianity: the story goes that Elekana's 1861 chance landing on the atoll was in fact announced the night before it happened by a female spirit medium of the "old religion" named Te Kafoa, whose vision of a new dawn enmeshed Christianity with spiritism right at its inception.

Spirits and what they enable are both far away and near, as I have discussed elsewhere at greater length (Besnier 1996b). Sorcery is far away because Nukulaelae Islanders, the inhabitants of Tuvalu's "chosen atoll" where Elekana and Christianity first landed, state that they know little (or, officially, nothing) about *vai laakau*, compared to, say, people of the northern islands of Nanumea and specially Niutao, and further afield "dark" Kiribati, in tune with the representations of the latter. The Nukulaelae cosmology of sorcery is therefore enmeshed with a national and transnational landscape, as well as a historical context of missionization, colonialism, and modernity-making.[6]

And indeed, a very different ethos underlies discourses of sorcery among northern Tuvaluans (cf. Chambers and Chambers 1985, 40–44; Finney 1976; Koch 1962), widely reputed throughout the country for their conservative stance toward traditional knowledge (medical, fishing, agricultural, wrestling, love magic, etc.). Witness, for example, the certainty with which an elderly gentleman from Nanumea, whom I interviewed while he was visiting Nukulaelae relatives (to attend to a sick relative, and thus suspect of knowing a thing or two beyond curing), asserts his belief in the existence of *vai laakau*:

Me i vai laakau nei laa, fai mai nei laa peelaa me seeai, peelaa, e see fakamaaoni-gina, nee? A ko toku fakama- toku iloa laa, e tonu eiloa mea kolaa. E isi eiloa ne vai laakau. [. . .] Kae nei laa, i ttou maaloo laa i te maaloo seki fakamaaonigina peelaa, nee? [. . .] A ko taku iloa laa, se mea tonu kkii. E isi loa ne agaaga. [T 1991:1: A:420–429]

Because as far as sorcery is concerned, it is said that it doesn't exist, that it's never been proved, right? But I know that these things [i.e., sorcery] are true. There is such a thing as sorcery. [. . .] But then our government, the government has not accepted it, right? [. . .] But I know that it is a true thing. Spirits very much exist.

Had the man been a Nukulaelae Islander, he would have categorically denied the existence of sorcery to me, a complete stranger to him and a non-Tuvaluan. Even at more relaxed moments, Nukulaelae discourse on *vai laakau* is rife with ambivalence and contradiction, as illustrated in the following two interview excerpts with someone I know well (the term *talitonu*, which I translate as "believe," is a borrowing from Samoan and thus has religious connotations):

Au laa see talitonu lele loo ki mea naa! See taaitai eeloo o talitonu! Konei taatou nei, e olo saale, e olo saale, kaiaa see vau ei te agaaga ki taatou nei? [L&S 1991:2: A:413–414]

I absolutely do not believe at all in those things [i.e., spirits]! I am not about to believe [in them]! [Look at] us here, [we] run around, [we] run around, why doesn't a spirit come to us here [if they really existed]?

Yet a few minutes later, the same interviewee affirms that spirits are selective in their manifestations, thus implying that they *do* exist:

Au e talitonu ki- i agaaga e mafai eeloo o olo ki tino kolaa e kaallaga saale ki agaaga. Kae see mafai o soo naa vau ua kia maatou kolaa see fiaffia atu kiaa ia, kae fano eeloo ki tino kolaa e fiafia a ia ki ei o fakataugaasoa ki ei, me ne kalaga atu kiaa ia kee vau. [L&S 1991:2:B:193–198]

I believe in- that spirits can go to people who are in the habit of calling out to spirits. But it [i.e., the spirit] can't come any old way to those of us who are not friendly with it, but it always comes to people who are happy to make friends with it, because they called out for it to come.

It is this kind of ambivalent and multivocal discourse, uncertain at times and certain at other times, that has led me to invoke, in a more extended analysis than I am able to develop here, Bakhtinian heteroglossia as a useful handle on the discursive complexities in which spirits and sorcery are embedded in Nukulaelae cosmology, complexities that cannot simply be explained away in terms of "context shifts" (Besnier 1996b): these things don't exist, but they also do; they don't affect me, but they touch people near me; I believe in them, but my tradition-steeped

Christian persona does not. There is strong "official" pressure to underplay the importance and relevance of sorcery, in close association with the discourse of Christianity and the state. But even public discourse, in which sorcery and spirit can only be mentioned to condemn them as things of the dark heathen past, is suffused with heteroglossia, as I will illustrate in chapter 7. The resulting complexities are not just a matter of cosmology, and the narratives I present in this and the next chapter offer striking illustrations of the fact that they can have very serious material consequences.

Odd Widows

The Nukulaelae people who had traveled to Funafuti to consult Saumaiafi were harboring suspicions about a lot of things, which they hoped that the spirit's omniscience would help them resolve. One question was what exactly was going on around a Nukulaelae woman in her mid-forties, whom I will call Loimata, who stood out as an unusual person when I met her for the first time that year (she had been living off-island for a long time). Twice widowed, she claimed a vast kinship network spanning several islands and island groups, of which she often deliberately reminded anyone who would listen. "*Tuaatina!*" (mother's brother!) she would call out to just about anyone who might possibly qualify (other than her avoidance cross-siblings) to make everyone laugh. Loimata was heir to substantial *logo* "customary knowledge" through these kin ties, particularly through her descent from one of the northern islands of the group known for its sorcerers. She was a midwife and bush doctor, knowledgeable in sought-after massage techniques and potions that brought her to the bedside of the sick, the pregnant, and the elderly. But she was also widely feared because of this knowledge, given the well-known inevitability that medicine goes hand in hand with sorcery. Her other inherited knowledge was of magic-supported wrestling holds *(te lima)*, which the island publicly sanctioned when she was the only woman asked to patrol, along with the men, during the sour-toddy rebellion of 1989 (chapter 3). No one seemed to share my view that her generous love handles might have made the practical implementation of this knowledge difficult. Her childlessness (except for an adoptive son, now adult) confirmed her status as the holder of powerful knowledge: recall that spirits demand a *taui* "reciprocity, compensation" for their assistance, childlessness being a common example.[7]

An issue of nagging concern was the mysterious ways in which her successive husbands had died. One, whom I knew reasonably well before I got to know her, went deep-sea fishing one day off Funafuti, where they were living at the time and where he was employed in the civil service, and never returned. He was known to be prone to psychotic episodes, but this complete disappearance raised questions. The second husband met an equally strange fate, suddenly falling ill and dying within hours, his calf muscles having become completely soft. In both cases, the unexpected demise of the husband had been preceded by a domestic quarrel (although this is unlikely to have been an unusual event, given Loimata's larger-than-life personality). In the second instance, the angry husband had thrown a coconut-husking stick (*koso*, a sharp instrument made of very hard wood) at her, but the stick had not reached its target and instead had fallen unexplainably at Loimata's feet.

Loimata had an adoptive sister, whom I will call Siuila, with whom she had always maintained a warm friendship despite the fact that the two women's presentations of self were polar opposites. While Loimata was loud, assertive, and extremely funny, Siuila was restrained (at least in mixed company), upstanding, and responsible. In the late 1980s, the two women were spending most of their time together, as Loimata had practically moved into Siuila's household. I say "practically" because, just as she claimed kinship ties to multiple islands and countries, Loimata also kept a foot in the (figurative) door of several households in which she theoretically had a residential claim, securing her foothold by leaving clumps of possessions from her extensive wardrobe. The renewed friendship between the women closely followed the death of Siuila's husband, a charismatic and important member of the atoll community, who had succumbed in his early fifties to throat cancer, undoubtedly the result of decades of smoking the virulently strong tobacco that almost all men smoke. Both Siuila and her late husband had been married before, and the bond between them was obviously very warm (second marriages are more likely than first marriages to be the product of agentive choice), despite the demure distance and mock snappiness that they maintained, as decorum calls for between spouses. At his death, Siuila had been devastated, and at intimate moments she continued to speak of how much she missed him. Siuila was also my adoptive mother, and we made up an odd little household, actually part of a larger household, but strained relations had called for some social and geographic distance as we spent most of the day in the cooking hut: Siuila, Loimata, a young distant male relative from another island posted on Nukulaelae as a civil servant, and the anthropologist. The children were away at school.[8]

The two widows were unusual in two additional respects. First, they clearly were not on their way to falling into the oblivion that aging women gradually sink into, particularly if they have few or no children. They maintained a strong presence on the atoll, playing an active role in church and *maneapa* when "women's affairs" were at stake. They were also considered fortunate in material terms: by a strange twist of kinship fate, Loimata had ended up being the sole heir of land of considerable size by atoll standards and had also cashed in on her first husband's government employee life insurance (though this money had quickly evaporated). Siuila had access to someone of wealth, namely me, who, it was well known, sent regular remittances for the household and the education of the children when away. At the same time, she continued staying with her former in-laws, who harbored barely concealed bad feelings about my continued privileging her rather than them. In short, both Loimata and Siuila were seen as fortunate *(manuia)* in that they were able to weather socioeconomic changes without having to depend on relatives working precarious jobs overseas and were able to survive by themselves despite their unlikely social status.

The second way in which the two women stood out is that they were attractive in various senses of the term, an attractiveness to which their economic security was not unrelated. To this they responded in divergent ways. Loimata would get as much mileage as she could out of it. Very coquettish, a brazen flirt *(fakafaafine)*, she often threw social conventions to the wind. She also had the gift of gab, often launching into long tirades of both elegant and hilarious speech making. Young men found her irresistible, including a twenty-year-old who, scandalously, had wanted to propose to her, before a good beating from his father persuaded him to change his mind. Siuila, in contrast, did not go out of her way to provoke any amorous or marital advances, yet she was the object of many. One unmarried young man, considerably younger than she, had followed her to the gardens when she went down to uproot some swamp taro for the family feast, and exposed himself to her. She cursed him and ran away, screaming at him to bring her swamp taro up to the cooking hut since he had interrupted her harvesting. The young man later claimed that she had invited his advances by joking in a risqué fashion. Various married men had also come to her one by one, proposing to divorce their wives in order to marry her. One of them had handed Siuila a letter, which she immediately gave to her stepdaughter to burn without opening it. This turned out to be a bad move: instead of burning the letter, the stepdaughter kept it and showed it to her own mother and her sisters, who were all too happy to gather ammunition against the problematic second wife. The author of the letter later decided to make a speech during a village moiety feast to deny rumors about the letter—a bad move as well. The pastor punished both him and Siuila by barring them from communion the following Sunday. Not only did these uninvited proposals and their aftermaths, so out of the bounds of the acceptable, taint Siuila's reputation, but they also made her the target of the ire of the wives threatened with desertion. In everyone's eyes, the men and boys who made moves on both Loimata and Siuila were acting *fakavalevale* "crazed, irrational." *Fakavalevale* is an interesting category because, since the term is etymologically a causative (*faka-* "cause to," *valevale* "disorderly, unsocialized"), it refers ambiguously to the characteristics of someone's actions and to the possibility that someone else is causing the behavior: one's *fakavalevale* can be one's own doing, or it can be the result of someone else causing the disorderliness.

Loimata and Siuila Implicated in Sorcery

The most obvious method of rendering someone *fakavalevale* with sexual desire is sorcery. So when Nukulaelae women consulted Saumaiafi, one of their first questions was whether Loimata "played with bad things" *(taafao ki mea maasei)*. The spirit's straightforward answer was yes. While Nukulaelae people were still sleeping before dawn, she elaborated, Loimata would tiptoe out to the bush to gather shoots of *talie (Terminalia samoensis)*, which she would crush to concoct a magical potion. One of the women confirmed that, when a young woman had gone out to the bush one morning to gather *talie* shoots to make medicine for a sick old woman, she had found them all plucked off. Unexplainable happenings conspired with a buildup of resentment (*loto maasei*, literally, "bad heart") from women threatened with divorce by their husbands, feathers repeatedly ruffled by Loimata's brashness, and a general envy of the widows' economic independence not commensurate with their respective status as childless widow and widow with only two unmarried children. Envy, fear, and greed—all the classic ingredients for allegations of sorcery were there (Robertson 2001, 100), but here as in southeast Colombia, "envy is not so much the cause of sorcery and misfortune as it is the immanent discursive force for raking over the coals of events in search of the sense (and senselessness) of their sociability" (Taussig 1987, 394).

The target of the allegation was Loimata. One of the spirit's interrogators was the woman who had read the love letter addressed to Siuila, and she did question the spirit about Siuila, perhaps in the hope of confirming a two-decades-old suspicion that there had been malevolent doings at play in the late husband's motivation to divorce her sister and marry Siuila. However, the spirit denied that the latter was a sorceress, but specified that she was the victim of Loimata's sorcery. This is also where my presence in the household complicated the situation. Following is the relevant excerpt of the interview I conducted with the spirit's interrogator, the disarming candor of which betrays her firm conviction that the spirit alone was responsible for the allegations:

Naa laa, au koi ssili atu peelaa, "A ko Niko?"

"Then I continue asking, 'And Niko?'"

Ana pati, "Oo! A Niko teelaa ne puke nee F mo Siuila?" Aku pati, "Ao!"

"She says, 'Ah! The Niko that F and Siuila adopted?' I say, 'Yes!'"

Mea loa koo fai mai, "Io, a Niko e- e fai nee Loimata kia- kia Siuila, e nnofo i- i Nukulaelae nei peelaa me he taumaatua. A kaafai e olo ki- ki tua,"

"Then she tells me, 'Ah, Loimata is doing something to Niko and Siuila, they are now living on Nukulaelae like mother and child. But when they leave for overseas,'"

. . .

A koo oti ne fai nee Loimata, kaa olo koulua ki tua, kee nnofo koulua peelaa me he tauaavaga.

"And Loimata has done things so that, when you go overseas, you'll live like a married couple." [Saumaiafi 1990:1:A, p. 2]

The anthropologist always cuts a liminal figure in fieldwork, of which people commonly make sense in reference to a preexisting social order, of which fictive kin ties is the most common example, and rationalizes his or her activities in terms of local symbolic logics. It is perhaps not surprising that spirits come into play so frequently, given the liminality that they share with the anthropologist. Maria Lepowsky's (1993, 23–28) experience of being taken persistently for an ancestral spirit on Vanatinai (Louisiades, Papua New Guinea) is one of the best-told examples of this association. Nukulaelae people's more long-standing cosmopolitanism (and less enduring home-grown cosmology) did not open the door to the same possibility, but it is clear that my repeated and prolonged presences on the atoll, cutting across different social arrangements and political phases, presented complexities that, for some, only a spirit like Saumaiafi would be able to resolve.[9]

Had I been a bona fide Nukulaelae young man at the time, the story would have been explosive. The relationship that Siuila and I had forged was patterned on a mother-child adoptive tie, so that a redefinition of it as spousal would have been considered Oedipal incest, customarily as well as legally. In my case, the allegations were in very poor taste to say the least, as they made light of the kinds of expectations and obligations that not only she and I, but also her deceased husband, had established over the years. The difference in age between us would also have made us a very odd pair, although it fell in line with the pattern of very young men falling head over heels in sorcery-induced rapture for the middle-aged Loimata. Finally, the allegation articulated the widely held expectation that I would eventually take the family to live overseas, occurring as it did at the dawn of Tuvaluans' migratory movement to New Zealand.

For Nukulaelae audiences in the Saumaiafi séances, the spirit's prescience had an undeniable logic that ties together a number of loose strands. One was the occasion of a speech during which, as I described in chapter 2, a member of my deceased adoptive father's family had bestowed onto me the name of the deceased. Despite the fact that he had no authority to do so, the family accepted, probably taking into account that my foreignness made the matter relatively inconsequential. But judgments about consequentiality are difficult to control, and the renaming did catch on as most people (save for the spirit) began calling me with no apparent facetiousness by the new name, and it created a potential blurring of persona that peopled joked about most of the time, although it also set the scene for the serious Oedipal interpretation that Saumaiafi attributed to it.[10]

Another loose strand was that, since the beginning of my fieldwork, as is the case of any outsider visiting Nukulaelae, I had been the object of immense efforts to marry me off to one of the atoll's many eligible young women. These efforts can be understood in the context of the near collapse of the population after the slavers' raid in the late nineteenth century, which left an island peopled by women and old people that only recovered thanks to enthusiastic exogamy with plantation workers brought in by Godeffroy und Sohn (chapter 2). On a more contemporary note, the increasing absence of young men working overseas as seamen has renewed the gender gap and altered marriage patterns. My apparent reluctance to have a *fekau* "marriage proposal" sent to the family of one of many eligible young women was difficult to account for, particularly as I grew older, in part because of my choice to generally keep issues of sexuality close to my chest during fieldwork. The best explanation some people came up with was that it was motivated by *kaiuu* "stinginess," not so much my own in this case but that of Siuila, who had the aggravating distinction of having descended patrilineally and matrilineally from people of Nanumaga, the northern island of Tuvalu whose stigma *(pona)* is stinginess.[11] Indeed, marriage would have opened new channels for the circulation of wealth and would have added affines to the adoptive family as recipients of my seemingly vast resources, but would have curbed the latter's access to them as well. Siuila, who had long made unarticulated sense of my lack of enthusiasm for marriage (incomprehensible to most Nukulaelae Islanders), would often snap back impatiently at questions about when she would send out a *fekau* on my behalf. Sadly, women had attributed self-centered motivations to the motherly protectiveness Siuila extended on my behalf, putting her own intentions on the line.

One event, three months before, had highlighted in everyone's consciousness the material implications of the relationship I had established over the years first with Siuila and her husband, and then her alone, as well as its potential exclusivity. The atoll's Council of Women had opened a competition to pool money *(lukugaa tupe),* to be used to purchase corrugated iron sheets and cement to complete the houses of the village. As I explained in chapter 2, this transformation had begun in the early 1980s, spurred on by the veritable invasion of development-aid organizations that followed independence, particularly by Save the Children USA, but a chronic lack of money had prevented households from finishing the work, and as a result most houses were sorry-looking construction sites, held together by tarpaulin sheets and other temporary materials. It was the completion of this work that the women had made their task. The funds would be raised competitively, first pitching two half-moieties against their respective half-moieties, which would then combine their respective proceeds and compete against each other, the Pepe-sala *ituuala* "village side" against the Nukualofa *ituuala*.

July was coming to a close, and the cut-off date that the Council of Women had decreed was fast approaching. Many women had worked themselves into a frenzy, having cajoled, coaxed, and threatened their younger relatives working overseas to wire them money, adding to the burden that Nukulaelae contract laborers complain so bitterly about. At stake was prestige, not just the women's, but the household's, the half-moiety's, and the moiety's, and this prestige is consequential in a society in which the egalitarian ideology leaves few avenues for claiming symbolic capital of any kind. Some women were clearly being driven to desperation by the meagerness of the sums they had managed to gather. I learned later that some had tried to persuade Siuila to ask me for more money, but she had refused, risking being reminded that she was from Nanumaga, having decided that the A$200 that she had already asked for sufficed.

On the morning of the deadline, I innocently went to the IEO's office, which doubles as an agency of the Bank of Tuvalu, to withdraw some money to pay my assistants, and I learned there that there was little cash left in circulation. I began suspecting that something was amiss when one young married man, to whom I was not particularly close, came to ask me for a loan. Several others followed him, and I had to explain that I was running low on cash and was thus unable to extend any loan. Finally, as evening was drawing near and I was on my way to put out the fishing net across our corner of the lagoon, an elderly woman came to me and sat down on the sand at my feet, explaining that she had been my father's very best friend while he had been alive, an explanation she was punctuating with the little whining exclamations that old women emit in such situations (*Mm! Toku mokopu:::na!* "Hm! My grandchild!"), and begged me to give her money for her contribution to the pooling. (I learned later that her two sons working overseas had both sent her money but that she had already spent it all.) I am retrospectively ashamed to admit that I replied with a magnificently histrionic performance (the theatricality of which all Nukulaelae people within hearing range probably secretly appreciated), threatening to go and hang myself from a coconut tree if people kept harassing me about money.

Siuila and Loimata had witnessed the last exchange and could barely suppress giggles, prompting the elderly woman to break frame and turn to them angrily ("What are you two stupid things laughing at?!"), after which they explained to me what had taken place during the day. One young woman had seen me at the IEO's office and had concluded that I had gone to withdraw money for Siuila's contribution, which she surmised would have amounted to A$50,000. The news went from cooking hut to cooking hut in a matter of minutes. While everyone I talked to expressed a mixture of annoyance and amusement at what amounted to the fabrication of a young woman's fertile imagination, the incident did leave a vague feeling in the air of the extent of the wealth I could possibly be controlling, the extent of Siuila's access to this wealth, and the fact that she could deny other people's access to it, including the entire atoll community.

Ambiguity and Marginality

People returning from Funafuti in September began talking about Saumaiafi's pronouncements as they were still wading through the lagoon from the *Nivaga*'s barge, which had dropped them off in the shallow waters of the outer reef. The rumors traveled so fast so far that within a few weeks people began writing letters back home from as far as Nauru:

E tonu laa tala kia Siuila?

"Are the stories about Siuila true?"

Maaua nei mo U see iloa atu me e tonu tala konaa, me seeai nemaa tusi.

"U and I don't know whether the stories are true, because we haven't received any letters [from Nukulaelae]."

A kaafai e tonu, au e ofo ma kaiaa e maua ei nee Siuila o fai peelaa i ana tama koo maattua, i ttoko lua e fakaaallofa.

"But if they are true, I am outraged, how can Siuila behave like this, her children are now older, the poor things."

Teenaa ko tena [tautali] kia Loimata.

"That's the result of her hanging out with Loimata." [Letters 1991:801]

One of Siuila's children, who was then away studying, wrote to her blaming her poor grades on the fact that Siuila was wasting time flirting instead of praying for her children's academic success.

Before long, both women found themselves severely ostracized by other women. A year later, Siuila described to me how clusters of women would suddenly stop talking when she walked up to them, an unpleasant situation in any society, but one that is particularly trying in a society that places so much importance on sociality (*sulu ki te fenua*, literally, "dive into the community"). For Siuila, a firm believer in sanctioned values, these responses were devastating. Other women would taunt her:

Paa, kaa- au peelaa me e fai fakaaattea oki eeloo mana fano ki koga kolaa i fakapotopotoga, nee?

"Like, and- I felt really odd when I had to go to where there were groups of people, see?"

Kee oko loo ki fono, me e isi ttaimi foki, [. . .] ko au siki fano i te fono teenaa, au paa me e tai fakalavelave,

"Even meetings, because one time, [. . .] I had skipped some meeting, I had been rather busy,"

kae teenaa koo fai mai te mea a V paa me e- e vau o fai mai ana pati fakalagona ki au,

"and then V comes along, she comes along and says to me, in a way that could be overheard [by others],"

"Oi! Ee Siuila! Kaiaa koo hee hano ei koe ki fono?"

"'Oh, Siuila! Why did you not come to the meeting?'"

Muna a- aku muna, "Ee, au e tai fakalavelave."

"I say, 'Because I was rather busy.'"

Muna a ia, "Io! I au laa e fai, iaa koe he tino fiafia ki fono, mo ko koe loo koo fia fakaasi ou taaofi, kae kau iloaaga koe, a koe koo paea i luga i au mea ne fai."

"She says, 'Oh, because I thought, given that you like going to meetings, because you like providing your opinions, but I figured that you were ashamed by what you have done.'" [S Interviews 1991:1:A:107–114]

More seriously, Siuila's affines, with whom she had been living since the loss of her husband five years before, were now threatening to expel her from the household, an action that did not happen because, I suspect, of my presence.

The two widows responded to their precarious circumstances differently. Siuila, being meek-mannered, church-oriented, and *loto fenua* "community hearted" and thus attentive to the approval of others, was crushed by the events, even though according to many (but not all) accounts, she was the victim of the sorcery rather than its agent. She characterized her emotional state as being extremely *loto mmae* "pained-hearted." Loimata, in contrast, continued her life of ostensible insouciance, going on with her ways, laughing and talking loudly in public, master of the sharp-tongued repartee *(gutu tapitapi)* and of studied indifference, seemingly disregarding the allegations even though they presented her as bearing the burden of responsibility. She had the gall of laughing at the allegations, a reaction that both confirmed their truthfulness and fueled further resentment. Here is the spirit's main interrogator's account of Loimata's response to being confronted:

Teelaa au koo oti ne faipati ki ei, kia Loimata, aku pati- me heki- tena- taku faipatiiga atuuga konaa ki mea konaa, heeai eeloo neana pati e hai mai peelaa, me e ssee me e ttonu! E katakata eiloo!

"So I've already spoken to her, to Loimata, I said, but she hadn't- her- when I spoke to her about these things, she said nothing about their being true or false! She just casually laughed!" [Saumaiafi 1990:1:A:420–423]

When Loimata explained this reaction to me, she told me that she wished to stand above the allegations:

Au ne sagasaga fua o fakalogologo, kae katakata au ki ana pati. [. . .] Aku muna, "Kiloko, saa fakatalitonugina nee koe a pati naa."

"I just sat there listening, and I just laughed at what she said. [. . .] I said, 'Look here, don't believe a word of all this.'" [Saumaiafi 1990:3:A:089–091]

Her accuser's different interpretation demonstrates that laughter here is as ambiguous as it is elsewhere, and Loimata clearly found these ambiguities useful. Not denying the allegation came at a cost, but it also increased the sort of defiant prestige that she actively sought through her norm-breaking activities and presentation of self. In addition (and this is my own interpretation), it increased her prestige as the heir and guardian of medical and other knowledge, given the tenuous boundary between beneficent and maleficent *vai laakau,* a prestige on which she depended given her prestige-depleting lack of concern for what others may think.

The spirit's interrogation of course did not take place in a social vacuum. The bad blood between Siuila on the one hand and, on the other, the spirit's main questioner and her immediate family should be understood in the context of Siuila's being the second wife of a man who had divorced the latter's sister upon his return from Nauru because of her alleged infidelity. Thus Siuila's and Loimata's unlikely economic independence and apparently irresistible attractiveness in the eyes of men young and old fell into the context of a two-decades-old low-level feud. How was one to deal with this feud twenty years on and not appear to violate too blatantly community and church norms of mutual empathy, forgiveness, and peace? Saumaiafi's pronouncements, and their inherent ambiguity with respect to the truth, came to the rescue of those harboring revenge. Witness how another active participant in the mediumship séances negotiates, in an interview with me (during which he was undoubtedly a little defensive), the issue of attribution of intentionality:

Ka ne fai foki loo taku pati peenaa, nee?, taku faipatiiga i konei, au ne faipati foki loo peelaa,

"So this is what I said, right?, what I said here, this is what I said,"

Mea naa ko pati a te agaaga, "kae hee hai peelaa kee olo koutou, peelaa, o fakamaa-sei nee koutou io me aa?", a ko pati hua ne llogo ei maatou i pati a te agaaga, nee?

"These were the spirit's words, [and I said to other people,] 'I'm not relating these things to you so that you can go, like, for you to go and denigrate or whatever,' but this is just what we heard the spirit say, right?"

Kae hee hai peelaa ne pati e-. Hee iloa atu loo nee taatou ne pati e ttonu, peelaa, ne mmai maatou o fakamatala i konei me ne pati e ttonu. Peelaa, nee?

"And these words are not as if they were-. We just don't know whether these words are true, like, we didn't repeat these things as if they were true. Like that, see?"

A ko te mea ne faippati eiloa maatou i pati ne llogo i ei, pati katoa loo, mea valevale, nee?, kolaa ne faipatiga nee te agaaga.

"But what we said is what we heard, everything we heard, right?, that the spirit had said."

Peelaa! Peelaa ne mmai maatou o faippati nee maatou i konei, nee?, kae hee hai peelaa ne faippati peelaa me ne mea eiloo koo iloa tonu nee maatou ne mea e ttonu, nee? Peelaa.

"Like that! Like what we said here, right?, it's not is if we presented these words as words that we know are true, right? Like that." [Saumaiafi 1990:2:A:159–166]

Saumaiafi's pronouncements thus emanate from multivocal sources, whose nature no one can quite agree on: does the responsibility for the pronouncements rest with the spirit, the medium, the questioner, or those who repeat them to others? It is precisely this heteroglossic uncertainty that makes the allegations repeatable as "facts," allowing the gossipers to spread the news while maintaining the role of morally neutral parties. But the factuality of having heard the spirit make the accusation easily slips into the factuality of the accusation. The power of sorcery allegations thus resides in the possibility that their heteroglossic ambiguity can easily transform into unambiguous action. The ethereal, extraworldly, and ambiguous can give rise to very concrete marginalization.

Materiality, Spirits, and the Ethnographer

This chapter has foregrounded several themes, which are closely interrelated. The first is the fact that gossip is not only a production, but also an instrument for the negotiation of existing social relationships. This negotiation, however, can take on ambitious proportions, as it invokes supernatural beings such as Saumaiafi and supernatural events such as Suunema's mediumship events, which fall outside the received version of the Nukulaelae sociocultural order. They are ambitious in another, not unrelated, way. While local social relations are mundanely colored by the jealousy of a divorced wife, the deceit of a stepdaughter, the general envy directed at women who, not knowing their place, either fling convention to the wind or have access to resources (largely imagined) incommensurate with their status as widows with few children, they also involve agents as far away as Funafuti, Nauru, Samoa, and cargo ships plying the world's waters. Nukulaelae is indeed at the center of a large transnational network of people, information, and material resources.

Secondly, gender suffuses the events I have described. Men, of course, knew about the allegations and took a guarded interest in them, but they remained on the sidelines, save for Siuila's affines, who considered expelling her from the household, and the pastor, who was following his script. Husbands had warned the spirit's questioners: don't spread gossip about the white man, he is very smart and could take you to court. But all agents in the sorcery allegations—spirits, medium, questioners, gossipers, victims, and bystanders—were women (the only man, cited in the last excerpt, who played a significant role is transgender). Gender is a familiar theme in sorcery allegations and accusations across societies and times, as the vast ethnographic and historical literature on the topic has demonstrated (e.g., Ankarloo and Henningsen 1993; Boyer and Nissenbaum 1974; Comaroff and Comaroff 1993; M. Douglas 1970; Gluckman 1972; Niehaus 2001, to cite but a few). What is perhaps a little out of the ordinary in this sequence of events is that, while historians and anthropologists have demonstrated that women who do not conform to expectations (e.g., spinsters, widows, homeless or childless women, women of inappropriate wealth) are prime magnets for witch hunts, in this case women are both perpetrators and victims, which may have softened the consequences of the allegations, particularly in contrast to the situation I will describe in the next chapter.

The third theme that this chapter has brought to the fore is that certain kinds of gossip, already suffused with the ambiguity inherent in all gossip, become further enmeshed with the epistemological and moral ambiguity of spirits, mediumship, and sorcery. In gossip about sorcery allegations, politics and culture become deeply intertwined. But gossip originating from a spirit has different qualities from ordinary gossip. It is still surrounded with secrecy and a dose of shame, but it no longer needs to be hidden from people in the cooking hut next door since its content is open knowledge for which no one is locally responsible, and thus the gossipers can confront its victims without apparent shame (although others are quick to point out that those who spread the gossip carry the burden of responsibility). Instead, this kind of gossip should be kept at a distance from the church-sanctioned forms of knowledge and ways of conducting social relations, and in particular from elderly men, the most obvious guardians of church-related epistemologies and social dynamics. Elderly men are most likely to distance themselves from talk of sorcery and to express disgust about "those things," in public at least, although in private they can prove to be captivated, if stone-faced, audiences. This stance becomes dramatically consequential in the events I relate in the next chapter, in which sorcery allegations break loose from their gendered intimacy and burst open into the male-dominated public sphere, with much more serious effects.

Deeply implicated in the events that I analyze in this chapter are matters of inequality and of the anxieties generated by new patterns of unequal distribution of wealth and the demands that collective expectation makes on people of unequal wealth. The harrowing pressure that women felt to contribute formidable sums of money, the number of zeros of which they could barely keep track, was not incidental to the spirit-inspired allegations. Pressure to produce money on Nukulaelae has increased far more quickly than the availability of money. The theme is not unique to the Nukulaelae situation: Geschiere's (1997) now classic analysis of Cameroonian witchcraft as a response to the immorality of individualistic capitalist accumulation and resulting inequalities (also Comaroff and Comaroff 1993) provides a blueprint for understanding comparable dynamics in other contexts, and stands in contrast to arguments about money as absorbed into patterns of continuity and localization (e.g., Parry and Bloch 1989). Nukulaelae anxiety about who has access to what wealth is a deeply troublesome issue, perhaps continuous with long-standing discourses of egalitarianism, but also aggravated in problematic ways by new patterns of access to resources, both real and imagined. Here as elsewhere (Robbins 2007), rupture may be more consequential than traditional anthropological accounts have traditionally been willing to take into account (Englund and Leach [2000] notwithstanding).

The consequences of spirit-inspired gossip can be as tangible and disturbing as the consequences of any other gossip, although it can also feed alternative ways of defining the self for those who are already marginalized because of descent, knowledge, and practices. To the now vast analytic corpus on the "effect" of sorcery allegations and accusations, the events I analyze in this chapter add an agentive dimension: whether gossip about sorcery has the effect of leveling or accentuating structures of inequality depends not only on structural definitions of sorcery or the intention of the accuser, but also on the victims of the allegations, who may have divergent reactions. For some, gossip can lead to serious suffering and a profoundly transformative experience of marginalization, which in the olden days probably would have translated into ostracism and death. For others, it fuels an alternative prestige built on ambiguously normative inherited knowledge and complex reputation.

The last theme that this chapter has animated is the extent to which gossip is needed to make sense of the ethnographer and the extent to which the ethnographer is thus responsible, through no particular "fault" of his own (other than wishing to be good to people who are good to him), for the envy, resentment, and jealousy that underlies a great deal of gossip. The situation I have described here differs from other researchers' attempts to make sense of the gossip about themselves, in that the gossip did not target me as much as it affected the people I was close to, the people who had been good to me over the years and had fallen on affective hard times. Perhaps it is time for anthropologists to begin to understand their place in local contexts, not so much in terms of the way in which they elicit particular responses, but also in terms of the consequences that their presence may have on those who choose to associate with them, or onto whom such an association is thrust by the luck of the draw.

7 Sorcery and Ambition

GOSSIP IS A PERFORMATIVE ACT, in both the literal sense of "performance" and the narrower sense of "performative" as ordinary language philosophers have theorized it. The starting point for discussions of performativity in the latter sense continues to be J. L. Austin's (1962) proposal that performatives have the effect of altering aspects of the context in which they operate. For example, the speech act "I now pronounce you husband and wife" creates a particular kind of affinal relation between persons (so that bystanders react to hearing it in a proper context by clapping and cheering), and is thus a performative. Performatives, says Austin, are successful if and only if certain "felicity conditions" are met. In the case of the wedding performative, the felicity conditions include its being authored by someone with the authority to wed others, the objects of the performative being entitled to undergo the transformation that the performative purports to enact, and so on.

The poststructuralist critique of the Austinian model of performativity, particularly Derrida's (1977) response to Austin and Butler's (1990, 1997) rereading of it, has altered our understanding of the workings of performativity in a significant way. It is not just that successful performatives presuppose that felicity conditions are met, but rather that their efficacy resides in iteration across contexts. In other words, performatives do not depend so much on the individual intentions that underlie felicity conditions as on the "repetition or citation of a prior and authoritative set of practices" (Butler 1997, 51). What conditions the success of performative acts is the extent to which they invoke prior utterances and actions that carry authorizing legitimacy and reinforce the performativity of the current utterance. From intentional acts, performatives become social acts in this rereading. This chapter seeks to elucidate how gossip, as a performative, is dependent on relevant authority-bestowing social acts that precede it.

As I have already alluded to in previous chapters, utterances and genres always operate in the context of other utterances and genres: public and private talk, official decrees and talk about them, mediated discourse and everyday discourse, political and off-the-record statements always address one another, leak onto one another, support or contradict each other, and collude with one another or resist each other's power. Agents utilize specific genres with the more or less conscious awareness that they are *not* utilizing other genres that are theoretically available to them in particular situations. The interconnectedness of discourse forms is embedded in Bakhtin's notion of heteroglossia, but it also conjures up a Foucauldian understanding of power as elusive, multifarious, and shifting (Foucault 1977, 1980, 1990). While this perspective on power has proved inspirational to many anthropologists and other social scientists (Aretxaga 1993), this inspiration has generally been implemented in analyses of the most formalized and institutionalized bodies that society has to offer: prisons, courtrooms, hospitals, laboratories, counselors' offices, and other bureaucratic, scientific, and educational institutions in industrial societies, and meetings, councils, and (post-)colonial bureaucracies in other societies. What is far less understood is how public institutions and intimate contexts (as well as what takes place within each) articulate with each other to create webs of power that are the property of no one but that nevertheless provides a relentless inequality-generating machinery. Indeed, as Keane (2003, 240) argues in a critique of anthropological texts that present intimacy as if it existed out of the reach of "distancing" words and actions (e.g., Abu-Lughod 1991), even the most private thoughts and deeds never operate beyond the reach of public discourse. This chapter focuses on the way in which gossip colludes with other forms of discourse and explores how intimate and official discourses constitute the warp and weft of the same power loom, in which one person, in the narrative I present, gets caught.

Death and Suspicion

In early 1991, a healthy-looking thirty-seven-year-old Nukulaelae man, whom I will call Ioopu, returned home from Nauru, where like many other Nukulaelae people he had been a laborer employed by the Nauru Phosphate Company. But Ioopu was returning before the end of his three-year contract because during a medical examination prompted by his frequent physical discomfort, the NPC's medical staff found him to have malfunctioning kidneys. The company, in accordance with its employment policies of non-Nauruan employees, immediately repatriated him.

Eight days after his return, Ioopu died. It is true that he had been diagnosed with kidney problems, but how could problems of the kind arise so suddenly, his relatives asked, like the Azande of the termites in the granary (Evans-Pritchard 1937)? Such things do not happen so unexpectedly to a healthy-looking younger man. While Nukulaelae Islanders do not invoke foul play to explain all deaths, as members of many Melanesian societies do (e.g., Knauft 1985; Riebe 1987), the specter of sorcery becomes conspicuous when death strikes suddenly or when its victims are in their prime. Slowly, things started falling into place as news from Nauru began trickling in: there were problems in the Nukulaelae community on the phosphate island, people not getting along, and power struggles. Much of this talk centered on one person, whom I will call Paanapa, an ambitious man who had served for three years as the *toeaina* "elder" of the Nukulaelae community on Nauru. Swift action was needed. Nukulaelae's Council of Elders met and decided to order Paanapa to resign from his employ with the NPC and return home in disgrace.

This chapter analyzes the events that led to and followed Paanapa's downfall, which bring to the fore the fundamental ambiguities in Nukulaelae's political makeup that I investigated in chapter 3. Alongside their overtly articulated idealization of a strong leadership structure and clear-cut hierarchy (the "discourse of nostalgia"), Nukulaelae Islanders see powerful and ambitious leaders like Paanapa as a threat to social order (the "discourse of egalitarianism"). Paanapa was guilty, in Nukulaelae eyes, of loving power and prestige too much. Yet because Nukulaelae people value strong leadership in some respects, he could not simply be disgraced for exerting authority. The solution was to invoke sorcery. And again, the "multiple orders of reality" (Tambiah 1990, 101–105) that background sorcery and its accompanying agents and practices (spirits, spirit mediumship) on Nukulaelae stretched a web of ideological complexity across the path of the victim that embedded gossip into a vast array of other communicative practices, with serious consequences.

Paanapa Implicated in Sorcery

As I discussed in chapter 3, Nukulaelae Islanders working on Nauru were of utmost economic importance for Nukulaelae, and their little community (in 1991, eight adult men and their spouses and up to the two children that the NPC allowed, and eight single men) represented a structural replica of the community back home. Its *toeaina*, appointed by the Nukulaelae Island Council, worked for the NPC but received an additional allowance, bringing his daily income to A$5.50, compared to the A$2.20 that low-level employees received. No one was as aware of the importance and cushiness of this position as Paanapa, who had already occupied it for several years. A retired police officer with the Gilbert and Ellice Islands Colony and, after separation and independence, with the government of Tuvalu, Paanapa brought to Nauru an impressive curriculum vitae. (Many former members of the colonial police force now occupy important positions in Tuvaluan politics and civil service.) In particular, his thirty-odd years of civil service gave him a clear economic advantage over others. A physically imposing man, an alleged womanizer, and an infamous liar and braggart, Paanapa was a natural target for envy-fueled gossip. With few friends and supporters, he had the bad fortune of having few kindred amongst the *sina o te fenua* "elders [literally, 'white-hair'] of the atoll." Yet his experience, age, and material comfort made him a good candidate for the position of *toeaina* on Nauru and from there eventually for the Nukulaelae chieftainship. Once again, the classic prerequisites were in place (envy, fear, greed) for a sorcery allegation.

One day, people spotted Paanapa at a deserted spot in Nauru's desolate landscape, ravaged by decades of indiscriminate mining. He was standing over one of the abandoned phosphate quarries and allegedly flaying his arms about, whereupon a large red cloud appeared and enveloped him. Without a doubt, Paanapa was dabbling in sorcery, since weather phenomena like sudden clouds are evidence of spirit activity. As time went on, the Nukulaelae community on Nauru began to unravel the details of his actions, and several facts converged to "prove" *(fakamaaonia, fakatalitonu)* the veracity of the allegation. Since spirits know who practices sorcery, people consulted a spirit medium on Nauru, a woman from, not surprisingly, Niutao. The spirit confirmed that Paanapa's sorcery was aimed at two families, headed by Naakala and Ioopu, both potential contenders for Paanapa's position of *toeaina*:

> *Ne fakalleo i Naaluu, nee? Kae faipati nee ia a te mea teenaa, ia Ioopu mo tena kaaiga e ttaa nee Paanapa, fakavailaakau nee Paanapa, mo Naakala mo tena kaaiga foki e ttaa nee Paanapa. Teenaa te mea [. . .] e fakatalitonu nee laatou a-, te fafine teenaa ne fakalleo, faipati mai loo peenaa i- ia Ioopu mo Naakala mo tena kaa- mo laa kaaiga ne- e fakavailaakau nee Paanapa.* [F 1991:2:A:109–120]

[She] made [the spirit] speak on Nauru, right? And [she] said that Ioopu and his relatives are being killed by Paanapa, ensorcelled by Paanapa, and Naakala and his kin group are also being killed by Paanapa. That's what [. . .] proved to them that the-, that woman through which [the spirit] spoke said that Ioopu and Naakala and his- and their kin groups were being ensorcelled by Paanapa.

Soon news reached Nukulaelae. Several Nukulaelae Islanders on visits to the capital went to consult Suunema, the Funafuti spirit medium I introduced in chapter 6, who confirmed the information. The allegations were already grounded in suspicions, held by many, that Paanapa was the owner of a *fagu*, which several claimed to have seen. Finally, and most damningly, both Ioopu and the wife of his other alleged victim were constantly sick around the time of the allegations:

> *[. . .] te aavaga a Naakala e ssoko loo te masaki i Naaluu, nee?, kee oko foki kia Ioopu. E ssoko loo te- te masaki, nee? Ia, teelaa laa, kee oko mai loo ki ttaimi teenei, teelaa koo- koo galo nei a Ioopu mo t-, te masakimaiiga loo mai Naaluu, masaki*

masaki masaki, oko mai ki Nukulaelae nei, ne masaki, mea loo koo- koo mate,
nee? Aati laa teenaa te suaa feituu peelaa e tai fakatalitonu atu ei ki te moolimau
teelaa, moi ne fai e- e ola nei a Ioopu, aati, peelaa, see fakatalitonugia te aa?, a te- te
mau a laatou teelaa mai koo, nee? Ia, kae nei, peelaa, kaa maafaufau atu taatou
ki- ki te fakalleo a te fafine teelaa, fai mai, me ttaa nee Paanapa, fakavailaakau nee
Paanapa, ka koo mafai foki nee taatou o tai fakatalitonu, me iaa Ioopu nei, koo seeai
nei, nee?, koo oti ne mate. [F 1991:2:A:127–143]

Naakala's wife kept getting sick on Nauru, see?, and Ioopu as well. He kept getting
sick, see? So, even now, now that Ioopu has- has died of the-, when he got sick all
the way back on Nauru, he was sick [and] was sick [and] was sick, [then] arrived
here on Nukulaelae, he was sick, and then he died, right? Perhaps that's another
thing that proves that account, [because] had Ioopu survived, perhaps, like, the-
the- the explanation they developed over there would not have been proven, right?
But now, if we think about what- what the woman said during her spirit mediumship, she said, Paanapa killed him, Paanapa ensorcelled him, so now it's been
proven for us, because Ioopu has now disappeared, see?, he's dead.

As Derrida and Butler would have predicted, the iterative citation of the assertions
across contexts, genres, authors, and locales all contributed to their truth. Even the
spirits confirmed it from over in the other world.

Several other incidents concerning Paanapa's and his family's behavior made
the gossip particularly worthy of attention. Their *fia maualuga* "arrogance" (literally, "having pretensions of being high up") appeared to know no bounds, and
the most oft-quoted example of it concerned the wife. During one of the many
quarrels pitting her against other Nukulaelae women, she declared in public that
she and her husband were the *tupu* "king" or *aliki* "chief" of Nukulaelae. Gossipers invariably specified that she had made this statement on the Nukulaelae
community's Nauru *malae* "public green," a location where words mean what they
mean. It was not necessarily a direct challenge to the current chieftainship, but
it nevertheless was serious because it invoked impossible-to-prove genealogical
legitimacy that people usually tiptoed around. Paanapa's adult daughter, who was
married to a Nauruan (never a very good start, in Nukulaelae opinions) and was
as quarrelsome as her mother, made similar claims.

Paanapa's wife allegedly treated single Nukulaelae men on Nauru poorly, failing to invite them to eat, for example, in violation of the expectation that she, as
the *toeaina*'s spouse, serve as a surrogate parent. Paanapa also favored *(faapito)*
his own son Fitilalo by looking after his welfare on the job while neglecting other
young men. Fitilalo himself frequently acted intolerably, but Paanapa did not discipline him. On one occasion, he came to a feast drunk, ate from the young men's
communal tray, and to everyone's utter disgust vomited the food back into the

tray, but he received no punishment. The common theme that underlies these stories is abuse of power and an inability to fulfill the obligations of a leader.

The sorcery allegation articulated with the other allegations in an ambiguous fashion. Nukulaelae people view sorcery as the antithesis of leadership, as leaders should be models of Christian enlightenment and modernity. Leaders ideally exert some control over nature through their *mmana* "mana," but spirits do not mediate this control. Sorcery undermines the foundational values of peacefulness and mutual empathy. So the sorcery allegation was congruent with other allegations leveled against Paanapa. However, it also played a particularly important role in that it was the only allegation of misconduct directed at Paanapa himself rather than at a family member. While a leader must keep the family under control, the failure to exert such control is not as serious as one's own misconduct. Furthermore, all discussion of Paanapa's and his family's behavior invariably centralized sorcery as the most scandalous and dangerous. It is one thing to be a poor leader and be surrounded by an unmanageable family, and quite another to use sorcery to murder. As one Nukulaelae respondent asserted, fear of Paanapa's sorcery subsumes the general discontent with his other reprehensible actions:

[Nukulaelae] people on Nauru are afraid, [. . .] people are afraid of sorcery. That's the simple reason. As for me, when I start to think about sorcery, I can't think how you-, why, is a spirit going to come and throttle you while you're just sitting around like this? Because spirits are afraid of people. And they grope around, [saying] that Paanapa does this, Paanapa does this [and] does this, but the real reason, they are afraid of Paanapa's sorcery. [N 1991:1:A:567–571]

Paanapa himself would later argue in public that the sorcery allegations underlay all other allegations, using this argument to put people to shame for their un-Christian anxieties:

Ne lafo peenei nee au te pati ki luga i te faanau a taatou mai koo, "Au e faipati ttonu atu, a te mea teenei ne tupu ki luga i toku faapito kia Fitilalo, e see fia maaina loo koe i ei, ona loo ko te mea teenaa e nofo mo koe, ia Paanapa e fai vai laakau, ia Paanapa e fai vai laakau." [Fono Taupulega 1991:1:B:533–535]

I said the following to our sons over there [on Nauru], "I am speaking straight to you, what really happened [that you interpret as] my having favored [my son] Fitilalo, you don't want to try to understand, because all you can think about is that Paanapa is a sorcerer, that Paanapa is a sorcerer."

But it is precisely the sorcery allegations that Paanapa would later have the greatest difficulty defending himself against.

This is where gossip begins to become enmeshed with other discursive forms, but in convoluted ways because sorcery can surface in public talk only if couched in condemnatory terms. In April 1991, Nukulaelae people on Nauru sent two telegrams to Nukulaelae's Council of Elders, the second more forceful than the first, outlining the various allegations against Paanapa and asking the council to order Paanapa to resign from the NPC, give up his position as Nukulaelae *toeaina* on Nauru, and return home. The second telegram, sent because the council had ignored the first, added the stipulation that if the council did not comply, all Nuku-laelae workers would quit and return home. The blackmail was explosive, since mass resignation would have meant the end of remittances, and left little choice to the council. Paanapa was forced to resign and, disgraced, returned to Nukulaelae in June 1991. Some of his own relatives refused to greet him. The following is his own public description of how his *tuagaene* "sister" (FFZSD) greeted him on Funafuti (classificatory cross-siblings are supposed to display mutual respect and support):

Ia, fanatu au, e sagasaga mai ko toku tuagaene teenaa ko Oolepa. Fakataalofa fakataalofa fakataalofa kia Oolepa, muna a Oolepa iaa ia e tapu kkii e fakataalofa ki au, me se aa te maumea o Ioopu ne fano ei au o fakavailaakau Ioopu. [Fono Taupulega 1991:2:A:440–442]

So, I come along, [and find] my classificatory sister Olepa sitting down. I greeted [and] greeted [and] greeted Olepa, [but] Olepa says that she absolutely wouldn't greet me, [asking me] on account of what wealth of Ioopu I had gone out and performed sorcery on Ioopu.

Paanapa will later bear witness to the agony *(loto mmae)* to which he was subjected in dramatic and, frankly, heart-rending terms, alluding to the allegations as shack-les around his ankles, and praying to God that he be given the fortitude to bear the pain of his ostracization:

[. . .] au e manako ki te seni teenei i oku vae, mo te seni teenei i vae o taku faanau, kee ttoo keaattea. [Fono Taupulega 1991:1:B:411–412]

[. . .] I want these shackles around my ankles, and these shackles around my children's ankles, to come away.

Au (n)e tuku taalosaga nee au ki te Atua, kee maua nee au o onosai, kee maua nee toku kaaiga o onosai. [Fono Taupulega 1991:1:B:550–551]

I gave my prayers to God so that I'd have the fortitude, so that my family would have the fortitude [to endure it all].

The Meeting in the *Maneapa*

From gossip to telegram to meeting to gossip, and now from telegram to face-to-face public confrontation. Upon his arrival on Nukulaelae, Paanapa immediately requested that the Council of Elders call an unscheduled meeting. It is significant that he did not attempt to seek redress through the court system, probably well aware that a number of Tuvaluans from other islands had attempted in the recent past to take issues of sorcery to court with little success, confirming the futility and danger of pitching sorcery against the power of modernity (cf. Rodman 1993 on Ambae, Vanuatu).[1] What transpired from this dramatic meeting, where I was present, my tape recorder to my side and the council's permission to record, is that talk of sorcery does not fare well there either. Scheduled at short notice, the meeting followed on the heels of a feast held to welcome the returnees, as is customary. Paanapa had requested that the entire atoll be present, an unusual occurrence. Riveted by the fact that history was in the making in front of its collective eyes, expecting (and probably hoping for) the worst, the community acted like a muffled-voiced Greek chorus, punctuating the proceedings with barely suppressed exclamations, murmuring its disapproval, and holding its collective breath at particularly dramatic moments.

The meeting first turned to a couple of routine matters. An hour and a half into the proceedings, the *ulu fenua* announced, almost as an afterthought, "Let us turn to the matter that was brought up to our attention by our son who has something to say, this opportunity is now open to him." Getting up to his feet to heighten the importance of the occasion, Paanapa began by asking the Council of Elders for an explanation for his disgrace.[2] The *ulu fenua* answered:

> *Ia, e fakailoa atu nee au, ee Paanapa, kiaa koe, a te aumai o koe nee ttaupulega,*
> *e seeai se vaa maasei o koe mo ttaupulega i konei. A te vaa maasei, (e) ia koutou*
> *loo i Naaluu. A ko te mea teelaa ne fakatoka nee ttaupulega, ko te llei- te nnofo llei*
> *o ana taagata. Teelaa ne avatu ei tena uaeelesi, kee fakamolemole, kee tuku aka koe*
> *kee vau.* [Fono Taupulega 1991:1:B:404–405]

> All right, I am making known to you, Paanapa, that you have being brought back by the Council of Elders, but that there are no bad feelings between you and this council. The bad feelings are among you all, over there on Nauru. What the council decided was meant to keep the peace between men. That's why it sent a telegram to the effect that you should please avail yourself to come home.

The theme underlying the chief's initial answer will surface time and again in the meeting: the council had no choice but to act as it did to keep the peace (*fiileemuu* "peace," *nofo llei* "stay well") among members of the Nukulaelae community on

Nauru. Other council members also stressed that the Nukulaelae community's threat to leave Nauru had left them little choice:

> Te mea fua teelaa ne saga ei taatou kia Paanapa, kae teenei eiloa Paanapa e fakalo-gologo, fakamunaaga- koo lua taimi ne aumai te fakamunaaga nee faanau a taatou i koo, "Kaafai e see fai nee koutou se faiga kia Paanapa kee avatu, a maatou kaa olo katoa atu." [Fono Taupulega 1991:2:A:159–163]

The only reason why we took notice of Paanapa, here you are Paanapa listening to this, were reports- our sons over there [on Nauru] sent us reports on two occasions [saying], "If you don't order Paanapa to come home, we'll all come home."

The Council of Elders could not afford, literally, to ignore the telegrams.

Paanapa then delivered several speeches in succession, arguing that the charges brought against him were all untrue. He began with allegations other than the sorcery allegations, denying, for instance, reports of the belligerence and arrogance imputed to his wife, Seeluta:

> Faipati ttonu atu au peenei, te mmalu o te fenua i konei, seeai eeloo se fafine ne taua mo taku aavaga i (taku)- maa nnofooga i Naaluu. Seeai, seeai eeloo se fafine ne taua mo taku aavaga, maa nnofooga i Naaluu. Seeai, seeai. E seeai ne pati a Seeluta ne fai peelaa iaa ia se aliki. Seeai, seeai. [Fono Taupulega 1991:1:B:551–554]

I am speaking straight to you, with due respect to this atoll community, my wife didn't fight with any woman while we were on Nauru. My wife didn't fight with a single woman while (I)- we were on Nauru. There is no such thing, there is no such thing. Seeluta never said anything about her being a chief. There is no such thing, there is no such thing.

In the course of his lengthy deliveries, Paanapa called upon a wide range of persuasive strategies. At times, his performance consisted in emotional displays of pain, vulnerability, and humility, complete with sobs, breaking voice, and trembling:

> I au se faanau fua. A kaa suesue koe ki luga- ki luga i au, toku tupumaiiga, au ne tupu mai fua i ika, mo aa?, mo niu. Kae kilo atu au ki luga i tau vau, see aamanaia ((voice breaking)) au nee koe i au ne (ave nee koe). Teelaa ne oko ifo ki luga i au, faipati ttonu atu peenei ki luga iaa koe ttaupulega, toku fakaalofa mo toku kaaiga see fakattau eeloo. [Fono Taupulega 1991:1:B:564–568]

I am just a son [of the community]. If one inquires who- who I am, how I grew up, I simply grew up on fish and- and coconuts. And then I look at how I came back, I am not appreciated ((*voice breaking*)) by you (who sent me away) [to work]. This is what has occurred to me, I am speaking straight to you, the Council of Elders, there are no bounds to the pitiful state that I and my family are in.[3]

At other moments, Paanapa made rather pointed allegations, in a tone of voice that betrayed his anger and frustration. For instance, he dramatically confronted the chief Tito and another elder, Faamalama. These confrontations drew disapproving murmurs from the audience and yielded the following dramatic exchange:

Paanapa	*Ttaimi ne nnofo ei koulua i Funaafuti, ne lagona nee au ki oku taliga, e isi se tino- se tino ne faipati atu peenei ki Naaluu- i Naaluu, "Koo fai foki aamioga a Paanapa ne fai i konei?" Fakamolemole, kooi laa ttino ia koulua teenaa ne faippati i koo? Ne faipati atu ki Fu- ki- ki Naaluu, mo kooi ia koulua ne faipati atu ki koo? Kaafai e- e fakafiti koulua, kaafai seeai, toku toe taimi nei e tuu atu ei au. (Fakatoetoega)* = ((sobs))*
	"When the two of you were on Funafuti, I heard with my own ears, someone- someone said the following to [someone on] Nauru, 'So Paanapa is again doing what he used to do here?' Please, who said that? Someone said that to- Fu- to- [someone on] Nauru, so which of the two of you said that? If you deny it, if there is no such thing, this is the last time I ask you about it. (Shorten) =" ((sobs))*
Tito	*= Paanapa, fakamolemole, koe koi fano koe i konaa, nee? Au fua e fia iloa nee au mo ko ia ttino teenaa ne fakasae aka nee ia toku igoa i koo?*
	"= Paanapa, please, you are still harping on this, are you? I just want to know who involved my name in this?"
Paanapa	*Te feituu teelaa. Feituu teelaa.*
	"This matter. This matter."
Tito	*Aa, ikaai, au seki faipati eeloo i se telefoni ki Naaluu. E see iloa nee au a feituu konaa.*
	"Ah, no, I never spoke over any telephone to Nauru. I know nothing about this matter."
Paanapa	*Au e fakafetai. ((turning to Faamalama)) Te ssuga a Faamalama, tou mmalu! E isi se pati peelaa ne lafo atu nee koe i loto i ttelefoni e peelaa?*
	"I thank you. ((turning to Faamalama)) Faamalama, your respected honor! Did you ever throw such words over the telephone?"

<table>
<tr><td>Faamalama</td><td>*Ee, Paanapa, kae mmalu a te fenua! Ia, kae koo fia iloa nee koe te feituu teelaa, au e aamene au ki ttou Tamana teenei i te lagi, seei saku faipatiiga i ttelefoni ne fai ei nee au se feituu peenaa.*</td></tr>
</table>

Faamalama   *Ee, Paanapa, kae mmalu a te fenua! Ia, kae koo fia iloa nee koe te feituu teelaa, au e aamene au ki ttou Tamana teenei i te lagi, seei saku faipatiiga i ttelefoni ne fai ei nee au se feituu peenaa.*
"Paanapa, with due respect to the atoll community! So since you want to know about this matter, I say amen to our Father in Heaven, I never said any such thing over the telephone."
[Fono Taupulega 1991:1:B:573–582]

Finally, Paanapa turned to what everyone was waiting for, the sorcery allegations. Opening his remarks by apologizing profusely to the atoll community for bringing up such an inappropriate topic in public, Paanapa went on to deny the allegations. As the emotional tension increased, he announced dramatically that he was about to show the atoll community the sorcery bottle he had taken with him to Nauru. As a dead hush fell over the entire audience, he picked up a lady's plaited handbag that was lying at his feet, and, searching it long enough to maximize the suspense, pulled out of it a Bible, opened it, and dramatically kissed it three times:

Te mmalu o ttaupulega, e teenei te fagu ne fano mo au ki- ki Naaluu. Faipati ttonu atu nee au, teenei te fagu ne fano mo au ki taku gaaluega ki Naaluu. ((takes Bible out of handbag, audience falls dead silent)) *Te mmalu o ttaupulega! Au e faipati ttonu i loto i ttaupulega, te mmalu o laaua konei e sagassaga mai. Au ko Paanapa! Au e faipati ttonu ki mua o te Atua e tapu! Au e ssogi fakatolu ki ttusi tapu! E see iloa nee au o fai vai laakau!* ((kisses open Bible three times)) [Fono Taupulega 1991:1:B:586–591]

Due respect to the Council of Elders, this is the [sorcery] bottle I took with me to Nauru. I am speaking straight to you, this is the [sorcery] bottle I took with me to Nauru. *((takes Bible out of handbag, audience falls dead silent))* Due respect to the Council of Elders! I am speaking straight to the Council of Elders, due respect to those sitting facing me. My name is Paanapa! I am speaking straight before Almighty God! I am kissing the Bible three times! I do not know how to do sorcery! *((kisses open Bible three times))*

Swearing on the Bible in public by oneself is certainly not common practice on the atoll, hence the suspense and amazement. It does bear witness to Paanapa's familiarity with Western legal practices, probably stemming from his long experience as a police officer. But while they were impressed by the seriousness of the act, Nukulaelae people remained dubious. Pastors swear on the Bible that they will devote their life to God, one cynical young Nukulaelae friend pointed out to me in 1994, and yet one witnesses pastors being greedy, adulterous, and otherwise ungodly, but no thunder and lightning come to strike them from above. So what's the big deal?

Almost as dramatic was his narrative, further along in the meeting, of his confrontation with several of the individuals primarily responsible for spreading sorcery rumors. Among these figures was Suunema, the Funafuti spirit medium who had confirmed that he had caused Ioopu's death and the death of several others. While waiting on Funafuti for the monthly ship to Nukulaelae, Paanapa wrote a letter to Suunema, a copy of which he read out in the meeting. Following are highlights:

"*I loto laa i taku tusi teenei, koo fakailoa atu ei kiaa koe, iaa koe kaa ave nee au ki te fono, [. . .]. Me i tala ne fai nee koe, koo oko ei ki au mo toku kaaiga te mmafa, mo te inoino mai o tino ki au mo te kaaiga katoa. Teenaa foki loa te auala ne fakafoki mai ei au mai Naaluu. Teenei laa, tou avanoaga kee vau koe o fakatooese mai ki au, kae fai mai foki nee koe ki au peenei, i tau tala ne fai se tala ppelo fua. [. . .] Kaafai laa see fai tau- tou avanoaga teenaa, [. . .] teelaa kaa tagi ei au ki te fono, kee ttogi mai nee koe ki au, e tolu afe taalaa.*" ((audience gasps audibly, general murmur)) [Fono Taupulega 1991:2:A:418–447]

"In this letter, I am informing you that I am intending to take you to court, [. . .]. Because the stories you told weigh very heavily on my family and me, and people are showing their disgust toward my family and me. It is also the reason why I was recalled from Nauru. So you have the opportunity to come and apologize, and to tell me that the story you fabricated is only a lie. [. . .] If you do not take this opportunity, [. . .] I will ask in court that you pay me three thousand dollars." *((audience gasps audibly, general murmur))*

At stake in the meeting was Paanapa's integrity and credibility. Symptomatic of this concern was his repeated insistence that he was *faipati ttonu* "speaking straight": in the course of the hour and fifteen minutes of deliberations (during which many members of the council spoke in addition to him), Paanapa uttered the statement *Au e faipati ttonu atu* "I am speaking straight to you," or variations of it, thirty-one times. Unfortunately for him, the position he was speaking from put him at a clear disadvantage, and his very insistence on the fact that he was speaking straight only added to the impression that he was lying. As I mentioned earlier, his *pona* "[behavioral] stigma" was his *gutu ppelo* "mouth full of lies," a well-known fact that, solidly confirmed by his past actions, was often talked about. Paanapa himself recognized that challenge, as evidenced by his attempt to confront the problem in a statement that blended together threats of lawsuits and emotion talk in a convoluted manner:

Soo se tino Nukulaelae e fai mai i au e ppelo, soo se tino Nukulaelae e fai mai i au
e ppelo, kee siki aka tena lima. Ttaimi nei. Faipati ttonu atu au, mea nei ko ttaimi
o toku alofa, Suaaliki! Kae mai tua, koe kaa ave nee au ki te fono. Tala konei koo
oti ne lagona nee au, ttala a ttino mo ttinoo mo ttinoo, au e tautoo atu ki mua o
te Atua, koe e fakamaagalo nee au, ((voice breaking)) *koe e fakamaagalo nee au.*
Kae fai atu au, moi ave koe nee au ki te fono, te taga nei e ffonu i tupe. Ka ko koe e
fakamaagalo nee au. [Fono Taupulega 1991:1:B:600–605]

Would any Nukulaelae person who thinks I'm lying, would any Nukulaelae
person who thinks I'm lying, please raise your hand. Now. I am speaking straight
to you, this is time for me to have empathy, Suaaliki! But later, I shall take you to
court. The stories I have heard, the stories [told] by one person to another person,
I swear before God, I forgive you, *((voice breaking))* I forgive you. But I am telling
you, had I taken you to court, this pocket [of mine] would be full of money. But I
forgive you.

Furthermore, Paanapa was in an awkward position to prove his integrity, because
members of the Council of Elders went to great lengths to distance themselves
from the various allegations leveled against him. The problems that arose, as elders
made clear over and over again, only concerned Paanapa and the Nukulaelae community on Nauru. Since no member of that community could come forth to confirm or contradict Paanapa's testimonies, the council could not rule on the veracity of Paanapa's defense. His denials were thus left in limbo, and the council stood
on safely neutral ground.[4]

Finally, and perhaps most effectively, the council brushed aside Paanapa's
oratorical performance as inappropriate to the context. While council members
responded variously to the sorcery allegations, all responses were geared toward
dismissing these allegations as not worthy of the council's attention. One stance
represented in the responses stated flatly that any talk of sorcery was inappropriate
to a council meeting. This stance was represented by the chief's forceful reaction:

Ia, a ko te mataaupu e tautoo atu ki luga i te fenua, au seeai soku fia saga ki te
mataaupu teenaa ki tau vai laakau. E seeai eiloa soku fia fakalogologo ki se tino
kee faipati ki ei ki seoku talitonuga, fia faipati ki ei. [Fono Taupulega 1991:2:
A:107–111]

Now, regarding the matter you swore about to the atoll community, I just have
no desire to pay attention to matters of you being a sorcerer. I have no desire to
listen to people speak about any belief of mine [in this matter], [or] desire to talk
about it.

While other reasons for the discord between Paanapa and the Nukulaelae community on Nauru could be discussed (although they never were in much detail, since they were also dismissed as matters that only concerned Paanapa and the workers on Nauru), sorcery and its attributes, as well as Paanapa's oath on the Bible, are ideologically censored from public forums.

A second stance, closely related to the first, maintained that individual members of the council simply did not believe *(talitonu)* in sorcery, that talk of sorcery was irrelevant to their lives, and that they did not want to be subjected to it in any shape or form. This stance was illustrated by the remarks of a mild-mannered elder who takes some pride in his worldliness and enlightenment, and hence his trust in the law and disbelief in sorcery:

> *Kae tasi te mataaupu mai mataaupu konaa, (e) seeai s-, peelaa, e fia tuku atu toku maafaufauga ki ei, io me seoku talitonuga ki ei, ko mea tau vai laakau. E seeai, e seeai lele eiloa seoku maafaufauga e tau ki te feituu teenaa, ko mea tau vai laakau. Kee oko foki eiloa ki toku olaga e nofo nei, seeai soku maafaufau e faipati eeloo ki ei, seeai soku maafaufauga e fia talitonu atu au ki mea konaa. Vaegaa mea foki konaa kaa ave ki ttuulaafono, e- e see taaitai eiloa o fakatalitonugina nee te tuulaafono mea tau vai laakau.* [Fono Taupulega 1991:2:A:037–053]

> As for there is one matter among these matters, I have no-, like, desire to put my thinking to it, nor do I have any belief in things relating to sorcery. I have no [thought], absolutely no thought whatsoever on things having to do with sorcery. And this is also true of the life I lead, I have no thoughts [about this] to talk about, I have no thought of believing in those things. That sort of thing, if you bring it up to the law, the- the law is not about to believe in things having to do with sorcery.

The third and most complex stance was represented by Sautia, a prominent member of the council and a recently retired pastor with barely concealed political ambition. Although not present at the original meeting during which the council decided to recall Paanapa, Sautia first addressed other members of the council and ridiculed them for having paid attention to talk of sorcery:[5]

> *Nukulaelae!* ((very slow)) *au faanoanoa faanoanoa loa au i ttaupulega o Nukulaelae, ne aumai nee koutou te faanau, ona ko te vai laakau.* ((falsetto)) *Koutou e talittonu ki vai laakau?* [Fono Taupulega 1991:2:A:299–301]

> Nukulaelae! *((very slow))* I am very very distressed, I am very distressed by Nukulaelae's Council of Elders. You recalled a son because he was a sorcerer. *((falsetto))* You believe in sorcery?

Then Sautia turned to Paanapa and engaged him in the following exchange, the swift tempo of which heightened the drama:

Sautia   ((addressing Paanapa, very fast)) *Paanapa, koe e fai vai laakau?*
            "Paanapa, are you a sorcerer?"
Paanapa   *Ikaai!*
            "No!"
Sautia   ((very fast)) *E tii taaua, maafai e tonu koe e fai vai laakau?*
            "Will you cast a die with me to see if you are a sorcerer?"
Paanapa   *See iloa nee au!*
            "I know nothing [of it]!"
[Fono Taupulega 1991:2:A:301–304]

Again turning to the Council of Elders, Sautia then ridiculed it for allowing talk of sorcery to be held in full light, and concluded by invoking a Christian discourse, to which his status as a recently retired pastor made him particularly entitled:

((falsetto)) *Au e ofo! Kaiaa e fakaffifi ei fua te vai laakau, Tinilau, ki luga i te aumai o Paanapa? Kaiaa seki aumai ei Paanapa i mea kolaa? [. . .] Ttuuvalu e nnofo, kae aumai e tasi eiloa te pati, "A Paanapa ne aumai, e fai vai laakau!"* ((slow)) *Maa::umau laa, Nukulaelae!, ffonu te fale saa i taeao mo afiafi, kae talittonu ua ki vai laakau?* [Fono Taupulega 1991:2:A:304–311]

((falsetto)) I am astounded! Why do you tangle up sorcery, Tinilau, with the issue of Paanapa's recall? Why didn't you recall Paanapa for those other reasons? [. . .] [All of] Tuvalu is here [listening], and [you] only say one thing, "Paanapa was recalled, [because] he's a sorcerer!" *((slow))* What a waste, Nukulaelae!, the church is full, mornings and afternoons, and [you] believe in sorcery?

The structure of this exchange is particularly complex: there are clear indications that Sautia was exploiting the opportunity at hand to accumulate political capital, as he had been doing since his recent return to Nukulaelae. (He was intending to run in the next parliamentary elections.) Suffice it to say that, while Sautia appeared on the surface to side with Paanapa against the council, the exchange was not of much help to Paanapa. Indeed, like the other statements made earlier, Sautia's tirade dismissed all talk of sorcery and was as effective as more transparent statements in silencing Paanapa's attempts to justify himself.

Underlying these various positions is a common reasoning: responsible adult men pay no attention to sorcery, and therefore the Council of Elders should not talk about sorcery allegations in meetings. Instead, meetings should be the voice of *maalamalama* "enlightenment," as embodied in Christian ideology, government law, and the maintenance of peace *(fiileemuu)* and mutual empathy *(feaalofani)*. Rumors that particular individuals engaged in sorcery practices were simply not worthy of the dignity of the council. In other words, the sorcery allegations, which Nukulaelae respondents identified in private as the main source of Paanapa's downfall, were simply dismissed as inconsequential and irrelevant, and talk of them inappropriate to the context. Yet what was so easily branded as inconsequential and irrelevant was the principal cause of Paanapa's disgrace, by now a fait accompli.

This reasoning hinges crucially on the contradictory and shifting nature of Nukulaelae discourses on sorcery. Paanapa was caught in the heteroglossic web created by these contradictions, which spans several communicative genres. On the one hand, he was utterly helpless before the overwhelming power of faceless gossip, as his own description bears witness to:

> *See fakattau eiloa te mmae i (te) koga teelaa. [. . .] ppoi fua maatou, maanu mai se tala, maanu mai se tala, kee oko loa ki luga i mea ttupu konei i luga i ttou fenua nei, maanu mai se tala, maanu mai se tala. Ia, kae fakalogologo faaka nei, kaati laa koo tai sili atu maalie ttou fenua teelaa mai koo, i te mea loa ki te fakalasilasi o tala.*
> [Fono Taupulega 1991:2:A:565–575]

The pain that stemmed from this was indescribable. [. . .] to our surprise, a story would come our way, a story would come our way, even things that would happen here on our atoll [Nukulaelae], a story [about these] would come our way. And now I hear that this atoll of ours is even worse than [the Nukulaelae community on Nauru] over there, in regard to blowing stories out of proportion.

On the other hand, his attempts to extricate himself in the meeting were stifled as inappropriate. Thus one communal voice can enact the demise of an individual through gossip in a way that no other voice can challenge it. But even in private interaction, Paanapa had trouble confronting his accusers. When his cousin refused to greet him upon his return, she was denying him the possibility of justifying himself before her. Another example of the impasse in which he found himself was his threat of a lawsuit against the Funafuti spirit medium, Suunema, who had hosted one of the spirits who had accused him. After receiving the letter of threats excerpted earlier, she went to see him and told him the following:

> *"Paanapa, au e faipati ttonu atu ki luga iaa koe, a mea kolaa ne faipati nee au, e see iloa nee au. Kaa oti faaka, koo fai mai a tino, 'A mea kolaa ne faipati nee koe, a mea kolaa ne faipati nee koe.'"* [Fono Taupulega 1991:2:A:458–459]

"Paanapa, I am speaking straight to you, I have no knowledge of what I said [during the mediumship session]. When it is finally over, people tell me, 'This is what you said, this is what you said.'"

It's the spirit that spoke, not her, which in her view exonerates her of any wrongdoing.

What did Paanapa actually achieve in the meeting, during which he pleaded, threatened, wept, took a formal oath, and displayed his grief for all to see? Remarks made by various members of the council at the close of the proceedings are particularly enlightening.[6] Praising Paanapa for his contentment *(malie)* with the council's decision to recall him (which he had not expressed), council members thanked him for his forgiving *(fakamaagalo)* attitude:

> *Ia, kae malie koe ki soo se mea teelaa koo oti (ne) faigia nee te fenua, kee malie tou loto. Te aofaga teelaa koo oko ki ei. [. . .] Teenaa, maallie (koulua) ki te koga teelaa. Ia, kae fakafetai, peelaa mo tau faipatimaiiga, maaggalo katoa katoa mea katoa. Paanapa, fakafetai! Fakamaagalo nee koe, manafai eiloa e tonu koe! Ia koe e tonu, kae fakamaagalo nee koe ou taina. Fakafetai.* [Fono Taupulega 1991:2:A:285–294]

So, you are content with any decision that the atoll community has made, let your heart be content. Any decree that it has made. [. . .] There, the two of you are content with it. And thank you for what you said, [that] everything is forgiven. Paanapa, thank you! You have forgiven everything, if you speak the truth! You are right, forgive your brothers. Thank you.

Other concluding statements invoked very general, normative ideas: "this day was of use," an elder proclaimed, because it enabled everyone to tidy up *(teu)* the community of conflict, after which it would return to beauty *(gali)*, mutual empathy *(feaalofani)*, and peace *(fiileemuu)*:

> *Kai!, e llei, koo aogaa te aso teenei! teu ei a fenua, teu ki te gali, teu ki te llei, teu ki te feaalofani, teu ki te loto o te Atua. [. . .] A ko te aso nei, koo aogaa, Tito! Koo gali. [. . .] Teu mea katoa loa ki te llei, fiileemuu, ka kee taakkato taatou i lima alofa o te Atua, e gali ei ttou fenua i moo taimi konei mai mua.* [Fono Taupulega 1991:2: A:339–342, 354–355, 357–359]

Yes!, good, this day was of use! The atoll community has been tidied up, tidied up to be beautiful, tidied up for mutual empathy, tidied up as God wishes it to be. [. . .] This day has been of use. Tito! It is beautiful. [. . .] Everything has been tidied up for the good, [for] peace, so we can rest in God's loving hands, in which our atoll community finds beauty for the few moments that remain [to be lived].

These remarks show that the meeting had somehow morphed into a conflict-management session. Potentially unsociable emotions, like anger and grief, had been displayed and talked through *faipati fakallei* "speaking properly," conflicting points of view have been presented, and all that was left to do was for the most senior among those present to *polopolooki* "admonish" other participants and lead them back to a sociality that could work on a day-to-day basis, transcending personal interests, interpersonal tensions, and the rancor of the past.

Aftermaths

It is difficult to know precisely the extent to which the Council of Elders meeting provided Paanapa with what he had sought in the first place (if indeed he had sought anything specific, which itself is open to question). Nukulaelae Islanders do place much value on ironing out together socially disruptive emotions and on providing a moral conclusion to conflicts that is also practical insofar as it enables people to face one another again daily, which they will inevitably do on an islet a few hundred meters long. The importance of emotional disentangling in resolving social difficulties is undeniable. However, it reestablishes a social order by always downplaying the relevance of an objective truth, which necessarily privileges some perspectives while sidelining or even silencing others. In the case of the meeting that had turned into a familiar session of *faipati fakallei*, key elders had in fact placed Paanapa in a subordinate position, in which they could subject him to their *polopolooki* "admonitions." One seriously wonders whether Paanapa found satisfaction in this meeting, given that it deprived him of a lucrative job, deprived his son of a job, and did not solve the ostracism of which he was the target.

The meeting in the *maneapa* closed with a profusion of statements to the effect that, thanks to the meeting, life had returned to its idealized state of beauty, trust, and peace. But had it? Gossip continued even more ferociously, fueled by the new juicy bits from the meeting, which had opened entirely new possibilities for interpretations and speculations. Gossipers gleefully pounced on Paanapa's public performance, ridiculing his inappropriate emotionality. In retrospect, what Paanapa may have hoped would be an opportunity to exonerate himself in public had turned into a degradation ceremony of the first order, despite token efforts on the part of some council members to frame it as a disentangling meeting. And like other degradation ceremonies, it had further rallied the community against Paanapa.

Three weeks after the meeting, the pastor asked Paanapa to lead the Sunday afternoon church service, ostensibly in an effort to reintegrate him into the community. Taking advantage of the temporary authority associated with sermonic discourse (Besnier 1995, 140–168), Paanapa delivered a highly emotional sermon. Abandoning his notes halfway through the performance, dropping his Bible to the floor in the process (someone had to go up to the pulpit to retrieve it), he became more and more pointed and precise in his allusions. Sobbing again, shouting at the top of his lungs, he urged the congregation to abandon the ways of the *poouliga* "darkness":

NUKULAELAE I TTAEAO TEENEI! NUKULAELAE E PELE I MANATU, NUKULAELAE E TAGI KI EI TE LOTO, I TE AFIAFI TEENEI! [. . .] I TE AFIAFI TEENEI, E FAKAPILIPILI ATU, NUKULAELAE, NE AA LEO KONEI E TTAGI I LUGA I TE FENUA? [. . .] ((voice breaking)) *TE FILIFILIGA A TE ATUA, KOO TONU MOO KOE, Nukulaelae! E fakapilipili atu i te afiafi teenei, kee SEE TOE AUMAI NE MANATU SSEE, E FAKASSEEGINA EI TAATOU MO TTOU FAANAU! Koa oti tausaga o te poouliga. Koa oti tausaga o* ((voice breaking)) *te ifo ki tupua! Koo oti tausaga o te talittonu ki luga i- i fatu mo aa!* [Sermons 1991:1:B:477–490]

NUKULAELAE THIS AFTERNOON! NUKULAELAE BELOVED IN ONE'S THOUGHTS, NUKULAELAE FOR WHICH THE HEART CRIES, THIS AFTER-NOON! [. . .] THIS AFTERNOON, [GOD] IS REACHING OUT, WHAT ARE THOSE VOICES CRYING ON THE ATOLL? [. . .] *((voice breaking))* GOD'S CHOOSING IS RIGHT FOR YOU, Nukulaelae! [God] is reaching out to you this afternoon, DO NOT BRING UP ERRONEOUS THOUGHTS AGAIN, WHICH MAKE US AND OUR CHILDREN ERR! The years of darkness are over. The years of *((voice breaking))* the adoration of heathen gods are over! The years of beliefs in stone icons and whatever else are over!

But, again, he had miscalculated. Shuffling their feet and staring at the floor, members of the congregation murmured their disapproval. One respondent later described her reaction to the sermon:

Like, I was not happy with the way he cried during his sermon! It was as if- it rested-, like, as he was speaking, like, later [in his sermon, he was saying things that] were offensive to people, and he was [aggravating it by] crying on top of it, see? It was like he was talking about what happened to him, and crying at the same time, [I wonder,] were these tears of anger, or what kind of tears were they that he shed this afternoon, see? [S 1991:1:A:129–134]

The emotional sermon only fueled further the scorn. People described his behavior as *fakalaukilivalea*, literally, "making one's skin crawl" because it was so off-color and excessive.

Koo aogaa te aso teenei! "This day was of use!" an elder had declared at the conclusion of the council meeting. Indeed, the day was of use in certain ways. For besides being reminded of the moral imperative to strive for harmony, enlightenment, and trust, so clearly articulated in the "official" version of Nukulaelae culture, Nukulaelae Islanders, and in particular one Islander, were shown what happens to men with too much personal ambition who let their spouses claim chiefly descent.

Three Years Later

I ran into Paanapa again during a brief visit to Funafuti at the end of 1994. He had come to Funafuti for a break from the monotony of outer island life and the continued gossip. It was his first trip away from the atoll in three years. For the first time, I felt comfortable enough to interview him about the events of 1991, and was able to complete the picture I had formed through conversations with other people and participation in the meetings. The gloom of the interview was heightened by a violent downpour that began fifteen minutes into the conversation, darkening the afternoon and rendering the recording almost inaudible.

At my request, he recounted his version of what had happened to him, reconstructing conversations and events in minute detail, as if he had been repeating them to himself over and over again, interspersing emotional descriptions of his suffering with biblical allusions ("Father, forgive them, for they know not what they do"). His ostracism continues, and only a few people remain civil to him. A few families exchange food with his, but his household is kept out of larger networks of reciprocity. He sits among the elders in the *maneapa* but, according to him, rarely speaks.

Talking to other people, I had the distinct impression that anything that Paanapa did or did not do pointed again and again to sorcery. One young man related to me that, when he had been summoned to the Council of Elders for violating prohibition (see chapter 3), Paanapa kept asking him over and over whether he had been drinking, from which the young man concluded that Paanapa already knew the answer through a spirit but that he was afraid to come out with a direct accusation lest he expose himself to another round of suspicions. When a song came on the radio that Paanapa had asked to dedicate to his grandchild recently arrived from Nauru, the women of the house where I was staying responded immediately with a loud expression of annoyance and disgust vocalized in perfect unison by all involved *("AAAAAAA!!")*. A year before, another young man had died under mysterious circumstances on Nukulaelae, and when his coffin was hauled up to shore upon return from his final hospital visit on Funafuti, Paanapa had watched, allegedly looking self-satisfied, as other men struggled under the weight. People inferred from his attitude that the death was another one of his murders.

Gossip, Genres, and the Shifting Nature of Power

Gossip, spirit mediumship, telegrams, meetings, more gossip, more meetings, sermons, more gossip, radio dedication, more gossip—Paanapa learned the hard way that communicative genres are deeply interconnected to one another in a

Bakhtinian web through which statements refer to one another, contradict each other, bleed onto one another, even deny each other from even having existed. The effect is not just a web of information circulating in capricious but relentless ways, but it also structures power as Foucault would have predicted, so that it is not anyone's property, it is never localized anywhere, but it remains ever-present in the social domain and the social relations with which it is interwoven. Furthermore, power and its relationship to knowledge and truth operate particularly effectively through negative structures of exclusion, denials, and prohibitions (Foucault 1980). It is thus not just the iterative citationality that made the performative aspects of the gossip "work," but the combination of citationality and denial of citationality.

There is nothing new in affirming that sorcery and witchcraft, accusations and confessions, and the concomitant gossip and rumor are all about power, as the point has been made in the now substantial corpus of anthropological writings on these topics beginning with British structural functionalists. Geschiere (1997, 219) laments the fact that traditional anthropological analyses of sorcery have generally focused on accusations (often of a direct nature that one would never witness on Nukulaelae) rather than sorcery itself, to methodological advantage of course since accusations are the most concrete manifestation of sorcery, but with the consequence that these analyses have invariably explained sorcery as reproducing social order. While the critique is well taken, a couple of issues need taking up in light of the present analysis. One is that accusations are the most concrete aspect of sorcery, if not its only manifestation, not only for the anthropologist, but also for Nukulaelae Islanders themselves: sorcery is what "those people" do (northern Islanders, Gilbertese, spirits from Samoa visiting Funafuti), and when it comes closer to the atoll's shore it is all about furtive gossip, alleged glimpses of sorcery bottles, and statements heard during Funafuti spirit mediumship. In fact, Nukulaelae allegations are quite different from the dramatic public accusations we read about in the classic works of E. E. Evans-Pritchard, Mary Douglas, Victor Turner, and Peter Geschiere, since they remain furtive and hidden, while people go to great lengths in public contexts to erase, with mitigated success, any reference to sorcery.

It is indeed the case that, as structural-functionalists would have us believe, sorcery allegations may serve conservative purposes. But on Nukulaelae they do and they don't. On the one hand, gossip about Paanapa's sorcery punished someone who was defying the social order. But already the situation was complicated by the fact that gossip became effective only after it had secured, through blackmail, the collaboration of Nukulaelae's Council of Elders, which understood that its ability to function was seriously threatened: had Nukulaelae workers resigned en masse from their Nauru employment, the island would have lost its access to remittances and the council its political foundation. Like the sour-toddy rebellion of 1989 (chapter 3), the case illustrates the powerlessness of the powerful in this society. On the other hand, the sorcery allegations leveled against Paanapa can be understood as "weapons of the weak" in the hands of the Nukulaelae community on Nauru, that is, as grassroots defiance of the abusive authority of the appointed leader. As Scott (1985) would have predicted, gossip about Paanapa's sorcery was effective in ways that more open forms of rebellion might not have been. The allegations are thus both dominance-reinforcing actions and contestations of preexisting power structures. This complexity is the direct result of the coexistence in Nukulaelae political ideology of a discourse of nostalgia and a discourse of egalitarianism: the success of socially leveling action, of which sorcery allegations are a superb example, depends on the authority of a chief and a Council of Elders; at the same time, these institutions are ultimately at the mercy of the community's gossip and blackmail. It is my analytic focus on allegations qua allegations (rather than treating them as the concrete "evidence" of sorcery as the classical literature does) that enables me to avoid simplistic functionalist explanations.

We cannot trivially explain the coexistence of the discourse of nostalgia and the discourse of egalitarianism as a tension between the public and the private, between onstage and offstage action. At first glance, this tension appears to be at play in the events I have described: one can talk feverishly about sorcery in private gossip, but the topic is off-limits in public meetings. However, the situation is more complicated. The censorship of sorcery talk in the meeting ensures the effectiveness of offstage allegations. While the "work" of sorcery allegations is performed in offstage gossip, talk and action in public forums collude with gossip in bringing about the sociopolitical consequences of the allegations. Thus the sabotage of an individual's ambitious quest for power takes place in both onstage and offstage settings. The successful collusion of the public meetings and private gossip, as well as the telegrams, the letters to and from Nauru, and the sermon, depends crucially on the heteroglossic ambiguities and contradictions of Nukulaelae discourse on sorcery, contradictions that make sorcery allegations attractive resources for political manipulation.

It is probably the case that large-scale sociohistorical dynamics are also implicated in the situation I have analyzed. Like anthropologists working in other regions of the world (e.g., Comaroff and Comaroff 1993; Geschiere 1997; Taussig 1980), I have been struck by the increased prominence that sorcery seemed to be acquiring as my fieldwork progressed. While this state of affairs may have something to do with my progressive understanding of Nukulaelae social life, it is striking that Nukulaelae Islanders themselves recognize that sorcery is a more prominent anxiety today than it was a decade ago. The link between the escalating anxiety and emergent capitalism, increased monetization, and modernity is as suggestive here as it is elsewhere, and it is clear that Paanapa's relative wealth and considerable swagger triggered the envious antipathy of the less fortunate. However, reading the antagonism directed at him solely as a text of a precapitalist community's reaction to creeping capitalism would be an oversimplification. Indeed, capitalism has been a reality in Nukulaelae society long enough that several of its prominent members owe their power and prestige to the accumulation of wealth. Furthermore, not all targets of sorcery insinuations are accumulators in any simple sense. The role of sorcery allegations in their broader sociocultural context is undoubtedly complex, and the association of sorcery with incipient capitalism is only one piece of the puzzle.

Throughout the events leading up to and following his disgrace, Paanapa was abiding by the standards of Nukulaelae politics: accumulating wealth on Nauru, walking the tightrope between ostentation and humility, and calling on multiple discourses of togetherness, sociability, and subservience of the individual to the welfare of society. Yet he miscalculated his timing. Between his immoderate ostentation on Nauru and his excessive humility after his forced return home, he only manages to irritate everyone. The basic principles underlying his personal strategy were normative, but his management of these principles was off-kilter. Relying too much on the discourse of nostalgia one day and invoking the discourse of egalitarianism excessively the next, Paanapa somehow failed to apprehend that both discourses must coexist at all times.

Finally, a brief comparison of the effect that sorcery allegations had on Paanapa and the effect they had on the two widows (chapter 6) is instructive. In both situations, the ambiguities of authorship and responsibility that are part and parcel of gossip, overlaid with the ideological complexities of Christian denial and experiential affirmation, created a stranglehold that was difficult to deny or accept. When they target a politically ambitious man like Paanapa, who attempts to play by the rules of Nukulaelae politics, rumors of sorcery can destroy a career. Unlike Paanapa, and probably more wisely, Siuila and Loimata did not attempt to confront the entire atoll community, and they perhaps exposed themselves to less enduring scorn. Siuila, the widow who played by the social game and depended for her well-being on the approval of others, had less to lose materially than Paanapa but was equally crushed emotionally. In contrast, when allegations were leveled at Loimata, a woman of loose morals who is widely suspected of having instigated the death of both her husbands, gossip about sorcery became a useful tool in the hands of its target, who can use it to increase the awe in which she is held because of the supernatural powers already attributed to her. In short, the more "mainstream" a personal image the alleged sorcerer strives for, the greater the fall after the sorcery allegation strikes. Gender positions play an important role in these dynamics: women accusing women is less consequential on Nukulaelae than everyone accusing a mature man, whose sense of self is considerably more dependent on his own image as an upstanding Christian who only refers to sorcery as *mea kolaa* "those things."

8 Gossip and the Everyday Production of Politics

IN THE TITLE OF THIS BOOK, which I recycle here as the title of the concluding chapter, I utilize the classic anthropological trope that juxtaposes seemingly incommensurable categories to announce that incommensurability is a fact of social life. Of the tensions between categories that I explored in this work, two merit additional attention in this conclusion: the micro–macro linkage between interaction and the larger social context, and the tension between emotion and politics.

Talk Matters

In its most simplified form, the argument I have developed in this book is that talk matters. In particular, talk matters in the conduct of politics, the assertion of power and its contestation, the construction and destruction of reputations, the manipulation of truths, and the formation of alliances and conflicts among people and positions. There is nothing terribly new about this insight, of course, given the long genealogy of debates about the importance of talk in political anthropology.[1] One early form that these debates took, for example, followed from the proposition that political oratory is a mere prop for the "real" work of politics, a means by which those in power announce decisions already taken prior to its deployment. This position, memorably espoused by Bloch (1975), downplayed the importance of talk as a vehicle for action, while highlighting its role as representation of decision making. The opposite stance is summarized by Murray Edelman's provocative assertion "Political language *is* political reality" (1988, 104; emphasis in the original), which maintains that all politics is talk, although Edelman immediately complicates the assertion by adding, "[T]hat statement poses the problem rather than resolving it for it challenges us to examine the complex link between language and meaning." It is this last challenge that political anthropologists who have focused on language in the last decades have taken up, many concluding that language can have both an instrumental and a creative relationship to politics, depending on situations, genres, and the political ideologies extant in society (Brenneis and Myers 1984). Political talk is not necessarily concerned only with coercion and decision making; it also is often implicated in negotiations about notions of legitimacy, how society should be organized, and the very definition of what counts as political. As Keesing (1990, 496) formulates succinctly, "[T]alk at once expresses and publicly iterates structures of power and constitutes them, at once reproduces existing constellations of political relationships and transforms them." This book has gone beyond merely asserting that political and communicative actions are dynamically related by seeking to demonstrate how this relationship operates.

The analysis I have developed in the preceding chapters has added a twist to the project by problematizing the very concept of "political language," a category whose constitution is generally taken for granted. I was drawn to this problematization by situations such as the one in which "heads roll" because of allegations that float in difficult-to-pin-down gossip: in these situations, there is a great deal of talk (whispered, uncompleted, falsettoed, written hurriedly), but there is no "political language" in the literal sense, quite the opposite in fact since sorcery is a morally out-of-bounds issue where political language is normally heard. My analysis demonstrates that, to arrive at an understanding of how language and politics are intertwined, we must expand our analytic focus from sites in which politics operates in canonical ways (e.g., meetings, councils, courtrooms) to sites that are much less straightforwardly political, including interactions that are woven into the ordinariness of everyday existence. Despite its stigmatized banality, gossip is political action, and by analyzing it as such I have sought to expand traditional anthropological ways of thinking about politics as located primarily in public life. One consequence of "politicizing" forms of interaction and social situations that are not political in a simple sense is that the old debate about the representative or performative nature of political language is rendered somewhat irrelevant: agents' intentions emerge as multilayered and potentially contradictory, the consequences of their actions articulate with their intentions in complicated ways, and production and reproduction become intertwined.

I do not claim, of course, that the politics that operates in the everyday is weightier than the politics that operates in the public arena. When people gossip, they are intensely aware of the fact that their words and actions articulate with (i.e., repeat, elaborate, comment on, contradict, ridicule) words and actions that take place in other contexts. More specifically, political action resides at the convergence of genres of speaking, rather than in any one genre (Brenneis 1984b), and we must seek to locate and understand it at this convergence. Thus, rather than focusing exclusively on gossip, I have embedded it in a broad context of other forms of interaction, which across the various chapters have included political meetings, letters, telegrams, church sermons, radio-telephone calls, spirit mediumship sessions, and ethnographic interviews, forms of interaction, incidentally, that link together several islands and several nations. Gossip articulates with these other forms of "doing" in different ways. It may operate in collusion with these other forms, as in the cases in which a particular piece of information bleeds from gossip to another context or vice versa, or in opposition to them. Alternatively, people may gossip about something that they know is morally out of bounds in other contexts, as is the case of sorcery allegations. In yet other cases, it is not merely the content of gossip that complements other genres and contexts but also such features as its personnel and its form: voices that are never heard in political meetings may be loud and clear in cooking huts, and the messiness of gossip discourse is the exact opposite of public oratory. Whatever forms the articulation between gossip and other kinds of action may take, it behooves the ethnographer to seek an understanding of the workings of politics in this articulation.

Context Matters

In my exploration of talk as political practice, I owe inspiration to works in linguistic anthropology that in the last decades have insisted on the fine-grained analysis of textual materials to reach beyond the impressionistic retellings of what the ethnographer thinks people say (or write) that characterize a great deal of works in political anthropology. At the same time, I have sought to embed the analysis of language and interaction in a world of material processes and cultural dynamics in such a way that the latter remain as much the focus of analysis as the structure of talk. It is amply clear that talk both reproduces and produces its context. More specifically, gossip reflects the social structures and cultural dynamics in which it is embedded, as is evident in the fact, for example, that its structural organization can be understood in terms of this sociocultural context, as I argue in chapter 4. At the same time, hand in hand with other forms of talk and action, gossip can "do things," just as an Austinian performative "does things." But like Butlerian performatives, gossip must also be embedded in the history of iteration from which it derives its power and truth. Between the productive capacity of gossip and its reproductive capacity there is a constant interplay, and this interplay demands that we problematize the sociocultural context in which it is based and that it actively creates.

This context, however, is not confined to the face-to-face social relations of immediate quotidian existence, but reaches beyond the confines of the local, encompassing much broader dynamics of migration, labor, dependence, and environmental challenges that link Nukulaelae to the wider world. That this wider world is of pressing relevance to gossip in cooking huts may seem surprising at first glance, both because of the intrinsic "localness" of gossip and because what strikes the casual observer is the smallness and remoteness of Nukulaelae. Characterizations of the atoll as tiny and out of the way suffuse all representations, historical and contemporary. They color the comments that modern-day civil servants make when they exclaim (in alternatively exasperated and resigned tones), "Such a small island, and so many words, so many meanings!" Nukulaelae people themselves, both jokingly and seriously, picture their home in terms of its small size and remoteness, often commenting on the fact that the MV *Nivaga II* often bypasses the island on its monthly round to the outer islands because it is the only atoll of Tuvalu (alongside tiny and supernumerary Niulakita to the south) that does not lie in the northwestern arc that runs from Funafuti, and thus it demands a special trip all its own.[2]

All aspects of social and political life on the atoll, from the public to the intimate, operate at the convergence of seemingly divergent forces: on the one hand, the forces of locality, smallness, sedentarism, and isolation, with which Nukulaelae people associate order, stasis, and continuity; and, on the other hand, the forces of nationhood, transnationalism, migrations, capitalism, modernity, and world-scale ecological change, in which one can generally read an orientation to the future and the outside world and one that islanders themselves associate, understandably, with uncertainty and discontinuity. In many contexts, these seemingly divergent forces are not divergent at all. The enthusiastic exogamy that followed the 1863 slavers' raid, tapping the fount of marriageable men that the German plantation on Niuooku made available, is a historical example of the happy "marriage" of local and extralocal dynamics. A much more recent illustration is the return to a "traditional" political order in the 1980s, while at the same moment the atoll was exporting its labor force more earnestly than ever, radically changing the appearance of the village, and abandoning its canoes for metal dinghies and outboard motors, so quickly and thoroughly that within a couple of years a man was writing pleading letters to his relatives employed off-island describing his shame at being the last person to go fishing in a canoe (Besnier 1995, 95–96).

In many situations, the copresence of forces of locality and those associated with a larger context do provoke anxiety and conflict. The new inequalities, real or perceived, that the changing distribution of economic opportunities have created drive people to consequential forms of action, questioning intentions, invoking spirits, competing in frantic fund-raising drives in which the stakes are well beyond what most can afford, and marginalizing one another in painful ways. The uncertainties that the future and the larger world present shape not only social relations among people on the atoll, but also the anxious impression management that the community engages in when confronting the outside world, which I document in chapter 2, foregrounding a harmony, cohesion, and vulnerability that is seriously at odds with the fractured and assertive realities of daily life. It is for all these reasons that I have located my understanding of Nukulaelae politics at the convergence of the intimacy of the local and the impersonality of large-scale dynamics. Methodologically, I have sought an understanding of political agency that packages together the minute details of the most intimate of interactions, events that take place in the local public arena, the circumstances of interisland and international connections, and the larger context of globality.

The Emotions of Politics

One theme that has run through the course of the discussion is the central role of emotions and morality in Nukulaelae understandings of political and social action. Emotions and morality mediate between agency, as the capacity for action, and subjectivity, the "specifically cultural and historical consciousness" constituted of the "inner feelings, desires, anxieties, intentions, and so on, of individuals" (Ortner 2005, 34). Islanders foreground emotions and morality when they evaluate each other's actions, reactions, and decisions. When they reach consensus, they declare, *koo malie te loto* "the heart is satisfied." They describe themselves as *faanoanoa* "sad" when there is disagreement, and characterize other people's disagreement as being manifestations of *ita* "angry, displeased" and *loto maasei* "bad-hearted." When Paanapa tried to obtain justice in the meeting of the Council of Elders and later chastise the island in his sermons, it was his highly emotional performance that the audience judged to be particularly inappropriate: his dramatic juxtaposition of the Bible and a sorcery bottle, his passionate kissing of the Bible, his tears, and the shouting at the top of his lungs in church. Political ideology is suffused with morality and emotion: moral action must strive to render society *fiileemuu* "peaceful," *feaalofani* "mutually empathetic," and *ola fiafia* "happy living." Discord, lack of consensus, and self-centeredness are all evidence of being *vaaivai* "weak," of needing counseling and *polopolooki* "admonition" by someone in greater control of his or her comportment, or at least *faipati fakallei* "speaking properly." Even when Nukulaelae people do not make them the topic of talk, emotions lurk in the background of all politically significant contexts: the simultaneous pleasure and shame of gossip are inscribed in the organization of the interaction, in the whispers, giggles, and scandalized interjections, and in its studied affectlessness and disorderliness. Emotion is the idiom through which, on a day-to-day basis, Nukulaelae people give shape and meaning to politics.

Why should emotion and politics not be intertwined, since emotion is deeply implicated with many other aspects of society and culture, such as social structure (Irvine 1990)? My choice of focus on agency as the lens through which to understand the practice of politics of course has something to do with the importance of emotion in the analysis, since agency implies subjectivity, and hence emotions. But this focus on agency and subjectivity is in a sense compelled by the ethnography itself, in the same manner that the great prominence of emotion in revolutionary-era French political theory and practice, as an object to celebrate at one historical moment and repress at another, makes emotion unavoidable if one is to seek an understanding of the historical forces of the time (Reddy 2001).

One important characteristic of emotion is its particular propensity to take on different forms, and the complexities of Nukulaelae politics can be understood through this propensity. In a basic way, emotion is malleable because it is so classically culturally relative. We know from the now vast analytic corpus in psychological anthropology from the 1970s to the 1990s that emotions differ across cultures, in their configuration, their "hypercognition" or "hypocognition" across societies (Levy 1984) and across social contexts in the same society (Besnier 1995, 110–112). But emotion is fickle in more subtle ways, because contradictory emotions, or at least different emotions that lead to different forms of action, can operate at the same moment, or in comparable contexts. Gossip is both pleasurable and shameful; both hierarchy and egalitarianism constitute a good society, even though they call for opposite kinds of emotional stances; being accused of sorcery can be devastating, but it can also increase one's prestige; most church sermons are delivered in a passionate tone, but the appropriation of this passion by one man makes congregants' skin crawl. Emotion is also unstable historically: the hyperemotionality of the "emotional regime" of one historical moment can rapidly give way to the suppression of emotion of another (Reddy 2001), giving emotion a time sensitivity that few anthropologists have managed to engage with (including myself, handicapped by the thinness of the historical record in the societies where I have conducted fieldwork). I have investigated in this book how we can understand the apparent contradictions and complexities of politics on a small atoll through the multiplex instability of emotions and of the morality attached to them. Emotion and morality are always unfinished projects that require constant reiteration, and it is this reiteration that I have attempted to document and make sense of in this book.

Notes

1. Gossip, Hegemony, Agency

1. The intellectual field relevant to the issues I touch on in the paragraph is vast. Emotions were of course not an "invention" of anthropology of the 1970s, since they occupied a central position among the concerns of the Culture and Personality school, although in that body of work they were only of interest as an entry into the organization of personality (Levy 1984, 214). Groundbreaking works of the 1970s and 1980s that animated debates on the anthropology of emotion include Abu-Lughod (1986), J. Briggs (1970), Caton (1990), Levy (1974), Lutz (1988), Myers (1986), Rosaldo (1980a), and White and Kirkpatrick (1985). Important explorations of the intertwining of emotion, politics, and history include Lutz and Abu-Lughod (1990), Reddy (2001), and G. White (1991), issues that contributors to Robbins and Wardlow (2005) have rekindled in particularly promising ways by focusing on emotions in the context of colonialism, modernity, and development. "Multisited" ethnography refers to Marcus' widely cited (1995) essay, as well as a plethora of other works on delocalized categories and actions. Keane (2003) is the most thought-provoking exploration I know of the tension between ethnography of the particular and deterritorialized ethnography, and I will return to this insightful essay periodically.

2. Duranti does quote a village chief saying that "there are now in Samoa two orders: the traditional structure at the village and district level, with its emphasis on hierarchy, public debate, and search for consensus, and the new order of the central government, with its implied and imported notions of equality, free elections, and secret ballot" (1994, 9). While it clearly represents some Samoans' understanding of these dynamics, accepting this picture uncritically obscures the deep interpenetration of these two "orders" and assumes that historical change can only be consequent of the forces of modernity originating elsewhere (cf. Tsing 2000).

3. I am intensely aware that any presentation of what people say is already an interpretation on the part of the analyst, since all transcripts are necessarily partial representations ("partial" in the sense of both "incomplete" and "biased"), and all analyses foreground some aspects of what people say while remaining deaf to others (Ochs 1979b; Tedlock 1983). But given the choice between a transcript and impressionist note-taking based on the vague recollection of what someone might have said, often

in a language of which the anthropologist has an imperfect command, I opt for the former, plus a strong dose of reflexivity, which I will strive to maintain in the pages that follow.

4. Friedman (1979) had proposed a comparable reanalysis of the same materials a few years before. The various critics of Barth's (1959) *Political Leadership and Swat Pathans*, principally Ahmed (1980) and Asad (1972), share Nugent's call for attention to material dynamics, although they do not embed them in large-scale processes as clearly as Nugent does with the material from Highland Burma (cf. Vincent 1990, 257–262; Street 1990; but see D. Edwards 1998).

5. Kulick (2006) argues that anthropologists' fixation on the suffering of the underdog is suffused with libidinal pleasure, and reads in the overrepresentation of women among "masochist anthropologists" evidence of the cultural expectation that women must engage in "emotional labor" (Hochschild 1983). The argument, which had been made previously (e.g., Olivier de Sardan 2001), calls for a useful reflexivity but also presents a number of problems, which comments published alongside the paper spell out. Dominguez in particular asks, "Is the 'emotional labor' he and others link to women [and to the anthropology they practice] a good thing or a bad thing?" (2006, 946), implicitly demanding that we tease apart "masochism" as methodology and "masochism" as ideology or morality. Kulick also overlooks a long historical tradition of anthropologists focusing on the "winners" in the society that they study (e.g., chiefs, big men, leaders), to the exclusion of the less fortunate, as I will elaborate later in this chapter. My view on the topic is that, as long as we keep our roles in reflexive perspective, anthropologists' siding with people in subordinate positions is not as problematic as Kulick proposes. If we don't, who will?

6. I read a statement of this indeterminacy in Foucault's oft-cited tautology, "Where there is power there is resistance, and yet, or rather consequently, this resistance is never in a position of exteriority in relation to power" (1990, 95).

7. On Pacific societies alone, classic and contemporary works on the ascription and achievement of rank, power, and prestige include B. Douglas (1979), Feinberg and Watson-Gegeo (1996), Firth (1936), Godelier (1986), Godelier and Strathern (1991), Marcus (1980, 1989), Sahlins (1963, 1981), A. Strathern (1975), and White and Lindstrom (1998). Work on political systems in Oceania that foreground the analysis of meetings and similar ritualized contexts include Arno (1993), Brenneis and Meyers (1984), Duranti (1994), Goldman (1983), Keating (1998), Lindstrom (1990), Merlan and Rumsey (1991), Salmond (1975), and many others. "Rubbish men" and comparable categories of sociopolitical abjection, particularly the modern-day Papua New Guinea *raskol* "bandit," are treated in Bowers (1965), Goddard (1992, 1995), Kulick (1993), Panoff (1985), Roscoe (1999), Sykes (1999), and Zimmer (1987).

8. The pervasive nature of gossip has prompted evolutionary psychologist Dunbar (1996) to surmise that it played a crucial role in the evolution of language and sociality, a hypothesis that has become confirmed truth in some circles, as is typical of research in that tradition (McKinnon 2005). Playwright Jane Wagner adds her own perspective on the issue in the one-person play *The Search for Signs of Intelligent Life in the Universe*, which comedian Lily Tomlin immortalized in her long-standing performances:

"Right after we started talking to each other we began to talk behind each other's backs. Sometimes it was vicious gossip, other times a casual critical remark, like 'Jeez, did you see the hair on his back?' When it dawned on everybody that not only could they talk, but they could also be talked *about*, primitive man began showing signs of paranoia. With everyone so paranoid, war soon broke out. With war came stress, and the rest is history" (1986, 134).

9. Haviland's (1977) monograph remained for many years the sole book-length anthropological treatment of gossip, alongside Rosnow and Fine's (1976) treatment from a social psychological perspective. These works have now been supplemented (to cite only books) by Brison (1992), J. Mintz (1997), Møhl (1997), Pietilä (2007), and Stewart and Strathern (2004) in anthropology; Goodwin (1990) in sociolinguistics; Bergmann (1993) in sociology; Tebbutt (1995) and L. White (2000) in history; Goodman and Ben-Ze'ev (1994) in social psychology; Dunbar (1996) in evolutionary psychology; Solove (2007) in legal studies; and Gordon (1996), Solomon and Chamayou (2006), and Spacks (1985) in literary criticism.

10. The personalization and contextualization of definitions is not confined to this particular topic: like members of many other societies, Nukulaelae Islanders understand social action or personal characteristics as tied to particular people, families, descent groups, or types of social relations (cf. Rumsey 1990).

11. Gender has figured prominently in analyses of gossip precisely because so many societies define it and denigrate it as "women's talk." Works on gender and gossip from an anthropological perspective include Cowan (1991), Faris (1966), Herzfeld (1991), Innes (2006), Rasmussen (1991), and Rogers (1975), and works in sociolinguistics include Cameron (1997), Coates (1988), and Johnson and Finlay (1997).

12. Notable examples of recent sociolinguistic works on gossip are Evaldsson (2002), Guendouzi (2001), Jaworski and Coupland (2005), Slade (2007), Tholander (2003), and Thornborrow and Morris (2004). Anthropological works that skirt around gossip and related dynamics include celebrated works such as Evans-Pritchard (1937), Favret-Saada (1977), and Taussig (1980), as well as more recent works such as Cornwall (2002), Ellis (1989), Fonseca (2001), Kray (2007), Kroeger (2003), Rebhun (2004), Scheper-Hughes (2002), Strating (1998), Van Vleet (2003), and L. White (2000). Most works in the latter category deal with rumor rather than gossip. It is telling, for example, that Stewart and Strathern's (2004) compilation, despite its title *(Witchcraft, Sorcery, Rumors, and Gossip)*, in fact barely touches gossip. The reason is that stories are more likely to have been told to the anthropologist rather than overheard or participated in activities that also require focused efforts to understand often very opaque conversations. In addition, in many societies, informants are likely to restrict what they share with ethnographers to only the most general stories.

13. Just as she or he is implicated in the production and circulation of gossip (whether through exclusion or complicity), the ethnographer is also often the topic of gossip, an observation that has provoked some fruitful analyzes of the "ethnographization" of ethnographers by those whose lives they study (Ashkenazi and Markowitz 1999; M. Murphy 1985; Rasmussen 1993; Rockefeller 2000). Nukulaelae Islanders did not miss the chance to involve me in their gossip, as either the target or a secondary

character. Indeed, "making sense" of the Other is not the anthropologist's monopoly, and the Other may spend as much effort in making sense of the outsider as the anthropologist does trying to understand the Other. We can trace the genealogy of mutual sense-making between autochthon and interloper to the Enlightenment, if not before (e.g., Obeyesekere 1997; Sahlins 1985; Salmond 2005).

14. Throughout this book, I use the term "gossiper" to refer to someone who gossips, rather than the more standard but potentially ambiguous term "gossip."

15. Firth's (1956) analysis of rumor on Tikopia and a brief article on "false rumors" in "Congo" (Leyder [1935], pointed out to me by Johannes Fabian), as well as in passim references to gossip in many classic ethnographies, in fact preceded the publication of Gluckman's (1963) paper. The latter appeared in the then newly created journal *Current Anthropology* as part of a series of essays honoring Melville Herskovits (other papers in the series were by Margaret Mead, Irving Hallowell, Jacques Maquet, and Francis Hsu), who had written about gossip in two of his now classic ethnographies, *Life in a Haitian Valley* (1937) and *Trinidad Village* (Herskovits and Herskovits 1947), and who shared with Gluckman intellectual and political views, on decolonization for example. Gluckman's paper is notable in a number of respects. Unlike in his other works, Gluckman here bases his arguments almost entirely on other scholars' ethnographic material. Among these figure prominently works by two of his students, Colson's (1953) ethnography of the Makah of the American northwest coast and Frankenberg's (1957) monograph on a Welsh village. But the paper also alludes discreetly to Gluckman's feelings of exclusion when "taking up the sport of riding and sailing," very possibly metaphors for the (either British or South African White) establishment that found Gluckman's Russian-Jewish background and left-wing politics seriously wanting.

16. Gluckman's (1968) reply to Paine (1967) reminded him that Durkheim had convincingly demonstrated a century before that, while individuals commit suicide, suicide is still a group phenomenon. The debate, cogently summarized in Merry (1984), was rekindled several years later by P. Wilson (1974, and ensuing correspondence), before the steam seems to have run out.

17. See, for example, the public controversy that Hanson's (1989) analysis of the nineteenth-century origin of Maori mythology triggered in New Zealand (aptly summarized in Goldsmith [1992], Hanson [1997], and Thomas [1997]), and the debate that Keesing (1989) triggered among Jolly (1992), Keesing (1991), Linnekin (1991, 1992), and Trask (1991).

18. The gross distortions embedded in Trask's representation of anthropologists' lives, field practices, social standing, and disregard of basic ethics have been commented on by others (e.g., Linnekin 1991), and I will not pursue these points here.

19. These cautions echo Haraway (1988, 583–584): "Many currents in feminism attempt to theorize grounds for trusting especially the vantage points of the subjugated; there is good reason to believe vision is better from below the brilliant space platforms of the powerful. . . . [But] to see from below is neither easily learned not unproblematic, . . . [and] the standpoints of the subjugated are not 'innocent' positions."

20. While unmistakably fair-skinned and blue-eyed, I find in the model of the halfie much to identify with. A citizen of three countries, only two of which I have resided in, I grew up multilingually in various parts of Europe, Asia, and North America, although not under particularly privileged conditions. I was born at the end of a colonial era in North Africa of parents in temporary residence there, which ensured that any link to my birthplace, including my birth certificate, would disappear promptly after my birth ("eaten by goats," as a French consular officer once contemptuously described the fate of the document). Everywhere I am treated like a foreigner or, at best, a halfie, often with ambiguous consequences. Of French, British, Irish, German, Mauritian, and other miscellaneous descent, with a Calvinist, Catholic, and above all Theosophist background, I find nothing and everything to identify with in my own heritage. But then "hybrids are the art form of the time" (Iyer 1993, 14), and rootlessness can sometimes turn out to be a superb advantage.

21. In mid-1998, I was asked to make a legal deposition in the criminal lawsuit of a young woman who had migrated to New Zealand from another island of Tuvalu who was accused of murdering her husband in a fit of jealous rage. My deposition, which focused on the loss of self-control that Tuvaluans may experience in certain contexts, as well as the isolation associated with the migrant experience, played a determinative role in the arguments of the defense. The accused was convicted of manslaughter instead of murder, and received a light sentence. (The Crown appealed and lost.) The deposition was the object of some coverage in the New Zealand press and appears to have acquired the status of legal precedent, although exactly how remains unclear to me, as it was certainly not the first time "culture" was invoked in a New Zealand courtroom. To my knowledge, it did not provoke any negative reaction from any quarters, including Tuvaluan immigrants, who may have objected to the implications that they could be violent "by nature," or conservative segments of New Zealand society anxious to eradicate what they view as politically correct invocations of "culture" from the social map of the nation. I am aware of the possibility that the "cultural defense" stance I took in my deposition, mediated by the defense attorneys' and journalists' oversimplified renditions of it, could ill serve the interests of those it is designed to protect (cf. Koptiuch 1996). It is in such contexts that "leaks" are most likely to occur from anthropological discourse to public discourse, to potentially damaging effect for the interest of those represented, since one loses control over public discourse very quickly.

22. Barbara Myerhoff provides a poignant vignette from her celebrated fieldwork among the residents of a Jewish old folk's home in Los Angeles, many of whom were Holocaust survivors and for whom "being remembered" was the subject of considerable anxiety: "When I told them that in transcribing the notes, their names would be changed, they were disappointed. Everyone wanted to leave a personal statement, wanted to be identified with an enduring record, some indication of what had happened to them, what they believed, that they had been here" (1979, 36). The following anecdote illustrates all too dramatically the futility of trying to achieve anonymity in a place like Nukulaelae. Having sent a copy of Besnier (1995) to a Tuvaluan friend, I was dismayed by his lighthearted report that his spouse and mother-in-law, both from

Nukulaelae, had had a great time guessing the identity of the authors of the personal letters I analyze in that work!

2. The World from a Cooking Hut

1. I am cheating somewhat. I had visited Nukulaelae briefly once a couple of weeks before, as part of the retinue, of which I was very clearly the supernumerary member, following the then-ambassador of the United States to Fiji, also accredited to Tuvalu, John Condon, an extraordinary man in his own right. Twenty years old at the time, I had been recruited to design training materials for the soon-to-come first group of Peace Corps volunteers sent to Tuvalu. This very strange journey by motor yacht took him, his spouse, the director of the Peace Corps in Fiji, the director of Save the Children USA (former actor David Geier), and a few others around the eight principal islands and atolls of Tuvalu, on a reconnaissance trip before NGOs invaded the country. John Condon was arguably the first high-ranking foreign dignitary to visit the outer islands of Tuvalu, and the backdrop of the visit was the fact that Pacific Island countries including Tuvalu were at the time playing the "USSR card" to parlay the United States into coughing up aid.

2. The beloved original MV *Nivanga* (Tuvaluan for "mirage"), to which I allude in the first paragraph, had been built in 1962, and was the one and only ship that the British colonial administration gave to Tuvalu when it separated from the Gilbert and Ellice Islands Colony against the wishes of the United Kingdom, as I will discuss below. It made the monthly round of the islands until Tuvalu managed to replace it with a newer ship, the thousand-ton MV *Nivaga II* (as it is now spelled to reflect modern orthographic usage), in 1988. The original MV *Nivanga* was acquired by a Fijian company, which sold it for NZ$200,000 to a pair of New Zealanders who apparently wanted to use it as a low-budget cruise ship to the Great Barrier Reef. The ship was, however, so rusty and poorly maintained that the buyers were unable to have it registered and went bankrupt. They sold it for the scrap value of NZ$500 and unsuccessfully sued the New Zealand Ministry of Transport for negligence in surveying the ship prior to sale, a case that has become a cause célèbre in international maritime law (Basedow and Wurmnest 2005, 21–22).

3. *Te tokoukega o tino i konei e fai peelaa me i te Ppaalagi se manu valea fua* "Most people here think that the white man is just a silly bird," one of the people closest to me declared.

4. Compare Harvey's (1992, 87) experience of being told by Quechua speakers that she spoke "purer" Quechua than themselves, because her Quechua was book-learned. The characterization of my linguistic competence probably has something to do with the fact that I continue to inadvertently pepper my spoken Tuvaluan with Tongan vocabulary and vice versa. While the two languages are not mutually intelligible, Tongan sounds vaguely familiar to Tuvaluans because of the historical linguistic connections between the two languages, but it also carries a distinct but hard-to-place "archaic" feel.

5. Various (invariably male) outsiders with differing degrees of connections to Nukulaelae have attempted to live on the atoll in recent memory, usually after mar-

rying a young Nukulaelae woman, but they were eventually defeated by structures of kinship obligation and assorted complexities of the cross-cultural encounter. One Norwegian yachter in this category wrote a book about his adventures in, of course, paradise (Dahl 1992).

6. The LMS was founded in 1795, originally as the Missionary Society, by Nonconformist and Anglican evangelicals, for the purpose of proselytizing to the colonies. It became very visible in South Africa (Comaroff and Comaroff 1991, 1997). In 1830, LMS missionary John Williams landed in Savai'i, Samoa, from which the society rapidly missionized all of Samoa, and then neighboring island groups, including the Ellice Islands thirty-five years later. While founded on Congregationalist principles, the society and the churches that it gave rise to, including the Christian Church of Tuvalu, would present many contradictions between these original principles and the needs and desires for hierarchy and centralization. The configuration of early missionization in Tuvalu certainly prefigured an authoritarian structure that would last to this day.

7. Keith and Anne Chambers (2000) centralize this last theme in their ethnography of Nanumea, the northernmost atoll of Tuvalu, to the point of making it part of the title of their monograph.

8. One notable exception is an amusing article in the *Boston Daily Journal* of August 8, 1865, entitled "Four Years among the Cannibals," which asserts that Nukulaelae people "were frequently at war with a neighboring tribe. Going forth to battle, they confined their captives in a stockade, releasing them on their return" (Ward 1967, 261–262). Who that neighboring tribe might be is a complete mystery, and the same report contains other items of doubtful veracity, from the attribution of cannibalism in the title to the assertion that "[c]orn, pumpkins, yams and oranges were abundant, and required but little cultivation" (1967, 261), a very unlikely description of a coral atoll. The newspaper obtained this information from Tom Rose (or Thomas Ross or, locally, Taumeesi), a beachcomber reputedly from Jamaica who had spent four years on Nukulaelae and undoubtedly had his own ax to grind (Goldsmith and Munro 1992, 33). The journalists who recorded the information may also have contributed their own exotic fantasies to the report. There were in fact instances in which Tuvaluans reacted violently to Westerners' visits and encroachments in the days of early contacts, but commentators subsequently played them down as isolated and uncharacteristic incidents. Violence in the other direction occurred dramatically in several important moments of Nukulaelae nineteenth-century history, as I will discuss.

9. Conversion narratives on Nukulaelae echo similar foundation narratives in many other Pacific Island societies (e.g., G. White 1991, 103–130), but they differ from them in that they lack a "resistance" thematic component, providing a sense of continuity and inevitability to both Christianity's arrival and Nukulaelae's anointed status. For example, narratives contend that a woman named Kafoa, a spirit medium of the "old" religion, had envisioned a bright new light from the east the night before Elekana's canoe beached itself on the east coast of the atoll. I have annoyed more than one Nukulaelae respondent by asking what my interlocutors considered senseless questions like "What if Elekana had missed the atoll?" and "What if he had carried the message of another religion?"

10. Nukulaelae preference for exogamy (*aavaga ki tai,* literally "seaward marriage") also has synchronic explanations: the tiny population, coupled with strong avoidance taboos between opposite-gender cousins, make exogamy almost inevitable, and the lack of "land hunger" in comparison to other islands of Tuvalu (Brady 1974) poses few barriers to it.

11. Tafalagilua appears in oral history both in 1861, when the first Christian missionary, a Manihiki Islander called Elekana (Goldsmith and Munro 1992, 2002), reached Nukulaelae, and in 1865, when he leased away Niuooku Islet. The LMS's Reverend A. W. Murray, who dropped off Samoan teacher Ioane in 1865, mentions that "the chief" (whose name he does not provide), "being a old man, had been rejected by the slavers" (1876, 382).

12. Throughout my years of fieldwork, Radio Tuvalu broadcast a weekly program entitled *Tala o te Lalolagi* "News of the World," which consisted of "news" stories, clearly translated from Western tabloids, about people abandoning their children, killing their own parents, or committing incest. The stories were clearly selected to cater to Tuvaluan sensibilities, and everyone on the atoll listened assiduously, delighting in the sense of outrage that they provoked and in the confirmation of the utter immoral wretchedness of the rest of the world. The only other "news of the world" that the station would broadcast was a retransmission of Radio Australia world news. The obscurity of the content even if one understood the English, combined with the short-wave crackling, made this program very unpopular with most.

13. The one exception to the local invisibility of the colonial administration in the Ellice Islands was Donald Gilbert Kennedy, a New Zealander who administered the colony's first secondary school from 1922 to 1932 and remained as district officer until 1940. Kennedy educated a generation of young men who would later become the politicians and civil servants of the late colonial and decolonization eras. Kennedy is vividly remembered for his irascible character, drunken violence, tyrannical management style, humiliating and sadistic punishments, womanizing, and tense rapport with Samoan pastors, but also for his paternalistic promotion of Ellice Islanders. He published the first ethnographic monograph on Tuvalu (1931) and the first description of the Tuvaluan language (1946), based on information he obtained from Vaitupu elders with an authoritarian sense of entitlement, according to elderly informants, that resembles Malinowski's two decades earlier (Young 2004, 538).

14. Cara David (1856–1951), later Lady Caroline David, was a British woman of modest background who had married a prominent scientist and held progressive views on many matters (Kyle 1993). However, in typical Victorian fashion, she devotes a significant portion of her account of Nukulaelae, based on her one-day visit, to commenting on the relative cleanliness of things and people. She thus characterizes the "king" as "a dirty old man in a filthy shirt and lavalava, with his head bound up in unclean rags," while she finds that "the pastor's wife ... set a splendid example of cleanliness and tidiness" (1899, 285, 287).

15. Charles Barnard, remembered today as Sale Panaata or Te Kuki "the cook," was one of the more colorful characters who had arrived as a contract laborer with the German plantation and stayed on after the plantation was closed, marrying a Nuku-

laelae woman. His fifth-generation Nukulaelae descendants continue to be teased for their dark complexion, gossiping skills, and love of drama. It is entirely possible that the group portrait includes in-married former plantation workers from other Pacific islands and beyond or their first-generation descendants, since most of the original male population had been enslaved thirty-five years before.

16. Two of the servicemen married young Nukulaelae women, the ultimate strategy to give local anchoring to persons, symbols, and memories from the outside. One of these alliances proved to be a great success, in that emotional and material ties were maintained through correspondence, remittances, and highly enjoyable visits back to Nukulaelae every few years. "Do you know Paul and Hank?" is a question that American visitors to Nukulaelae are invariably asked.

17. The striking candor of this passage, in an official report whose audience was the British Parliament, would be somewhat toned down in subsequent official reports. The remark about the Ellice inferiority "in all things that really matter" is puzzling, but it is also revealing of the British colonial officer's ambivalence toward the colonized in general, as well as, undoubtedly, the ambivalence of both Ellice and Gilbert Islanders toward him and what he represents. In particular, because of their situation as a doubly colonized group, Ellice Islanders played on their multiple allegiances as the occasion suited, ingratiating themselves to the British colonizers at one moment and underscoring their bonds of solidarity with Gilbert Islanders at another. Such "footing" (Goffman 1979) between collaboration and resistance, between acquiescence and defiance, is hardly unique to this situation, and indeed characterizes any structure of dominance (Ortner 1995, 175–176).

18. Nukulaelae Islanders invoke a rich body of contemporary evidence of Gilbertese violence, which they link to the persistence of heathenish practices like sorcery in Kiribati, the slow historical acceptance of Christianity, and of course the darker pigmentation of most Gilbertese complexions. A favorite theme is the violent jealous rage named *koko* in Gilbertese, during which a man sometimes bites off the nose of his spouse to disfigure her (see Brewis 1996, 46–52). To balance this picture, however, they also speak of the wonderful sense of hospitality and unshakable sense of loyalty that characterize the Gilbertese.

19. As Barrie Macdonald reports, "[P]erhaps the cultural arguments, especially in translation, might sound facile and trifling to a European but many Ellice Islanders believe that having said 'we are different people' they had explained their desire to separate" (1982, 255). Also invoked as part of the same body of arguments was the fear that Gilbert Islanders in a joint independent state would seek revenge on Ellice Islanders for the British favoritism they had enjoyed for decades. These fears are not unfounded, as similar situations have given rise to patterns of serious discrimination in postindependence times elsewhere in the colonial world (e.g., Luhrmann 1996).

20. In writing this section, I benefited from discussions with Heather Lazrus, whose forthcoming University of Washington Ph.D. dissertation, based on extensive fieldwork on Nanumea Atoll in northern Tuvalu, analyzes local representations of environmental change.

21. One could retort that the draconian immigration policies of John Howard's

right-wing Australian government (1996–2007) and refusal to consider the possibility of atoll dwellers' relocation are worthy of critical scrutiny. New Zealand, in contrast, has been accepting migrants from Tuvalu on temporary work visas, although it is not enthusiastic about permanent mass migration.

22. Until 2000, Tuvalu's diplomatic missions were limited to a high commissioner in Suva, Fiji, and a "roving ambassador to all major capitals of the world," who was also the secretary of state. Since its accession to United Nations membership in 2000, an ambassador has represented the country in New York.

23. The vulnerability of gardens and of the food supply gets no comment either in articles about Tuvalu that are appearing with increasing frequency in popular or middle-brow magazines (e.g., L. Allen 2004; Lynas 2004; Patel 2006; Price 2003), generally authored by journalists after short trips to Funafuti to "meet the locals" (Patel 2006, 734), but in fact citing the same small group of articulate civil servants and politicians.

3. Hierarchy and Egalitarianism

1. Events such as this one, in which the (re)creation of political institutions is closely tied to a particular person, are not uncommon in the Pacific Islands (e.g., G. White 1991, 218), and militate against placing too much weight on the contrast between Melanesian big men and Polynesian chiefs (Sahlins 1963).

2. The anthropological literature on these categories is vast. Anthropological attention to them was probably first drawn by Keesing and Tonkinson's (1982) edited collection of papers, whose publication in fact preceded that of the much more widely quoted Hobsbawm and Ranger volume (1983). For additional references, see chapter 1, note 17.

3. While the MIRAB "model" has generated vigorous debate among development experts, particularly Down Under, it has generally not captured anthropologists' imagination. For example, a search I conducted (April 2008) on the term "MIRAB" in AnthroSource, which combs the content of thirty-two key North American journals in the discipline, returned one mention of MIRAB in an article and two in reviews. The reason for this interest differential (besides academic provincialism) is that, while MIRAB may be a useful top-down descriptor of Pacific economies, it elides Islanders' agentive role in the conduct of their economic lives. The model depicts Islanders as passive recipients of overseas money, contrary to the highly agentive picture I develop in this paper, and confines them to an inappropriate reactive utilitarianism (cf. Connell 2007, 130), also treating them as an undifferentiated grouping acting in Durkheimian unison.

4. The letters cited here are part of a large corpus of letters gathered in the field in 1985 and 1991 (Besnier 1995, 72–115). The reference following the extract (e.g., Letters 1985:558) refers to the location of the extract in this corpus.

5. I use "egalitarianism" as a characteristic of *discourse,* not as a possible type of political organization. Problems with the belief that egalitarianism is a possible political type are well known (e.g., Flannagan [1989] among many others). However, as Joel Robbins explains, inspiring himself from Dumont (1980), "[A]n egalitarian society

would be one in which equality is the paramount value, in which equality encompasses inequality at the level of ideology and serves to structure the relations between other values. But note, an egalitarian society would not be one where there were no empirical inequalities, not even one where there were empirical inequalities but no ideological charter for them" (1994, 29).

6. The arguments presented here are reminiscent of Shore's (1982) analysis of dissociation and ambivalence in Samoan ideologies of personhood and social action. In a Samoan theory of social action, for example, there is room for *both* compliance to and rebellion against authority, and the coexistence of these ideologies, which has given rise to sharp debates among ethnographers, is rendered possible by a cultural conceptualization of the person as a bundle of more or less autonomous facets. I differ from Shore in viewing "contradiction" as an appropriate characterization of the material I present here, maintaining, with Abu-Lughod (1991) and others, that culture is often a system of unresolved contradictions.

7. The term *fenua* itself has telescopic meaning. Like its cognates in other Polynesian languages, its primary meaning is "atoll, island, country." It is also frequently used metonymically to refer to the inhabitants of an atoll or island as a corporate, bounded group.

8. As in ancient Greek polities (Forsdyke 2005), ostracism in the atolls of Tuvalu is perhaps the most serious punishment that can be inflicted on a person. In the olden days, in its most severe form, the offender was placed in a leaky canoe and set adrift, a fate that few survived (although some, like Elekana, managed to reach distant lands). This practice, called *fakataapea* "to set adrift," was last implemented in historical times but is viewed as evidence of un-Christian "darkness" *(pouliuli),* although at moments of tense conflicts between particular persons and the majority, some recall it with a certain nostalgia. *Fakataapea* is still a favorite way of committing suicide (cf. Firth 1961 on Tikopia).

9. Awareness of human rights as a concept was awakened on Nukulaelae in large part by the establishment in the mid-1980s of the office of People's Lawyer on Funafuti, filled by a succession of British and later Australian volunteers—one of whom later published amusing memoirs (Ells 2006)—who acted essentially as public defenders. The office became a "human rights translator" (Goodale and Merry 2007; Merry 2006), for example by publishing in 1990 a widely distributed booklet in Tuvaluan entitled *Ko Koe mo te Tulafono* "You and the Law," which "vernacularized" human rights for Nukulaelae Islanders and other Tuvaluans. Islanders learned from it that Tuvalu's constitution protects human rights, but also calls for the protection of *tuu mo aganuu* "customs and traditions," leaving much unresolved in cases where what fall under the latter rubric (e.g., authoritarian control by the Council of Elders) conflicts with human rights.

4. Morality and the Structure of Gossip

1. When I was living in Wellington, New Zealand, in the late 1990s, Tuvaluan migrants teased me mercilessly for not owning a television, which they attributed to my being tight-fisted *(kaiuu),* a trait that they linked to my adoptive mother's genealogical

links to Nanumaga, a northern Tuvalu island where people are reputed not to share (food, in particular, probably because it is scarce). Similar allegations of Nanumaga-style stinginess had more serious consequences in 1990, as I discuss in chapter 6.

2. Jamaican blood is a decidedly recurrent bad omen when it comes to being associated with gossip in Tuvalu. Lucille Iremonger, wife of the Ellice Islands administrative officer before World War II and author of memoirs of her years on Funafuti, tells of the wireless operator, "a tall, coal-black negro, with nothing Polynesian about him, with a lame leg" (1948, 66) named Falavii, descendant of a "buck negro" named George, a sailor from Jamaica (where Iremonger herself was born, of a slave-owning family, which may explain her obsession with race). Falavii's principal character trait? "Falavi loved gossip, especially malicious gossip, and had to be shut up almost by force. He was as slippery as an eel" (1948, 67).

3. Bourdieu's (1970) classic analysis of the symbolism of space in the Kabyle house already prefigures an understanding of multiple self-embeddings as indexes of social inequality.

4. The practices governing bodily hexis in Tuvalu relax much more readily than in neighboring societies (Samoa, Tonga, Fiji), where people are expected to sit up cross-legged in many more circumstances and for much longer than in Tuvalu. What I have translated here as "take a load off your feet" is a common expression that Nukulaelae people use to encourage each other to relax, fakapaa (ou tua) ki lalo, literally, "flop down your back to the ground," equivalent to "don't stand on ceremony."

5. See chapter 1 for references of relevance.

6. Reisman's (1974) analysis must be contextualized in a long-standing theme in the ethnographic representation of Caribbean societies, the cultural tension between "reputation," that is, independence, fast life, and verbal prowess, and "respectability," that is, sedentarism, hard work, and churchgoing (P. Wilson 1969). Contrapuntal conversation fits well into the "reputation" scheme and its carefree disorder. Notions of both "contrapuntal" and "reputation" have been subjected to criticism: Sidnell (2001) provides a trenchant sociolinguistic critique demonstrating that Guyanese conversation that "looks" contrapuntal is in fact very orderly, while Freeman (2000, 108–112) shows that the reputation vs. respectability contrast is not just a simple "cultural model," but that it implicates slavery, colonialism, gender, and race.

7. I invoke intentionality as a relevant analytic category here, perhaps in contrast to claim that some Polynesian societies downplay. For example, Duranti (1993) documents a general reluctance among his Samoan informants to talk about other people's intentions, a reluctance in which Ochs (1988) finds echoes in Samoan adults' lack of interest in attributing meaning to children's early utterances. This lack of interest in others' intentions contrasts in fascinating ways with the conviction, found among many Papua New Guinea societies, for example, that multiple, laminated, and often sinister intentions underlie people's words and deeds (e.g., Brison 1992; Merlan and Rumsey 1991, 225; Stroud 1992). While in earlier publications I concurred that Nuku-laelae people downplayed intentionality, my view today is more mitigated. Factors such as status and context play a pivotal role in the relative importance of intentionality: like

the high-ranking male Samoan villagers among whom Duranti spent time, older male Nukulaelae Islanders who see themselves as part of the "establishment" may find it beneath their dignity to speculate about the intentions of the lower ranking, but women, younger men, and marginal adult men take great pleasure in doing so. As in Samoa, the intentions of low-ranking people (such as children) are of little consequence, but those of high-ranking people (such as influential elderly men) are. It is unwise to speculate about intentions in contexts where such speculations may have serious consequences, as in meetings or in conversation with the ethnographer, but away from prying ears people are very interested in intentions and very eager to speculate about them. In fact, a lot of Nukulaelae gossip is designed to attribute intentions to others, as I will illustrate copiously in the remainder of this text (particularly chapters 6 and 7), although this is often accomplished not through linguistic symbolism (i.e., in the literal meaning of what is said), but through the other semiotic means that I document in this chapter. And Tuvaluans from other islands who spend time on Nukulaelae often remark that people are prone to *fakauiga* "give meaning to" behavior, hence its love of gossip. "Both a minefield and a goldmine" (Herzfeld 2001, 46), intentionality is perhaps too complex to lend itself to simple societywide generalizations (Gluckman 1972; Hill and Irvine 1993; Rosen 1995). I find particularly useful Paul's (1995, 19–21) distinction between *discussing* intentions, which people often avoid for a variety of reasons, and actually *attributing* intentions, which no one probably finds particularly difficult.

8. Because the colonial lady dispensed with the subtlety of using pseudonyms, we know exactly whom is she is talking about. Falavii, wireless operator from Vaitupu already mentioned in note 2 (this chapter), would later play an important role in the Gilberts during the war, which earned him a British decoration (McQuarrie 1994, 129). Melitiana, of Nukulaelae, was a former pupil of Douglas Gilbert Kennedy (see chapter 2, note 13) and an influential schoolteacher, who would later become Nukulaelae's representative to the House of Representatives at the end of the colonial era.

9. A substantial body of conversation analytic literature focuses on repairs, which now includes works based on conversation in other than the hegemonic languages of the West, to which they were long confined (see Sidnell 2006 for an overview).

10. For the "victim," a good-natured response to this kind of teasing is to express annoyance and shame while also laughing. Younger people, who are less and less concerned about cross-sibling avoidance, employ a broader range of responses. I remember one instance, in 1980, of a middle-aged man teasing a young woman strolling with her friends on the path by calling out to her, with feigned disinterest, a question as to her cross-sibling's whereabouts, to which she retorted, turning the tables on him, *Teenei!* "He's right here!" The teaser then reacted, in a jokingly scandalized tone, "Hey! Don't you know that kind of behavior is *tapu?*"

11. Important works on reported speech in literary criticism include Banfield (1982), Chatman (1978), and Pascal (1977); in sociolinguistics, Coulmas (1986), Holt and Clift (2007), and Tannen (1989); and in linguistic anthropology, Hill and Irvine (1993), Lucy (1993), and Silverstein and Urban (1996).

12. Sometimes jokes are fictionalized embellishments of real-life events, or com-

pletely fictional, but people who are too much in the habit of telling such jokes risk being accused of *loi* "lying" or, if persistent, of being *looia* "lawyers."

13. True to normal conversational practices, Peifaga and his hosts would often engage in detailed identification of the unfortunate protagonists, who are listening in alongside the entire country ("'You know So-and-so?' 'Ah! So-and-so's grandchild, from Nukufetau?' 'Yes yes yes, that's the one! The one with the mole on her forehead!'"). Since Peifaga is a public figure, I am using his real name.

5. The Twenty-Dollar Piglets

1. Tuvaluan oratory does not involve elaborate canonical references, genealogical recitations, honorific vocabulary, or similes and conventionalized allusions, and thus is not as formally elaborated as certain forms of oratory in rigidly ranked Polynesian societies like Samoa and Tonga (e.g., Duranti 1994; Philips 2000, 2004). It is considerably more open to creativity, despite the fact that older Tuvaluan interviewees often insist on the existence of a rigid formal code, undoubtedly the result of a century of subservience to Samoan pastors.

2. Many scholars have demonstrated that informal conversation can have an aesthetic structure, which resides in the spontaneous use of such features as parallelisms and repetitions (Jakobson 1960; also Silverstein 1984). Nukulaelae gossip, however, has few if any of these features, so not *all* everyday interaction is necessarily poetic, even in the broadest sense of this term.

3. The strategic use of diffuseness in establishing a particular relationship between a text and the truth is, of course, not an exclusive characteristic of Nukulaelae gossip, as Terry Eagleton argues:

> Many modernist literary works . . . make the 'act of enunciating' the process of their own production, part of their actual 'content.' They do not try to pass themselves off as unquestionable, . . . but as the Formalists would say 'lay bare the device' of their own composition. They do this so that they will not be mistaken for absolute truth— so that the reader will be encouraged to reflect critically on the partial, particular ways they construct reality, and so to recognize how it might all have happened differently. (1983, 170)

4. In the 1979 national census, 222 Tuvaluans out of a total population of 7,271 declared membership in religious groups other than the Church of Tuvalu (mostly Seventh-Day Adventism and the Baha'i Faith), with one "undeclared" on Nukulaelae at the time (Iosia and MacCrae 1980, 194). The 2002 census enumerated 892 residents of Tuvalu declaring not to be members of the majority denomination (total population 9,499), the overwhelming majority living on Funafuti. Seventh-Day Adventists and Baha'is were the most numerous (185 and 184 respectively), followed by 167 members of the evangelical Brethren Assembly, 169 of "other denominations," and smaller numbers of Jehovah's Witnesses, Catholics, and adherents of the Apostolic Church and New Testament Church. Nukulaelae continues to have only a single Baha'i fam-

ily in residence, although Nukulaelae Islanders residing elsewhere have joined other denominations.

5. A woman, Looine, was *ulu fenua* for a brief period in the 1950s. Any mention of her invariably segues to the narrative of her inability to *fakafeagai* with the captain of a New Zealand ship that called at Nukulaelae during her tenure because she did not speak English. In addition to high rhetoric, knowledge of some English, or at least the ability to demonstrate an entitlement to speak some English without being laughed at, is a prerequisite for positions of social salience. There is a great deal of subtle footing involved in these demonstrations, and some opt for the trickster role, garbling English utterances probably on purpose to control laughter, while others make a serious attempt that their charisma backs up (cf. Besnier 2003 on Tonga).

6. The terms "covert prestige" and "negative prestige" acquired currency in early forms of variationist sociolinguistics (Labov 1972; Trudgill 1974) to refer to linguistic production that the establishment devalues, but that are subculturally valued. These labels are problematic because they assume a pretheoretical model of power and prestige (Bourdieu 1991): "negative" implies that this prestige is not the product of agency, and "covert" implies that "overt" forms acquire prestige in more transparent ways than "covert" forms, which Gal's (1995) critique of the resistance literature (discussed in chapter 1) demonstrates is not the case.

7. The expression is made up of the adverbial or verbal deictic *peelaa* "thus," which has a variety of meanings (it appears repeatedly in the transcript with the place-holding meaning of the hesitation marker "like"). As a comparative conjunct, *peelaa* takes an object marked *mo*, which in other grammatical contexts functions as the coordinator "and, with" (Besnier 2000, 224–226). The object marker *mo* is repaired twice here.

6. The Two Widows

1. In Samoa, Sauma'iafi is a voracious devourer of men, whom she lures into the bush. She is associated with the subdistrict of Saleimoa in Samoa (Unasa Va'a, personal communication). She appears in Western lore in a short story by R. L. Stevenson's stepson, Lloyd Osbourne (1900).

2. The alien nature of spirits is a recurring theme in ethnographies of spirits, spirit mediumship, and possession cults. From the Zâr cult in Sudan (Boddy 1989), the Hauka cult in Ghana (Rouch 1955; Stoller 1995), and the Spirit Movement of eastern Nigeria (Pratten 2007) to American New Age spirit channeling (M. Brown 1997), spirits are frequently associated with alterity, although what kind of alterity is the potential subject of debate (Henley 2006), and often derive their political meaning from this alterity. It is tempting to relate these themes to the quintessentially nonlocal and modernity-suffused nature of witchcraft and sorcery, as Ashforth (2005), Comaroff and Comaroff (1993), Geschiere (1997), and Niehaus (2001), among others, argue convincingly. The association, however, is far from universal as, in other contexts like Mayotte, spirits are ancestral and very familiar (Lambek 1981, 1993).

3. Few ethnographies of Melanesian societies fail to at least mention sorcery, witchcraft, and magic. The anthropological corpus on the subject based on Melanesian material is consequently vast. It includes epoch-making works such as Fortune (1932),

Malinowski (1935), and Munn (1986); important ethnographies such as Knauft (1985), Lindenbaum (1979), Stephen (1994), Tuzin (1980), and Young (1983); and edited collections that include Herdt and Stephen (1989), Stephen (1987), and Zelenitz and Lindenbaum (1981). In the anthropology of Polynesia, sorcery is almost entirely confined to antiquarian reconstructions of another age (e.g., Buck 1936), although it does figure with some prominence in analyses of the gift, particularly the return gift or *utu* (also "retribution, vengeance"), among the Māori (e.g., Firth 1959, 417–421; Sahlins 1972, 162–165).

4. We owe our current theoretical understanding of the distinction between sorcery and witchcraft to Evans-Pritchard (1937) and the Azande: sorcery is the (predominantly male) achieved and voluntary use of tangible or symbolic tools for maleficent purposes, while witchcraft is the (predominantly female) ascribed ability to perform otherwise impossible tasks. However, because notions of instrumentality and, in particular, the intentionality on which it rests are notoriously complex (see chapter 4, note 7), this contrast is problematic as a theoretical and cross-cultural distinction (cf. Geschiere 1997, 225). It does not correspond to any identifiable contrast on Nukulaelae, where supernatural capacities are both ascribed and achieved, and passed on through both women and men, and what I refer to as "sorcery" here bears affinities to both sorcery and witchcraft as others have discussed them.

5. This theme is elaborated throughout the ethnography of sorcery in Africa (e.g., Bastian 1993; Bleek 1976; Geschiere 1997, 2003; Niehaus 2001). Also relevant is Marwick's (1964) classic comparison of African sorcery as group-internal and Melanesian sorcery as group-external, although later ethnography (e.g., Knauft 1985) contradicts it. Child stealing and organ stealing and trafficking, globalization-infused parallels of witchcraft and sorcery in many parts of the world (e.g., Adams 1998; Niehaus 2000; Scheper-Hughes 2000, 2002), have yet to appear in Tuvalu's consciousness.

6. Interestingly, the law book of 1894 (the first page of which is reproduced in chapter 3), published when the Ellice Islands still constituted a separate protectorate, is silent about sorcery. In contrast, the next edition, revised after the merger of the Ellice Islands with the Gilbert Islands and Tokelau and the establishment of the colony, is specific: "Law No. 19. Any native found guilty of the offence of sorcery shall, on conviction, be imprisoned with hard labour for a term of not less than six months and not exceeding two years" (Gilbert and Ellice Islands Colony 1916, 9). Clearly, the colonial authorities played a role in constructing the Gilbertese as sorcery-prone, in contrast to the gentle and civilization-oriented Ellice Islanders.

7. I have left the most clearly identifying details vague in this chapter, although I realize that anyone familiar with Nukulaelae will be able to identify the people I am writing about. However, I secured in 1991 the permission of the principal agents to retell this narrative, and I waited a significant amount of time to ensure that the narrative of what were then difficult events would lose its edge.

8. Anthropologists who have conducted fieldwork in neighboring, hierarchy-obsessed Samoa tell me that my continued link to such a skeletal household would never have been allowed there.

9. By that time, I had acquired some visibility all over Tuvalu, in part because of the

adoption (which went to national Parliament, where it was declared to have no legal weight when it came to issues of land inheritance) and in part because of my linguistic ability. For example, as I mention in chapter 4, I had appeared several times on the national radio program *Tala Fakkata,* to which the entire nation listens rapturously. So the fact that the omniscient spirit knew me was not surprising, even though I had met neither her nor the medium.

10. Anthropologists all over the Pacific Islands and other foreigners have been named and renamed since the beginning of contact, and some have even caught on to the multilayered irony potentially embedded in these events, such as Serge Tcherkézoff (personal communication), onto whom a Samoan family bestowed the chiefly title of *Sāmoa 'Ua Tasi* "Samoa has become one" (a joke at the expense of the white man, at the expense of the fractious nature of Samoan politics, or at the expense of the ever-expanding Samoan chiefly system?). Similarly, Samoan tattooing families, smelling a good thing in the emergence of the Western tattooing industry since the 1990s, have sold for considerable amounts of money their chiefly titles to American and European tattoo artists, who then use this symbolic capital to market their studios in Los Angeles, Berlin, and Amsterdam (Mallon 2005, 163–167).

11. See also chapter 4, note 1. A stereotypical example of Nanumaga *kaiuu* is the allegation that fishing partners on that island do not pool and redistribute the fish, but take home their own individual catches. On Nukulaelae, the practice is called *faka-Nanumaga* "[act] in Nanumaga fashion."

7. Sorcery and Ambition

1. Philip Ells, Tuvalu's former VSO-funded people's lawyer, informs me that legal attempts to seek redress for sorcery-related libel on Funafuti could begin with a writ, heard by the resident magistrate (an experienced and respected Tuvaluan with no formal legal training), demanding monetary compensation, which in the early 1990s typically amounted to A$500. Generally, perhaps always, such cases ended with the magistrate lecturing both parties and the parties making a tear-soaked mutual apology, probably akin to the *faipati fakallei* "speaking properly" through which conflicts are managed in nonlegal settings.

2. Elders normally deliberate while sitting on the floor, and only get up to their feet to make formal speeches on special occasions, for example, at feasts or dances. By standing up, Paanapa was bracketing his performance as a formal speech, rather than a routine contribution to the meeting.

3. An interesting detail of Paanapa's speeches is his consistent use of the singular pronoun *koe* "you" to address the Council of Elders, instead of the usual honorific dual pronoun *koulua* "you [two]." This is the only instance of this practice I ever witnessed in the course of many years spent recording council meetings. I did not ask my Nukulaelae respondents about their views on this, but I propose that Paanapa eschewed polite forms because civility was not what the meeting was about, in his view. In addition, referring to the council in the singular may have indexically emphasized the dyadic nature of the conflict, pitching Paanapa against one other entity, the island community.

4. Several people who had come to the end of their contract on Nauru had come home on the same ship as Paanapa. These people were unusually silent during these events, and the council never asked any of them to come forth and testify.

5. There is contradictory evidence as to whether the council had addressed sorcery in the original meeting, which took place before my return to the atoll. In the meeting I analyze here, some council members claimed that no such thing occurred. Others stated that the council considered the sorcery allegations alongside the many other problems that had arisen between Paanapa and the Nukulaelae community on Nauru. In private, interviewees told me that the allegations were the central theme of the original discussion.

6. Clearly anxious to put an end to the meeting as quickly as possible, several members of the council attempted to close the proceedings at various stages. But Paanapa ignored their efforts and continued presenting additional aspects of his misfortunes.

8. Gossip and the Everyday Production of Politics

1. I refer, for example, to the groundbreaking works anthologized in Bloch (1975), Brenneis and Myers (1984), and Grillo (1989), and reviewed in Ahearn (2001), Brenneis (1988), Gal (1989), Mertz (1994), and Parkin (1984), to cite only a few.

2. In addition, when their representative in the national Parliament is a member of the opposition, Nukulaelae Islanders often feel that they are being denied transportation and supplies as collective punishment for their MP's not supporting the government.

References

Abrahams, Roger D. 1970. A Performance-Centered Approach to Gossip. *Man* [n.s.] 5: 290–301.

———. 1983. *The Man-of-Words in the West Indies: Performance and the Emergence of Creole Culture.* Baltimore, MD: Johns Hopkins University Press.

Abu-Lughod, Lila. 1986. *Veiled Sentiments: Honor and Poetry in a Bedouin Society.* Berkeley: University of California Press.

———. 1990. The Romance of Resistance: Tracing Transformations of Power through Bedouin Women. *American Ethnologist* 17: 41–55.

———. 1991. Writing against Culture. In *Recapturing Anthropology: Working in the Present.* Richard G. Fox, ed. Pp. 137–162. Santa Fe, NM: School of American Research Press.

———. 1993. *Writing Women's Worlds: Bedouin Stories.* Berkeley: University of California Press.

Adams, Abigail E. 1998. Gringas, Ghouls, and Guatemala: The 1994 Attacks on North American Women Accused of Body Organ Trafficking. *Journal of Latin American Anthropology* 4: 112–133.

Addo, Ping-Ann, and Niko Besnier. 2008. When Gifts Become Commodities: Pawn Shops, Valuables, and Shame in Tonga and the Tongan Diaspora. *Journal of the Royal Anthropological Institute* [n.s.] 14: 39–59.

Ahearn, Laura M. 2001. Language and Agency. *Annual Review of Anthropology* 30: 109–137.

Ahmed, Akbar. 1980. *Pukhtun Economy and Society: Traditional Structure and Economic Development in a Tribal Society.* London: Routledge & Kegan Paul.

Allen, Charlotte. 1997. Spies Like Us: When Sociologists Deceive Their Subjects. *Lingua Franca* 7(9): 31–39.

Allen, Leslie. 2004. Will Tuvalu Disappear Beneath the Sea? *Smithsonian* 35(5): 44–52.

Allison, Anne. 1991. Japanese Mothers and *Obentōs*: The Lunch-Box as Ideological State Apparatus. *Anthropological Quarterly* 64: 195–208.

Almirol, Edwin B. 1981. Chasing the Elusive Butterfly: Gossip and the Pursuit of Reputation. *Ethnicity* 8: 293–304.

Althusser, Louis. 1971. Ideology and Ideological State Apparatus (Notes toward an Investigation). In *Lenin and Philosophy, and Other Essays*. Ben Brewster, trans. Pp. 127–186. New York: Monthly Review Press.

American Anthropological Association. 1998. Code of Ethics of the American Anthropological Association. http://www.aaanet.org/committees/ethics/ethcode.htm, accessed August 2007.

Ankarloo, Bengt, and Gustav Henningsen, eds. 1993. *Early Modern European Witchcraft: Centres and Peripheries*. Oxford: Clarendon Press.

Apte, Mahadev L. 1985. *Humor and Laughter: An Anthropological Approach*. Ithaca, NY: Cornell University Press.

Aretxaga, Begoña. 1993. Maddening States. *Annual Review of Anthropology* 32: 393–410.

Arno, Andrew. 1993. *The World of Talk on a Fijian Island: An Ethnography of Law and Communicative Causation*. Norwood, NJ: Ablex.

Asad, Talal. 1972. Market Model, Class Structure and Consent: A Reconsideration of Swat Political Organization. *Man* [n.s.] 7: 75–94.

Ashforth, Adam. 2005. *Witchcraft, Violence, and Democracy in South Africa*. Chicago: University of Chicago Press.

Ashkenazi, Michael, and Fran Markowitz. 1999. Sexuality and Prevarication in the Praxis of Anthropology. In *Sex, Sexuality, and the Anthropologist*. Fran Markowitz and Michael Ashkenazi, eds. Pp. 1–21. Urbana: University of Illinois Press.

Atkinson, J. Maxwell, and John Heritage. 1984. Transcript Notation. In *Structures of Social Action: Studies in Conversation Analysis*. J. Maxwell Atkinson and John Heritage, eds. Pp. ix–xvi. Cambridge: Cambridge University Press; Paris: Éditions de la Maison des Sciences de l'Homme.

Austin, J. L. 1962. *How to Do Things with Words*. Oxford: Clarendon Press.

Bailey, F. G. 1960. *Tribe, Caste and Nation: A Study of Political Activity and Political Change in Highland Orissa*. Manchester: Manchester University Press.

———. 1971a. Gifts and Poison. In *Gifts and Poison: The Politics of Reputation*. F. G. Bailey, ed. Pp. 1–25. Oxford: Basil Blackwell.

———. 1971b. The Management of Reputation and the Process of Change. In *Gifts and Poison: The Politics of Reputation*. F. G. Bailey, ed. Pp. 281–301. Oxford: Basil Blackwell.

———. 1988. *Humbuggery and Manipulation: The Art of Leadership*. Ithaca, NY: Cornell University Press.

Bakalaki, Alexandra. 1997. Students, Natives, Colleagues: Encounters in Academia and in the Field. *Cultural Anthropology* 12: 502–526.

Bakhtin, Mikhail M. 1981 [1934]. Discourse in the Novel. In *The Dialogic Imagination: Four Essays*. Michael Holquist, ed. and trans. Pp. 259–422. Austin: University of Texas Press.

Banfield, Ann. 1982. *Unspeakable Sentences: Narration and Representation in the Language of Fiction*. Boston: Routledge & Kegan Paul.

Barnard, Alan. 2006. Kalahari Revisionism, Vienna and the "Indigenous Peoples" Debate. *Social Anthropology* 14: 1–16.

Barnes, John. 1980. *Who Should Know What? Social Science, Privacy and Ethics.* Cambridge: Cambridge University Press.

Barth, Fredrik. 1959. *Political Leadership among Swat Pathans.* London: Athlone Press.

———. 1966. *Models of Social Organisation.* London: Royal Anthropological Institute of Great Britain and Northern Ireland.

Basedow, Jürgen, and Wolfgang Wurmnest. 2005. *Third-Party Liability of Classification Societies: A Comparative Perspective.* New York: Springer.

Bashkow, Ira. 2006. *The Meaning of Whitemen: Race and Modernity in the Orokaiva Cultural World.* Chicago: University of Chicago Press.

Bastian, Misty L. 1993. "Bloodhounds Who Have No Friends": Witchcraft, Locality, and the Popular Press in Nigeria. In *Modernity and Its Malcontents: Ritual and Power in Africa.* Jean Comaroff and John L. Comaroff, eds. Pp. 129–166. Chicago: University of Chicago Press.

Bauman, Richard. 1986. *Story, Performance, and Event: Contextual Studies of Oral Narrative.* Cambridge: Cambridge University Press.

———, and Charles L. Briggs. 1990. Poetics and Performance as Critical Perspectives on Language and Social Life. *Annual Review of Anthropology* 19: 59–88.

———. 2003. *Voices of Modernity: Language Ideologies and the Politics of Inequality.* Cambridge: Cambridge University Press.

Bayer, Julie, and Josh Salzman, directors. 2005. *Time and Tide.* Wavecrest Films. 59 minutes.

Becker, Alton. 1988. Language in Particular: A Lecture. In *Linguistics in Context: Connecting Observation and Understanding.* Deborah Tannen, ed. Pp. 17–35. Norwood, NJ: Ablex.

Bergmann, Jörg R. 1993. *Discreet Indiscretions: The Social Organization of Gossip.* John Bednarz, Jr., trans. New York: Aldine de Gruyter. (Originally published as *Klatsch: Zur Socialform der diskreten Indiskretion.* Berlin: Walter de Gruyter, 1987.)

Bertram, I. Geoffrey. 2006. The MIRAB Model in the Twenty-First Century. *Asia Pacific Viewpoint* 47: 1–13.

———, and Ray F. Watters. 1985. The MIRAB Economy in South Pacific Microstates. *Pacific Viewpoint* 26: 497–519.

Besnier, Niko. 1989. Information Withholding as a Manipulative and Collusive Strategy in Nukulaelae Gossip. *Language in Society* 18: 315–341.

———. 1990a. Conflict Management, Gossip, and Affective Meaning on Nukulaelae. In *Disentangling: Conflict Discourse in Pacific Societies.* Karen A. Watson-Gegeo and Geoffrey M. White, eds. Pp. 290–334. Stanford, CA: Stanford University Press.

———. 1990b. Language and Affect. *Annual Review of Anthropology* 19: 419–451.

———. 1992. Reported Speech and Affect on Nukulaelae. In *Responsibility and Evidence in Oral Discourse.* Jane H. Hill and Judith T. Irvine, eds. Pp. 161–181. Cambridge: Cambridge University Press.

———. 1994. The Truth and Other Irrelevant Aspects of Nukulaelae Gossip. *Pacific Studies* 17(3): 1–39.

————. 1995. *Literacy, Emotion, and Authority: Reading and Writing on a Polynesian Atoll*. Cambridge: Cambridge University Press.

————. 1996a. Gossip. In *Encyclopedia of Cultural Anthropology*. David Levinson and Melvin Ember, eds. Vol. 2, pp. 544–547. New York: Henry Holt.

————. 1996b. Heteroglossic Discourses on Nukulaelae Spirits. In *Spirits in Culture, History, and Mind*. Jeannette M. Mageo and Alan Howard, eds. Pp. 75–97. London: Routledge.

————. 2000. *Tuvaluan: A Polynesian Language of the Central Pacific*. London: Routledge.

————. 2003. Crossing Genders, Mixing Languages: The Linguistic Construction of Transgenderism in Tonga. In *Handbook of Language and Gender*. Janet Holmes and Miriam Meyerhoff, eds. Pp. 279–301. Oxford: Blackwell.

————. 2004a. Consumption and Cosmopolitanism: Practicing Modernity at the Second-Hand Marketplace in Nuku'alofa, Tonga. *Anthropological Quarterly* 77: 7–45.

————. 2004b. The Social Production of Abjection: Desire and Silencing among Transgender Tongans. *Social Anthropology* 12: 301–323.

Billig, Michael. 1999. Whose Terms? Whose Ordinariness? Rhetoric and Ideology in Conversation Analysis. *Discourse and Society* 10: 543–558.

————. 2005. *Laughter and Ridicule: Towards a Social Critique of Humour*. London: Sage.

Bleek, Wolf [pseudonym for Sjaak van der Geest]. 1976. Witchcraft, Gossip and Death: A Social Drama. *Man* [n.s.] 11: 526–541.

Bloch, Maurice, ed. 1975. *Political Language and Oratory in Traditional Society*. London: Academic Press.

Blommaert, Jan. 2003. Context Is/as Critique. *Critique of Anthropology* 21: 13–32.

Boddy, Janice. 1989. *Wombs and Alien Spirits: Women, Men, and the Zar Cult in Northern Sudan*. Madison: University of Wisconsin Press.

————. 1994. Spirit Possession Revisited: Beyond Instrumentality. *Annual Review of Anthropology* 23: 407–434.

Boissevain, Jeremy. 1968. The Place of Non-Groups in the Social Sciences. *Man* [n.s.] 3: 542–556.

Bolinger, Dwight. 1982. Intonation and Its Parts. *Language* 58: 505–533.

Borovnik, Maria. 2006. Working Overseas: Seafarers' Remittances and Their Distribution in Kiribati. *Asia Pacific Viewpoint* 47: 151–161.

Bourdieu, Pierre. 1970. The Berber House or the World Reversed. *Social Science Information* 9(1): 151–170.

————. 1977. *Outline of a Theory of Practice*. Richard Nice, trans. Cambridge: Cambridge University Press.

————. 1991. *Language and Symbolic Power*. Raymond Gino and Matthew Adamson, trans., John B. Thompson, ed. Cambridge: Polity Press.

Bowers, Nancy. 1965. Permanent Bachelorhood in the Upper Kaugel Valley of Highland New Guinea. *Oceania* 36: 27–37.

Bowman, Glenn. 1989. Fucking Tourists: Sexual Relations and Tourism in Jerusalem's Old City. *Critique of Anthropology* 9: 77–93.

Boyer, Paul, and Stephen Nissenbaum. 1974. *Salem Possessed: The Social Origins of Witchcraft*. Cambridge, MA: Harvard University Press.

Brady, Ivan A. 1974. Land Tenure in the Ellice Islands: A Changing Profile. In *Land Tenure in Oceania*. Henry P. Lundsgaarde, ed. Pp. 130–178. Honolulu: University of Hawai'i Press.

———. 1975. Christians, Pagans, and Government Men: Culture Change in the Ellice Islands. In *A Reader in Culture Change*. Ivan A. Brady and Barry L. Isaacs, eds. Vol. 2, pp. 111–145. New York: Schenkman.

———. 1976. Socio-Economic Mobility: Adoption and Land Tenure in the Ellice Islands. In *Transactions in Kinship: Adoption and Fosterage in Oceania*. Ivan A. Brady, ed. Pp. 120–163. Honolulu: University of Hawai'i Press.

———. 1978. Stability and Change: Wherewithal for Survival on a Coral Island. In *Extinction and Survival in Human Populations*. Charles Laughlin, Jr., and Ivan A. Brady, eds. Pp. 245–281. New York: Columbia University Press.

Brenneis, Donald L. 1984a. Grog and Gossip in Bhatgaon: Style and Substance in Fiji Indian Conversation. *American Ethnologist* 11: 487–506.

———. 1984b. Straight Talk and Sweet Talk: Political Discourse in an Occasionally Egalitarian Community. In *Dangerous Words: Language and Politics in the Pacific*. Donald L. Brenneis and Fred R. Myers, eds. Pp. 69–84. New York: New York University Press.

———. 1987a. Performing Passions: Aesthetics and Politics in an Occasionally Egalitarian Community. *American Ethnologist* 14: 236–250.

———. 1987b. Talk and Transformation. *Man* [n.s.] 22: 499–510.

———. 1988. Language and Disputing. *Annual Review of Anthropology* 17: 221–237.

———. 1989. Gossip. In *International Encyclopedia of Communications*. Erik Barnouw et al., eds. Vol. 2, pp. 225–226. New York: Oxford University Press.

———. 1990. Shared and Solitary Sentiments: The Discourse of Friendship, Play, and Anger in Bhatgaon. In *Language and the Politics of Emotions*. Catherine A. Lutz and Lila Abu-Lughod, eds. Pp. 113–125. Cambridge: Cambridge University Press; Paris: Éditions de la Maison des Sciences de l'Homme.

———, and Fred R. Myers, eds. 1984. *Dangerous Words: Language and Politics in the Pacific*. New York: New York University Press.

Brettell, Caroline B., ed. 1993. *When They Read What We Write: The Politics of Ethnography*. Westport, CT: Bergin & Garvey.

Brewis, Alexandra. 1996. *Lives on the Line: Women and Ecology on a Pacific Atoll*. Fort Worth, TX: Harcourt Brace.

Briggs, Charles L. 1992. "Since I Am a Woman, I Will Chastise My Relatives": Gender, Reported Speech, and the (Re)construction of Social Relations in Warao Ritual Wailing. *American Ethnologist* 19: 337–361.

———. 2007. Mediating Infanticide: Theorizing Relations between Narratives and Violence. *Cultural Anthropology* 22: 315–356.

Briggs, Jean. 1970. *Never in Anger: Portrait of an Eskimo Family*. Cambridge, MA: Harvard University Press.

Brison, Karen J. 1992. *Just Talk: Gossip, Meetings, and Power in a Papua New Guinea Village*. Berkeley: University of California Press.

Brown, Carolyn H. 1996. Contested Meanings: Tantra and the Poetics of Mithila Art. *American Ethnologist* 23: 717–737.

Brown, Michael F. 1996. On Resisting Resistance. *American Anthropologist* 98: 729–735.

———. 1997. *The Channeling Zone: American Spirituality in an Anxious Age.* Cambridge, MA: Harvard University Press.

Buck, Peter (Te Rangi Hiroa). 1936. *Regional Diversity in the Elaboration of Sorcery in Polynesia.* Yale University Publications in Anthropology, 2. New Haven, CT: Yale University Press.

Bustos-Águilar, Pedro. 1995. Mister Don't Touch the Banana: Notes on the Popularity of the Ethnosexed Body South of the Border. *Critique of Anthropology* 15: 149–170.

Butler, Judith. 1990. *Gender Trouble: Feminism and the Subversion of Identity.* New York: Routledge.

———. 1997. *Excitable Speech: A Politics of the Performative.* New York: Routledge.

Calhoun, Craig. 1993. *Habermas and the Public Sphere.* Cambridge, MA: MIT Press.

Cameron, Deborah. 1997. Performing Gender: Young Men's Talk and the Performance of Heterosexual Masculinity. In *Language and Masculinity.* Sally Johnson and Ulrike H. Meinhof, eds. Pp. 47–64. Oxford: Blackwell.

Carrier, James G. 1992. Occidentalism: The World Turned Upside-Down. *American Ethnologist* 19: 196–212.

Carsten, Janet. 1995. The Politics of Forgetting: Migration, Kinship and Memory on the Periphery of a Southeast Asian State. *Man* [n.s.] 11: 317–335.

Caton, Steven C. 1990. *"Peaks of Yemen I Summon": Poetry as Cultural Practice in a North Yemeni Tribe.* Berkeley: University of California Press.

Cerroni-Long, E. L. 1995. Introduction: Insider or Native Anthropology? In *Insider Anthropology.* E. L. Cerroni-Long, ed. Pp. 1–16. N.p.: National Association for the Practice of Anthropology.

Chambers, Anne F., and Keith S. Chambers. 1985. Illness and Healing in Nanumea, Tuvalu. In *Healing Practices in the South Pacific.* Claire D. F. Parsons, ed. Pp. 16–50. Lāʻie, HI: Institute for Polynesian Studies.

———. 2007. Five Takes on Climate and Cultural Change in Tuvalu. *The Contemporary Pacific* 19: 194–306.

Chambers, Keith S., and Anne F. Chambers. 1975. A Note on the Ellice Referendum. *Pacific Viewpoint* 16: 221–222.

———. 2000. *Unity of Heart: Culture and Change in a Polynesian Atoll Society.* Prospect Heights, IL: Waveland Press.

Chatman, Seymour B. 1978. *Story and Discourse: Narrative Structure in Fiction and Film.* Ithaca, NY: Cornell University Press.

Coates, Jennifer. 1988. Gossip Revisited: Language in All-Female Groups. In *Women in Their Speech Communities.* Jennifer Coates and Deborah Cameron, eds. Pp. 94–122. London: Longman.

Collier, Jane F., and Sylvia J. Yanagisako, eds. 1987. *Gender and Kinship: Essays toward a Unified Analysis.* Stanford, CA: Stanford University Press.

Colson, Elizabeth. 1953. *The Makah Indians: A Study of an Indian Tribe in Modern American Society*. Minneapolis: University of Minnesota Press.

Comaroff, Jean, and John Comaroff. 1991. *Of Revelation and Revolution*. Vol. 1: *Christianity, Colonialism, and Consciousness in South Africa*. Chicago: University of Chicago Press.

———. 1992. *Ethnography and the Historical Imagination*. Boulder, CO: Westview.

———, eds. 1993. *Modernity and Its Malcontents: Ritual and Power in Africa*. Chicago: University of Chicago Press.

Comaroff, John L., and Jean Comaroff. 1997. *Of Revelation and Revolution*. Vol. 2: *The Dialectic of Modernity on a South African Frontier*. Chicago: University of Chicago Press.

Conklin, Beth A. 1997. Body Paint, Feathers, and VCRs: Aesthetics and Authenticity in Amazonian Activism. *American Ethnologist* 24: 711–737.

———, and Laura R. Graham. 1995. The Shifting Middle Ground: Amazonian Indians and Eco-Politics. *American Anthropologist* 97: 695–710.

Connell, John. 2007. Islands, Idylls and the Detours of Development. *Singapore Journal of Tropical Geography* 28: 116–135.

Cornwall, Andrea. 2002. Spending Power: Love, Money, and the Reconfiguration of Gender Relations in Ado-Odo, Southwestern Nigeria. *American Ethnologist* 29: 963–980.

Coulmas, Florian, ed. 1986. *Direct and Indirect Speech*. Berlin: Mouton de Gruyter.

Cowan, Jane K. 1991. Going Out for Coffee? Contesting the Grounds of Gendered Pleasures in Everyday Sociability. In *Contested Identities: Gender and Kinship in Modern Greece*. Peter Loizos and Evthmios Papataxiarchis, eds. Pp. 180–202. Princeton, NJ: Princeton University Press.

Cox, Bruce A. 1970. What Is Hopi Gossip About? Information Management and Hopi Factions. *Man* [n.s.] 5: 88–98.

Creed, Gerald W. 2006. Reconsidering Community. In *The Seduction of Community: Emancipations, Oppressions, Quandaries*. Gerald W. Creed, ed. Pp. 3–22. Santa Fe, NM: School of American Research Press; London: James Currey.

Dahl, Terje. 1992. *Paradiset Jeg Fant*. Oslo: Grøndahl & Dreyer.

David, Mrs. Edgeworth [Lady Caroline M. David]. 1899. *Funafuti, or Three Months on a Coral Island: An Unscientific Account of a Scientific Expedition*. London: John Murray.

Derrida, Jacques. 1977 [1972]. Signature Event Context. *Glyph* 1: 172–197.

Doane, Molly. 2007. The Political Economy of the Ecological Native. *American Anthropologist* 109: 452–462.

Dominguez, Virginia R. 2006. Comment on Kulick 2006. *Current Anthropology* 47: 945–946.

Douglas, Bronwen. 1979. Rank, Power, Authority: A Reassessment of Traditional Leadership in South Pacific Societies. *Journal of Pacific History* 14: 2–27.

Douglas, Mary. 1966. *Purity and Danger: An Analysis of the Concepts of Pollution and Taboo*. London: Routledge & Kegan Paul.

———, ed. 1970. *Witchcraft Confessions and Accusations*. London: Tavistock.

Drew, Paul, and John Heritage, eds. 2006. *Conversation Analysis.* 4 vols. Thousand Oaks, CA: Sage.

Dumont, Louis. 1980. *Homo Hierarchicus: The Caste System and Its Implications.* Rev. English ed. Chicago: University of Chicago Press.

Dunbar, Robin. 1996. *Grooming, Gossip, and the Evolution of Language.* Cambridge, MA: Harvard University Press.

Duranti, Alessandro. 1993. Truth and Intentionality: Towards an Ethnographic Critique. *Cultural Anthropology* 8: 214–245.

———. 1994. *From Grammar to Politics: Linguistic Anthropology in a Western Samoan Village.* Berkeley: University of California Press.

Dwyer, Kevin. 1982. *Moroccan Dialogues: Anthropology in Question.* Baltimore, MD: Johns Hopkins University Press.

Eagleton, Terry. 1983. *Literary Theory: An Introduction.* Oxford: Basil Blackwell.

Edelman, Murray. 1988. *Constructing the Political Spectacle.* Chicago: University of Chicago Press.

Edwards, David B. 1998. Learning from the Swat Pathans: Political Leadership in Afghanistan, 1978–97. *American Ethnologist* 25: 712–728.

Edwards, Jane A. 1993. Principles and Contrasting Systems of Discourse Transcription. In *Talking Data: Transcription and Coding in Discourse Research.* Jane A. Edwards and Martin D. Lampert, eds. Pp. 3–31. Hillsdale, NJ: Lawrence Erlbaum.

Elekana. 1872. Elikana's [*sic*] Story. *The Juvenile Missionary Magazine,* June–October: 101–105, 123–127, 147–150, 175–177, 196–198.

Ellice Islands Protectorate. 1894. *Tulafono o le Atu Elisa* [Laws of the Ellice Islands]. Suva: Edward John March, le Lomitusi a le Malo [in Samoan].

Ellis, Stephen. 1989. Tuning In to Pavement Radio. *African Affairs* 88: 321–330.

Ells, Philip. 2006. *Where the Hell Is Tuvalu? How I Became the Law Man of the World's Fourth Smallest Country.* London: Virgin Books.

Englund, Harri, and James Leach. 2000. Ethnography and the Meta-Narratives of Modernity. *Current Anthropology* 41: 225–248.

Etienne, Mona, and Eleanor Leacock, eds. 1980. *Women and Colonization: Anthropological Perspectives.* New York: Bergin & Garvey.

Evaldsson, Ann-Carita. 2002. Boys' Gossip Telling: Staging Identities and Indexing (Unacceptable) Masculine Behavior. *Text* 22: 199–225.

Evans-Pritchard, E. E. 1937. *Witchcraft, Oracles and Magic among the Azande.* Oxford: Clarendon Press.

———. 1940. *The Nuer: A Description of the Modes of Livelihood and Political Institutions of a Nilotic People.* Oxford: Clarendon Press.

Fabian, Johannes. 1983. *Time and the Other: How Anthropology Makes Its Object.* New York: Columbia University Press.

Farbotko, Carol. 2005. Tuvalu and Climate Change: Constructions of Environmental Displacement in the *Sydney Morning Herald. Geografiska Annaler* 87B(4): 279–293.

Fardon, Richard. 1990. Localizing Strategies: The Regionalization of Ethnographic Accounts. In *Localizing Strategies: Regional Traditions of Ethnographic Writing.*

Richard Fardon, ed. Pp. 1–35. Edinburgh: Scottish Academic Press; Washington, DC: Smithsonian Institution Press.

Faris, James C. 1966. The Dynamics of Verbal Exchange: A Newfoundland Example. *Anthropologica* [n.s.] 8: 235–248.

Favret-Saada, Jeanne. 1977. *Les mots, la mort, les sorts.* Paris: Gallimard.

————, and Josée Contreras. 1981. *Corps pour corps.* Paris: Gallimard.

Feinberg, Richard, and Karen Ann Watson-Gegeo, eds. 1996. *Leadership and Change in the Western Pacific: Essays Presented to Sir Raymond Firth on Occasion of his Ninetieth Birthday.* London: Athlone.

Finin, Gerard A. 2002. *Small Is Viable: Global Ebbs and Flows of a Pacific Atoll Nation.* Pacific Islands Development Working Paper Series, 15. Honolulu: East-West Center.

Finney, Joseph. 1976. *Vai Laaqau* and *Aitu:* Healing in a West Polynesian Village. In *Culture-Bound Syndromes: Ethnopsychiatry and Alternate Therapies.* William Lebra, ed. Pp. 115–129. Honolulu: University Press of Hawai'i.

Firth, Raymond. 1936. *We the Tikopia: A Sociological Study of Kinship in Primitive Polynesia.* London: Allen and Unwin.

————. 1956. Rumour in a Primitive Society, with a Note on the Theory of "Cargo Cults." *Journal of Abnormal and Social Psychology* 53: 122–132.

————. 1959 [1929]. *Economics of the New Zealand Maori.* 2nd ed. Wellington: R. E. Owen, Government Printer.

————. 1960. Succession to Chieftainship in Tikopia. *Oceania* 30: 161–180.

————. 1961. Suicide and Risk-Taking in Tikopia Society. *Psychiatry* 24: 1–17.

Flanagan, James G. 1989. Hierarchy in Simple "Egalitarian" Societies. *Annual Review of Anthropology* 18: 245–266.

————, and Steve Rayner, eds. 1988. *Rules, Decisions, and Inequality in Egalitarian Societies.* Aldershot: Avebury.

Fluehr-Lobban, Carolyn. 1994. Informed Consent in Anthropological Research: We Are Not Exempt. *Human Organization* 53: 1–10.

Fonseca, Claudia. 2001. Philanderers, Cuckolds, and Wily Women: Reexamining Gender Relations in a Brazilian Working-Class Neighborhood. *Men and Masculinities* 3: 261–277.

Forsdyke, Sara. 2005. *Exile, Ostracism, and Democracy: The Politics of Expulsion in Ancient Greece.* Princeton, NJ: Princeton University Press.

Fortune, Reo. 1932. *Sorcerers of Dobu: The Social Anthropology of the Dobu Islanders of the Western Pacific.* New York: E. P. Dutton.

Foucault, Michel. 1977. *Discipline and Punish: The Birth of the Prison.* Alan Sheridan, trans. New York: Pantheon.

————. 1980. *Power/Knowledge: Selected Interviews and Other Writings, 1972–1977.* Colin Gordon, ed.; Colin Gordon et al., trans. New York: Pantheon.

————. 1990. *The History of Sexuality: An Introduction.* New York: Vintage.

Frankenberg, Ronald. 1957. *Village on the Border: A Social Study of Religion, Politics and Football in a North Wales Community.* London: Cohen & West.

Freeman, Carla. 2000. *High Tech and High Heels in the Global Economy: Women, Work, and Pink-Collar Identities in the Caribbean.* Durham, NC: Duke University Press.

―――. 2001. Is Local:Global as Feminine:Masculine? Rethinking the Gender of Globalization. *Signs* 26: 1007–1037.

Friedman, Jonathan. 1979. *System, Structure, and Contradiction in the Evolution of "Asiatic" Social Formations.* Copenhagen: National Museum of Denmark.

Gal, Susan. 1989. Language and Political Economy. *Annual Review of Anthropology* 18: 345–357.

―――. 1995. Language and the "Arts of Resistance." *Cultural Anthropology* 10: 407–424.

―――, and Kathryn A. Woolard, eds. 2001. *Languages and Publics: The Making of Authority.* Manchester: St. Jerome's Press.

Gamson, Joshua. 1994. *Claims to Fame: Celebrity in Contemporary America.* Berkeley: University of California Press.

Garfinkel, Harold. 1956. Conditions of Successful Degradation Ceremonies. *American Journal of Sociology* 61: 420–424.

Geest, Sjaak van der. 2003. Confidentiality and Pseudonyms: A Fieldwork Dilemma from Ghana. *Anthropology Today* 19(1): 14–18.

Geschiere, Peter. 1997. *The Modernity of Witchcraft: Politics and the Occult in Postcolonial Africa.* Charlottesville: University Press of Virginia.

―――. 2003. Witchcraft as the Dark Side of Kinship: Dilemmas of Social Security in New Contexts. *Etnofoor* 16(1): 43–62.

Gewertz, Deborah, and Frederick Errington. 1999. *Emerging Class in Papua New Guinea: The Telling of Difference.* Cambridge: Cambridge University Press.

―――. 2007. The Alimentary Forms of the Global Life: The Pacific Island Trade in Lamb and Mutton Flaps. *American Anthropologist* 109: 496–508.

Ghosh, Anjan. 1996. Symbolic Speech: Towards an Anthropology of Gossip. *Journal of the Indian Anthropological Society* 31: 251–256.

Giddens, Anthony. 1979. *Central Problems in Social Theory: Action, Structure and Contradiction in Social Analysis.* Berkeley: University of California Press.

Gilbert and Ellice Islands Colony. 1916. *Revised Native Laws of the Gilbert, Ellice and Union Groups—O Faatonuga o Mea Faalemalo, ma Tulafono ua faaaogaina mo motu o te Atu Kilipati ma Elise ma Tokelau.* Suva: S. Bach, Printer to the Government of His Britannic Majesty's High Commission for the Western Pacific.

Gilbert and Ellice Islands Protectorate. 1916. *Report for 1914–1915, Presented to both Houses of Parliament by Command of His Majesty.* Annual Colonial Reports, 884. London: Barclay and Fry, under the Authority of His Majesty's Stationery Office.

Gilmore, David. 1978. Varieties of Gossip in a Spanish Rural Community. *Ethnology* 17: 89–99.

Gilsenan, Michael. 1996. *Lords of the Lebanese Marches: Violence and Narrative in an Arab Society.* London: I. B. Tauris.

Gluckman, Max. 1963. Gossip and Scandal. *Current Anthropology* 4: 307–315.

————. 1968. Psychological, Sociological and Anthropological Explanations of Witchcraft and Gossip: A Clarification. *Man* [n.s.] 3: 20–34 (followed by correspondence by Robert Paine, *Man* [n.s.] 3: 305–308).

————, ed. 1972. *The Allocation of Responsibility.* Manchester: Manchester University Press.

Goddard, Michael. 1992. Bigman, Thief: The Social Organization of Rascal Gangs in Port Moresby. *Canberra Anthropology* 15(1): 20–34.

————. 1995. The Rascal Road: Crime, Prestige, and Development in Papua New Guinea. *The Contemporary Pacific* 7: 55–80.

Godelier, Maurice. 1986. *The Making of Great Men: Male Domination and Power among the New Guinea Baruya.* Rupert Swyer, trans. Cambridge: Cambridge University Press.

————, and Marilyn Strathern, eds. 1991. *Big Men and Great Men: Personifications of Power in Melanesia.* Cambridge: Cambridge University Press.

Goffman, Erving. 1959. *The Presentation of Self in Everyday Life.* New York: Doubleday.

————. 1963. *Stigma: Notes on the Management of Spoiled Identity.* New York: Prentice-Hall.

————. 1967. *Interaction Ritual: Essays on Face-to-Face Behavior.* New York: Anchor.

————. 1974. *Frame Analysis: An Essay on the Organization of Experience.* New York: Harper Colophon.

————. 1979. Footing. *Semiotica* 25: 1–29.

Goldman, Laurence. 1983. *Talk Never Dies: The Language of Huli Disputes.* London: Tavistock.

Goldsmith, Michael. 1985. Transformation of the Meeting-House in Tuvalu. In *Transformations of Polynesian Culture.* Antony Hooper and Judith Huntsman, eds. Pp. 151–175. Auckland: Polynesian Society.

————. 1992. The Tradition of Invention. In *Other Sites: Social Anthropology and the Politics of Interpretation.* Michael Goldsmith and Keith Barber, eds. Pp. 29–41. Palmerston North: Department of Social Anthropology, Massey University.

————, and Doug Munro. 1992. Encountering Elekana Encountering Tuvalu. In *Pacific History: Papers from the 8th Pacific History Association Conference.* Donald H. Rubinstein, ed. Pp. 25–41. Mangilao: University of Guam Press and Micronesian Area Research Center.

————. 2002. *The Accidental Missionary: Tales of Elekana.* Christchurch: MacMillan Brown Centre for Pacific Studies, University of Canterbury.

Goodale, Mark, and Sally Engle Merry, eds. 2007. *The Practice of Human Rights: Tracking Law between the Global and the Local.* Cambridge: Cambridge University Press.

Goodman, Robert F., and Aaron Ben-Ze'ev, eds. 1994. *Good Gossip.* Lawrence: University Press of Kansas.

Goodwin, Marjorie H. 1990. *He-Said-She-Said: Talk as Social Organization among Black Children.* Bloomington: Indiana University Press.

————. 1997. Byplay: Negotiating Evaluation in Story-Telling. In *Towards a Social Science of Language: Papers in Honor of William Labov.* Gregory R. Guy, Crawford

Feagin, Deborah Schriffin, and John Baugh, eds. Vol. 2, pp. 77–102. Amsterdam: John Benjamins.

Gordon, Jan B. 1996. *Gossip and Subversion in Nineteenth-Century British Fiction: Echo's Economies.* New York: St. Martin's Press.

Gramsci, Antonio. 1991–2007. *Prison Notebooks.* Joseph A. Buttigieg, ed.; Joseph A. Buttigieg and Antonio Callari, trans. 3 vols. New York: Columbia University Press.

Grillo, Ralph D., ed. 1989. *Social Anthropology and the Politics of Language.* London: Routledge.

Guendouzi, Jackie. 2001. "You'll Think We're Always Bitching": The Function of Cooperativity and Competition in Women's Gossip. *Discourse Studies* 3: 29–51.

Guerin, Bernard, and Yoshihiko Miyazaki. 2003. Rumores, Chisme y Leyendas Urbanas: Una Teoría de Contingencia Social. *Revista Latinoamericana de Psicología* 35: 257–272.

Gupta, Akhil, and James Ferguson. 1997a. Culture, Power, Place: Ethnography at the End of an Era. In *Culture, Power, Place: Explorations in Critical Anthropology.* Akhil Gupta and James Ferguson, eds. Pp. 1–29. Durham, NC: Duke University Press.

———. 1997b. Discipline and Practice: "The Field" as Site, Method, and Location in Anthropology. In *Anthropological Locations: Boundaries and Ground of a Field Science.* Akhil Gupta and James Ferguson, eds. Pp. 1–46. Berkeley: University of California Press.

Habermas, Jürgen. 1991. *The Structural Transformation of the Public Sphere: An Inquiry into a Category of Bourgeois Society.* Thomas Burger, trans. Cambridge, MA: MIT Press.

Halbwachs, Maurice. 1992 [1925]. *On Collective Memory.* Lewis Coser, trans. Chicago: University of Chicago Press.

Handelman, Don. 1973. Gossip in Encounters: The Transmission of Information in a Bounded Social Setting. *Man* [n.s.] 8: 210–227.

Hanks, William. 2005. Pierre Bourdieu and the Practices of Language. *Annual Review of Anthropology* 34: 67–83.

Hannerz, Ulf. 1967. Gossip, Networks and Culture in a Black American Ghetto. *Ethnos* 32: 35–60.

Hanson, F. Allan. 1989. The Making of the Maori: Cultural Invention and Its Logic. *American Anthropologist* 91: 890–902.

———. 1997. Empirical Anthropology, Postmodernism, and the Invention of Tradition. In *Present Is Past: Some Uses of Tradition in Native Societies.* Marie Mauzé, ed. Pp. 195–214. Lanham, MD: University Press of America.

Haraway, Donna. 1988. Situated Knowledge: The Science Question in Feminism as a Site of Discourse on the Privilege of Partial Perspective. *Feminist Studies* 14: 575–599.

Harvey, Penelope. 1991. Drunken Speech and the Construction of Meaning: Bilingual Competence in the Southern Peruvian Andes. *Language in Society* 20: 1–36.

———. 1992. Bilingualism in the Peruvian Andes. In *Researching Language: Issues of Power and Method.* Deborah Cameron et al., eds. Pp. 65–89. London: Routledge.

Haugerud, Angelique. 1995. *The Culture of Politics in Modern Kenya.* Cambridge: Cambridge University Press.

Haviland, John B. 1977. *Gossip, Reputation, and Knowledge in Zinacantan.* Chicago: University of Chicago Press.

Henley, Paul. 2006. Spirit Possession, Power, and the Absent Presence of Islam: Reviewing *Les maîtres fous. Journal of the Royal Anthropological Institute* [n.s.] 12: 731–761.

Herdt, Gilbert, and Michele Stephen, eds. 1989. *The Religious Imagination in New Guinea.* New Brunswick, NJ: Rutgers University Press.

Hereniko, Vilsoni. 1995. *Woven Gods: Female Clowns and Power in Rotuma.* Honolulu: University of Hawai'i Press.

Herskovits, Melville J. 1937. *Life in a Haitian Valley.* New York: Albert A. Knopf.

———, and Frances S. Herskovits. 1947. *Trinidad Village.* New York: Albert A. Knopf.

Herzfeld, Michael. 1991. Silence, Submission, and Subversion: Towards a Poetics of Womanhood. In *Contested Identities: Gender and Kinship in Modern Greece.* Peter Loizos and Evthmios Papataxiarchis, eds. Pp. 79–97. Princeton, NJ: Princeton University Press.

———. 2001. *Anthropology: Theoretical Practice in Culture and Society.* Malden, MA: Blackwell.

———. 2003. *The Body Impolitic: Artisans and Artifice in the Global Hierarchy of Value.* Chicago: University of Chicago Press.

Hill, Jane H. 1995. The Voices of Don Gabriel: Responsibility and Self in a Modern Mexicano Narrative. In *The Dialogic Emergence of Culture.* Dennis Tedlock and Bruce Mannheim, eds. Pp. 97–147. Urbana: University of Illinois Press.

——— and Judith Irvine, eds. 1993. *Responsibility and Evidence in Oral Discourse.* Cambridge: Cambridge University Press.

Hobsbawm, Eric, and Terence Ranger, eds. 1983. *The Invention of Tradition.* Cambridge: Cambridge University Press.

Hochschild, Arlie. 1983. *The Managed Heart: Commercialization of Human Feeling.* Berkeley: University of California Press.

Holt, Elizabeth, and Rebecca Clift, eds. 2007. *Reporting Talk: Reported Speech in Interaction.* Cambridge: Cambridge University Press.

Hornberger, Julia. 1998. Die Kraft des Tratschens: Versuch einer Definition. *Etnofoor* 11(2): 7–24.

Horner, Christopher, and Gilliane Le Gallic, directors. 2004. *The Disappearing of Tuvalu: Trouble in Paradise.* European Television Center. 75 minutes.

Hotchkiss, John C. 1967. Children and Conduct in a Ladino Community of Chiapas, Mexico. *American Anthropologist* 69: 711–718.

Howe, Leo. 1998. Scrounger, Worker, Beggarman, Cheat: The Dynamics of Unemployment and the Politics of Resistance in Belfast. *Journal of the Royal Anthropological Institute* [n.s.] 4: 531–550.

Hutchby, Ian. 1998. *Conversation Analysis: Principles, Practices and Applications.* Oxford: Polity.

Hutchinson, Sharon E. 1996. *Nuer Dilemmas: Coping with Money, War, and the State.* Berkeley: University of California Press.

Innes, Pamela. 2006. The Interplay of Genres, Gender, and Language Ideology among the Muskogee. *Language in Society* 35: 231–259.

Iosia, Simeona, and Sheila Macrae, eds. 1980. *A Report of the Results of the Census of the Population of Tuvalu, 1979.* Funafuti: Government of Tuvalu.

Iremonger, Lucille. 1948. *It's a Bigger Life.* London: Hutchinson.

Irvine, Judith T. 1982. The Creation of Identity in Spirit Mediumship and Possession. In *Semantic Anthropology.* David Parkin, ed. Pp. 241–260. New York: Academic Press.

———. 1989. When Talk Isn't Cheap: Language and Political Economy. *American Ethnologist* 16: 248–267.

———. 1990. Registering Affect: Heteroglossia in the Linguistic Expression of Emotion. In *Language and the Politics of Emotions.* Catherine A. Lutz and Lila Abu-Lughod, eds. Pp. 126–161. Cambridge: Cambridge University Press; Paris: Éditions de la Maison des Sciences de l'Homme.

———. 1996. Shadow Conversations: The Indeterminacy of Participant Roles. In *Natural Histories of Discourse.* Michael Silverstein and Greg Urban, eds. Pp. 131–159. Chicago: University of Chicago Press.

———, and Susan Gal. 2000. Language Ideology and Linguistic Differentiation. In *Regimes of Language: Ideologies, Politics, and Identities.* Paul V. Kroskrity, ed. Pp. 35–83. Santa Fe, NM: School of American Research; Oxford: James Currey.

Iyer, Pico. 1993. The Soul of an Intercontinental Wanderer. *Harper's Magazine* 286(1715): 13–17.

Jackson, Michael. 1995. *At Home in the World.* Durham, NC: Duke University Press.

———. 1996. Introduction: Phenomenology, Radical Empiricism, and Anthropological Critique. In *Things as They Are: New Directions in Phenomenological Anthropology.* Michael Jackson, ed. Pp. 1–50. Bloomington: Indiana University Press.

———. 1998. *Minima Ethnographica: Intersubjectivity and the Anthropological Project.* Chicago: University of Chicago Press.

Jakobson, Roman. 1960. Concluding Statement: Linguistics and Poetics. In *Style in Language.* Thomas A. Sebeok, ed. Pp. 350–377. Cambridge, MA: MIT Press.

Jaworski, Adam, and Justine Coupland. 2005. Othering in Gossip: "You Go Out You Have a Laugh and You Can Pull Yeah Okay but Like . . ." *Language in Society* 34: 667–694.

Jefferson, Gail. 1979. A Technique for Inviting Laughter and Its Subsequent Acceptance Declination. In *Everyday Language: Studies in Ethnomethodology.* George Psathas, ed. Pp. 79–96. New York: Irvington.

———. 1984. On the Organization of Laughter in Talk about Troubles. In *Structures of Social Action: Studies in Conversation Analysis.* J. Maxwell Atkinson and John Heritage, eds. Pp. 346–369. Cambridge: Cambridge University Press.

Johnson, Sally, and Frank Finlay. 1997. Do Men Gossip? An Analysis of Football Talk on Television. In *Language and Masculinity*. Sally Johnson and Ulrike U. Meinhof, eds. Pp. 130–143. Oxford: Blackwell.

Jolly, Margaret. 1992. Specter of Inauthenticity. *The Contemporary Pacific* 4: 49–72.

Joseph, Miranda. 2002. *Against the Romance of Community*. Minneapolis: University of Minnesota Press.

Keane, Webb. 1997. *Signs of Recognition: Powers and Hazards of Representation in an Indonesian Society*. Berkeley: University of California Press.

———. 2003. Self-Interpretation, Agency, and the Objects of Anthropology: Reflection on a Genealogy. *Comparative Studies in Society and History* 45:222–248.

Keating, Elizabeth. 1998. *Power Sharing: Language, Rank, Gender and Social Space in Pohnpei, Micronesia*. New York: Oxford University Press.

Keenan [Ochs], Elinor. 1974. Norm-Makers, Norm-Breakers: Use of Speech by Men and Women in a Malagasy Community. In *Exploration in the Ethnography of Speaking*. Richard Bauman and Joel Sherzer, eds. Pp. 125–143. Cambridge: Cambridge University Press.

Keesing, Roger M. 1985. Kwaio Women Speak: The Micropolitics of Autobiography in a Solomon Islands Society. *American Anthropologist* 87: 27–39.

———. 1989. Creating the Past: Custom and Identity in the Contemporary Pacific. *The Contemporary Pacific* 1: 19–42.

———. 1990. The Power of Talk. In *Disentangling: Conflict Discourse in Pacific Societies*. Karen A. Watson-Gegeo and Geoffrey M. White, eds. Pp. 493–499. Stanford, CA: Stanford University Press.

———. 1991. Reply to Trask. *The Contemporary Pacific* 3: 168–171.

———, and Robert Tonkinson, eds. 1982. Reinventing Traditional Culture: The Politics of Kastom in Island Melanesia. *Mankind* 13(4), special issue.

Kennedy, Donald G. 1931. *Field Notes in the Culture of Vaitupu, Ellice Islands*. New Plymouth, N.Z.: Polynesian Society.

———. 1946. Te Ngangana a Te Tuvalu: *Handbook of the Language of the Ellice Islands*. Suva: Government Printer.

Kirch, Patrick V. 2002. *On the Road of the Winds: An Archaeological History of the Pacific Islands before European Contact*. Berkeley: University of California Press.

Kirsch, Stuart. 2001. Lost Worlds: Environmental Disaster, "Culture Loss," and the Law. *Current Anthropology* 42: 167–198.

Knauft, Bruce. 1985. *Good Company and Violence: Sorcery and Social Action in a Lowland New Guinea Society*. Berkeley: University of California Press.

Koch, Gerd. 1962. Alte Glaubensvorstellungen und Magie auf den Ellice-Inseln (Westpolynesien). *Baessler-Archiv* [n.f.] 10: 45–62.

Koptiuch, Kristin. 1996. "Cultural Defense" and Criminological Displacements: Gender, Race, and (Trans)Nation in the Legal Surveillance of U.S. Diaspora Asians. In *Displacement, Diaspora, and Geographies of Identity*. Smadar Lavie and Ted Swedenburg, eds. Pp. 215–233. Durham, NC: Duke University Press.

Kray, Christine A. 2007. Women as Border in the Shadow of Cancún. *Anthropology Today* 23(4): 17–21.

Kroeger, Karen A. 2003. AIDS Rumors, Imaginary Enemies, and the Body Politic in Indonesia. *American Ethnologist* 30: 243–257.

Kroskrity, Paul V., ed. 2000. *Regimes of Language: Ideologies, Politics, and Identities.* Santa Fe, NM: School of American Research Press.

Kulick, Don. 1993. Heroes from Hell: Representations of "Rascals" in a Papua New Guinean Village. *Anthropology Today* 9(3): 9–14.

———. 1995. The Sexual Life of Anthropologists: Erotic Subjectivity and Ethnographic Work. In *Taboo: Sex, Identity and Erotic Subjectivity in Anthropological Fieldwork.* Don Kulick and Margaret Willson, eds. Pp. 1–28. London: Routledge.

———. 2006. Theory in Furs: Masochist Anthropology. *Current Anthropology* 47: 933–944, 948–952.

Kyle, Noeline J. 1993. Cara David and the "Truths" of Her "Unscientific" Travellers' Tales in Australia and the South Pacific. *Women's Studies International Forum* 16: 105–118.

Laban, Luamanuvao Winnie, and Peter Swain. 1997. Consumer Focus on Tuvalu. *South Pacific Consumer's Report* 8(4): 12–13.

Labov, William. 1972. *Language in the Inner City.* Philadelphia: University of Pennsylvania Press.

Lambek, Michael. 1981. *Human Spirits: A Cultural Account of Trance in Mayotte.* Cambridge: Cambridge University Press.

———. 1990. Certain Knowledge, Contestable Authority: Power and Practice on the Islamic Periphery. *American Ethnologist* 17: 23–40.

———. 1993. *Knowledge and Practice in Mayotte: Local Discourses of Islam, Sorcery, and Spirit Possession.* Toronto: University of Toronto Press.

———. 1996. The Past Imperfect: Remembering as Moral Practice. In *Tense Past: Cultural Essays in Trauma and Memory.* Paul Antze and Michael Lambek, eds. Pp. 235–254. New York: Routledge.

Larmouth, Donald W.; Thomas E. Murray; and Carmin R. Murray. 1992. *Legal and Ethical Issues in Surreptitious Recording.* Tuscaloosa: University of Alabama Press.

Leach, Edmund. 1954. *Political Systems of Highland Burma: A Study of Kachin Social Structure.* London: Athlone Press.

———. 1983. Imaginary Katchins. *Man* [n.s.] 18: 191–199.

Leacock, Eleanor, and Richard Lee, eds. 1982. *Politics and History in Band Societies.* Cambridge: Cambridge University Press.

Leggett, Jeremy K. 2001. *The Carbon War: Global Warming and the End of the Oil Era.* London: Routledge.

Lepowsky, Maria. 1993. *Fruit of the Motherland: Gender in an Egalitarian Society.* New York: Columbia University Press.

Levi, Jerome M. 1999. Hidden Transcripts among the Rarámuri: Culture, Resistance, and Interethnic Relations in Northern Mexico. *American Ethnologist* 26: 90–113.

Levy, Robert I. 1974. *Tahitians: Mind and Experience in the Society Islands.* Chicago: University of Chicago Press.

————. 1984. Emotion, Knowing, and Culture. In *Culture Theory: Essays on Mind, Self, and Emotion*. Richard A. Schweder and Robert A. LeVine, eds. Pp. 214–237. Cambridge: Cambridge University Press.

Lewin, Ellen, and William L. Leap. 1996. Introduction. In *Out in the Field: Reflections of Lesbian and Gay Anthropologists*. Ellen Lewin and William L. Leap, eds. Pp. 1–28. Urbana: University of Illinois Press.

Leyder, Jean. 1935. La fausse nouvelle chez les primitifs du Congo belge. In *Mélanges offerts à Ernest Mahaim, professeur émérite de l'Université de Liège*. Vol. 1, pp. 334–338. Paris: Librairie du Recueil Sirey.

Limón, José E. 1994. *Dancing with the Devil: Society and Cultural Poetics in Mexican-American South Texas*. Madison: University of Wisconsin Press.

Lindenbaum, Shirley. 1979. *Kuru Sorcery: Disease and Danger in the New Guinea Highlands*. Mountain View, CA: Mayfield.

Lindsay, Paul, director. 2005. *Before the Flood*. Stampede Ltd. 59 minutes.

Lindstrom, Lamont. 1990. *Knowledge and Power in a South Pacific Society*. Washington, DC: Smithsonian Institution Press.

————. 1992. Context Contexts: Debatable Truth Statements on Tanna (Vanuatu). In *Rethinking Context: Language as an Interactive Phenomenon*. Alessandro Duranti and Charles Goodwin, eds. Pp. 101–124. Cambridge: Cambridge University Press.

Linnekin, Jocelyn. 1991. Text Bites and the R-Word: The Politics of Representing Scholarship. *The Contemporary Pacific* 3: 172–177.

————. 1992. On the Theory and Politics of Cultural Construction in the Pacific. *Oceania* 62: 249–263.

Lucy, John A., ed. 1993. *Reflexive Language: Reported Speech and Metapragmatics*. Cambridge: Cambridge University Press.

Luhrmann, T. M. 1996. *The Good Parsi: The Fate of a Colonial Elite in a Postcolonial Society*. Cambridge, MA: Harvard University Press.

Lutz, Catherine A. 1988. *Unnatural Emotions: Everyday Sentiments on a Micronesian Atoll and Their Challenge to Western Theory*. Chicago: Chicago University Press.

————. 1990. Engendered Emotion: Gender, Power and the Rhetoric of Emotional Control in American Discourse. In *Language and the Politics of Emotions*. Catherine A. Lutz and Lila Abu-Lughod, eds. Pp. 69–91. Cambridge: Cambridge University Press; Paris: Éditions de la Maison des Sciences de l'Homme.

————, and Lila Abu-Lughod, eds. 1990. *Language and the Politics of Emotions*. Cambridge: Cambridge University Press; Paris: Éditions de la Maison des Sciences de l'Homme.

————, and Jane L. Collins. 1993. *Reading National Geographic*. Chicago: University of Chicago Press.

————, and Geoffrey M. White. 1986. The Anthropology of Emotions. *Annual Review of Anthropology* 15: 405–436.

Lynas, Mark. 2004. Warning from a Warming World. *Geographical* 76(5): 51–54.

Macdonald, Barrie. 1982. *Cinderellas of the Empire: Towards a History of Kiribati and Tuvalu*. Canberra: Australian National University Press.

MacLeod, Arlene E. 1992. Hegemonic Relations and Gender Resistance: The New Veiling as Accommodating Protest in Cairo. *Signs* 17(3): 533–557.

Mahmood, Saba. 2005. *Politics of Piety: The Islamic Revival and the Feminist Subject.* Princeton, NJ: Princeton University Press.

Makihara, Miki, and Bambi B. Schieffelin, eds. 2007. *Consequences of Contact: Language Ideologies and Sociocultural Transformations in Pacific Societies.* New York: Oxford University Press.

Malinowski, Bronislaw. 1922. *Argonauts of the Western Pacific: An Account of Native Enterprise and Adventure in the Archipelagoes of Melanesian New Guinea.* London: Routledge & Kegan Paul.

————. 1935. *Coral Gardens and Their Magic: A Study of the Methods of Tilling the Soil and of Agricultural Rites in the Trobriand Islands.* London: G. Allen & Unwin.

Mallon, Sean. 2005. Samoan Tatau as Global Practice. In *Tattoo: Bodies, Art, and Exchange in the Pacific and the West.* Nicholas Thomas, Anna Cole, and Bronwen Douglas, eds. Pp. 145–169. Durham, NC: Duke University Press.

Marcus, George E. 1980. *Nobility and the Chiefly Tradition in the Modern Kingdom of Tonga.* Wellington: Polynesian Society.

————. 1989. Chieftainship. In *Development in Polynesian Ethnology.* Alan Howard and Robert Borofsky, eds. Pp. 175–211. Honolulu: University of Hawai'i Press.

————. 1995. Ethnography in/of the World System: The Emergence of Multi-Sited Ethnography. *Annual Review of Anthropology* 24: 95–117.

Marshall, Mac. 1975. The Politics of Prohibition on Namoluk Atoll. *Journal of Studies on Alcohol* 36: 597–610.

————. 1979. *Weekend Warriors: Alcohol in a Micronesian Culture.* Palo Alto, CA: Mayfield.

Marwick, Max. 1964. Witchcraft as a Social Strain-Gauge. *Australian Journal of Science* 26: 263–268.

Maude, Harry E. 1970. Baiteke and Binoka of Abemama: Arbiters of Change in the Gilbert Islands. In *Pacific Islands Portraits.* J. W. Davidson and Deryck Scarr, eds. Pp. 201–224. Canberra: Australian National University Press.

————. 1981. *Slavers in Paradise: The Peruvian Labour Trade in Polynesia, 1862–64.* Canberra: Australian National University Press.

Mauss, Marcel. 1967 [1925]. *The Gift: Forms and Functions of Exchange in Archaic Societies.* Ian Cunnison, trans. New York: W. W. Norton.

McDermott, Ray. 1988. Inarticulateness. In *Linguistics in Context: Connecting Observation and Understanding.* Deborah Tannen, ed. Pp. 37–68. Norwood, NJ: Ablex.

McKinnon, Susan. 2000. Domestic Exceptions: Evans-Pritchard and the Creation of Nuer Patrilineality and Equality. *Cultural Anthropology* 15: 35–83.

————. 2005. *Neo-Liberal Genetics: The Myths and Moral Tales of Evolutionary Psychology.* Chicago: Prickly Paradigm Press.

McLean, R. F., and Doug Munro. 1991. Late 19th Century Tropical Storms and Hurricanes in Tuvalu. *South Pacific Journal of Natural Science* 11: 203–219.

McQuarrie, Peter. 1994. *Strategic Atolls: Tuvalu and the Second World War.* Christchurch: Macmillan Brown Centre for Pacific Studies, University of Canterbury.

Medvedev, Pavel N. 1985 [1928]. *The Formal Method in Literary Scholarship: A Critical Introduction to Sociological Poetics.* Albert J. Wehrle, trans. Cambridge, MA: Harvard University Press.

Meijl, Toon van. 2000. The Politics of Ethnography in New Zealand. In *Ethnographic Artifacts: Challenges to a Reflexive Anthropology.* Sjoerd R. Jaarsma and Marta A. Rohatynskyj, eds. Pp. 86–103. Honolulu: University of Hawai'i Press.

Merlan, Francesca, and Alan Rumsey. 1991. *Ku Waru: Language and Segmentary Politics in the Western Nebilyer Valley, Papua New Guinea.* Cambridge: Cambridge University Press.

Merry, Sally Engle. 1984. Rethinking Gossip and Scandal. In *Toward a General Theory of Social Control.* Donald Black, ed. Vol. 1, pp. 271–302. New York: Academic Press.

———. 1995. Resistance and the Cultural Power of Law. *Law and Society Review* 29: 11–26.

———. 2006. Transnational Human Rights and Local Activism: Mapping the Middle. *American Anthropologist* 108: 38–51.

Merton, Robert K. 1957. *Social Theory and Social Structure.* Rev. ed. Glencoe, IL: Free Press.

Mertz, Elizabeth. 1994. Legal Language: Pragmatics, Poetics, and Social Power. *Annual Review of Anthropology* 23: 435–455.

Mintz, Jerome R. 1997. *Carnival Song and Society: Gossip, Sexuality and Creativity in Andalusia.* Oxford: Berg.

Mintz, Sidney. 1985. *Sweetness and Power: The Place of Sugar in Modern History.* New York: Viking Penguin.

Mitchell, Timothy. 1990. Everyday Metaphors of Power. *Theory and Society* 19: 545–577.

Mitchell, William, ed. 1992. *Clowning as Critical Practice: Performance Humor in the South Pacific.* Pittsburgh, PA: University of Pittsburgh Press.

Møhl, Perle. 1997. *Village Voices: Coexistence and Communication in a Rural Community in Central France.* Copenhagen: Museum Tusculanum.

Munn, Nancy. 1986. *The Fame of Gawa: A Symbolic Study of Value Transformation in a Massim Society.* Cambridge: Cambridge University Press.

Munro, Doug. 1978. Kirisome and Tema: Samoan Pastors in the Ellice Islands. In *More Pacific Islands Portraits.* Deryck Scarr, ed. Pp. 75–93. Canberra: Australian National University Press.

———. 1990. The Peruvian Slavers in Tuvalu, 1863: How Many Did They Kidnap? *Journal de la Société des Océanistes* 90: 43–52.

———, Suamalie N. T. Iosefa, and Niko Besnier. 1990. *Te Tala o Niuoku: The German Plantation on Nukulaelae Atoll, 1865–1990.* Suva: Institute of Pacific Studies of the University of the South Pacific.

Murphy, Michael D. 1985. Rumors of Identity: Gossip and Rapport in Ethnographic Research. *Human Organization* 44: 132–137.

Murphy, William. 1998. The Sublime Dance of Mende Politics. *American Ethnologist* 25: 563–582.

Murray, A. W. 1865. Missionary Voyage to the Lagoon Islands. *Missionary Magazine,* December: 335–345.

———. 1876. *Forty Years Mission Work in Polynesia and New Guinea, from 1835 to 1875.* London: James Nisbet.

Myerhoff, Barbara. 1979. *Number Our Days.* New York: E. P. Dutton.

Myers, Fred R. 1986. *Pintupi Country, Pintupi Self: Sentiment, Place, and Politics among Western Desert Aborigines.* Washington, DC: Smithsonian Institution Press.

Nader, Laura. 1990. *Harmony Ideology: Justice and Control in a Zapotec Mountain Village.* Stanford, CA: Stanford University Press.

Narayan, Kirin. 1993. How Native Is a "Native" Anthropologist? *American Anthropologist* 95:671–686.

Niehaus, Isak. 2000. Coins for Blood and Blood for Coins: From Sacrifice to Ritual Murder in the South African Lowveld, 1930–2000. *Etnofoor* 13(2): 31–54.

———, with Eliazaar Mohlala and Kally Shokane. 2001. *Witchcraft, Power and Politics: Exploring the Occult in the South African Lowveld.* London: Pluto Press.

Norrick, Neal R. 1995. *Conversational Joking: Humor in Everyday Talk.* Bloomington: Indiana University Press.

Nugent, David. 1982. Closed Systems and Contradiction: The Kachin in and out of History. *Man* [n.s.] 17: 508–527.

Obeyesekere, Gananath. 1997. *The Apotheosis of Captain Cook: European Mythmaking in the Pacific.* Princeton, NJ: Princeton University Press.

Ochs, Elinor. 1979a. Planned and Unplanned Discourse. In *Discourse and Syntax.* Talmy Givón, ed. Pp. 51–80. New York: Academic Press.

———. 1979b. Transcription as Theory. In *Developmental Pragmatics.* Elinor Ochs and Bambi B. Schieffelin, eds. Pp. 43–72. New York: Academic Press.

———. 1988. *Culture and Language Development: Language Socialization in a Samoan Village.* Cambridge: Cambridge University Press.

Olivier de Sardan, Jean-Pierre. 2001. Populisme méthodologique et populisme idéologique en anthropologie. In *Le goût de l'enquête: Pour Jean-Claude Passeron.* Jean-Louis Fabiani, ed. Pp. 195–246. Paris: L'Harmattan.

Ong, Aihwa. 1987. *Spirits of Resistance and Capitalist Discipline: Factory Women in Malaysia.* Albany: State University of New York Press.

Ortner, Sherry B. 1995. Resistance and the Problem of Ethnographic Refusal. *Comparative Studies in Society and History* 37: 173–193.

———. 1997. Fieldwork in the Postcommunity. *Anthropology and Humanism* 22: 61–80.

———. 2005. Subjectivity and Cultural Critique. *Anthropological Theory* 5: 31–52.

Osbourne, Lloyd. 1900. *The Queen versus Billy and Other Stories.* New York: Charles Scribner's Sons.

Paeniu, Bikenibeu. 1995. *Traditional Governance and Sustainable Development in the Pacific.* Economics Division Working Papers, South Pacific Series, 95/6. Canberra: Economics Division, Research School of Pacific Studies, Australian National University.

Paine, Robert. 1967. What Is Gossip About? An Alternative Hypothesis. *Man* [n.s.] 2: 278–285.

Panoff, Michel. 1985. Une figure de l'abjection en Nouvelle-Bretagne: Le *rubbish-man*. *L'homme* 25(2): 57–71.

Parkin, David. 1984. Political Language. *Annual Review of Anthropology* 13: 345–365.

Parry, Jonathan, and Maurice Bloch, eds. 1989. *Money and the Morality of Exchange.* Cambridge: Cambridge University Press.

Pascal, Roy. 1977. *The Dual Voice: Free Indirect Speech and Its Functioning in the Nineteenth-century European Novel.* Manchester: Manchester University Press.

Patel, Samir S. 2006. A Sinking Feeling. *Nature* 440: 734–736.

Paul, Robert A. 1995. Act and Intention in Sherpa Culture and Society. In *Other Intentions: Cultural Contexts and the Attribution of Inner States.* Lawrence Rosen, ed. Pp. 15–45. Santa Fe, NM: School of American Research Press.

Peirce, Charles Sanders. 1932. *Collected Papers of Charles Sanders Peirce.* Vol. 2: *Elements of Logic.* Charles Hasthorne and Paul Weiss, eds. Cambridge: Cambridge University Press.

Philips, Susan U. 2000. Constructing a Tongan Nation-State through Language Ideology in the Courtroom. In *Regimes of Language: Ideologies, Politics, and Identities.* Paul V. Kroskrity, ed. Pp. 229–257. Santa Fe, NM: School of American Research Press; Oxford: James Currey.

———. 2004. The Organization of Ideological Diversity in Discourse: Modern and Neotraditional Visions of the Tongan State. *American Ethnologist* 31:231–250.

Pietilä, Tuulikki. 2007. *Gossip, Markets, and Gender: How Dialogue Constructs Moral Value in Post-Socialist Kilimanjaro.* Madison: University of Wisconsin Press.

Poirine, Bernard. 1998. Should We Hate or Love MIRAB? *The Contemporary Pacific* 10: 65–106.

Pollock, Elizabeth, director. 2005. *Tuvalu: That Sinking Feeling.* PBS *Frontline.* 16 minutes.

Pratt, Mary Louise. 1986. Fieldwork in Common Places. In *Writing Culture: The Poetics and Politics of Ethnography.* James Clifford and George E. Marcus, eds. Pp. 27–50. Berkeley: University of California Press.

Pratten, David. 2007. Mystics and Missionaries: Narratives of the Spirit Movement in Eastern Nigeria. *Social Anthropology* 15: 47–70.

Price, Tom. 2003. High Tide in Tuvalu. *Sierra* 88(4): 34–37, 66–67.

Radio New Zealand International. 2006. Most Tuvaluans and i-Kiribati on Nauru Should Be Repatriated by End of July. http://www.rnzi.com/pages/news.php?op=read&id=25252, accessed August 2007.

Rappaport, Joanne. 1990. *The Politics of Memory: Native Historical Interpretation in the Columbian Andes.* Cambridge: Cambridge University Press.

Rasmussen, Susan J. 1991. Modes of Persuasion: Gossip, Song, and Divination in Tuareg Conflict Resolution. *Anthropological Quarterly* 64: 30–46.

———. 1993. Joking in Researcher-Resident Dialogue: The Ethnography of Hierarchy among the Tuareg. *Anthropological Quarterly* 66: 211–220.

Rebel, Herman. 1989. Cultural Hegemony and Class Experience: A Critical Reading of Recent Ethnological-Historical Approaches. *American Ethnologist* 16: 117–136, 350–365.

Rebhun, L. A. 2004. Sexuality, Color, and Stigma among Northeast Brazilian Women. *Medical Anthropology Quarterly* 18: 183–199.

Reddy, William M. 2001. *The Navigation of Feeling: A Framework for the History of Emotions.* Cambridge: Cambridge University Press.

Reed-Danahay, Deborah. 1993. Talking about Resistance: Ethnography and Theory in Rural France. *Anthropological Quarterly* 66: 221–229.

Reisman, Karl. 1974. Contrapuntal Conversations in an Antiguan Village. In *Explorations in the Ethnography of Speaking.* Richard Bauman and Joel Sherzer, eds. Pp. 110–124. Cambridge: Cambridge University Press.

Riebe, Inge. 1987. Kalam Witchcraft: A Historical Perspective. In *Sorcerer and Witch in Melanesia.* Michele Stephen, ed. Pp. 211–245. New Brunswick, NJ: Rutgers University Press.

Robbins, Joel. 1994. Equality as a Value: Ideology in Dumont, Melanesia and the West. *Social Analysis* 36: 21–70.

———. 2007. Continuity Thinking and the Problem of Christian Culture. *Current Anthropology* 48: 5–38.

———, and Holly Wardlow, eds. 2005. *The Making of Global and Local Modernities in Melanesia.* Aldershot: Ashgate.

Robertson, A. F. 2001. *Greed: Gut Feelings, Growth, and History.* Cambridge: Polity Press.

Rockefeller, Stuart A. 2000. On Hearsay and Ethnography: Why We Should Study Rumors. Presented at the Biannual Meeting of the American Ethnological Society, Tampa Bay, FL.

Rodman, William. 1993. Sorcery and the Silencing of Chiefs: "Words on the Wind" in Post-Independence Ambae. *Journal of Anthropological Research* 49: 217–235.

Rogers, Susan C. 1975. Female Forms of Power and the Myth of Male Dominance: A Model of Female–Male Interaction in Peasant Society. *American Ethnologist* 2: 727–756.

Rosaldo, Michelle Z. 1974. Women, Culture, and Society: A Theoretical Overview. In *Women, Culture, and Society.* Michelle Z. Rosaldo and Louise Lamphere, eds. Pp. 14–42. Stanford, CA: Stanford University Press.

———. 1980a. *Knowledge and Passion: Ilongot Notions of Self and Social Life.* Cambridge: Cambridge University Press.

———. 1980b. The Use and Abuse of Anthropology: Reflections on Feminism and Cross-Cultural Understanding. *Signs* 5: 389–417.

Roscoe, Paul. 1999. The Return of the Ambush: "Raskolism" in Rural Yangoru, East Sepik Province. *Oceania* 69: 171–184.

Rosen, Lawrence, ed. 1995. *Other Intentions: Cultural Contexts and the Attribution of Inner States.* Santa Fe, NM: School of American Research Press.

Rosnow, Ralph L., and Gary A. Fine. 1976. *Rumor and Gossip: The Social Psychology of Hearsay.* New York: Elsevier.

Rouch, Jean, director. 1955. *Les maîtres foux*. 30 mins. Originally produced and distributed by Les films de la Pléiade.

Rumsey, Alan L. 1986. Oratory and the Politics of Metaphor in the New Guinea Highlands. In *Semiotics, Ideology, Language*. Terry Threadgold, E. A. Grosz, Gunther Kress, and M. A. K. Halliday, eds. Pp. 283–296. Sydney: Sydney Association for Studies in Society and Culture.

———. 1990. Wording, Meaning, and Linguistic Ideology. *American Anthropologist* 91: 346–361.

Sabini, John, and Maury Silver. 1982. *Moralities of Everyday Life*. Oxford: Oxford University Press.

Sacks, Harvey. 1978. Some Technical Considerations of a Dirty Joke. In *Studies in the Organization of Conversational Interaction*. Jim Schenkein, ed. Pp. 249–269. New York: Academic Press.

Sahlins, Marshall. 1958. *Social Stratification in Polynesia*. Seattle: University of Washington Press.

———. 1963. Poor Man, Rich Man, Big-Man, Chief: Political Types in Melanesia and Polynesia. *Comparative Studies in Society and History* 5: 285–303.

———. 1972. The Spirit of the Gift. In Marshall Sahlins, *Stone Age Economics*. Pp. 149–183. New York: Aldine.

———. 1981. The Stranger-King: Dumézil among the Fijians. *Journal of Pacific History* 16: 107–132.

———. 1985. *Islands of History*. Chicago: University of Chicago Press.

Said, Edward. 1991. The Politics of Knowledge. *Raritan* 11(1): 17–31.

Salmond, Anne. 1975. Hui: *A Study of Maori Ceremonial Gatherings*. Wellington: A. H. & A. W. Reed.

———. 2005. Their Body Is Different, Our Body Is Different: European and Tahitian Navigators in the 18th Century. *History and Anthropology* 16: 167–186.

Schegloff, Emmanuel A. 1987. Between Micro and Macro: Contexts and Other Connections. In *The Micro-Macro Link*. Jeffrey C. Alexander, Bernhard Giesen, Richard Münch, and Neil J. Smelser, eds. Pp. 193–206. Berkeley: University of California Press.

———. 1992. In Another Context. In *Rethinking Context: Language as an Interactive Phenomenon*. Alessandro Duranti and Charles Goodwin, eds. Pp. 191–227. Cambridge: Cambridge University Press.

———. 2007. *Sequence Organization in Interaction: A Primer in Conversation Analysis*. Cambridge: Cambridge University Press.

———, Gail Jefferson, and Harvey Sacks. 1977. The Preference for Self-Correction in the Organization of Repair for Conversation. *Language* 53: 361–382.

Scheper-Hughes, Nancy. 2000. The Global Traffic in Human Organs. *Current Anthropology* 41: 191–224.

———. 2002. Min(d)ing the Body: On the Trail of Organ-Stealing Rumors. In *Exotic No More: Anthropology on the Front Lines*. Jeremy MacClancy, ed. Pp. 33–63. Chicago: University of Chicago Press.

Schieffelin, Bambi B.; Kathryn A. Woolard; and Paul V. Kroskrity, eds. 1998. *Language Ideologies: Practice and Theory*. New York: Oxford University Press.

Scott, James C. 1979. *The Moral Economy of the Peasant: Rebellion and Subsistence in Southeast Asia*. New Haven, CT: Yale University Press.

———. 1985. *Weapons of the Weak: Everyday Forms of Peasant Resistance*. New Haven, CT: Yale University Press.

———. 1986. Everyday Forms of Peasant Resistance. *Journal of Peasant Studies* 13(2): 5–34.

———. 1990. *Domination and the Arts of Resistance: Hidden Transcripts*. New Haven, CT: Yale University Press.

———. 1998. *Seeing like a State: How Certain Schemes to Improve the Human Condition Have Failed*. New Haven, CT: Yale University Press.

Seidel, Gill. 1975. Ambiguity in Political Discourse. In *Political Language and Oratory in Traditional Society*. Maurice Bloch, ed. Pp. 205–226. London: Academic Press.

Sennett, Richard, and Jonathan Cobb. 1972. *The Hidden Injuries of Class*. New York: Alfred A. Knopf.

Seymour, Susan. 2006. Resistance. *Anthropological Theory* 6: 303–321.

Shostak, Marjorie. 1981. *Nisa: The Life and Words of a !Kung Woman*. New York: Vintage.

Shore, Bradd. 1982. *Sala'ilua: A Samoan Mystery*. New York: Columbia University Press.

———. 1996. The Absurd Side of Power in Samoa. In *Leadership and Change in the Western Pacific: For Sir Raymond Firth on the Occasion of his Ninetieth Birthday*. Richard Feinberg and Karen A. Watson-Gegeo, eds. Pp. 142–186. London: Athlone Press.

Sidnell, Jack. 2001. Conversational Turn-Taking in a Caribbean English Creole. *Journal of Pragmatics* 33: 1263–1290.

———. 2006. Repair. In *Handbook of Pragmatics*. Jef Verschueren and Jan-Ola Östman, eds. N.p. Amsterdam: John Benjamins.

Silverstein, Michael. 1981. *The Limits of Awareness*. Sociolinguistic Working Papers, 84. Austin, TX: Southwest Educational Development Laboratory.

———. 1984. On the Pragmatic "Poetry" of Prose: Parallelism, Repetition, and Cohesive Structure in the Time Course of Dyadic Conversation. In *Meaning, Form, and Use in Context: Linguistic Applications*. Deborah Schiffrin, ed. Pp. 181–199. Washington, DC: Georgetown University Press.

———. 2003. Indexical Order and the Dialectics of Sociolinguistic Life. *Language and Communication* 23: 193–229.

———, and Greg Urban, eds. 1996. *Natural Histories of Discourse*. Chicago: University Of Chicago Press.

Slade, Diana. 2007. *The Texture of Casual Conversation: A Multidimensional Interpretation*. London: Equinox.

Smith, Bernard. 1985. *European Vision and the South Pacific: A Study in the History of Art and Ideas*. New Haven, CT: Yale University Press.

Solomon, Nathalie, and Anne Chamayou, eds. 2006. *Potins, cancans et littérature.* Perpignan: Presses Universitaires Perpignan.

Solove, Daniel J. 2007. *The Future of Reputation: Gossip, Rumor, and Privacy on the Internet.* New Haven, CT: Yale University Press.

Solway, Jacqueline. 1998. Taking Stock in the Kalahari: Accumulation and Resistance on the Southern African Periphery. *Journal of Southern African Studies* 24:425–441.

Spacks, Patricia M. 1985. *Gossip.* Chicago: University of Chicago Press.

Spitulnik, Debra. 1996. The Social Circulation of Media Discourse and the Mediation of Communities. *Journal of Linguistic Anthropology* 6: 161–187.

Spivak, Gayatri C. 1988. Can the Subaltern Speak? In *Marxism and the Interpretation of Culture.* Cary Nelson and Lawrence Grossberg, eds. Pp. 271–313. Urbana: University of Illinois Press.

Stephen, Michele. 1994. *A'aisa's Gifts: A Study of Magic and the Self.* Berkeley: University of California Press.

———, ed. 1987. *Sorcerer and Witch in Melanesia.* Melbourne: Melbourne University Press.

Stevenson, Robert Louis. 1924. *In the South Seas, Being an Account of Experiences and Observations in the Marquesas, Paumotus, and Gilbert Islands in the Course of Two Cruises, on the Yacht 'Casco' (1888) and the Schooner 'Equator' (1889).* London: Tusitala Editions.

Stewart, Pamela J., and Andrew Strathern. 2004. *Witchcraft, Sorcery, Rumors, and Gossip.* Cambridge: Cambridge University Press.

Stoller, Paul. 1995. *Embodying Colonial Memories: Spirit Possession, Power, and the Hauka in West Africa.* London: Routledge.

Strathern, Andrew. 1975. *Big-Men and Ceremonial Exchange in Mount Hagen New Guinea.* Cambridge: Cambridge University Press.

Strathern, Marilyn. 1987. The Limits of Auto-Anthropology. In *Anthropology at Home.* Anthony Jackson, ed. Pp. 16–37. London: Tavistock.

———. 2005. *Partial Connections.* 2nd ed. Walnut Creek, CA: Altamira Press.

Strating, Alex. 1998. Roddelen en de verbale constructie van gemeenschap. *Etnofoor* 11(2): 25–40.

Street, Brian V. 1990. Orientalist Discourses in the Anthropology of Iran, Afghanistan and Pakistan. In *Localizing Strategies: Regional Traditions of Ethnographic Writing.* Richard Fardon, ed. Pp. 240–259. Edinburgh: Scottish Academic Press; Washington, DC: Smithsonian Institution Press.

Stroud, Christopher. 1992. The Problem of Intention and Meaning in Code-Switching. *Text* 12: 127–155.

Sykes, Karen. 1999. After the "Raskol" Feast: Youths' Alienation in New Ireland, Papua New Guinea. *Critique of Anthropology* 19: 157–174.

Szwed, John F. 1966. Gossip, Drinking, and Social Control: Consensus and Communication in a Newfoundland Parish. *Ethnology* 5: 434–441.

Tambiah, Stanley J. 1990. *Magic, Science, Religion, and the Scope of Rationality.* Cambridge: Cambridge University Press.

Tannen, Deborah. 1989. *Talking Voices: Repetition, Dialogue, and Imagery in Conversational Discourse.* Cambridge: Cambridge University Press.

Taussig, Michael. 1980. *The Devil and Commodity Fetishism in South America.* Chapel Hill: University of North Carolina Press.

———. 1987. *Shamanism, Colonialism, and the Wild Man: A Study of Terror and Healing.* Chicago: University of Chicago Press.

Tcherkézoff, Serge. 2003. *Faa-Samoa: Une identité polynésienne (économie, politique, sexualité): L'anthropologie comme dialogue culturel.* Paris: L'Harmattan.

Tebbutt, Melanie. 1995. *Women's Talk? A Social History of "Gossip" in Working-Class Neighbourhoods, 1880–1960.* Aldershot, England: Scholar Press.

Tedlock, Dennis. 1983. *The Spoken Word and the Work of Interpretation.* Philadelphia: University of Pennsylvania Press.

Tholander, Michael. 2003. Pupils' Gossip as Remedial Action. *Discourse Studies* 5: 101–129.

Thomas, Nicholas. 1989. The Force of Ethnology: Origins and Significance of the Melanesia/Polynesia Division. *Current Anthropology* 30: 27–41.

———. 1997. *In Oceania: Visions, Artifacts, Histories.* Durham, NC: Duke University Press.

Thompson, E. P. 1966. *The Making of the English Working Class.* New York: Vintage.

Thornborrow, Joanna, and Deborah Morris. 2004. Gossip as Strategy: The Management of Talk about Others on Reality TV Show "Big Brother." *Journal of Sociolinguistics* 8: 246–271.

Tourell, Wayne; Mike O'Connor; and Savana Jones-Middleton, directors. 2001. *Paradise Drowned: Tuvalu, the Disappearing Nation.* New Zealand Natural History Ltd. 47 minutes.

Trask, Haunani-Kay. 1991. Natives and Anthropologists: The Colonial Struggle. *The Contemporary Pacific* 3: 159–167.

———. 1993. *From a Native Daughter: Colonialism and Sovereignty in Hawai'i.* Monroe, ME: Common Courage Press.

Trinh, T. Minh-ha. 1989. *Woman, Native, Other: Writing Postcoloniality and Feminism.* Bloomington: Indiana University Press.

Trudgill, Peter. 1974. *The Social Differentiation of English in Norwich.* Cambridge: Cambridge University Press.

Tsing, Anna. 2000. The Global Situation. *Cultural Anthropology* 15: 327–360.

Turner, George. 1865. Narrative of Elikana [*sic*], a Native Christian of Manahiki [*sic*]. *The Juvenile Missionary Magazine* 22(255): 338–343, 367–372.

Turner, Terence S. 1979. Anthropology and the Politics of Indigenous Peoples' Struggles. *Cambridge Anthropology* 5(1): 1–43.

Tuzin, Donald F. 1980. *The Voice of the Tambaran: Truth and Illusion in Ilahita Arapesh Religion.* Berkeley: University of California Press.

Urban, Greg. 1986. *Rhetoric of a War Chief.* Working Papers and Proceedings of the Center for Psychosocial Studies, 5. Chicago: Center for Psychosocial Studies.

Van Vleet, Krista. 2003. Partial Theories: On Gossip, Envy, and Ethnography in the Andes. *Ethnography* 4: 491–519.

Velsen, J. van. 1967. The Extended-Case Method and Situational Analysis. In *The Craft of Social Anthropology*. A. L. Epstein, ed. Pp. 129–149. London: Tavistock.

Vincent, Joan. 1990. *Anthropology and Politics: Visions, Traditions, and Trends*. Tucson: University of Arizona Press.

Voloshinov, Valentin N. 1978 [1929]. Reported Speech. In *Readings in Russian Poetics: Formalist and Structuralist Views*. Ladislav Matejka and Krystyna Pomorska, eds. Pp. 176–196. Ann Arbor: Michigan Slavic Publications.

Wagner, Jane. 1986. *The Search for Signs of Intelligent Life in the Universe*. New York: Harper & Row.

Wallerstein, Immanuel. 1974–1988. *The Modern World-System*. 3 vols. New York: Academic Press.

Ward, R. Gerard, ed. 1967. *American Activities in the Central Pacific, 1790–1870: A History, Geography and Ethnography pertaining to American Involvement and Americans in the Pacific Taken from Contemporary Newspapers, Etc.* Vol. 5. Ridgewood, NJ: Gregg Press.

Wardlow, Holly. 2006. *Wayward Women: Sexuality and Agency in a New Guinea Society*. Berkeley: University of California Press.

Warner, Michael. 2005. *Publics and Counterpublics*. New York: Zone.

Watson-Gegeo, Karen A., and Stephen T. Boggs. 1977. From Verbal Play to Talk Story: The Role of Routines in Speech Events among Hawaiian Children. In *Child Discourse*. Susan Ervin-Tripp and Claudia Mitchell-Kernan, eds. Pp. 67–90. New York: Academic Press.

———, and Geoffrey M. White, eds. 1990. *Disentangling: Conflict Discourse in Pacific Societies*. Stanford, CA: Stanford University Press.

Wetherell, Margaret. 1998. Positioning and Interpretative Repertoires: Conversation Analysis and Post-Structuralism in Dialogue. *Discourse and Society* 9: 387–412.

White, Geoffrey M. 1991. *Identity through History: Living Stories in a Solomon Islands Society*. Cambridge: Cambridge University Press.

———, and John Kirkpatrick, eds. 1985. *Person, Self, and Experience: Exploring Pacific Ethnopsychologies*. Berkeley: University of California Press.

———, and Lamont Lindstrom, eds. 1990. *The Pacific Theater: Island Representations of World War II*. Washington, DC: Smithsonian Institution Press.

———. 1998. *Chiefs Today: Traditional Pacific Leadership and the Postcolonial State*. Stanford, CA: Stanford University Press.

White, Luise. 2000. *Speaking with Vampires: Rumor and History in Colonial Africa*. Berkeley: University of California Press.

Whitehead, Neil L., and Robin Wright. 2004. Introduction: Dark Shamans. In *In Darkness and Secrecy: The Anthropology of Assault Sorcery and Witchcraft in Amazonia*. Neil L. Whitehead and Robin Wright, eds. Pp. 1–20. Durham, NC: Duke University Press.

Whitmee, S. J. 1871. *A Missionary Cruise in the South Pacific, Being the Report of a Voyage Amongst the Tokelau, Ellice, and Gilbert Islands, in the Missionary Barque "John Williams," During 1870*. Sydney: Joseph Cook.

Williams, Maslyn, and Barrie Macdonald. 1985. *The Phosphateers: A History of the Brit-*

ish Phosphate Commissioners and the Christmas Island Phosphate Commission. Melbourne: Melbourne University Press.

Willis, Paul. 1977. *Learning to Labour: How Working Class Kids Get Working Class Jobs.* Farnborough: Saxon House.

Wilmsen, Edwin N. 1989. *Land Filled with Flies: A Political Economy of the Kalahari.* Chicago: University of Chicago Press.

Wilson, John. 1990. *Politically Speaking: The Pragmatic Analysis of Political Language.* Oxford: Blackwell.

Wilson, Peter J. 1969. Reputation and Respectability: A Suggestion for Caribbean Ethnography. *Man* [n.s.] 4: 70–84.

———. 1974. Filcher of Good Names: An Enquiry into Anthropology and Gossip. *Man* [n.s.] 9: 93–102 (followed by correspondence by Barrie Machin, 9: 625–626; William Lancaster, 9: 626–627; Peter Wilson, 10: 615–616; E. Kolig, 10: 616–617; Bruce Kapferer, 10: 617–618).

Wolf, Eric R. 1982. *Europe and the People without History.* Berkeley: University of California Press.

Woolard, Kathryn A., and Bambi Schieffelin. 1994. Language Ideology. *Annual Review of Anthropology* 23: 55–82.

Yanagisako, Sylvia, and Carole Delaney, eds. 1995. *Naturalizing Power: Essays in Feminist Cultural Analysis.* New York: Routledge.

Young, Michael W. 1983. *Magicians of Manumanua: Living Myth in Kalauna.* Berkeley: University of California Press, 1983.

———. 2004. *Malinowski: Odyssey of an Anthropologist, 1884–1920.* New Haven, CT: Yale University Press.

Zelenietz, Marty, and Shirley Lindenbaum, eds. 1981. Sorcery and Social Change in Melanesia. *Social Analysis* 8, special issue.

Zimmer, Laura J. 1987. "Who Will Bury Me?" The Plight of Childless Elderly among the Gende. *Journal of Cross-Cultural Gerontology* 2: 61–77.

Index

aesthetics, 16, 19, 101, 124–125, 135, 138, 140, 208n.2. *See also* oratory
agency, 1, 3, 5–12, 17–18, 61, 82–83, 90, 137, 140, 193
alcohol. *See* prohibition
Althusser, Louis, 6, 11
anger *(ita, kaitaua)*, 89, 175–176, 193
antipoetics. *See* oratory
arrogance *(fia maualuga)*, 170
Austin, J. L., 166, 191

Baha'i Faith, 125–127, 130, 134, 208n.2
Bailey, F. G., 14, 16, 84, 118
Bakhtin, Mikhail, 28, 97, 109, 118, 151, 167, 185–186
beauty *(gali)*, 32, 73, 82, 96–97, 112, 182
Blackbirders. *See* slavery
Bourdieu, Pierre, 3, 45, 129, 206n.3, 209n.6
Brenneis, Donald, 17, 19, 83, 101, 102, 135, 190
Burma, Highland, 5–6
Butler, Judith, 19, 24, 166, 170, 191

chieftainship. *See* hierarchy
Christianity, 43–45, 47–48, 91, 122, 185, 201n.9, 208n.4; antithetical to sorcery, 149–150, 176–177, 179–180
citationality, 166, 170, 186
colonialism, 20–23, 46, 51–53, 64, 66–68, 91, 102–103, 202n.11, 203n.17, 206n.6, 210n.6
conflict management, 40–41, 89–90, 96–97, 134, 183, 193, 211n.1
contrapuntal, 101–102
conversation analysis, xiii, 98–99, 116, 135–137
cooking huts, 33–36, 96, 97, 103, 124, 129–130, 191

David, Cara (Mrs. Edgeworth David), 52–53, 68, 202n.14
Derrida, Jacques, 166, 170
development, 32, 58, 60, 62, 67, 72, 92, 157, 195n.1, 204n.3
dialogism, 109
Douglas, Mary, 147, 186
Duranti, Alessandro, 3, 195n.2, 206n.7

egalitarianism, 5–6, 12, 19, 25, 76–80, 96, 101–102, 104, 123, 125, 164–165, 187–188
Elekana, 47–48, 125, 150, 201n.9, 202n.11
emotions, 1–2, 18–19, 78–79, 161–163, 174–176, 193–194, 195n.1. *See also* anger; arrogance; beauty; empathy; envy; fortune; laughter; peace
empathy *(alofa, feaalofani)*, 45, 73, 112, 127, 182, 193

envy *(kaimanako, kaisanosano)*, 78–79, 125, 155
ethics. *See* fieldwork, ethics of
Evans-Pritchard, E. E., 5, 6, 167, 186, 210n.4

felicity conditions, 166
feminist anthropology, 6, 9, 28, 196n.5, 197n.11, 198n.19
fieldwork, 1, 29–31, 37–42, 144, 150, 157; ethics of, 19–27, 129–130, 139, 141–142, 199nn.21, 22
Fiji, 24, 31, 57, 200n.1, 204n.22; Indians, 16–17, 19, 83, 135
fortune *(manuia)*, 74
Foucault, Michel, 8, 22, 28, 167, 186, 196n.6
fractal recursivity, 96
Funafuti, 4, 21, 31, 39, 40, 52, 53, 57, 58, 60, 71, 145–146, 208n.4

Gal, Susan, 4, 9, 10–11, 96, 209n.6
gender, 6, 8–9, 14, 34–35, 58–59, 85–90, 96, 128–129, 149–150, 152–154, 163–164, 188, 197n.11. *See also* feminist anthropology
genre, 121, 166–167, 185–186, 190–191. *See also* literacy; oratory; sermon, church
Geschiere, Peter, 164, 186, 210n.4
Giddens, Anthony, 11
Gilbert Islands. *See* Kiribati
global warming, 4–5, 31, 59–63, 72
Gluckman, Max, 15–16, 143, 198n.15
gossip: definition of, 12–14, 95; as stereotype, 26, 94–96, 129, 206n.2; structural-functionalist vs. transactionalist theories of, 15–16, 119
Gramsci, Antonio, 6

Haviland, John, 14, 15, 197n.9
heterodoxy, 137–140
heteroglossia, 109, 114, 117, 118, 124, 151–152, 163, 167, 181, 187
hierarchy, 64–76
human rights, 205n.9

information withholding, 104–109
intentionality, 102, 108, 162, 166, 190, 206n.7
Internet, 31, 70
intersubjectivity, 22, 114, 118
Iremonger, Lucille, 102, 206n.2
Irvine, Judith, 10, 96, 99, 147, 193

Jamaica, 52–53, 95–96, 201n.8, 206n.2
jealousy. *See* envy

Kiribati, 51, 53–55, 57, 67, 95, 150, 203nn.18, 19, 210n.6

language ideology. *See* linguistic anthropology
laughter *(kata)*, 107–108, 114–117, 124, 129, 134–135, 137, 161, 207n.10, 209n.5
Leach, Edmund, 5–6
leadership. *See* hierarchy
letter-writing. *See* literacy
linguistic anthropology, 3–4, 10–11, 99, 191
literacy, 26, 46, 143, 154, 159, 172
London Missionary Society, 43–44, 47–48, 125–127, 201n.6, 202n.11
lying *(loi, ppelo)*, 95, 100, 177–178, 207n.12

maneapa, 36, 39, 67, 69, 81, 96, 121; meeting in the, 173–183
mediumship. *See* spirits
meeting. See *maneapa*, meeting in the
migration, 2, 3, 55–56, 57–59, 70–73, 91–92, 156, 191–192, 199n.21, 203n.21
MIRAB. *See* migration; remittances
modernity, 9, 32, 52–59, 97, 105, 115, 146, 173, 187–188, 192, 195n.2
morality, 1–2, 94–99, 108, 114, 118–119, 194

Naisali, Henry F., 70, 125
Nauru, 57–58, 71–73, 91, 168–172
New Zealand, 23, 24, 31, 55–56, 71, 92, 156, 198n.17, 203n.21, 205n.1

Nivanga, MV and MV Nivaga II, 29, 30, 31, 73, 192, 200n.2
nostalgia. *See* hierarchy
Nuer, 6

Ochs, Elinor, xiii, 113, 195n.3, 206n.7
oratory, 121–125, 127–129
orthodoxy, 137–140
Ortner, Sherry, 9, 11–12, 21, 23, 27, 193, 203n.17
ostracism *(faleesea)*, 86–87, 159–163, 205n.8

Paeniu, Bikenibeu, 62, 68–69
peace *(fiileemuu)*, 45, 73, 86, 97, 112, 127, 182, 193
Peirce, C. S., 11, 18, 28
performativity, 19, 28, 166–167
plantation, 48–49, 202n.15
poetics. *See* oratory
political anthropology, 5–7, 196n.7; language and, 189–190
politics *(poolitiki)*, 95, 126
prohibition, 35, 83–90
pronouns, 81, 82–83, 211n.3
psychological anthropology. *See* emotions

Radio Tuvalu, 60, 115, 125–126, 185, 202n.12, 210n.9
relocation. *See* migration
remittances, 4, 32, 58–59, 71–73, 84, 168, 172, 186, 204n.3
reported speech, 109–114
resistance, 7–12, 17, 138, 187, 201n.9, 203n.17, 209n.6
resources of jurisdiction, 31, 70, 140

rubbish men, 12
rumor, 13, 17, 90, 144, 186, 197n.12, 198n.15

Samoa, 3, 32, 43–44, 47–48, 52, 64–65, 67, 79–80, 146–147
Saumaiafe *or* Saumaiafi. *See* spirits
Scott, James, 7–12, 187
seamen, 21, 58–59, 71, 73, 87, 146, 157
sermon, church, 183–184
slavery, 48–50, 206n.6
sorcery *(vai laakau)*, 147–152, 155–163, 168–188; contrasted with witchcraft, 210n.4
speak properly *(faipati fakallei)*. *See* conflict management
spirits, 32, 35, 143, 145–152, 155–157, 161–165, 169–171, 181–182, 201n.9
stereotype *(pona)*, 95–97
stinginess *(kaiuu)*, 157, 205n.1
subaltern. *See* resistance
subjectivity, 22, 193–194

Tafia, Faiva, 67–68, 121–123
Tannen, Deborah, 109, 111
teasing, 107–108
telegraph. *See* literacy
tradition, 39, 40, 68–69, 81, 88, 192, 195n.2; invention of, 20, 198n.17, 204n.2
Trinh Minh-ha, 15, 20
truth *(tonu)*, 26, 120, 123–125, 137–140, 147, 161–163, 170, 177, 208n.3

weapons of the weak. *See* resistance
witchcraft. *See* sorcery
World War II, 43, 53, 57

About the Author

NIKO BESNIER is professor of cultural anthropology at the University of Amsterdam. He has previously taught at the University of Illinois at Champaign-Urbana, Yale University, Victoria University of Wellington, and the University of California, Los Angeles, and has held temporary appointments at the University of Hawai'i at Mānoa, the University of Auckland, the École des Hautes Etudes en Sciences Sociales, and Kagoshima University. Trained in anthropology, linguistics, and mathematics, his current research focuses on identity formation at the intersection of the global and the local, concepts of modernity in non-Western contexts, and the transnational movement of professional athletes. He has conducted extensive field research in the Pacific Islands, principally on Nukulaelae Atoll, Tuvalu, where he has spent a total of four years since 1979, as well as Tonga, where he began fieldwork in 1977. Among his previous books figure *Literacy, Emotion, and Authority* (Cambridge University Press, 1995) and *Tuvaluan* (Routledge, 2000). He has also authored articles published in a wide range of major journals in anthropology, linguistics, gender studies, and Pacific Islands studies. He has been the recipient of major research funding in the United States, New Zealand, and the Netherlands.

Production Notes for **Besnier / Gossip and the Everyday Production of Politics**

Designed by University of Hawai'i production staff with Minion text and Helvetica Rounded display

Composition by Josie Herr

Printed on 50# Glatfetter Offset D37, 400 ppi